Leading Sustainable

MW01292707

Leading Sustainable Change

An Organizational Perspective

Edited by

Rebecca Henderson, Ranjay Gulati,
and Michael Tushman

OXFORD
UNIVERSITY PRESS

OXFORD
UNIVERSITY PRESS

Great Clarendon Street, Oxford, OX2 6DP,
United Kingdom

Oxford University Press is a department of the University of Oxford.
It furthers the University's objective of excellence in research, scholarship,
and education by publishing worldwide. Oxford is a registered trade mark of
Oxford University Press in the UK and in certain other countries

© Oxford University Press 2015

The moral rights of the authors have been asserted

First published 2015
First published in paperback 2016

Published in the United States of America by Oxford University Press
198 Madison Avenue, New York, NY 10016, United States of America

British Library Cataloguing in Publication Data
Data available

Library of Congress Cataloging in Publication Data
Data available

ISBN 978–0–19–870407–2 (Hbk.)
ISBN 978–0–19–878372–5 (Pbk.)

■ FOREWORD

David Jones

The world often changes suddenly and dramatically under our noses almost without us being aware of it and quite quickly things are seen as normal that up until then were not.

When I was CEO of an advertising agency in Australia in the 1990s, we launched a digital agency inside the advertising agency. The reaction of most people at the time was, "Why are you doing that? You're not an IT or software business." Today, no one would ever admit to having said that. It was a similar thing five or six years ago with social media, which a lot of people dismissed as a childish fad. And I'd argue that for many people it's the same today with social responsibility in business.

Now, I'm not claiming to have some magic crystal ball that sees the future (I freely admit that in 2008 I told the person who was teaching me about Twitter that I was only doing it because I had to and that it would never catch on), but the movement towards socially responsible business is irrevocable. It is starting to truly gain momentum and we can no more turn it back or slow it down than King Canute could hold back the tide.

For many businesses, the path to being more socially responsible is not an easy one and it is important to understand the reasons behind why it has become today's business imperative.

The new world of business

We are at an inflection point in the world, in the wake of a financial crisis during which the world saw all too clearly that the ruthless pursuit of profit at all costs led us to the brink of the total collapse of the global financial system. And in my opinion, we are in the midst of a revolution that is every bit as significant as the Industrial Revolution; but while the Industrial Revolution empowered corporations, the digital and social revolution is empowering people. Through the power of social media, they can and do reward those who act responsibly and punish those who don't.

Two key groups are driving the movement to more responsible business, the first of which are 'prosumers.' 'Prosumer' is a term originally coined by the futurologist Alvin Toffler in 1980 to describe the producer-consumer but has now evolved to define people who are more proactive, more influential, and more cynical of marketing and who now, due to social media, hold the power.

The second and most important group are the brilliant younger generation, often called millennials. From my work with One Young World—the global youth organization and charity that I co-founded with Kate Robertson, described by CNN as "the young Davos"—I know that this generation is different from any that have gone before. Technology has made them the most informed, the most responsible, and the most powerful generation of young adults that has ever existed. They understand better than anyone how to use and leverage the power of digital and social media to effect positive change.

They will not buy products from companies that don't behave to the standards they set, nor will they work for them. Just ask the banks today how hard it is to recruit the best young talent. This generation isn't a generation of naïve idealists. They understand that business has to make money—there is a huge unemployment problem facing them in many countries and they clearly see the benefits of growth—but they believe business can and should make money in the right way. Not only that, they are the ones creating the new tools that are enabling and driving change.

And business dramatically needs to change. Havas's recent Meaningful Brands global study of 130,000 people found that only 20 percent of brands are seen to meaningfully, positively impact people's lives and that the majority of people worldwide wouldn't care if 73 percent of brands disappeared tomorrow. Just think about that for a moment; the vast majority of brands in the world could disappear tomorrow and people wouldn't care.

The Edelman Trust Barometer 2014 found that just one in five people (21 percent) trust business leaders to make ethical and moral decisions, and a similarly low number (20 percent) trust them to tell the truth regardless of how complex or unpopular it is.

Not a great position to be in, and the fact the same study shows people are even less favorable about governments only tinges the issue with irony, given that it is the governments that they expect to regulate businesses.

The age of damage

We have now entered headlong into what I call the Age of Damage, an era where businesses that are not socially responsible will suffer damage as a result. The most successful businesses will increasingly be those that demonstrate the ability to add value in a socially responsible way.

It is a world of radical transparency. From BP to News International, from bankers' bonuses to tax evasion, people will sanction you if you behave in the wrong way. There is a new example almost every day of a company that is being held to account by ordinary people using the power of social media—just ask JP Morgan, Starbucks, Barilla, Abercrombie & Fitch, Benetton, or

Fedex. Business can't avoid this: social media has taken corporate social responsibility out of the silo and put it firmly in the P&L statement.

It's not the old definition of "business as usual," then giving something away at the end of the year out of guilt, nor is it about some nice, siloed "Corporate Social Responsibility" activity. It means putting social responsibility at the very heart of business strategy as the Unilevers, Wholefoods, TOMS, and Patagonias of the world have.

In this era, the most successful businesses will increasingly be those that demonstrate the ability to lead and add value in a socially responsible way. The new price of doing well will be doing good.

We already know what doing the wrong thing can lead to, from BP, which in the wake of the Deepwater Horizon disaster was fined a record amount of US $4.5bn, charged with 14 criminal offences, and two employees with manslaughter, to News International forced to axe the *News of the World* and to a single disgruntled former Goldman Sachs employee publishing his resignation letter which promptly wiped US $2bn off the company's market cap—and we will see many more examples of the cost of not doing the right thing in this era.

But there will also be many winners; those that can embrace the open and collaborative world are well placed. Open business models such as Wikipedia, Facebook, Instagram, and Kickstarter have already been hugely successful. But the big opportunity for that sector, and key to avoiding it being seen as the new Wall Street, is that they demonstrate that a tech business can have a purpose and be socially responsible.

Power has changed

Part of the change in business has been driven by the fact that the very nature of power has changed and evolved. This is something Henry Timms talks very eloquently about. Today people who are the most influential and powerful are the ones who share the most, rather than the ones who try to keep control and close doors.

Whether you like this new world or not, you cannot opt out of it. Everything is now completely open; it's "always on," with no separation between public

Table F.1

Old power	New power
Closed	*Open*
Top-down	*Bottom-up*
Off the record	*Radical transparency*
No comment	*Always on*
Discrete channel reputations Corporations	*One reputation across everything People*

and private, between customers and shareholders, or between internal and external. The "top-down" world of command and control of the past no longer works and we all have to move to a more collaborative approach.

It's not all bad news though—far from it. Businesses also get rewarded for their good behavior, and for those excited about the change there is a big opportunity to out-behave the competition. There are some real stars emerging who understand that success will come from behaving differently in the future—those that have placed responsibility and doing the right thing at the core of their business models.

The new model: doing good and doing well

For example, the clothing company Patagonia has an overarching message of using less and making things that last. Their Common Threads project involved creating a channel on eBay to sell second-hand Patagonia clothing. Patagonia ran a campaign stating that buying second-hand clothing was much more socially responsible than buying something new. Similarly, it has a refreshingly honest, transparent, and socially responsible way of openly talking about the levels of toxic chemicals in its products and what they are doing about it. For many businesses, the instinct would have been to hide or gloss over information like this, but what Patagonia understands is that people are not looking for perfection, they are looking for honesty. And it is perhaps not surprising that in their video describing this approach they talk about how "it added credibility to the company"—a company already probably seen as the most responsible clothing company in the USA.

TOMS is another great example of a company that totally understands today's world. Alongside the highly successful and pioneering one-for-one model—where for each pair of shoes bought they give one to a poor person in need—TOMS launched TOMS Marketplace, using the reach of its huge network to showcase and sell the work of social entrepreneurs all around the world. And its latest venture into coffee, where the purchase of a bag of TOMS coffee pays for water for one person for a week, looks set to be equally successful.

I was recently at the airport queuing for a flight and the young girl in the queue in front of me had a battered old TOMS sticker on her laptop—a pretty clear sign that the badge brands of today's young people are the ones doing good. Blake Mycoskie, the TOMS founder, sums this philosophy up nicely in his book *Start Something that Matters*.

While Patagonia and TOMS are comparatively small and were both founded on the idea of social responsibility, huge and long-established businesses can transform themselves around the vision of social responsibility and doing the right thing. Unilever is one example of a massive organization that is, through its Sustainable Living Plan, actively putting socially responsible business practices at the core of business strategy, moving from marketing to mattering—and in Unilever's case, making somewhat of a return to its original values—while at the same time aiming to double the size of the business. Paul Polman, Unilever's CEO, is probably doing more than any single individual in business to drive change. But it's not for charitable reasons, it's because he understands that people—and especially young people—will reward you for it. And while Unilever are out ahead on their own, many other major companies such as Google, Starbucks, Marks & Spencer, Estee Lauder, Nike, GE, Wal-mart, Anheuser–Busch InBev, and P&G have realized too that it's about smart business and ensuring future success, and have made, are making, or are trying to make significant changes to their businesses to succeed in this new world.

These companies all understand that we're moving from image being all-important to reality being the key, from a focus that's solely on profit to a focus on purpose, or perhaps more accurately to a world where purpose drives profit.

I do often wonder how we would view Microsoft today and how well they would be doing if, instead of leaving Microsoft to create the Gates foundation and do so much good in the world, Bill Gates had done it through Microsoft.

The challenges for today's leaders

Let's turn now to some of the difficulties that may be encountered en route for those embarking on this journey. Social responsibility and sustainability are both inherently mid- to long-term propositions, with impacts sometimes taking years to be seen. Having run a listed company for several years, it often seems that for the financial markets, short-term is today, mid-term is this month, and long-term this quarter!

It's probably the hardest time in history to run a business. Leaders are increasingly caught in the middle of a tug of war between customers pushing the business to be more socially responsible on the one hand, and the board and shareholders pushing for greater and greater returns at any cost on the other hand.

This is compounded by the fact that many boards today are still composed of people who grew up in a different era with different values. You only need to look at the very low percentage of female executives on most boards to see that. I have had several conversations with progressive CEOs who have added sustainability to the bonus criteria of their key direct reports, but whose board had little or no interest in making it part of their own CEO's compensation.

Further complexity is added by the fact that several of the quick wins that do have an immediate impact on the business are one-offs. Major progress on reducing transport and fuel costs or on reducing packaging tends to have a significant impact in year one, but the benefit of that is lost after a year, when the new comparatives kick in.

Furthermore, there are challenges of marrying social responsibility with competition. Even when a leader has a free hand to implement change to create a more sustainable business, drive efficiencies, cut down on waste and so on, the most efficient thing to do might be to replace people with technology or machines. If you do this, it clearly has a human cost and could hardly be described as being socially responsible. If you don't do it, the negative impact on the business may be so great that many more people lose their jobs, or the business might not even survive.

There are no easy answers, and business leaders travelling this path will be forced to tackle many unenviable dilemmas. There is a need for strength, audacity, and commitment.

Naturally, there are a number of questions anyone embarking on this journey will have:

Will my customers really reward me for this?
Will my employees?
Will my board?
Will my shareholders?

I believe they will, and moreover, the danger of being one of the companies punished in the Age of Damage is much greater than the challenge of changing to be a better business.

The best businesses have always succeeded by delivering what people want. And people, especially young people, are demanding change. A major global study recently found that three-quarters (74 percent) of people think that business bears as much responsibility for driving positive social change as governments and that 86 percent believe that business should stand for more than just profit. This supports my view that Milton Friedman's assertion in the 1970s that business's only responsibility is to maximize profits for shareholders, and therefore social responsibility is anti-business, is obsolete. It may have cut it for that generation, but it won't with today's young adults.

For an increasing number of business leaders today, earlier conflicts between doing the right thing and making a profit no longer exist. The erosion of the Friedman argument has come about as a natural evolution, enabled by our growing interconnection, spurred by the economic meltdown, as well as a widening acknowledgment of the plight of our planet and its inhabitants.

As someone once said, there's no business to be done on a dead planet.

A crucial factor on the road to a more socially responsible future is going to be the action and evolution of the investment and shareholder communities. The optimistic hope that the entire world of finance would learn from the lessons of the financial and economic meltdown and change has proven not to be, but it definitely sent shockwaves through the entire sector and has them open to looking at new models.

Another issue is the speed of change in the world today. Businesses such as Google, Facebook, and Twitter have come along and changed the world in a matter of years, and once dominant market leaders from Nokia to Dell to

Yahoo to Blackberry have fallen very hard in a similar time. It is clear that as the world has become faster and faster, it is harder and harder to focus on the long term.

In a recent survey of major CEOs by the CECP, CEOs reported that the two biggest issues preventing them from focusing on the long term were pressure from boards and the increasing speed with which the world is now moving.

For now, quarterly performance is still the dominant barometer for share price movement. And sustainable or socially responsible business doesn't have the tangible positive effect in 12 weeks in the way that a merger or acquisition announcement can. But this shouldn't, and increasingly doesn't, mean that the most responsible businesses don't have better share price performance.

There is a growing body of evidence that shows that the most responsible companies are outperforming the market—by 16 percent over three years, according to Accenture's global study.

"Past performance is no guarantee of future success" is the disclaimer written across every piece of communication from the financial services industry, and nowhere is that more true than when related to the future of the world of business.

However, this is what is creating the opportunity for business to show that doing good and making money don't have to be at opposite ends of the spectrum. In simple terms, if in the twentieth century NGOs and charities had great intentions but not always great execution, and business had great execution but not always great intentions, then this century can be about, and needs to be about, great intentions and great execution.

Key issues and how to overcome them

My own journey along the path to trying to be a more socially responsible business person hasn't always been an easy one. I still remember being told by one senior executive when I was first appointed CEO of the publicly listed company that they hoped I realized that I'd now have to stop all of that doing good nonsense and just talk about maximizing profits.

So here are a few lessons learned that I've gathered along the way that hopefully you may find useful.

YOUR PURPOSE IS TO DRIVE PERFORMANCE

Ensure that everyone is clear that driving your business to be more sustainable and socially responsible is about performance and competitive advantage, not simply a personal crusade to save the planet. I witnessed first hand one company who, despite having cracked the most brilliant strategic plan for their business, never got to execute it because the CEO gave the impression that it was just about saving the planet and not about selling more product. He lost the support of the board, his employees, and management team, and sadly the plan went the same way as the CEO.

GET THE BOARD ON BOARD

Demonstrate to the board and management team in very clear and tangible terms why this will lead to better performance and ensure they understand and are aligned with the strategic direction. Take the time upfront to explain it—it will be more than worth it. Also every company goes through some tougher times and people look for an immediate and easy excuse for why. "Oh he/she is focusing too much on doing good and not enough on driving growth or running the company" will quickly be the default reason if you do not manage that issue—but if you take the board with you on the journey and give them the ammunition to support you and the company's direction to the naysayers, life will be a lot easier.

HARNESS THE POWER OF YOUR PEOPLE

Take the time to make sure your employees understand where you want to take the company. In fact make them a part of helping define it—good leaders should also be good followers and you will get some great input and ideas from within your organization. And then when you have nailed your strategy, over-communicate it. The one thing politicians understand is that if you want to get your message across you need to say it repeatedly and consistently. As business leaders we often make the mistake of thinking that because we've said something a few times everyone now knows it by heart and is bored of us saying it. That is rarely the case. And even less when you are embarking on something where you will need to clearly explain why you are heading on a more socially responsible path and why that will allow your business to do better. Also, make sure that your vision is simple to understand and easy to remember in the way that GE's Ecomagination, Chipotle's "Food With Integrity," or TOM's "one for one" all are. And check regularly that people in the company know and understand it. The most impressive thing I find when I talk to various different people at Unilever is how everyone throughout the company understands and can articulate the vision. If you want your employees to feel passionate and excited about your company, then be the kind of company people get excited and passionate about working for.

From my experience, employees are much more motivated and excited about being in a company with a clear purpose beyond just profit, and it is also a key retention and recruitment tool. I lost count of the number of people who told me how proud they were that we had created One Young World and how good it made them feel about the company.

THINK YOUNG

The one group of people who get all of this better than anyone are today's young adults, or millennials. Shortly after having finished my book on why "good business" was the future, seeing book sales and media coverage go well, I was perhaps feeling a little too proud of myself. An interview with a 26-year-old journalist from Fortune brought me back down to the ground when he said: "David I liked your book but it was really obvious." And he was right. To his generation it is. I explained to him that while to him and his generation it was obvious, to many of the boards I was talking to it was business heresy. But therein lies a real key to success. Your brilliant young talent can help you to drive change throughout the organization. They are the ones who understand how business needs to change to appeal to them, as customers and employees. They understand better than anyone the digital and social revolution that is changing the world and, importantly, they can help you convince your more cynical management colleagues and employees that this is where the company needs to go to ensure its future success. One of the characteristics I have seen amongst the more progressive and successful CEOs is how they see the potential of this generation and are harnessing it to drive change in their companies from Antony Jenkins, the new CEO at Barclays and his passionate desire to show the world that banking can be a force for good to Jean-Paul Agon at L'Oreal—recently named as one of the world's most ethical companies.

LEAD BY EXAMPLE

Finally, it's essential to lead by example. Have the courage of your convictions. Accept that there will always be critics. But merchandise very overtly the tangible success that being more socially responsible as a business delivers. Ensure that your behavior, actions, and calendar reflect your priorities and beliefs. And as with anything, if it's important measure it and incentivize it. Finally, be patient. One of the most rewarding things that happened to me was when a very senior, smart, but cynical and highly vocal executive came up to me a little while ago and said "David you know when you first started talking about all of this several years ago I thought you were so full of shit, but I have to tell you that you were right, and I've now seen beyond doubt the unbelievable impact it has had. Thank you for your patience."

So as you can see, it's not always an easy journey. But it is one that is worth it. My overall view is that it is somewhat akin to running a marathon. You have to hit certain split times along the way or you can't win the marathon. Those who do the business equivalent of just focusing on the short-term and sprint off fast may lead for a little while, but will be nowhere to be seen in the long run. But similarly, a smart leader understands that you can't use focusing on the long term as a reason to justify your poor short-term performance. We are at the start of a movement, but the key to driving fast change is to prove beyond doubt the business case for it: that you will do better by doing good.

Unilever's Polman summed it up well in a recent results announcement: "The consumer is able to identify responsible businesses from less responsible businesses. The pressure is higher but if you then deliver you will be rewarded more. Unilever has one of its fastest growth rates now.

We have just passed the €50bn barrier—since 2011 we have created a Heinz or a Campbell Soup in incremental turnover without affecting the bottom line."

Unilever have outperformed their competitors over the past few years—and have done that since abandoning quarterly earnings reporting and switching to twice annually to discourage short-term shareholders.

If you don't want to believe the positive story of the business and share price performances of the Unilever's, TOMS, Patagonias or Chipotles, then you only have to look at the share price performance of those who have been undone by the age of damage—such as BP or News Int'l—to see the price that the business leader who fails to embrace this new world will pay. And remember, not so long ago doctors were advertising cigarettes and no one thought that was odd!

The digital and social revolution has created a much more open, transparent, and connected world. And, while that is a massive challenge for the world of business, it is a hugely positive thing for the world in general because it will drive the behavior of businesses and leaders to a new and better standard.

From success to significance

Far from being bad news for businesses, it represents a golden opportunity. In the twentieth century we built business and brands through marketing; in this one we will build them through behavior. Smart businesses will out-behave the competition—and act before someone acts on their behalf. And we will move from a world of "marketing to consumers," to a world of "mattering to people." In fact, we should try and kill the word consumer altogether—it's a symbol for the ills of the 1980s and 90s as businesses viewed people as if their sole purpose in life was to consume their advertising messages or products. If you view people just as consumers, then that's probably how you'll treat them.

The next Apple will probably be the company that understands all of this; that in the future it will be impossible to do well without doing good. And if Unilever carries on its current path it might just assume that mantle—they certainly have made fantastic progress, recently being named by LinkedIn as the third most attractive company to work for in the world.

It's an incredibly exciting opportunity for business to drive the world to a better place. It's also an incredibly exciting opportunity for you to make your business more competitive. If you can align your board and management team, then together not only will you outperform your competitors, but you will do it knowing that you are also playing a small part in being a force for good in the world.

Recently, a journalist asked me what advice I would give to my kids. I borrowed a wonderful quote I'd seen cartoonist Hugh Macleod use. I think it's great advice for my kids but it's also great advice for all of us in the business world too, if we want to succeed in the future.

When we look back on what we've achieved, can we answer yes to the following:

"Did I live? Did I love? Did I matter?"

David Jones is Founder of One Young World, Founder and CEO of You & Mr Jones and Ex-Global CEO of Havas.

◼ CONTENTS

■ LIST OF FIGURES

■ LIST OF TABLES

■ LIST OF CONTRIBUTORS

Deborah Ancona is the Seley Distinguished Professor of Management, a Professor of Organization Studies, and the faculty director of the MIT Leadership Center at the MIT Sloan School of Management. Her pioneering research into how successful teams operate has highlighted the critical importance of managing outside, as well as inside, the team's boundary. Ancona's work also focuses on the concept of distributed leadership and on the development of research-based tools, practices, and teaching/coaching models that enable organizations to foster creative leadership at every level. This work has been published in a range of scholarly journals, including *Administrative Science Quarterly*, *Organization Science*, and the *Academy of Management Journal*, and in the book, *X-Teams: How to Build Teams That Lead, Innovate, and Succeed* (Harvard Business School Press, June 2007).

Elaine Backman is a Research Affiliate at the MIT Leadership Center.

Amy C. Edmondson is the Novartis Professor of Leadership and Management at the Harvard Business School. The Novartis Chair was established to enable the study of human interactions that lead to the creation of successful business enterprises for the betterment of society. She is an expert on leadership, teams, and organizational learning. Her recent work explores teaming—the dynamic forms of collaboration needed in environments characterized by uncertainty and ambiguity. Her prior work focused on the role of psychological safety in teamwork and innovation. Her books include *Organizational Learning and Competitive Advantage* (Sage, 1996), *Teaming: How Organizations Learn, Innovate and Compete in the Knowledge Economy* (Jossey-Bass, 2012), and *Teaming to Innovate* (Jossey-Bass, 2013).

Mary Ann Glynn is the Joseph F. Cotter Professor of Management and Organization, a Professor of Sociology (by courtesy), and the Research Director for the Winston Center for Leadership and Ethics at Boston College. She is a Fellow of the Academy of Management, as well as Vice President-Elect and Program Chair-Elect. Her research focuses on processes of leadership, organizational change, and entrepreneurship, as well as their embeddedness in broader cultural and institutional systems. Her research has been published in the leading management journals and received Thought Leader Awards in 2011 and 2012.

Royston Greenwood is the Telus Professor of Strategic Management in the School of Business, University of Alberta. His research interests focus upon institutional and organizational change, although recently he has begun to explore the institutional foundations of corporate fraud. He has a particular interest in the professions and professional firms and their role in modern society. His work has appeared in journals such as the *Administrative Science Quarterly*, the *Academy of Management Journal*, *Academy of Management Review*, and the *Strategic Management Journal*. He is a co-editor of the SAGE Handbook of Organizational Institutionalism.

Ranjay Gulati is the Jaime and Josefina Chua Tiampo Professor and the Unit Head of the Organizational Behavior Unit at Harvard Business School. He is an expert on leadership, strategy, and organizational issues in firms. His recent work explores leadership and strategic challenges for building high-growth organizations in turbulent markets. Some of his prior work has focused on the enablers and implications of within-firm and inter-firm collaboration. His previous works are *Managing Network Resources: Alliances, Affiliations, and Other Relational Assets* (Oxford University Press, 2007) and *Reorganize for Resilience: Putting Customers at the Center of Your Organization* (Harvard Business Press, 2009).

Martine Haas is an Associate Professor of Management at the Wharton School, University of Pennsylvania. She received her Ph.D. in Organizational Behavior from Harvard University. Her research focuses on global collaboration, with an emphasis on knowledge sharing and team effectiveness. Her publications have appeared in journals including the *Academy of Management Journal, Administrative Science Quarterly, Management Science, Organization Science*, and *Strategic Management Journal*.

Bruce Harreld assists organizations in building new businesses and turning ideas into organizational action. From 2008 to 2014 he was a senior lecturer at Harvard Business School, where he taught a popular second-year course entitled Executing Strategy. For 15 years prior to that he was senior vice president of IBM, where he was responsible for strategy, global marketing, and IBM's Emerging Business Opportunities program. He has also served as president of Boston Market and an officer and director of Boston Consulting Group. He is the co-author of numerous articles in *Harvard Business Review, California Management Review, MIT Sloan Management Review*, and *CFO Magazine*.

Rebecca Henderson is one of 24 university professors at Harvard University, and a research fellow at the National Bureau of Economic Research. She is also faculty co-chair of HBS's Initiative for Business and the Environment. Her research focuses on the economics of R&D, technology strategy, and the difficulties large organizations encounter in attempting to innovate and change, particularly in response to the challenge of sustainability. She sits on the boards of Amgen, Inc. and of Idexx Laboratories, and in June 2013 she became a member of the World Economic Forum's global agenda council on the role of business. Her most recent book is *Accelerating Innovation in Energy: Lessons from Other Sectors* (University of Chicago, 2011).

Bob Hinings is a Professor Emeritus in the Department of Strategic Management and Organization, Faculty of Business, University of Alberta. He has made contributions to the study of organizational design, power in organizations, organizational change, professionals in organizations, and institutional theory. He is involved in research into the organization of the Canadian wine industry in the Okanagan Valley and Ontario. He is a Fellow of the Royal Society of Canada and the US Academy of Management.

Kate Isaacs completed her Ph.D. in 2013 and is currently a postdoctoral research fellow at the MIT Center for Biomedical Innovation. She conducts research in two broad domains. One involves new organizational forms of "distributed leadership", in which many individuals, not just formal leaders, work across boundaries to mobilize the collective intelligence of a social system to attain desired goals. She also works on questions of multi-stakeholder collaboration, in which firms and their stakeholders, or larger groups of diverse organizations work together to achieve a desired outcome. Her research articulates the structural principles and the social psychological processes that influence outcomes in these collaboration settings. She is an expert on multi-stakeholder collaboration, having studied, designed, and facilitated multi-stakeholder processes for the past ten years.

P. Devereaux (Dev) Jennings is a Professor of Business at the Alberta School of Business, where he teaches strategy and organization theory. Dev does research in three areas: environmental regulation and management from an institutional angle; entrepreneurial processes in nano and clean technology; and family business dynamics from the embeddedness perspective. Over the years he and his diverse groups of co-authors have published work in *Administrative Science Quarterly*, the *Academy of Management Journal*, the *Academy of Management Review*, and the *American Journal of Sociology*. Dev has been involved in the OMT, ONE, and ENT Divisions at the Academy of Management, and is currently incoming Program Chair for ONE. He is also Associate Editor at *Administrative Science Quarterly*. Dev received his Ph.D. and M.A. from Stanford University and his A.B. from Dartmouth College.

Rosabeth Moss Kanter holds the Ernest L. Arbuckle Professorship at Harvard Business School, and is also the Chair and Director of the Harvard University Advanced Leadership Initiative, a collaboration across Harvard's professional schools to help successful leaders at the top of their professions apply their skills to addressing challenging national and global problems in their next stages of life. She is an expert on strategy, innovation, and leadership for change, and explores these topics in her various award-winning and best-selling works. Her latest book, *SuperCorp: How Vanguard Companies Create Innovation, Profits, Growth, and Social Good* (Crown Business, 2009), is a manifesto for leadership of sustainable enterprises. Her previous book, *Confidence: How Winning Streaks & Losing Streaks Begin & End* (Crown Business, 2004), describes the culture and dynamics of high-performance organizations as compared with those in decline, and shows how to lead turnarounds, whether in businesses, hospitals, schools, sports teams, community organizations, or countries. Past prizewinning books include *When Giants Learn to Dance* (Simon & Schuster, 1989), *Men & Women of the Corporation* (Basic Books, 1993), and *World Class: Thriving Locally in the Global Economy* (Free Press, 1997).

Christi Lockwood is a doctoral student in Management and Organization at Boston College's Carroll School of Management. Her research examines different facets of cultural processes as they come to define organizations, as well as their relationship to broader institutional and social systems. She is studying luxury hotels and how they balance organizational legitimacy and local authenticity to create 'indigenous luxury.' She is also conducting research on how culture enabled collective action and community resilience in the aftermath of the Boston Marathon bombings. Christi has published "Organizations Culture," a review of culture in management research over the past four decades (Oxford University Press, 2012), and is working on a synthesis of cultural perspectives (Academy of Management Annals).

John Macomber is a Senior Lecturer in the Finance Unit at Harvard Business School. His professional experience is in real estate and construction. He is an expert on sustainability in real estate and infrastructure in both developed and emerging economies. His recent work explores the application of finance, urban design, property, and infrastructure entrepreneurship to contribute to resource efficient, economically competitive cities. Writings include "Building Sustainable Cities" and "You CAN Manage Construction Risk," both published in *Harvard Business Review*.

Alfred A. Marcus is the Edson Spencer Endowed Chair in Strategy and Technological Leadership at the Carlson School of Management and at the Technological Leadership

Institute (TLI) College of Science and Engineering University of Minnesota. Since 2006, he also has taught in the MBA program of the Technion Israel Institute of Technology. Professor Marcus' research has been published by the *Strategic Management Journal, Organizational Science,* the *Academy of Management Journal,* the *Academy of Management Review,* and other academic journals. He is also the author or editor of 15 books, including *Big Winners and Big Losers: The Four Secrets of Long-Term Business Success and Failure* (The Wharton School Press, 2005), *Managing Beyond Compliance: The Ethical and Public Policy Dimensions of Business* (Northcoast Publishers, 2006), *Winning Moves* (Marsh Books, 2nd edn, 2008), *Strategic Foresight: A New Look at Scenarios* (Palgrave MacMillan, 2009), *Management Strategy* (McGraw Hill, 2nd edn, 2010), and *Cross-Sector Leadership for the Green Economy: Integrating Research and Practice on Sustainable Enterprise* (Palgrave MacMillan, 2011). His current research focuses on sustainable innovation and clean tech venture capital.

Kathleen Miller Perkins is the CEO of Miller Consultants, a management consulting firm. Her expertise is in corporate organizational culture, organizational change, and corporate sustainability. Her recent work focuses on how leadership, along with dimensions of corporate and organizational culture, are linked with successful sustainability strategies and outcomes. Currently, she is engaged in research on the role of the Chief Sustainability Officer in leading change in organizations. Her publications include *Retraining the American Workforce, How to Become a Sustainable Company* (Sloan Management Review, 1989), "Sustainability and Innovation: Creating Change That Engages the Workforce," in the *Journal of Corporate Citizenship* (2012) and "Sustainability at Dow Chemical," in the *Journal of Applied Corporate Finance* (2012).

Charles A. O'Reilly III is the Frank E. Buck Professor of Management at the Graduate School of Business at Stanford University. His recent research focuses on organizational culture, leadership, organizational ambidexterity, executive compensation, and gender issues in organizations. His previous books include *Winning Through Innovation: A Practical Guide to Leading Organizational Change and Renewal* (with Michael Tushman) (Harvard Business School Press, 2002) and *Hidden Value: How Great Companies Achieve Extraordinary Performance With Ordinary People* (with Jeff Pfeffer) (Harvard Business School Press, 2000).

Ryan Raffaelli is an Assistant Professor of Organizational Behavior at Harvard Business School. His research examines how innovation, identity, and institutions affect the dynamics of emerging and re-emerging fields, market categories, technologies, and organizational practices. He is currently investigating how industries and organizations on the brink of collapse are able to re-emerge and thrive, and how organizations manage their identity during periods of instability.

George Serafeim is an Associate Professor of Business Administration at Harvard Business School. He teaches in the MBA and doctoral programs and co-chairs the Executive Education program "Aligning Sustainability with Corporate Performance." He is an expert in equity valuation, corporate governance, and corporate reporting. His work on how organizations integrate sustainability issues into their business models, integrated reporting, and sustainable investing has won numerous awards and has been published in prestigious academic and practitioner journals.

Luciana Silvestri is a doctoral candidate in Management at Harvard Business School. She is broadly interested in uncovering how members of organizations operating in complex, dynamic, and ambiguous settings create viable structures. Her current research explores the relationship between organizational identity ("who we are and what we do") and organizational structure ("how we do it") at a leading social media company. Luciana holds an MBA and an undergraduate degree in business sciences. She was previously a management consultant in Latin America and Europe.

John Sterman is the Jay W. Forrester Professor of Management and Director of the System Dynamics Group at the MIT Sloan School of Management. His research spans systems thinking and organizational learning, computer simulation of corporate strategy and public policy issues, and environmental sustainability. He is the author of many scholarly and popular works on the challenges and opportunities facing organizations today, including the award-winning textbook, *Business Dynamics* (McGraw Hill, 2000). He has won multiple awards for teaching excellence and is often featured in the media for development and innovative use of interactive simulations in education and policymaking, including, with ClimateInteractive, award-winning interactive simulations now used by climate policy negotiators around the world.

Donald Sull is a Senior Lecturer at the MIT Sloan School of Management. He is an expert on how complex organizations execute strategy in volatile markets. His recent works include *Why Good Companies Go Bad and How Great Managers Remake Them* (Harvard Business School Press, 2005), and *The Upside of Turbulence* (Harper Business, 2009). His most recent book, co-authored with Kathleen Eisenhardt, is *Simple Rules: How to Thrive in a Complex World* (Houghton Mifflin, 2015).

Michael Tushman is the Paul R. Lawrence, Class of 1942 Professor at the Harvard Business School. His research and teaching focuses on issues of innovation, senior teams, organization architectures, and leading change. His new book with Charles O'Reilly on ambidextrous designs builds on his earlier books *Competing by Design* (Oxford University Press, 1998) and *Winning Through Innovation* (Harvard Business School Press, 2002).

Andrew H. Van de Ven is Vernon H. Heath Professor of Organizational Innovation and Change in the Carlson School of the University of Minnesota. His research and writings over the years have examined Nominal Group brainstorming techniques, program planning and problem solving, organization design and assessment, inter-organizational relationships, processes of organizational innovation and change, and engaged scholarship. He has published numerous journal articles and 12 books, including *The Innovation Journey* (Oxford University Press, 1999, 2008) and *Engaged Scholarship* (Oxford University Press, 2007), winner of the 2009 Terry Book Award from the Academy of Management. He was President of the Academy of Management in 2000–2001, and now serves as founding editor of the *Academy of Management Discoveries*.

Tiona Zuzul is an Assistant Professor of Strategy and Entrepreneurship at London Business School. Her research explores the micro-foundations of strategy and innovation in highly ambiguous settings. Her current research projects focus on individuals and organizations operating, innovating, and collaborating in new or nascent industries, including the smart cities industry and the air taxi market. In particular, her research examines how individuals' cognitive and emotional responses to ambiguity influence the performance of their projects and firms.

Part I
Introduction

1 Leading Sustainable Change

An Introduction

Rebecca Henderson, Ranjay Gulati, and Michael Tushman

Introduction

Building an environmentally sustainable economy is one of the most fundamental challenges facing our society today. We need to transition from a world powered by cheap fossil fuels, seemingly unlimited water and raw materials and almost no constraints on the disposal of waste to a low-carbon, input-efficient economy that generates as little waste as possible. This cannot be done unless the world's largest organizations are fundamentally transformed. We live in an organizational society (Barley, 2010). If organizations and their surrounding institutions are central to building a sustainable economy, we must connect what we know about large-scale organizational and institutional change to the sustainability challenge. This book pulls together a range of academics whose research has long explored the determinants of successful systemic change efforts. Between them our contributors explore the drivers of change from a wide range of perspectives and very different units of analysis, grappling with the challenge of building sustainable organizations from the executive leadership, organizational, and institutional points of view. Together they point towards a range of powerful solutions, and our hope is that this book is both a springboard for future research and a guide for managers looking to initiate change in their firms and institutional contexts.

This chapter begins by briefly reviewing the environmental challenges that make the transition to sustainability so important, before turning to the question of why large-scale transformation on the part of the private sector in response to these issues is both so critical and so difficult. We sketch out the business case for change, and then suggest that responding to it effectively will require not only significant shifts in the strategy, structure, and processes of most firms, but also the transformation of the institutional logic that currently pervades most large, private-sector organizations. We then turn to a brief summary of the book, highlighting the approaches that our contributors suggest are most likely to accelerate these kinds of changes.

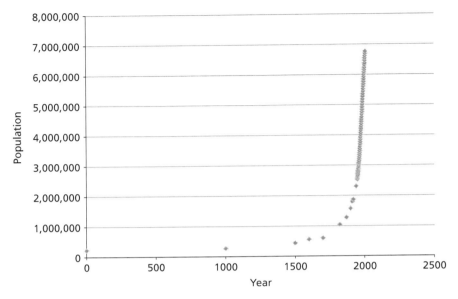

Figure 1.1. World population

THE ENVIRONMENTAL CHALLENGE

The environmental challenges we face are both daunting and imminent. The 1987 Brundtland report coined a definition of "sustainability" that has been widely cited ever since:

Sustainable development is development that meets the needs of the present without compromising the ability of future generations to meet their own needs.[1]

Unfortunately, as the twenty-first century unfolds it is becoming increasingly clear that our current economy is not—by this definition—sustainable. In the past hundred years the world's population has increased from roughly 1.6 billion to about 7 billion, with some estimates suggesting that it may reach 9 billion before leveling off (Figure 1.1) (MIT "Joint Program Energy and Climate Outlook 2012").

At the same time, the economy has grown exponentially. Since 1950, population has nearly tripled, but GDP has risen more than ninefold (Figure 1.2).

This expansion has brought billions of people out of starvation and given hundreds of millions lives that their grandparents could not have imagined, but it has also placed significant pressure on the physical environment on which the economy ultimately relies. Agricultural production has tripled since 1950 (Figure 1.3), and 38 percent of the earth's land area is now under cultivation (World Bank, 2014, available at <http://wdi.worldbank.orgtable/3.2>).

---

[1] World Commission on Environment and Development (WCED) (1987) *Our Common Future.* Oxford: Oxford University Press, 43.

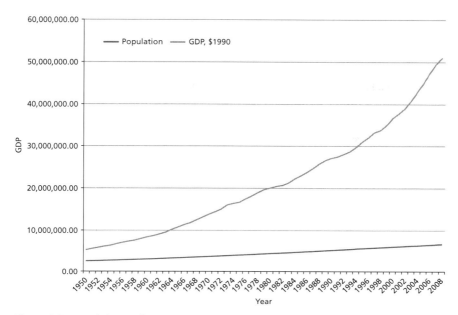

Figure 1.2. Population and GDP since 1950

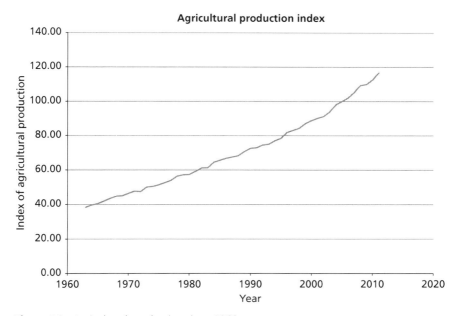

Figure 1.3. Agricultural production since 1960

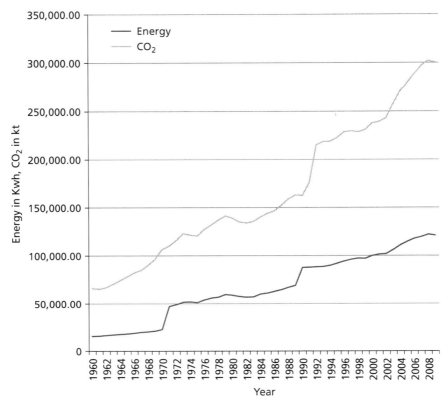

Figure 1.4. Energy production and CO_2 emissions since 1960

By one estimate, world water needs will increase over 50 percent by 2030 and exceed existing supply by 40 percent.[2] The Millennium eco-system assessment suggests that approximately 60 percent of the world's ecosystems are being degraded or used unsustainably, including fresh water, capture fisheries, air and water purification, and the regulation of regional and local climate, natural hazards, and pests. The full costs of the loss and degradation of these ecosystem services are difficult to measure, but the available evidence suggests that they are substantial and growing (Millennium EcoSystem Assessment, 2005). Several estimates suggest that we are in the midst of the "sixth great extinction" and that it is possible that as many as half of the world's species will be extinct by 2100 (Barnosky et al., 2011).

At the same time, energy consumption has more than doubled over the past forty years and is forecast to nearly triple again over the next fifty. Rates of carbon dioxide emission have increased enormously as a result (Figures 1.4 and 1.5).

---

[2] The 2030 Water Resources Group, The World Bank "Charting Our Water Future, Economic Frameworks to Inform Decision-Making." The 2030 Water Resources Group, The World Bank, 2009. Available at: <http://www.mckinsey.com/client_service?sustainability/latest_thinking/charting_our_water_future>, (accessed July 2014).

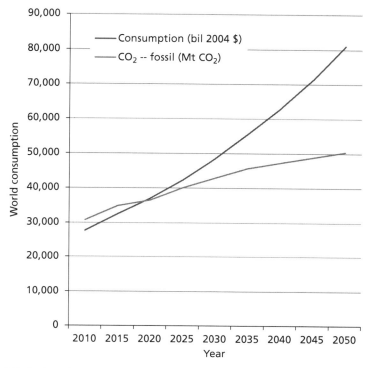

Figure 1.5. Projected energy use and CO_2 emissions

Source: MIT Joint Program on the Science and Policy of Global Climate Change, Outlook 2012. Available at: <http://globalchange.mit.edu/files/documents/MITJPSPGC=Outlook2012.pdf>.

Atmospheric carbon levels are now at levels that the earth has not experienced for nearly a million years, and while the complexity of the problem is such that no one can be sure what is likely to happen as a result, global temperatures have recently been rising significantly (Figure 1.6), and the majority of the world's climate scientists believe that we are facing an increasingly significant risk of global warming and large-scale climate disruption.[3]

For example, a report issued by the Department of Defense in 2011[4] suggested that the effects of climate change are likely to include:

- more frequent and longer droughts;
- increasing frequency of heavy precipitation events, flooding, and landslides;
- extreme temperatures becoming more common;
- tropical cyclone intensity increasing.

Other studies have focused on the possibility that sea levels will rise significantly, that ocean acidification will have adverse effects on the marine food

[3] Available at: <http://whatweknow.aaas.org/get-the-facts/> (accessed July 2014).
[4] Available at: <http://www.fas.org/irp/agency/dod/dsb/climate.pdf> (accessed July 2014).

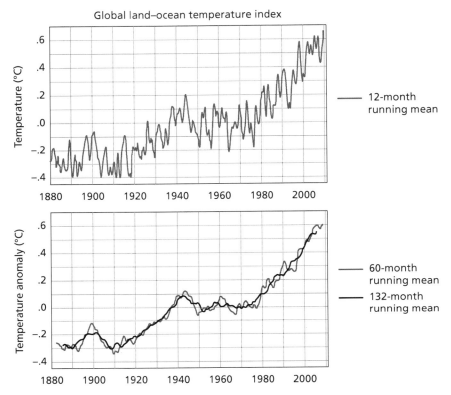

Figure 1.6. Global temperatures since 1880

Source: NASA Goddard Institute for Space Studies. Available at: <http://data.giss.nasa.gov/gisternp/>.

chain, and that increasing temperatures will accelerate the dissemination of pests and disease. Taken together, these kinds of changes would have very significant implications for the stability of the world's food system, particularly in the developing regions of the world, but as the costs of responding to Hurricane Sandy suggest, they are also likely to have significant implications for the developed nations.

IMPLICATIONS FOR THE PRIVATE SECTOR

These kinds of pressures clearly challenge us on multiple fronts, but do they have immediate implications for the private sector? After all, a powerful stream of research suggests that the most effective way to address these kinds of issues is to rely on the public sector to create the prices and property rights that will enable firms to internalize environmental costs as a cost of doing business (Stavins, 2011) and it is clear that public-sector action will be immensely important in solving our environmental challenges. However, as the near-collapse of the Kyoto protocol and the recent failure of the Copenhagen negotiations suggests, the global nature of the problems that we face make it unlikely that public-sector action will be either sufficiently fast or sufficiently comprehensive to provide a solution in the near term.

A failure of public regulation does not, of course, necessarily imply that there is a case for private-sector action. Indeed, the public goods nature of many environmental problems means that in many cases it may be difficult or impossible to build such a case. Rebecca Henderson tackles this issue in depth in Chapter 2 Making the Business Case for Environmental Sustainability. Here, she suggests that, given the ways in which the world is changing, three business models—increasing operational efficiency, selling to the environmentally engaged, and responding to potential threats—are already multi-billion-dollar opportunities.

She then uses the technique of scenario analysis to suggest that even in those cases in which becoming more sustainable is not obviously profitable in today's world, it is possible to build a compelling case for action by taking into account the ways in which continued environmental degradation is likely to significantly change the competitive context. She argues that on the one hand, demand for sustainable products and services is likely to increase, since there is a significant risk that the combination of increasing environmental pressure and the kind of "radical transparency" discussed by David Jones in the foreword will lead consumers to demand "green products" and governments to implement increasingly stringent regulatory policies. On the other hand, she suggests that the costs of becoming more sustainable are likely to fall as the need for new ways of working accelerates technological change. She suggests that the combination of these trends is leading thousands of firms to invest aggressively in becoming more sustainable, and indeed that there is increasing evidence that this is the case. In one recent survey of top managers, for example, 72 percent of respondents said they considered sustainability "extremely" or "very important" for managing their organizations' corporate reputation and brands (Bonini et al., 2010), compelling qualitative evidence that businesses everywhere are beginning to think—and to think hard—about how they can respond to these threats. Some business leaders are undoubtedly motivated by a desire to make a difference or to do the right thing (for example, Jones, 2012), others are responding to the challenge of doing well while doing good (for example, Hinings and Greenwood, 2002; Marquis et al., 2007; Battilana and Dorado, 2010), and still others are responding to the business opportunities that the challenge of building a sustainable economy is creating.

At the same time, there is increasing evidence that for many of these firms sustainability is a peripheral or marginal concern. The same survey suggested, for example, that 20 percent of respondents said their organizations had no clear definition of sustainability, and 56 percent of respondents worked with two or more definitions at the same time (Bonini et al., 2010). If the case for change is so compelling, why is change so slow?

Simply announcing that a firm has committed itself to becoming more sustainable is, of course, only a first step. Moving sustainability from the fringe of the organization, where it is often viewed as an exercise in philanthropy or PR, to the center, and then executing effectively on its promise are much more complex tasks. For example, in a 2013 survey of nearly 200 global corporations, changing the company's core business operations to integrate sustainable practices was cited as the single greatest obstacle to sustainability. The same survey revealed that only one-fifth of companies in the sample were close to fully integrating sustainable practices in their operations, with the rest in the midst of transformation, or just getting started (see Chapter 7 Two Tales of One City: Samsung, Daewoo, and Lessons on Large-Scale Transformation).

THE CHALLENGE OF BUILDING SUSTAINABLE ORGANIZATIONS

One of the reasons that building truly sustainable organizations is difficult is that it often requires a significant shift in the identity of the firm, as well as in its core structure and processes. Also, as a long tradition of research has established, large-scale organizational change of any magnitude is always hard. Existing cognitive frames shape perceptions of the world, so that possible threats are denied or discounted (Henderson and Clark, 1990; Tripsas and Gavetti, 2000). Firms are reluctant to cannibalize their existing businesses, or to explore new business models that might yield lower rates of return (Christensen, 1997; Tushman and O'Reilly, 1997; Bresnahan et al., 2012). Core capabilities become core rigidities (Leonard-Barton, 1992), and complementarities between existing organizational practices make adopting new configurations particularly difficult (Hannan and Freeman, 1989; Rivkin and Siggelkow, 2003). Any strategic change must deal with the power and politics, organizational processes, capabilities, and embedded agency dilemmas associated with inertia both within the firm and within its institutional context (for example, Nadler et al., 1997; Greenwood and Suddaby, 2006; Benner, 2007). Embracing sustainability implies changing deeply embedded, taken-for-granted assumptions about what organizations do and how they compete (Thornton et al., 2012). The senior team needs to be able to manage "ambidextrous" change—managing both the operational excellence of business as usual and the entrepreneurial ambiguity of the new approach. Change is hard!

It is this issue that our remaining chapters tackle in some depth. We begin with three chapters that focus on the "big picture," exploring the range of issues that must be tackled simultaneously if organizations are to change successfully, and outlining a variety of techniques that can be used to ensure that this is managed well. The next three chapters dive more deeply into the issues by exploring the role of the senior team in leading change, while the two that follow focus on the ways in which change must be supported by shifts in processes and structure throughout the organization. Our last three chapters discuss the ways in which firms can drive change in the broader system in which they are embedded. Three broad themes recur throughout the volume:

the need to balance financial logic with social or sustainability based logic; the need to build a deep understanding of the processes of change throughout the firm, at multiple levels of analysis; and the potential for the private sector to trigger change at the level of the system, the industry, and the broader economy.

The modern firm is rooted in "financial logic"—or in a focus on the economic and competitive implications of action, and several authors explore the ways in which external threats to this logic, coupled with the development of a viable business case are, in nearly every case, a necessary precondition to the decision to make sustainability a central strategic imperative. But our authors also suggest that the firm's adoption of the perspective that action that improves the health of the environment is intrinsically valuable in its own right and thus an important source of the values, ultimate purpose, and the identity of the firm is also a critically important component of this shift. Several of the chapters explore how successful firms hold the tension between these two logics, exploring ambidexterity, hybridity, and even complete integration between them as possible solutions.

Building a deep understanding of the processes by which change is successfully enacted is a central concern of many of the chapters. Several authors focus on the role of top management in driving change, while stressing that top management effort alone is a necessary but not sufficient condition for success. Others explore the ways in which firms reshape their identity to embrace sustainability without losing the historical elements of identity that have been central to their success. Several stress the interplay between identity, strategy, and organizational design, focusing particularly on the organizational processes that allow the organization to experiment with new approaches and to embrace new ideas in ways that may lead to the fundamental transformation of the firm.

Last but by no means least, several contributors explore both the necessity for change in the broader system in which firms are embedded if the problems of sustainability are to be tackled successfully, and the ways in which firms can affect these higher levels of analysis in productive ways. Some authors focus on the intersection between firms and their environment, exploring the ways in which certain kinds of firms and projects can act as catalysts for broader change. Others explore questions of governance, exploring the ways in which firms can drive industry self-regulation, common standards, and ultimately government regulation, while still others focus on the ways in which changes within the private sector can trigger cultural shifts and changes in the broader institutional senses of what is "appropriate."

Taken together, the chapters make a compelling case that large-scale organizational change in response to the challenge of environmental sustainability is not only necessary but eminently possible, laying out a road map that we hope will support both organizational researchers and business leaders in grappling with the coming transition.

Plan of the book: chapter summaries

INTRODUCTION

This chapter and the chapter that follows—Rebecca Henderson's review of the business case for acting sustainably—serve as the introduction to the book.

THE BIG PICTURE

In Part II, The Big Picture, three chapters—by John Sterman, by Luciana Silvestri and Ranjay Gulati, and by Rosabeth Kanter—stress the importance of thinking of organizational change as a holistic process that unites identity and vision with strategy and design, and draw on the examples of a number of firms to discuss how this can be accomplished.

In Chapter 3 Stumbling towards Sustainability, John Sterman reminds us that most process improvement initiatives designed to reduce cost or improve productivity and quality fail, and that many attempts to introduce radically new technologies also seem unable to deliver on their promise. Sterman asks what can be done to ensure that efforts to improve sustainability do not share the same fate. He highlights the role of the "capability trap" in preventing firms from investing in apparently highly profitable opportunities. Firms fall into the capability trap when they focus only on the short-term costs and benefits of action, failing to recognize that costly investments now will increase performance later. He suggests that successful firms frame the resources needed to get started as investments, not expenditures, and that they use life-cycle costs instead of up-front costs to assess the return to proposed initiatives, forging agreements with senior management to reinvest at least a portion of any savings in further improvement and using savings from initial programs to begin work on the programs that may be more difficult and take longer but that offer larger potential benefits. They train their employees to understand the roots of the capability trap, and they reduce the bias towards focusing only on the short term by changing incentives throughout the firm to reward improvement and investments in capabilities.

Sterman then turns his attention to the problems inherent in implementing radically new technologies, such as electric vehicles or renewable energy at scale. He suggests that these kinds of changes are unusually difficult because they imply change in large-scale coupled systems, and thus require coordinated change by many players. He points out that organizations and governments have successfully responded to these kinds of challenges in a variety of settings, relying on the establishment of common standards, industry self-regulation, and government regulation, but that if we are to respond to the challenges of sustainability effectively it will be particularly important to develop multiple, nested organizations and management processes, or what Elinor Ostrom described as "polycentric governance" (Poteete et al., 2010).

In Chapter 4 From Periphery to Core: A Process Model for Embracing Sustainability, Luciana Silvestri and Ranjay Gulati draw on the research literature to develop a model of the steps that are required for a firm to embrace sustainability. They suggest that organizations that relegate sustainability to the periphery differ from those that incorporate it into their core in their approaches to identity (how they think about sustainability), strategy (how they plan for sustainability), and design (how they act toward sustainability). They suggest that embedding sustainability into the identity of the organization is critical if firms are to make this transition, suggesting that many firms still think of sustainability as a way of managing their relationships with external constituencies, rather than as a fundamental component of the member's personal and collective commitment to what the organization is and what it strives to become. They hypothesize that unless identity is transformed it fails to guide members' thinking as they identify issues, make decisions, and take action, and that this failure relegates sustainability to a secondary concern that cannot transform the organization. They suggest that bringing sustainability to the core requires moving through four stages—imagining, experimenting, planning, and consolidating—and illustrate the model through a rich description of the successful transformation of the Ford motor company.

In Chapter 5 How Purpose-Based Companies Master Change for Sustainability: A Systemic Approach to Global Social Change, Rosabeth Moss Kanter suggests that many of the world's leading companies are moving beyond passive conformity to societal standards to instead actively seeking positive societal change. She suggests that this requires adding a social logic to the existing financial logic. Drawing on fieldwork conducted in 18 large global companies, she explores the role that strong values-based legacies, a decision to use purpose and values as a source of identity, and a focus on growth can play in allowing a firm to successfully balance these competing tensions. Focusing attention on the "Change Wheel", a dynamic model that shows the interconnections between ten key elements of any organizational system, she highlights the importance of conceptualizing change as much more than an episodic, top-down-driven process.

Kanter then turns her attention to the question of how this kind of organizational change may drive societal or ecosystem change. Expanding on Sterman's theme, she suggests that there are five ways in which firms can play a role in these kinds of change. First, private-sector innovation can change the broader context through the development of infrastructure. Second, alliances and partnerships forged across the supply chain and with strategic partners can provide a platform for action across multiple firms. Third, the success of any one firm can encourage both competition and imitation, and fourth, sustainably orientated firms can convene actors across sectors to attempt to develop a sense of shared responsibility for solving problems, potentially leading to the creation of cross-sector coalitions and/or the creation of new stand-alone organizations dedicated to action.

THE ROLE OF THE SENIOR TEAM

The three chapters in Part III explore the role of the senior team in driving change. In Chapter 6 Staying the Same While Changing: Organizational Identity in the Face of Environment Challenges, Mary Ann Glynn and her co-authors draw on two examples from the hospitality industry to explore the role of senior management in driving the identity change that is fundamental to embracing sustainability. In Chapter 7 Two Tales of One City: Samsung, Daewoo, and Lessons on Large-Scale Transformation, Donald Sull contrasts the role of the leader at Samsung and Daewoo to draw some general lessons about how leaders can best make a difference, while in Chapter 8 Chief Sustainability Officers: Who are They and What Do They Do?, Kathleen Miller and George Serafeim explore the critical role that the chief sustainability officer can play in driving sustainable change.

In Chapter 6 Staying the Same While Changing: Organizational Identity in the Face of Environmental Challenges, Mary Ann Glynn, Christi Lockwood, and Ryan Raffaelli draw on an in-depth study of the transformation of two hotel chains to expand on Silvestri and Gulati's suggestion that a shift in organizational identity is a fundamental pre-condition to a firm's fully embracing sustainability. Focusing on two exemplar hotels—one of which transformed its identity from a luxury hotel to a hotel focused simultaneously on both luxury and sustainability, and the other of which was founded as an "eco-friendly" chain—and using a host of detailed examples, they explore the contrast between "identity hybridicity" and "identity ambidexterity," suggesting that at both hotels the logic of sustainability and the logic of the market were initially experienced as being in significant tension with each other, but that as the two firms gained experience they learned to treat the two as largely complementary, enabling them to distinguish themselves from their competitors and to ensure their financial sustainability over the longer term. Echoing both Henderson's and Sterman's suggestions that one of the keys to becoming more sustainable is the ability to focus productively on future as well as on current challenges, they suggest that identity ambidexterity places emphasis not only on current identity attributes but also enables the organization to go about assimilating additional elements that may be critical to the organization's future survival and legitimacy.

In Chapter 8 Two Tales of One City: Samsung, Daewoo, and Lessons on Large-Scale Transformation, Donald Sull develops the concept of "managerial commitments" as a central tool in transforming the firm. He compares the histories of Samsung and Daewoo (two firms that initially followed very similar trajectories but that later diverged significantly, with Samsung evolving to become one of the world's most successful global firms, while Daewoo was forced into bankruptcy) to suggest that one of the most important ways in which successful leaders drive change is to make costly commitments to strategic frames, processes, resources, relationships, and values that cannot be easily reversed. He explores the ways in which Daewoo's refusal to relinquish its historical commitments led it to a state of what he describes as "active inertia," in which the firm doubled down on a strategy that left it unable to meet the challenges that threatened its existence, and contrasts the actions of Daewoo's CEO with those of Lee Kun Hee, Samsung's CEO at its moment of crisis.

Sull details the ways in which Lee embodied "inside–outside" leadership— the ability to combine the knowledge and organizational sophistication of an insider with the perspective and the willingness to take risks of an outsider. He draws on a detailed history of Samsung's evolution to suggest that Lee was able to combine this perspective with the ability to develop a cohort of leaders within the firm who could support the transformation he championed, to communicate a visceral understanding of his view for the firm and the ways in which this vision was linked to the potential for economic value creation, and to both make transformational commitment and to sustain the momentum behind his efforts as they unfolded. He closes by speculating as to the ways in which leaders who are determined to make their organizations more sustainable might be able to make similar kinds of transformational commitments to drive change.

In Chapter 8 Chief Sustainability Officers: Who are They and What Do They Do?, Kathleen Miller and George Serafeim explore the ways in which firms are using the position of "Chief Sustainability Officer (CSO)" to move sustainability into the core of the organization. Drawing on a recently completed survey of 66 CSOs, they map CSO responsibilities to the degree to which sustainability has become a core concern of the organization, distinguishing between organizations that are still at the "compliance" stage from those who have moved to a focus on "efficiency" and those who have progressed to a focus on "innovation." They demonstrate that in firms in the last, most advanced stage of development, the CSO is significantly *less* likely to have responsibility for facilities management, learning from external sources, reporting, and stakeholder relations or employee education, although it is significantly *more* likely that the person with primary responsibility for sustainability will have the title of CSO. They interpret these somewhat counter-intuitive results as consistent with the hypothesis that one of the most important roles of the CSO is to embed operational responsibility for sustainability into the routine operations of the company, so that sustainability becomes a line, rather than a staff responsibility.

Drawing on a number of rich, qualitative interviews with sitting CSOs, Miller and Serafeim go on to hypothesize that CSOs who succeed in supporting their firm's transition to the third or "innovation" stage not only become deeply involved in shaping the firm's sustainability strategy, but also help to develop the innovation strategy of the firm and to master the art of overseeing "the never-ending evolution" of the business case. They learn to plan for transformational change in a way that takes account of the multiple subcultures that characterize most large firms, and they also play an important role in legitimizing the sustainability effort with stakeholders beyond the firm.

EXPLORING THE PROCESSES OF CHANGE

The next two chapters focus in depth on the nature of the organizational processes that underlie successful strategic transformations towards sustainability. In Chapter 9 Two Roads to Green: A Tale of Bureaucratic versus Distributed Leadership Models of Change, Deborah Ancona, Elaine Backman, and Kate Isaacs contrast the efforts of two firms—"Alpha" and "Beta"—to develop viable "green" initiatives. Drawing on detailed ethnographies of the change efforts at the two firms, they document how, despite the fact that in many ways the firms were very similar to each other, Alpha and Beta occupied different positions on the continuum of leadership logics that ranges from "command and control" to "cultivate and coordinate."

These differences in logic led the green initiatives in the two companies to unfold in very different ways, creating critical differences in how each company decided to adopt green as a strategic priority, the selection of initiative leaders, and the execution of key leadership functions. Although Alpha had been moving towards a "cultivate and coordinate" logic, bureaucratic rules and a top-down mindset kept hijacking attempts at collaborative influence. What began as a bottom-up green initiative moved quickly to an implementation effort cascading down from the top, and this shift led relatively quickly to a concentrated effort on a few high-priority projects approved by top managers, each designed to lead to radical improvements in the company's environmental performance. At Beta, the challenge was how to cultivate organization-wide excitement in a coordinated fashion without imposing change. Successful implementation required creating space and support for bottom-up green initiatives by individuals and small teams working within the company's business divisions. This leadership style led to a slower start-up process, but to an organization that encouraged and connected small, bottom-up innovations throughout the organization.

In Chapter 10 Leading Proactive Punctuated Change, Michael Tushman, Charles O'Reilly, and Bruce Harreld draw on their first-hand experience of punctuated change at IBM between 1999 and 2008 to develop the hypothesis that strategic renewal is best managed as "an engineered social process anchored by an overarching aspiration and a paradoxical strategic intent that unfolds over time" and thought of as a "top down/bottom up engineered social movement." Describing this process in detail, they explore the ways in which—consistent with the suggestions of Sull, Miller, and Serafeim—transformation change must be simultaneously enabled from the top and embedded in the extended management team through collective cross-level and cross-firm experiences and conversations. In so doing they offer another perspective on the ways in which a leadership logic that had historically been focused on incremental innovation or on something more like "command and control" can be transformed towards something closer to the distributed logic of "cultivate and coordinate."

They describe two distinct but related interventions: Strategic Leadership Forums (SLFs) and Emerging Business Opportunities (EBOs). SLFs were intensive workshops designed to engage both strategic and operational issues within and across IBM's business units, while EBOs were a series of efforts to take advantage of cross-line-of-business opportunities in order to strategically explore new business opportunities at the corporate level. They suggest that IBM's experience—and in particular its ability to use exploratory innovation as a catalyst for strategic renewal—may provide a powerful model for firms attempting to respond to the challenge of becoming more sustainable. Echoing Silvestri, Gulati, Kanter, and Glynn, they suggest that this kind of change requires not only senior management ownership and the ability to internalize change across the organization by creating a context for experimentation and learning, but also the ability to appeal to aspirations, emotion, and organizational identity. The CEO's aspiration to make IBM a great firm again through both disciplined execution and experimentation helped unleash energy throughout the firm to lead innovation streams and, in turn, proactive punctuated change.

LEADING CHANGE IN THE BROADER SYSTEM

The final section of the book, Part IV: Leading Change in the Broader System, builds on the critical questions raised by both Sterman and Kanter as to whether and how firms may be able to play a role in helping to transform the broader economic and political context in more sustainable directions. In Chapter 11 The Role of Multiplier Firms and Megaprojects in Leading Change for Sustainability, Amy C. Edmondson, Martine Haas, John Macomber, and Tiona Zuzul define multiplier firms as organizations that develop, disseminate, and facilitate sustainability initiatives for a range of client or partner organizations. They argue that by working with many organizations, multiplier firms help to build networks between organizations that can accelerate the spread of sustainability knowledge and practices across industries and geographies, and thereby have an exponentially growing impact on other firms over an extended period that can enable them to catalyze change for sustainability throughout multiple organizations within, and even across, industries.

They define megaprojects as finite-duration initiatives involving multiple entities in the design and delivery of large-scale developments that may last for many years. Edmondson and her co-authors suggest that the size of a megaproject can often justify spending more effort in early stage planning, optimization, analysis, and team building, and as they simultaneously require collaboration and alignment of interests they can achieve better long-term results than smaller-scale efforts. Megaprojects also tend to be one-offs with little precedent—so their development requires innovation on many fronts at once. This creates an opportunity for multiple teams (representing multiple organizations) to realize new levels of sustainability performance. By working together across professional and industry boundaries, these teams and organizations have the potential to arrive at innovative solutions for environmental, social, and economic sustainability above and beyond what individual firms might generate. Drawing on four illustrative case studies of multiplier firms and megaprojects engaged in sustainability-related initiatives in the built environment (that is, in the development of buildings and urban infrastructure) the authors argue that the size and visibility of these initiatives leads them to have the potential to stimulate and encourage transformational change for sustainability.

Reinforcing the observations of both Ancona and her collaborators and Tushman and his, Edmondson and her collaborators explain the value of what they define as a "learning logic"—in contrast to "blueprint logic"—for leading change for sustainability. They suggest that leading change following a learning logic requires taking an observant and tentative stance. Given that few answers are known in advance, the essential leadership task is to motivate people to work hard to discover new answers together, and this requires articulating a vision, inviting participation, and encouraging experimentation.

In Chapter 12 Managing Shifting Goal Consensus and Task Ambiguity in Making the Transition to Sustainability, Alfred Marcus and Andrew Van de Ven use Thompson and Tuden's classic (1959) typology to explore the ways in which effective decision and change strategies vary as a function of in task ambiguity and goal consensus. They define four different cases: "computational," in which the means to achieve given project ends are generally known and there is agreement about project goals; "collegial," in which there is also agreement about goals but the means to a desired project end are ambiguous; "bargaining," in which means are well understood but there is little agreement about goals; and "partisan mutual adjustment," in which there is deep disagreement about both goals and means. In the first case, decisions can usually be handled routinely, and in the second, decisions are typically made via processes that emphasize discretionary collegial decision making among experts and/or professionals, but they suggest that effective progress in the third and fourth cases requires managing significant conflict across and beyond the boundaries of the firm, an issue that the authors suggest too much sustainability research fails to acknowledge or explore.

Drawing on the cases of Google, BP, and the German feed-in tariff, the authors explore the way in which the pursuit of sustainability entails moving between these different kinds of cases, requiring a leadership style that emphasizes "running in packs," or building coalitions with firms across the industry and with NGOs and regulators as appropriate. They suggest that this requires sharing leadership among conflicting actors and creating an atmosphere of information sharing, trust, and joint problem solving, and echo the conclusions of many of the earlier chapters in proposing that managing sustainability projects requires not only hierarchical leadership and the ability to plan change, but also the ability to include pluralistic leadership and dialectical change and the ability to shift between these strategies as support for sustainability projects changes over time.

Finally, in Chapter 13 Sustainability and Organizational Change: An Institutional Perspective, Royston Greenwood, Dev Jennings, and Bob Hinings draw on a comprehensive review of recent institutional research to explore the interaction between organizational and field-level change. They focus particularly on the ways in which organizations are shaped by the institutional fields in which they are embedded, where fields are " . . . a community of organizations that partakes of a common meaning system and whose participants interact more frequently and fatefully with one another than with actors outside the field." They explore the way in which institutional logics are as much properties of the institutional field in which organizations are embedded as properties of the organization themselves. Viewed from this perspective, organizational efforts to transition from a purely financial logic to the adoption of a hybrid or ambidextrous logic that combines the logic of sustainability with the logic of finance is likely to be as much a field-level process as an organizational-level process.

The authors draw on a wide range of examples, exploring this transition for both firms and industries, focusing particularly on three questions: how change occurs, and in particular the way in which change in field-level logic can be driven both by exogenous shocks and by the ways in which tension and contradiction between multiple logics can trigger improvisation; the importance of "theorization," or of the question of how new logics come to be expressed in ways that can compel legitimacy; and the question of the implications of this perspective for our understanding of the determinants of organizational change. They suggest that just as field-level institutional change requires "reflexivity" or the ability to create spaces in which actors can reflect on the institutional logics by which they are constrained, successful "theorization," and a supportive institutional infrastructure, so the implementation of change *inside* the organization involves similar processes and mechanisms to those operating at the field level. Thus using language and mobilizing actors around new ideas and practices are essential skills for senior managers hoping to generate institutional change.

Conclusions to leading sustainable change

This book is first and foremost written as a call to arms for business leaders to make sustainability a central mandate for their business. We make the case for change not only as essential to the long-term survival of our planet, but also as an increasingly important means to build long-term competitive advantage.

At the same time that we make a business case for enterprises embracing sustainability, we also highlight the challenges of doing so. Such a strategic shift requires systemic change that goes significantly beyond mere symbolic moves like hiring a CSO. We demonstrate that for most companies such a shift requires senior leadership to first articulate and shape the goals and purpose of the organization and then to move to the strategy and operations of the enterprise. Reconfiguring the very DNA of an enterprise is difficult, but we hope that by showing how others have led systemic change, we can help those who follow to decipher this road map more easily.

This book also has relevance for scholars who are interested in sustainability. Much has been written and debated about the science behind global warming. Others have explored the local and global policies that may be necessary to drive change. Here we focus on the critical role that business is likely to play in transforming our economy. Business academics have in general been slow to see these shifts, but we are now on the cusp of a growing social movement of scholarship on this very important topic. They can play a role both in documenting firms that are at the leading edge and in sketching a path to those who may follow. It is our hope that this book plays a small part in serving as a catalyst for this growing movement.

This book comes at a time when many scholars and policy makers are asking fundamental questions about the future of capitalism in our global economy. While modern capitalism has contributed to an unprecedented increase in prosperity around the world, its impact on the environment is becoming increasing unsustainable. It is our hope that as business leaders wrestle with the challenge of building a sustainable economy they will find this book a useful guide to the organizational changes that must be a fundamental part of the coming transformation.

■ REFERENCES

Barley, S. R. (2010) "Building an Institutional Field to Corral a Government: A Case to Set an Agenda for Organization Studies," *Organization Studies*, 31: 777–805.

Barnosky, Anthony D., Matzke, Nicholas, Tomiya, Susumu, Wogan et al. (2011) "Has the Earth's Sixth Mass Extinction Already Arrived?," *Nature* 471 (7336): 51–7.

Battilana, J. and Dorado, S. (2010) "Building Sustainable Hybrid Organizations: The Case of Commercial Microfinance Organizations," *Academy of Management Journal*, 53 (6): 1419–40.

Benner, Mary J. (2007) "The Incumbent Discount: Stock Market Categories and Response to Radical Technological Change," *Academy of Management Review*, 32: 703–20 (lead article).

Bonini, S., Görner, S., and Jones, A. (2010). *McKinsey Global Survey Results: How Companies Manage Sustainability*. New York: McKinsey & Company. Available at: <http://www.mckinsey.com/insights/sustainability/how_companies_manage_sustain ability_mckinsey_global_survey_results> (accessed July 2014).

Bresnahan, Tim, Greenstein, Shane, and Henderson, Rebecca. (2012) "Schupeterian Competition and Diseconomies of Scope: Illustrations from the History of Microsoft and IBM," in J. Lerner and Scott Stern (eds), *The Rate and Direction of Inventive Activity Revisited*. Chicago, IL and London: University of Chicago Press, 203–76.

Christensen, Clayton. (1997) *The Innovator's Dilemma*. Boston, MA: Harvard Business School Press.

Greenwood, R. and Suddaby, R. (eds). (2006) "Institutional Entrepreneurship in Mature Fields: The Big Five Accounting Firms." *Academy of Management Journal* 49 (1): 27–48.

Hannen, M. T. and Freeman, J. H. (1989) *Organizational Ecology*. Cambridge, MA: Harvard Business School Press.

Henderson, R. M. and Clark, K. B. (1990) "Architectural Innovation: The Reconfiguration of Existing Product Technologies and the Failure of Established Firms," *Administrative Science Quarterly* 35: 9–30.

Hinings, C. R. and Greenwood, R. (2002) "Disconnects and Consequences in Organization Theory?" *Administrative Science Quarterly*, 47 (3): 411–21.

Jones, D. (2012) *Who Cares Wins: Why Good Business is Better Business*. New York: Pearson.

Leonard-Barton, Dorothy. (1992) "Core Capabilities and Core Rigidities: A Paradox in Managing New Product Development," *Strategic Management Journal*, 13 (summer): 111–26.

Marquis, C., Glynn, M. A., and Davis, G. F. (2007) "Community Isomorphism and Corporate Social Action," *Academy of Management Review*, 32 (3): 925–45.

Millennium Ecosystem Assessment. (2005) *Ecosystems and Human Well-Being: Synthesis*. Washington, DC: Island Press.

MIT. (2012) "Joint Program Energy and Climate Outlook 2012." MIT. Available at: <http://globalchange.mit.edu/files/document/MITJPSPGC-Outlook2012.pdf>.

Nadler, David, Tushman, Michael L., and Nadler, Mark B. (1997) *Competing by Design: The Power of Organizational Architecture*. Oxford: Oxford University Press.

Poteete, Amy, Janssen, Marco, and Ostrom, Elinor. (2010) *Working Together*. Princeton, NJ: Princeton University Press.

Rivkin, Jan W. and Nicolaj Siggelkow. (2003) "Balancing Search and Stability: Interdependencies Among Elements of Organizational Design," *Management Science* 49 (3): 290–311.

Stavins, Robert. (2011) "The Problem of the Commons: Still Unsettled after 100 Years," *American Economic Review* 101: 81–108.

Thompson, J. D. and Tuden, A. (1959) "Strategies, Structures, and Processes of Organization Decision," in J. D. Thompson et al. (eds) *Comparative Studies in Administration*. Pittsburgh, PA: University of Pittsburgh Press.

Thornton, Patricia, Ocasio, William, and Lounsbury, Michael. (2012) *The Institutional Logics Perspective: A New Approach to Culture, Structure and Process*. Oxford: Oxford University Press.

Tripsas, Mary and Gavetti, Giovanni. (2000) "Capabilities, Cognition and Inertia: Evidence from Digital Imaging," *Strategic Management Journal* 21 (Fall): 1147–1161.

Tushman, Michael and O'Reilly, C. (1997) *Winning Through Innovation*. Boston, MA: Harvard Business School Press.

The World Bank. (2009) "Charting Our Water Future, Economic Frameworks to Inform Decision-Making." The 2030 Water Resources Group, The World Bank. Available at: <http://www.mckinsey.com/client_service/sustainability/latest_thinking/charting_our_water_future>.

World Commission on Environment and Development. (1987) *Our Common Future*. Oxford: Oxford University Press.

2 Making the Business Case for Environmental Sustainability

Rebecca Henderson

Can a business case be made for acting sustainably? This is a difficult question to answer precisely, largely because there is no generally accepted definition of the term "sustainability." Is it acting sustainably to protect the human rights of the firm's workforce? To invest in education in local communities? To switch to renewable power? All of these actions might improve social welfare, and some of them might improve profitability, but they are very different, and the business case for each of them is similarly likely to look quite different. Here I begin to explore the issue by focusing on a more limited question, namely whether a business case can be made for acting in an *environmentally* sustainable way, which I define as acting in any way that reduces a firm's environmental footprint.

An accumulating body of research suggests that reducing the environmental impact of the private sector is likely to have significant social returns (Stern, 2008; Jorgenson et al., 2013). Reducing the use of fossil-fuel-based energy and hence of CO_2 emissions reduces the risk of climate change, for example, and using fewer raw materials and adopting more sustainable fishing or farming practices reduces pressure on the world's ecosystems. However it is not immediately clear that these kinds of actions are likely to yield significant private returns. The risks of climate change or of eco-system destruction are classic "externalities" in that their costs accrue to the broader society and not to a particular firm, so that in a competitive market firms that invest to reduce their environmental footprint—by, for example, reducing the amount of waste they generate, using renewable energy, or investing in more efficient equipment—are running the risk of putting themselves at a competitive disadvantage if these actions simply contribute to the public good.

The substantial scholarly literature that has attempted to measure the relationship between economic returns and sustainable behavior underlines this tension, finding that at the very least the relationship between addressing environmental issues and immediate financial returns is a complex one. Margolis and Walsh (2003), for example, in one of the best summaries of this literature, find no evidence that embracing sustainability increases profitability, and although some recent papers suggest that these kinds of investments can increase returns (see, for example, Eccles et al., forthcoming), other work continues to find no correlation between financial returns and investments in

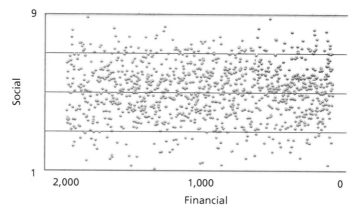

Figure 2.1. Long-term financial performance of ~1,100 CEOs against their companies' social and environmental performance for their last two years in office

Source: Reprinted with permission from "The Best-Performing CEOs in the World ©" by Morten T. Hansen, Herminia Ibarra, and Urs Peyer. Harvard Business Review, January 2013. Copyright © 2013 by Harvard Business Publishing; all rights reserved.

sustainability. Figure 2.1, for example, maps the relationship between a comprehensive set of social and environmental indicators and financial performance over the previous two years for 1,100 CEOs (Hansen et al., 2010). It suggests—and the authors confirm—that the correlation between them is very close to zero.

Does this evidence imply that the business case for investing in environmental sustainability cannot be made? Certainly, some observers have suggested that this is the case, arguing that the public sector is much better equipped to handle environmental problems than the private, and that at best those private firms who invest in environmental sustainability (hereafter simply "sustainability") are engaged in sophisticated green washing (Stavins, 2011).

In this chapter, however, I argue that this conclusion is fundamentally mistaken. The push to transform our economy from one based on the premise that natural resources are inexhaustible and that waste can be freely disposed of to one that acknowledges natural limits and actively minimizes waste is fundamentally disruptive, requiring firms to make sustainability a central strategic concern and to change their operations, strategies, and organizational processes in fundamental ways. As such, it will require business leaders to actively manage the tension between "exploitation," or the need to continue to exploit current ways of doing things, and "exploration," and the need to invest in preparing for a major shift. One of the reasons that these kinds of discontinuities challenge the status quo is that the investments required to prepare for the future are rarely immediately profitable (Tushman and Romanelli, 1985; Christensen, 1997; Bresnahan et al., 2012). The business case for making them cannot rely on immediate, short-term returns. Instead it rests on a sophisticated understanding of the risks entailed in doing nothing and on the opportunities inherent in moving early to prepare for a range of plausible futures.

It is thus not surprising that cross-sectional analyses of the relationship between financial returns and investments in sustainability do not—as yet—yield any easy answers. In a number of industries—particularly in energy, the built environment, agriculture, and consumer goods—investments to increase environmental sustainability have compelling economics on short time frames. But in many sectors these kinds of investments are best thought of as experiments, strategic hedges, or plausible bets against a coming world, rather than as investments that are likely to shift overall corporate performance today. The recognition that this is the case has significant implications for not only how leaders should make the case for change, but also for the ways in which the strategy-making process should be managed and for the ways in which investments in sustainability should be organized.

To make this case, I begin by focusing on those instances in which investing in sustainability already yields immediate, predictable returns. Building on a range of examples and the typology developed in Esty and Winston's *Green to Gold* (2006) I suggest that three business models have emerged to date as particularly powerful ways to make money from acting sustainably: forestalling risk; increasing operational efficiency; and selling to the environmental niche. I then draw on a scenario technique developed by Peter Schwartz (1996) to highlight the way in which increasing environmental degradation is likely to create the conditions under which these models will become increasingly compelling across a wide range of industries.

I argue that in many industries increasing environmental pressures may lead to major changes in the competitive context—including significant shifts in the nature of consumer demand, in the regulatory environment, and in the availability of cost-effective environmentally friendly technology. I suggest that these uncertainties mean that most firms face (at least) four possible futures, in three of which investing in sustainability is likely to be a significant source of competitive advantage. Using the examples of Unilever, M&S, Nissan, Duke, and BP, I suggest that leading firms are already using this perspective to make the case for investing in sustainability, despite the fact that these kinds of investments may not be immediately profitable in a "business-as-usual" scenario. I suggest that the key to building a business case in these circumstances is to make investments that are *robust*—to make investments that are at least marginally profitable in today's world, and that simultaneously position the firm for significant competitive advantage as and when the competitive context changes.

I close by suggesting that this perspective has important implications for the effective leadership of sustainable change, since it implies that investing in sustainability requires the explicit recognition that the firm faces a multiplicity of possible futures. Leading effectively in the face of this kind of uncertainty requires both challenging the conventional strategy process and the ability to hold the organizational tension inherent in investing in any "exploratory" project (March, 1991). Rather than insisting that environmental investments are certain to yield returns, leading effective change requires senior leaders to create both organizational and strategic flexibility inside the firm, and to create the capability to be both efficient and sustainable. These are precisely the kinds of capabilities highlighted so effectively in this book (see for example, Silvestri and Gulati (Chapter 4), Kanter (Chapter 5), Tushman et al. (Chapter 10), Ancona et al. (Chapter 9), and Edmondson, et al. (Chapter 11).

Investing in environmental sustainability: the case for current action

A lively, practitioner-orientated literature—including *Green to Gold* (Esty and Winston, 2006), "Creating Shared Value" (Porter and Kramer, 2011), *Resource Revolution* (Heck, 2014) and *The Big Pivot* (Winston, 2014) argues that the environmental crisis is creating very significant opportunities for the private sector. One particularly compelling example of this stream of work is the "Global GHG abatement cost curve"—an analysis by McKinsey & Company, the global consulting firm, which suggests that nearly half of all of the currently available opportunities for reducing emissions of greenhouse gases are NPV positive, or economically viable right now (Figure 2.2).

Indeed many firms claim to be actively investing in becoming more environmentally sustainable. For example, nearly 6,000 report issuing some form of sustainability report under the Global Reporting Initiative (GRI).[1] "Sustainability" is a broad term, and many of these firms may be focused more on social and governance issues than on environmental concerns, but nonetheless there is increasingly compelling evidence that environmental sustainability is big business. A recent front-page article in the *New York Times* suggested that "Industry Awakens to the Threat of Climate Change," and for many firms investments in sustainability appear to have yielded immediate returns.[2] Three business models have emerged as particularly promising: forestalling risk; increasing operational efficiency; and selling to the environmental niche.[3]

FORESTALLING RISK: PREVENTING BRAND DAMAGE AND/OR PRESERVING "LICENSE TO OPERATE"

The combination of an increasingly global media, the widespread penetration of social networks, and an increasingly concerned consumer base has led

---

[1] Available at: <http://database.globalreporting.org/> (accessed July 2014).
[2] Available at: <http://www.nytimes.com/2014/01/24/science/earth/threat-to-bottom-line-spurs-action-on-climate.html?_r=0> (accessed July 2014).
[3] How does this typology relate to G-to-G typology?

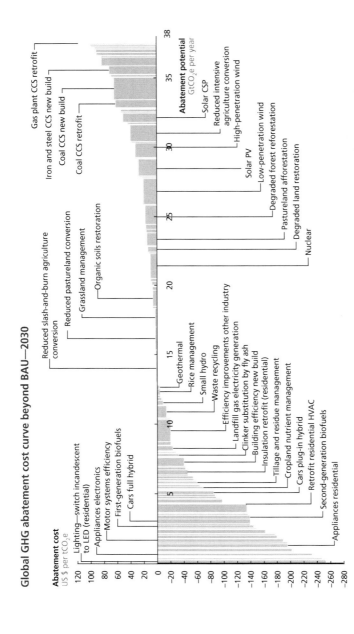

Figure 2.2. The McKinsey cost curve

Source: McKinsey Institute, 2011.

many firms with large, consumer-facing brands to invest aggressively in sustainable business practices to forestall potential brand damage. Similarly, firms facing tight regulatory environments or potentially hostile communities have also invested heavily in the attempt to head off potential regulation and/or the loss of the firm's "license to operate".

For example, allegations that Nike's factories were polluting local waterways were a major factor in persuading the firm to invest heavily in sustainability. Nike now employs more than 135 people in its sustainability group, and has publicly committed to a range of aggressive targets in the area. Similarly, some years ago Greenpeace accused both McDonalds and Kimberly Clark of contributing to deforestation (of the Amazon and of old-growth forest in the US, respectively). In response, McDonalds took the lead in spearheading industry-wide efforts to preserve the Amazon, and both firms have committed to sourcing policies that promise to steadily increase the environmental sustainability of their supply chains.[4]

Coca Cola's engagement with the question of water scarcity is another striking example. Nearly ten years ago, Coca Cola—whose brand is estimated to be worth more than $77bn, nearly half of the firm's entire capitalization—was accused by Indian activists of depleting local water supplies, and was the target of widespread local action and global criticism as a result.[5] While the firm disputed the accuracy of the underlying charges, it has since launched a major effort focused on water, announcing a commitment to become "water neutral."[6]

Similar dynamics have led a number of firms—particularly in the chemical and extractive industries—to invest in reducing their environmental impact in an attempt to preclude community pressure and/or additional regulation. The evidence is mixed as to whether such "self-regulation" is as effective as more standard regulation in reducing pollution (Toffel and Short, 2011), but there is compelling evidence that the chemical industry's extensive investments in both waste reduction and improvements in organizational efficiency have more than covered their costs through the delivery of significant improvements in operational efficiency (Hoffman, 2002).

INCREASING OPERATIONAL EFFICIENCY

As the introduction to this volume suggested, one of the most immediate impacts of the environmental crises we face has been increasing input costs. For example, Figure 2.3 shows the recent increase in commodity prices.

---

[4] Available at: <http://www.aboutmcdonalds.com/mcd/sustainability/library/policies_programs/sustainable_supply_chain/Rainforest_Conservation.html> (accessed July 2014).
[5] Available at: <http://www.nytimes.com/2008/01/16/business/16coke.html?ref=asia&_r=0> (accessed July 2014).
[6] Available at: <http://www.coca-colacompany.com/stories/our-water-conservation-goal> (accessed July 2014).

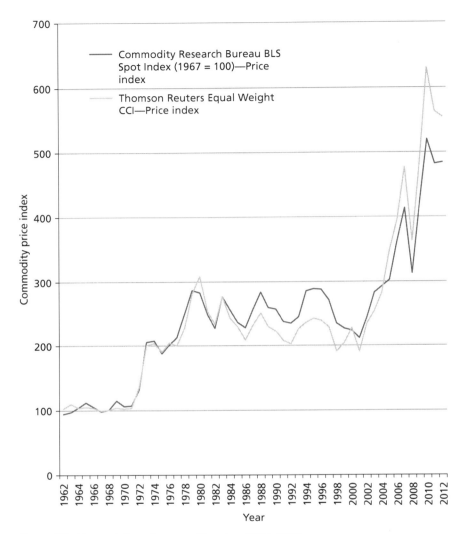

Figure 2.3. The evolution of commodity prices 1962–2012

Source: Thomson Datastream.

As a result, many firms are finding that there is a great deal of money to be made in increasing the efficiency with which resources are used. As Figure 2.1 suggested, this dynamic is particularly salient in the case of energy, where both anecdotal evidence and a number of careful comparative studies suggest that a compelling business case for increasing energy efficiency exists in many contexts. For example, a recent National Academies study conducted on behalf of the Department of Defense concluded that using LEED-Silver or equivalent standards in the design and construction of new buildings increased the costs of initial construction between 0 and 8 percent, but that since construction costs are typically only 5–10 percent of total life-cycle costs, building "green" or "high-performance" buildings increased total costs by less than 1 percent, while reducing energy costs by between 5 and 30 percent and water use by 8–11 percent over the life of the building. The commission recommended that all new Department of Defense buildings or major renovations use these standards.[7]

The widespread recognition of this opportunity has fueled the growth of hundreds of new firms. For example, Johnson Controls, one of the largest players in the space, had 2012 revenues of over $14bn in their energy efficiency business, while Schneider Electric, a €23bn global energy giant, recently repositioned itself as the "only global specialist in energy management," and claimed that more than 35 percent of its revenues were derived from its integrated solutions business. Similarly, an increasing fraction of new construction is being built with an eye to increased energy efficiency, and heavy equipment manufacturers across a range of industries have introduced energy-efficient products, including aerospace engines (GE, Rolls Royce) and compressors (Ingersoll R and United Technology).

Many firms have also reported significant savings from individual efforts to reduce energy. For example, KKR claims that the imposition of a systematic process of energy and water reduction across their portfolio companies has yielded returns of at least $150m a year for each of the past five years (Eccles et al., 2012), while between 1990 and 2012 IBM reduced electricity consumption by 6.1 billion kWh, saving $477 million through energy conservation alone.[8] Maersk, the world's largest container shipping company, forecasting that the cost of fuel was likely to rise from $250/ton in 2008 to $700/ton by 2020, committed to an aggressive program of energy efficiency, introducing "slow steaming" by its ships and reducing fuel use by 7 percent between 2009 and 2012 (Reinhardt et al., 2012). One report from the UN Foundation estimated that an investment of $US3.2 trillion worldwide in energy conservation would avoid new supply investments of $3 trillion and would pay for itself within three to five years.[9]

Similarly, technologies that enable reductions in water use are opening up new markets. For example, Jain Irrigation, an Indian firm specializing in "micro-irrigation" techniques, saw revenues grow at a 41 percent compound growth rate between 2005 and 2010 (Goldberg et al., 2012). Waste reduction is also emerging as a significant opportunity. For example, Walmart claims to have reduced waste by more than 80 percent, and in doing so to have returned $231m to the business in 2013.[10] Recycling is also an increasingly important

---

[7] National Research Council. (2013) *Energy-Efficiency Standards and Green Building Certification Systems Used by the Department of Defense for Military Construction and Major Renovations.* Washington, DC: The National Academies Press.

[8] Available at: <http://www.ibm.com/ibm/environment/climate/> (accessed July 2014).

[9] Available at: <http://www.globalproblems-globalsolutions-files.org/unf_website/PDF/realizing_potential_energy_efficiency.pdf> (accessed July 2014).

[10] Available at: <http://corporate.walmart.com/global-responsibility/environment-sustainability/zero-waste> (accessed July 2014).

business. Seventy percent of the feedstock to the aluminum industry, for example, is now derived from recycled materials, saving 95 percent of the energy required to make new aluminum from bauxite ore, and Waste Management estimates it could generate $15 billion of revenue annually if it could effectively separate and resell all the material in the roughly 100 million tons of rubbish it collects each year—something that would more than double the size of the company (Hecht, 2014).

SELLING TO THE ENVIRONMENT NICHE

A number of firms have been able to build successful businesses by developing highly differentiated offerings targeted specifically to consumers who value environmental performance. While only a relatively small proportion of consumers appear to be willing to pay more today for sustainable products, they are supporting some sizeable businesses. Stonyfield Farm, for example, had 2012 revenues of $360m and revenues at Patagonia, a leader in this space, are estimated to be about $500m. Some of the fastest-growing restaurant chains are claiming "sustainability" as a key identity. Starbucks is a particularly well-known example, but Chipotle had 2012 revenues of almost $3bn, while Panera Bread had 2012 revenues close to $2bn. Only 10 percent of Clorox's approximate $5b of sales are of "green" products, but they have been providing much of the firm's recent growth (Ofek and Barley, 2012).

On an even larger scale, Toyota sells more than 230,000 Priuses every year, making it a roughly $4.5bn business. Whole Foods had 2012 revenues of $11.7bn, while in the same year the sustainably orientated Triodos Bank had €8.0bn of assets under management, much of it provided by retail investors committed to the Bank's core mission.

Several opportunities to build entirely new kinds of businesses meeting entirely new needs have also emerged in the environmental space. The "clean tech" sector is both the most well known and the largest example. Renewable energy is still a relatively small share of the total energy supply, but it is a multi-billion dollar business. Walmart, for example, recently announced that they were planning to source 100 percent of their energy needs from renewable sources by 2020, while Verizon has committed to spending $100m on solar power and fuel cell technologies to power their operations.[11] Solar and wind have been growing at double-digit rates, and now provide 12 percent of total electric power in the US, with world-wide revenues in 2013 on the order of $100bn for each of them.[12]

---

[11] Available at: <http://www.mckinsey.com/insights/energy_resources_materials/the_disruptive_potential_of_solar_power?cid=ResourceRev-eml-alt-mkq-mck-oth-1404> (accessed July 2014).

[12] Pew Charitable Trust. (2013) "Manufacture, Compete: A Clean Energy Action Plan." Available at: <http://cleantechnica.com/2013/03/12/biofuel-wind-and-solar-global-market-values-set-to-double-by-2012/> (accessed July 2014).

Actively seeking to reduce consumption by building the so-called "shared economy" is another source of opportunity. For example, Avis recently bought Zipcar, the pioneering provider of "wheels when you want them" for $96m, and Zipcar's success has drawn in a host of new competitors, including firms such as Car2Go and Mint Cars on demand. Uber, the leading car hailing company, is reported to have revenues of over $20m a week, or more than $1bn a year, while Airbnb, the online room rental service, is expected to reach $1bn in revenues this year.[13]

Building a business case in the face of uncertainty

Thus in the case of a number of industries—including energy, chemicals, the built environment, transportation, and consumer goods—building a business case to act in the face of the environmental crisis is already relatively straightforward, and this perhaps explains why so many consultants and observers insist that "green is the new gold." In many sectors of the economy and for many firms, however, the business case for investments in sustainability rests much more on their ability to position the firm for advantage in anticipation of the ways in which an increasingly visible environmental crisis is likely to change the competitive context.

First, investing in anticipation of major shifts is always risky, but it is often also a powerful source of competitive advantage—or, at the least, a useful means of avoiding competitive disadvantage. In this case, for example, the case for investing to forestall potential brand damage or regulatory costs is likely to become increasingly compelling as consumers become increasingly concerned about sustainability, and as regulators respond to their concerns. Second, investing "ahead of the curve" may also allow firms to create first-mover advantage: investing in sustainability before it is required, for example, may enable firms to build brand advantage, or to create relationships or assets that will serve them well as the world shifts. Third, leading-edge firms often shape the future to their advantage. No one can be sure what will drive the kinds of technical, cultural, and political shifts that would make many sustainable business models profitable, but in many cases it seems plausible that private-sector action—particularly if it can be coordinated with other stakeholders—may play an important role in making them happen. Lastly, the increases in employee engagement that often emerge as the result of a commitment to sustainability may more than cover the usually minimal costs of making some of these pre-emptive or exploratory investments.

---

[13] Available at: <http://allthingsd.com/20131204/uber-essentially-confirms-revenue-estimates-but-bristles-over-source-of-valleywag-report/> (accessed July 2014).

I develop this argument in more depth using scenario analysis, an approach that was first developed at Shell, the oil major, as a tool for thinking about how a firm might frame strategy in the face of very significant uncertainties, when the common assumption that the future is likely to look like a slightly modified version of today is unlikely to hold (Wilkinson and Kupers, 2014). In these situations, it is much more useful to think of the firm as facing several different scenarios, or future worlds, in each of which it might be optimal to adopt a very different strategy, rather than being faced with a single future for which it must plan.

I explore three sources of uncertainty whose resolution would have a significant effect on the profitability of sustainable action: whether and when mainstream consumers come to value sustainable products and services enough to pay for them; whether and when increasingly acute environmental pressures generate political pressure for additional environmental regulation; and whether and when scientific and technological advances across a range of fields are likely to make responding to environmental issues significantly cheaper.

AN EMERGING CONSUMER MOVEMENT?

One of the major uncertainties surrounding the development of sustainable business models is the extent to which consumers will be willing to pay a premium for sustainable products and services. At the moment, the evidence on this point is mixed. On the one hand, one study has reported that two-thirds of consumers in six countries say that "as a society, we need to consume a lot less to improve the environment for future generations" (66 percent), and that they feel "a sense of responsibility to purchase products that are good for the environment and society" (65 percent).[14] The same study suggested that consumers in developing markets (Brazil, China, India) were more than twice as likely as their counterparts in developed markets (Germany, UK, US) to report purchasing products because of environmental and social benefits, being willing to pay more for sustainable products and encouraging others to buy from companies that are socially and environmentally responsible.

Careful experimental research similarly suggests that in some situations, some consumers will pay a significant premium for some products—although this work is still at a sufficiently early stage that we don't yet have a clear sense for the common factors that are at work across them. For example, two large-scale field experiments conducted with the apparel manufacturer Gap suggested that labels with information about a program to reduce water pollution increased sales by 8 percent amongst female shoppers, although

---

[14] Available at: <http://www.sustainablebrands.com/news_and_views/articles/rethinking-consump tion-finds-consumers-buying-less-and-better> (accessed July 2014). The findings are based on an online survey of 6,224 consumers across Brazil, China, India, Germany, the United Kingdom, and the United States conducted in September and October 2012.

they apparently had no such effect in outlet stores or on male shoppers (Hainmueller and Hiscox, 2012). Experiments in a major US grocery store chain suggested that sales of the two most popular bulk coffees sold in the store rose by almost 10 percent when the coffees were labeled as Fair Trade (Hainmueller et al., 2014) and an experiment on eBay suggested that shoppers were willing to pay a 23-percent premium for coffee labeled Fair Trade (Hiscox et al., 2011). Similarly, several studies of consumers' willingness to pay for "green power" suggest that some consumers are willing to pay a premium for sustainably produced electricity (Borchers et al., 2007; Bigerna and Paolo, 2011).

On the other hand, "green" products and services remain a niche product in many markets, with many firms reporting that consumers are not willing to pay more for them. For example, Walmart has not marketed its (extensive) green supply chain initiatives directly to consumers, apparently fearing that the "green" or "sustainable" label may be interpreted as either "expensive" or "lower quality" (Humes, 2011). Whether and when consumer preferences shift in this regard clearly has immediate implications for the profitability of acting sustainably.

POTENTIAL SHIFTS IN POLITICAL AND REGULATORY REGIMES

Similar uncertainties surround whether and when local, state, and national governments are likely to react to the threat of environmental degradation. For example, some US states have imposed their own "cap-and-trade" regimes in an attempt to limit the emissions of greenhouse gases, while others have mandated renewable portfolio standards. Europe has been experimenting with several different forms of carbon regulation, while some countries—including Norway and Australia—have imposed significant carbon taxes. The Chinese government appears to be attempting to shift its power sector towards a less carbon-intensive mix. Attempts to create a global carbon regime have so far been unsuccessful, but if the effects of climate change are as significant as some forecast, they may one day succeed.

Governments across the world are also exploring the possibility of increasing regulatory protection for natural systems such as water, clean air, and a variety of natural habitats, as well as potentially tightening up rules for the disposal of many different kinds of waste, with recent Australian and Chinese activity in this space perhaps the most far-reaching example.[15] Since these kinds of regulations are often viewed as constraints on short-term economic growth, it is very difficult to predict how they will evolve going forward, but historically significant increases in living standards have been accompanied by political pressure to raise environmental standards, so that accelerating growth in the developing world may well increase the pressure for environmental

---

[15] Available at: <http://www.economist.com/news/briefing/21583245-china-worlds-worst-polluter-largest-investor-green-energy-its-rise-will-have> (accessed July 2014).

regulation. Appropriate regulation can, of course, completely shift the land-scape for private-sector action. In the US, for example, investments in wind power have fluctuated significantly in response to the presence or absence of tax credits,[16] while the installation of solar power in Germany has been entirely dependent on the provision of generous incentives from the German government.[17]

TECHNOLOGICAL RESPONSES

Yet another critically important uncertainty is the question of how rapidly technological solutions are likely to emerge in response to the kinds of environmental pressures we are likely to face, since investing pre-emptively in these kinds of opportunities can often create advantage as costs come down. For example, Duke Energy's investments in renewable energy have forced them to explore both the technological challenges and the policy hurdles inherent in moving to distributed power generation, while both IBM and Cisco are investing aggressively in exploring the potential for technology to enable the creation of "Smart Cities." New technologies can rarely be adopted off the shelf, since their successful adoption usually requires the development of detailed knowledge about how they are likely to be used and how they can best be integrated into existing systems.

This issue is particularly salient since humans are almost infinitely resourceful, and it is possible that the next ten years will see major break-throughs in resource use, in agriculture, and in energy production that will dramatically lower their costs. For example, the cost of both solar and wind power has fallen dramatically over the past ten years—some estimates suggest that the cost of solar power has fallen by over 80 percent,[18] and some experts have predicted that the next few years will see a "resource revolution" in which investments of more than $1 trillion may lead to $3–4 trillion of potential efficiency gains.[19] Similarly, new approaches to the generation of nuclear power may significantly reduce costs, waste generation, and the threat of nuclear proliferation (Sahlman et al., 2012), while in Singapore, introducing "smart" transportation systems may cut the number of vehicles on the road by over 60 percent, while improving levels of service.[20] Investing in advance of these kinds of trends can allow the firm to develop the kind of on-the-ground

---

[16] Available at: <http://www.businessweek.com/articles/2014-01-09/wind-energy-companies-prepare-for-tax-credits-end> (accessed July 2014).

[17] U.S. National Renewable Energy Lab. (2010) *Policymaker's Guide to Feed-in Tariff Policies*. Available at: <www.nrel.gov/docs/fy10osti/44849.pdf>.

[18] Available at: <http://cleantechnica.com/2013/05/06/solar-pv-module-prices-have-fallen-80-since-2008-wind-turbines-29/> (accessed July 2014).

[19] Available at: <http://www.mckinsey.com/features/resource_revolution> (accessed July 2014). See also National Research Council (2013).

[20] Available at: <http://app.mot.gov.sg/page_land.aspx?p=/Land_Transport/Sustainable_Development/Promoting_Sustainable_Transport.aspx&AspxAutoDetectCookieSupport=1> (accessed July 2014).

experience, customer knowledge, and regulatory relationships that can allow them to take advantage of technological change as it occurs.

Scenario analysis: exploring the interaction between these trends

Following Peter Schwartz (1996), one can use these uncertainties to define a 2×2 grid defining four possible future worlds. I assume that the possibility that consumers will be willing to pay for products and services that prevent or mitigate environmental harm is so closely correlated with the possibility that there will be increasing political pressure for increased regulation that the two are effectively equivalent. This is clearly an enormous simplification, and if one was conducting this analysis for a single industry, or for a single geography, one could be much more precise—but at this very broad level of analysis it's not an unreasonable first cut. Figure 2.4 shows the results of mapping this possibility against the possibility of significant technological change.

Any such mapping is necessarily a simplification of a hugely complex underlying reality. This particular map, for example, doesn't explicitly focus on the question of how rapidly environmental degradation is likely to occur going forward, and here I thus make the implicit assumption that from a

Figure 2.4. One possible scenario grid

business perspective the key issue is not how rapidly the environmental crisis is likely to unfold but whether and how such degradation will feed through into consumer response or political action. Despite its simplicity, however, this map immediately highlights a number of critically important strategic and organizational dynamics.

Between them, the two uncertainties define four possible scenarios: "business as usual"; "green goes mainstream"; "demand-driven opportunity"; and "supply-driven opportunity." "Business as usual" is a world in which neither consumer demand nor regulatory pressure leads to any significant increase in the demand for sustainable products or services, and in which implementing sustainable solutions remains relatively expensive. Notice that it could still be a world in which there was very substantial environmental degradation—in this world, however, such degradation does not lead to any pressure for action. This is the world that most firms experience at present, and it appears to be the future that is taken for granted by many business people. For example, Exxon Mobil recently released a report asserting that the firm does not believe that there is a significant risk that any of their current reserves will become "stranded," or valueless, as a result of future changes to regulatory policy.[21]

Even those business people who do not believe that "business as usual" is the most likely future often act as if it were. As decades of organizational research have taught us, assumptions about how the world works and how it is likely to evolve are often deeply embedded in the structure of an organization—in its identity, in its information-processing routines, and in its organizational capabilities (Nelson and Winter, 1982; Hannan and Freeman, 1989; Tushman and O'Reilly, 1997). The identity and mental models of an organization often evolve only very slowly (Tripsas and Gavetti, 2000; Kaplan, 2008; Glynn et al., Chapter 6 (this volume)).

"Green goes mainstream" is a world in which accelerating technological change in combination with robust demand driven either by consumer preference or political pressure has opened up large markets for sustainable products and services. For those parts of the solar energy and wind power industry with strong political support and for those businesses such as Zipcar or Uber that already sell to sustainably orientated consumers and for whom the technologies necessary to support their business are already in place, this world is already a reality, but for many firms it remains only a possibility.

In "demand-driven opportunity," the technological progress necessary to develop new products is slow in coming and/or costly, but consumer or voter concern has led to an increasing demand for green products and/or for policies that penalize conventional offerings. Firms such as Patagonia and Seventh Generation, which sell more expensive products to those consumers who currently care about sustainability, are already experiencing this world,

---

[21] Available at: <http://cdn.exxonmobil.com/~/media/Files/Other/2014/Report%20-%20Energy%20and%20Carbon%20-%20Managing%20the%20Risks.pdf>.

but to date these kinds of products remain a relatively small share of the market.

"Supply-driven opportunity" is a world in which significant technical change has opened up opportunities, but neither consumers nor politicians are willing to allocate resources to pay more for sustainable products. The very large efforts focused on reducing energy demand are already experiencing this world—acting sustainably is economically viable even in the absence of consumer demand, and many observers believe that acceleration in raw material prices of all kinds will drive significant activity to this space going forward.

Mapping these examples to industries highlights the way in which the current case for sustainability differs enormously across the economy, with the major opportunities currently occurring in energy, buildings, water, agriculture, and consumer goods. In these cases, the uncertainties I have mapped are increasingly no longer uncertainties—firms can be sure that technological progress will occur, or that consumer or regulatory demand will enable them to offer a more highly priced product. But framing the strategic space in this way also focuses attention on the fact that for many industries, the case for becoming more sustainable rests on the assumptions one makes about how these uncertainties are likely to play out.

In many industries, raw materials and energy are a relatively small percentage of value added, and there is as yet only nascent consumer and political pressure to become more sustainable. One way to approach the development of sustainable business models in these contexts is to simply insist that the world is changing, and that becoming more sustainable is a far-sighted anticipatory response. But as this discussion suggests, we cannot be certain how the world is likely to evolve. It might prove to be the case, for example, that technological change triggers such significant improvements in resource productivity, and/or such dramatic reductions in the costs of carbon-free energy, that we can arrest or reverse the environmental decline and resource productivity that might otherwise occur. Similarly, environmental degradation could continue to accelerate, but economic pressure may make mainstream consumers very reluctant to pay for green products, and there may never be sufficient political will to impose appropriate regulation. Even if one believes that both trends are inevitable, there can be significant disagreement about the pace of change. It is much easier to make a business case if one is reasonably certain that major regulation is likely to be imposed next year than if one believes it is likely, but not for another twenty years. This kind of uncertainty is a constant feature of disruptive or discontinuous change, but it is not, in itself, a reason to do nothing. Nokia, for example, lost its phone business because of its inability to make a compelling case to make the investments necessary to compete with Apple in the smart phone business, while Corning survived the dot-com crash because it had invested in the technology necessary to make large displays many years in advance of their becoming commercially viable.

This uncertainty has very significant implications for the leadership of sustainable change. In the first place, it highlights the importance of distinguishing between models that are profitable now, given today's prices and technology, and models that represent strategic bets against possible future states of the world. Persuading a firm to make investments that are likely to be immediately profitable, while by no means always easy, presents a fundamentally different kind of strategic and organizational challenge from persuading firms to develop models whose success is contingent on some uncertain future state. In the second place, it focuses attention on the contingent nature of plausible sustainable business models. Their profitability in any particular context is going to be dependent on the rate at which the relevant uncertainties resolve themselves and their salience for the nature of the business. In any particular industry, the potential profitability of sustainable business models will be dependent on how much pressure these forces can exert, and on how rapidly they resolve.

Consider, for example, Unilever's move to introduce "sustainable tea." In 2007, Unilever became the first major tea company to commit to sustainable sourcing on a large scale. Unilever's tea business is substantial—Unilever sells roughly €3.5bn worth of tea, approximately 30 percent of the world's market for branded tea, and buys approximately 12 percent of the world's supply of black tea. The firm is committed to sourcing 100 percent of its tea sustainably by 2020, and, in partnership with the Rainforest Alliance, has developed an auditable standard. As of February 2014, 39 percent of Unilever's tea purchases were sourced from Rainforest Alliance-certified farms.[22]

Estimating the economic returns to this effort is complicated by the fact that it is impossible to know what would have happened to Unilever's share of market without the adoption of Rainforest Alliance certification, but those numbers that are available suggest that by 2011 the effort had roughly broken even. Moving to certified tea required training farmers—between 2007 and the end of 2012, for example, 450,000 farmers had been trained to Rainforest Alliance standards—and also meant paying a small premium for certified tea. However, in some markets the introduction of certified tea was associated with significant market share gains, at least in the short term. For example, in the UK the introduction of Rainforest Alliance-certified tea was associated with a share gain of 1.8 percent (Henderson, 2011). These introductions were not costless—for example, in the UK Unilever spent the entire €12m marketing budget on launching the new product—but given the difficulty of making share gains in such a hotly contested space these results are suggestive. The move to sustainable sourcing also generated economic gains for the farmers involved, as in many cases yields increased significantly and costs fell.

Has this strategy been successful? It has since been widely imitated by Unilever's competitors, with many of the world's largest tea brands announcing a commitment to sustainability. Such rapid imitation would suggest that the idea has gained some traction amongst consumers, and there is some evidence that Unilever's commitment to sustainability has significantly

---

[22] Available at: <http://www.unilever.com/sustainable-living/sustainablesourcing/tea/Accessed 2/1/2014> (accessed July 2014).

increased employment commitment and engagement.[23] Moreover, there is no evidence that it has harmed the brand, and some that it may even have increased brand equity.

But to think about it this way is to miss the point. Thinking about Unilever's strategy in the context of the scenario grid of Figure 2.4 suggests that it is better thought of as an experiment or as a well-designed strategic option. If the world does *not* change significantly—if the next five years see the "business-as-usual" scenario playing out—then Unilever has lost nothing. But should the world change—if, for example, consumer preferences switch aggressively towards sustainable brands—then Unilever may have established a first-mover position in consumers' minds that could be tremendously valuable. Less plausibly but still possibly, should climate change indeed have a negative effect on the productivity of tea plantations, Unilever's moves may have given it an advantage in accessing worldwide tea supplies. And, of course, if both should happen— should the tea industry move to the "green-goes-mainstream" future—then in retrospect Unilever's investment will come to be seen as a brilliant strategic move.

Another intriguing example is that of the Nissan Leaf. The Leaf—an all-electric, five-passenger compact car—was launched in December 2010. By the end of June 2013, the firm had cumulative sales of roughly 70,000 units (Nissan, 2013: Annual report), and installed capacity of 250,000 units/year.[24] The firm claimed that the Leaf was a profitable product,[25] but with estimates of Nissan's commitment to the car running as high as €4bn, and cumulative sales probably no greater than $2.2bn, it seems hard to argue that—at least so far— the Leaf has achieved a positive rate of return on its investment.[26]

But the Leaf, too, can be viewed as a strategic option against an uncertain future. Carlos Ghosn, Nissan's CEO, defends the Leaf as a long-term investment, and as an "asset to the brand".[27] He hopes to use it to enter the Chinese market, and he also believes that the company's head start in electric vehicle battery technology may give it a long-term advantage (Burgelman and Schifrin, 2011). As in the case of Unilever's tea business, in the "business as usual" scenario it's hard to see the Leaf as a huge success. But Nissan can certainly afford the investment—in 2012, Nissan's revenues were $94bn, and net income was over $5bn (Nissan AR, 2012)[28]—and again, should consumer

---

[23] Available at: <http://www.unilever.com/sustainable-living/betterlivelihoods/developing-and-engaging-our-people/> (accessed July 2014).

[24] Available at: <http://insideevs.com/nissan-leaf-production-starts-at-3rd-assembly-plant-in-sunderland-uk-factory-video/> (accessed January 2014).

[25] Available at: <http://www.sustainablebusiness.com/index.cfm/go/news.display/id/25362> (accessed January 2014).

[26] Available at: <http://www.plugincars.com/ghosn-defends-nissan-leaf-calling-electric-cars-future-automobile-126844.html> (accessed January 2014).

[27] Available at: <http://www.plugincars.com/ghosn-defends-nissan-leaf-calling-electric-cars-future-automobile-126844.html> (accessed January 2014).

[28] Available at: <http://www.nissan-global.com/EN/DOCUMENT/PDF/AR/2012/AR2012_E_All.pdf> (accessed July 2014).

preferences shift towards sustainability, or should the political climate shift to support widespread carbon regulation, Nissan's first-mover position may give it a very significant advantage in a "demand-driven opportunity" world.

A number of other major consumer-orientated companies similarly appear to be preparing for a world in which consumers increasingly value sustainable products. For example, it is probably not the case that Chipotle's recent remarkable growth has been driven by its commitment to "Food with Integrity," since in a 2007 interview the CEO of Chipotle estimated that only about 5 percent of his consumers knew about the campaign and the company conducts only minimal advertising.[29] But the firm's positioning both give it an edge with those consumers who do value sustainable agriculture and means that should consumer tastes shift, the company will be well positioned to meet them.

The renewable energy strategies currently being pursued by many of the large energy suppliers can similarly be best understood as strategic hedges, placed against the possibility that carbon will be regulated or taxed in the foreseeable future, and/or that the price of conventional energy will rise dramatically. For example, the economics of Duke Energy's plan to build a nuclear reactor look only marginally profitable given today's energy prices and regulatory regime, but would look a great deal better should either shift (Vietor and Reinhardt, 2014), while BP's $2.9bn investment in a range of renewable technologies including wind, solar, and biofuels,[30] almost certainly has a similar strategic rationale.

Implications for leading sustainable change

This framing has a number of important implications for the leadership of sustainable change. In the first place it suggests that developing a deep understanding of key uncertainties—and incorporating them directly into the firm's strategic thinking—may be critically important to building an accurate and persuasive business case for sustainability. In many contexts it is a mistake to blindly insist that acting sustainably is simply "the right thing to do" or that it is always likely to be profitable. Some of the discussion around "shared value", for example, can be construed as suggesting that the set of actions that simultaneously makes a difference in the world and creates value for the firm is clearly delineated. In reality, however, this boundary is both fuzzy and constantly changing—and this has important implications both for how the strategic process should be led and for how organizational efforts designed to improve the sustainability of the firm should be managed.

---

[29] Available at: <http://www.businessweek.com/stories/2007-02-16/chipotle-fast-food-with-integritybusinessweek-business-news-stock-market-and-financial-advice> (accessed January 2014).
[30] Available at: http://www.bp.com/sectiongenericarticle.do?categoryId=9030041&contentId=7055175 (accessed July 2014).

MANAGING THE STRATEGY PROCESS

In established businesses dominated by incremental change, strategic planning is often difficult to distinguish from budgeting, and is largely a matter of planning incremental extensions to the current business. Indeed, in many firms the immediate needs of the firm's largest customers dominate the strategic agenda, making it very difficult to invest in anything significantly different (Christensen, 1997). The fact that the business case for sustainability is—for many sectors and firms—likely to be dependent on the recognition of the uncertainties facing the world and the potential advantage that may be realized by anticipating them suggests that one of the most important tasks for leaders trying to drive their organization towards sustainability is the development of a strategic process that incorporates the time and expertise necessary to do the kind of uncertainty-driven strategic framing I outlined earlier. Such a process, for example, would invest heavily in understanding the nature of the most salient uncertainties facing the business, would carefully track them over time (Wilkinson and Kupers, 2014), and would focus attention on those investments that are likely to be "robust," in that they are worth making in a range of possible futures.

Developing such a process is also likely to have a number of important organizational benefits. Strategic discontinuities must be coupled with organizational discontinuities if they are to be navigated successfully. Large, successful firms often react to them first with denial ("it's not happening"), then with skepticism ("even if it does happen we won't be able to make any money"), and then with incompetence and inertia, as old identities, structures, and processes make the execution of new strategies difficult (Tushman and Romanelli, 1985; Hannan and Freeman, 1989).

Effective strategic framing can be a powerful tool to help overcome these kinds of barriers. In the first place, new frames can help to confront denial. The reluctance to admit the possibility that the world is fundamentally changing is deeply rooted in both individual cognition and in the dynamics of firm identity. In this context, simply asserting that the world is changing and expecting the organization to shift is unlikely to be successful. But using a tool like scenario analysis—one that moves the debate away from the question "Is global warming real?" to "Is there a real possibility that an increased public perception that global warming is real may lead to increased regulation of global warming gases?" can be enormously helpful in reframing perceptions. Figure 2.5, for example, shows the probabilities two groups of executives estimated characterized the uncertainties identified in Figure 2.4 in the context of a discussion of the energy supply business and the consumer goods industry, respectively.[31]

---

[31] Both figures are composites derived from teaching and consulting to a large number of global executives.

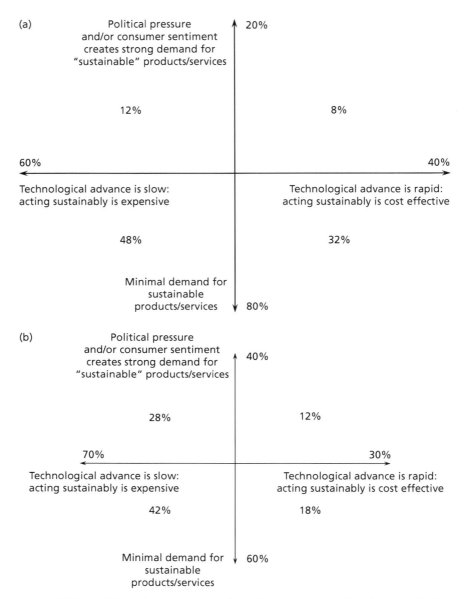

Figure 2.5 (a) and (b). Estimated uncertainties in the consumer goods industry and in the energy supply industry respectively

In both cases, the "business-as-usual" scenario—no major shift in the technological opportunity set and no major shift in either consumer demands or the regulatory context—is the most likely scenario. But in both cases, the odds of its coming to pass—if one believes these executives—is less than 50 percent. My experience has been that this recognition—that *by their own reckoning* the odds of the "business-as-usual" scenario continuing into the indefinite future are less than 50/50—changes the conversation amongst a group in significant ways. Indeed, in some cases I have seen it support a major shift in orientation—away from "It isn't going to happen" to "It might happen"—and—most importantly—to the idea that assuming that there is no real chance that sustainable business models will be important is a mistake. This kind of analysis can be also be organizationally helpful in that it immediately highlights the business case for investing in "experiments," and for developing the organizational capabilities that will be required to make these experiments a success.

Another benefit of thinking through the potential for sustainable business models from this perspective is that it also focuses attention on the factors that are likely to resolve the uncertainties that are central to any decision, and most importantly on the degree to which firms themselves can affect these uncertainties. For example, Unilever's decision to put its entire tea business on a sustainable footing has been followed by similar announcements from all of its major competitors. What might have been a competitive disadvantage for the firm has thus been transformed into table stakes—and possibly into an advantage, since Unilever has a very significant head start in greening its supply chain. While one cannot be sure that Unilever's behavior has caused this shift, it certainly seems within the realms of possibility. Similarly, Nissan's investment in electric vehicles has been accompanied by a commitment to sell the technology that it develops as a result to the rest of the industry, thus significantly reducing the costs of other firms and potentially accelerating the adoption of the infrastructure needed to support them. The private-sector investments in clean energy that have played a huge role in driving down the cost of both wind and solar energy—some observers now believe that solar energy may be cost competitive with fossil-fuel-based energy by 2020 in most applications—have similarly changed the political climate surrounding carbon regulation.

More broadly, it seems plausible that many of the shifts in consumer preferences and/or in the political environment that are likely to make the widespread deployment of sustainable models profitable are unlikely to happen without coordinated action at either the level of the industry or the state. Building the basis for a sustained conversation about sustainable business models thus has the potential to support the firm's engagement in these broader networks and levels of action. For example, Nike has been central to the apparel industry's effort to improve both environmental and labor standards, while HP and IBM appear to have played similarly critical roles within the IT industry. There is some evidence that these kinds of efforts can play a crucial role in complementing local, state-based regulation (Locke, 2013). Thinking about strategic efforts within this kind of contingent framework may thus be a means for engaging the organization in the kinds of long-term, multiple-player-based effort that is almost certainly critical to long-term sustainable change.

ORGANIZATIONAL IMPLICATIONS

Thinking of many sustainability orientated investments as hedges against risk or as strategic bets against future states of the world also highlights the fact that they may need to be managed quite differently from investments designed to pay off in the near future, in ways that are orientated towards the support of flexibility and innovation. Shifts in strategy must be coupled with shifts in organizational architectures. This is a theme that is taken up extensively in the other chapters of this volume, but the scenario-based perspective provides a particularly useful lens through which one can understand quite how important this is likely to be and why it is likely to be particularly difficult because it makes explicit the fact that there is no guarantee that these efforts will be successful.

As a long literature has suggested, the organizational structures best suited to exploit the existing business are quite distinct from those required to explore new possibilities (Henderson and Clark, 1990; March, 1991; Tushman and O'Reilly, 1997; Ancona et al., Chapter 9 (this volume); Tushman et al., Chapter 10 (this volume); Edmondson et al., Chapter 11 (this volume)). Running the existing business well requires well-developed skills in operational excellence and the ability to execute rapidly and effectively, while building entirely new businesses often requires abandoning existing routines and procedures in favor of new ways of operating that support creativity, flexibility, and the ability to fail. These two modes typically require quite different organizational structures, quite different incentive structures, and quite different time frames and formal metrics.

If it is indeed the case that in many firms, environmental investments are strategic bets against possible futures, managing them will require holding the tension between these two very distinct modes of organizing. Opportunities within the "business-as-usual" quadrant may challenge the organization, but they have the great advantage of being at least minimally profitable according to the firm's established metrics. Opportunities in the other three quadrants are—by definition—only likely to be significant sources of financial return in the potentially quite distant future and in some—very uncertain—states of the world. They are exploratory by their very nature, and investing effectively in them is likely to require both the implementation of local mechanisms that ensure they are managed to allow for creativity and flexibility, and the development of the capability at the most senior level of the firm to manage two very different kinds of project simultaneously. In this context, effective leadership must be "ambidextrous"—able to support the evolution of the firm's identity and organization in a way that both honors the firm's pasts and invests against its probable future. This is the task explored in the subsequent chapters of this volume.

Conclusion

In this chapter I have argued that making the business case for sustainable environmental change is both more complex and more interesting than is generally assumed. I have argued that, as many observers have suggested, in some industries and for some firms the benefits of environmental action can be directly internalized today, focusing particularly on the benefits of using raw materials more efficiently, securing supply, preventing brand damage, selling to the sustainable niche, and building entirely new businesses. But I have further suggested that for many firms, the case for sustainable change is better understood as a strategic bet against a number of possible future states. I have suggested that if this is the case it not only explains why cross-sectional studies of the relationship between environmental action and financial returns have yielded such mixed results, but also has important implications for the ways in which one should think about leading and learning how to execute sustainable change.

▤ REFERENCES

Bigerna, Simona and Polinori, Paolo. (2011) *Italian Consumers' Willingness to Pay for Renewable Energy Sources. Working paper, MPRA*. Available at: <http://mpra.ub.uni-muenchen.de/34408/> (accessed July 2014).

Borchers, Allison, Duke, Joshua, and Parsons, George. (2007) "Does Willingness to Pay for Green Energy Differ by Source?," *Energy Policy* 35 (6): 3327–34.

Bresnahan, Tim, Greenstein, Shane, and Henderson, Rebecca. (2012) "Schumpeterian Competition and Diseconomies of Scope: Illustrations from the History of Microsoft and IBM," in J. Lerner and S. Stern (eds), *The Rate and Direction of Inventive Activity Revisited*, NBER conference volume. Chicago and London: University of Chicago Press, 203–76.

Burgelman, Robert and Schifrin, Debra. (2011) "Nissan's Electric Vehicle Strategy in 2011," June. HBS Case No. SM189. Stanford, CA: Stanford Business School Press.

Christensen, Clayton. (1997) *The Innovator's Dilemma*. Boston, MA: Harvard Business School Press.

Eccles, Robert G., Ioannou, Ioannis, and Serafeim, George. (forthcoming) "The Impact of Corporate Sustainability on Organizational Processes and Performance," *Management Science*.

Eccles, Robert G., Serafeim, George, and Clay, Tiffany. (2012) "KKR: Leverage Sustainability," HBS Case No. 112032. Boston, MA: Harvard Business School Press.

Esty, Daniel and Winston, Andrew. (2006) *Green to Gold: How Smart Companies Use Environmental Strategy to Innovate, Create Value, and Build Competitive Advantage*. Princeton, NJ: Wiley.

Goldberg, Ray, Knoop, Carin-Isabel, and Preble, Matthew. (2012) "Jain Irrigation Systems Limited: Inclusive Growth for India's Farmers," HBS Case 912403. Boston, MA: Harvard Business School Press.

Hainmueller, Jens and Hiscox, M. (2012) "The Socially Conscious Consumer? Field Experimental Tests of Consumer Support for Fair Labor Standards," Working paper. Stanford, CA: Stanford University.

Hainmueller, Jens, Hiscox, M. and Sequeira, S. (2014) "Consumer Demand for the Fair Trade Label: Evidence from a Field Experiment," *Review of Economics and Statistics* (forthcoming).

Hannen, M. T. and Freeman, J. H. (1989) *Organizational Ecology*. Cambridge, MA: Harvard University Press.

Hansen, Morten T., Ibarra, Herminia, and Peyer, Urs. (2010) "The Best-Performing CEOs in the World," *Harvard Business Review*, January–February.

Heck, Stefan, Rogers, Matt, and Carroll, Paul. (2014) *Resource Revolution: How to Capture the Biggest Business Opportunity in a Century*. Seattle, Washington: New Harvest.

Henderson, Rebecca. (2011) "Sustainable Tea at Unilever," HBS Case 9-712-438. Boston, MA: Harvard Business School Press.

Henderson, R. M. and Clark, K. B. (1990) "Architectural Innovation: The Reconfiguration of Existing Product Technologies and the Failure of Established Firms," *Administrative Science Quarterly* 35: 9–30.

Hiscox, Michael, Broukhim, Michael, and Litwin, Claire. (2011) "The Premium for Fair Trade: New Evidence from a Field Experiment Using Ebay Auctions." Available at <http://papers.ssrn.com/sol3/papers.cfm?abstract_id=1811783> (accessed July 2014).

Hoffman, Andrew. (2002) *From Heresy to Dogma: An Institutional History of Corporate Environmentalism*. Stanford, CA: Stanford University Press.

Humes, Edward. (2011) *Force of Nature: The Unlikely Story of Wal-Mart's Green Revolution*. New York, NY: Harper Business.

Jorgenson, Dale, Goettle, Richard, Ho, Mun, and Wilcoxen, Peter. (2013) *Double Dividend: Environmental Taxes and Fiscal Reform in the United States*, Cambridge, MA: MIT Press.

Kaplan, Sarah. (2008) "Framing Contests: Making Strategy Under Uncertainty," *Organization Science* 19 (5): 729–52.

Locke, Richard M. (2013) *The Promise and Limits of Private Power Promoting Labor Standards in a Global Economy*. Cambridge: Cambridge University Press.

March, James G. (1991) "Exploration and Exploitation in Organizational Learning," *Organizational Science* 2 (1): 71–87.

Margolis, Joshua D. and Walsh, James P. (2003) "Misery Loves Companies: Rethinking Social Initiatives by Business," *Administrative Science Quarterly* 48: 268–305.

McKinsey Global Institute. (2011) "Resource Revolution: Meeting the World's Energy, Food and Water Needs." Available at: <http://www.mckinsey.com/features/resource_revolution> (accessed July 2014).

National Research Council. (2013) *Energy-Efficiency Standards and Green Building Certification Systems Used by the Department of Defense for Military Construction and Major Renovations*. Washington, DC: The National Academies Press.

Nelson, R. and Winter, S. (1982) *An Evolutionary Theory of Economic Change*. Cambridge, Mass: Harvard University Press.

Ofek, Elie and Barley, Lauren. (2012) "The Chlorox Company: Leveraging Green for Growth," Case study. Boston, MA: Harvard Business School Press.

Pew Charitable Trust. (2013) "Manufacture, Compete: A Clean Energy Action Plan." Available at: <http://cleantechnica.com/2013/03/12/biofuel-wind-and-solar-global-market-values-set-to-double-by-2012/> (accessed July 2014).

Porter, Michael and Kramer, Mark. (2011) "Creating Shared Value," *Harvard Business Review* 89 (1/2): 62–77.

Reinhardt, Forest, Casadesus-Masanell, Ramon, and Nelleman, Frederick. (2012) "Maersk Line and the Future of Container Shipping," HBS Case No. 712449.

Sahlman, W., Nanda, R., Lassiter, J., and McQuade, J. (2012) "Terrapower," HBS case 9-813-108. Boston, MA: Harvard Business Press Review.

Schwartz, Peter. (1996) *The Art of the Long View: Planning for the Future in an Uncertain World*. New York: Doubleday.

Stavins, Robert. (2011) "The Problem of the Commons: Still Unsettled after 100 Years," *American Economic Review* 101: 81–108.

Stern, Nicholas. (2008) "The Economics of Climate Change," *American Economic Review* 98: (2): 1–37.

Toffel, Michael W. and Jodi L. Short. (2011) "Coming Clean and Cleaning Up: Does Voluntary Self-Reporting Indicate Effective Self-Policing?," *Journal of Law & Economics* 54 (3): 609–49.

Tripsas, Mary and Gavetti, Giovanni. (2000) "Capabilities, Cognition and Inertia: Evidence from Digital Imaging," *Strategic Management Journal* 21: 1147–61.

Tushman, M. L. and Romanelli, E. (1985) "Organizational Evolution: A Metamorphosis Model of Convergence and Reorientation," *Research in Organizational Behavior* 7: 171–222.

Tushman, Michael and O'Reilly, C. (1997) *Winning Through Innovation*. Boston, MA: Harvard Business School Press.

United Nations Foundation. (2007) "Realizing the Potential of Energy Efficiency," co-chair Eberhard Jochem and Zhou Dadi. Available at: <http://www.globalproblems-globalsolutions-files.org/unf_website/PDF/realizing_potential_energy_efficiency.pdf> (accessed July 2014).

U.S. National Renewable Energy Lab. (2010) *Policymaker's Guide to Feed-In Tariff Policies*. Available at: <http://www.nrel.gov/docs/fy10osti/44849.pdf> (accessed July 2014).

Vietor, Richard and Reinhardt, Forest. (2014) "Duke Energy and the Nuclear Renaissance," HBS Case No. 712002. Boston, MA: Harvard Business Press Review.

Wilkinson, Angela and Kupers, Roland. (2014) *The Essence of Scenarios: Learning from the Shell Experience*. Amsterdam: Amsterdam University Press.

Winston, Andrew. (2014) *The Big Pivot: Radically Practical Strategies for a Hotter, Scarcer, and More Open World*. Boston, MA: Harvard Business Press Review.

Part II
The Big Picture

3 Stumbling Towards Sustainability

Why Organizational Learning and Radical Innovation are Necessary to Build a More Sustainable World—But Not Sufficient

John Sterman

Our civilization is unsustainable and it is getting worse fast. Humans now appropriate 38 percent of net primary production. Most of the rest is unavailable, leaving only 9 percent for future growth. Humanity has exceeded sustainable boundaries for greenhouse gases (GHGs), nitrogen, biodiversity loss, and other critical resources and ecosystem services. The ecological footprint of humanity is now 1.5 times the sustainable carrying capacity of the Earth.[1] At the same time, population is expected to grow by 2 billion by 2050 and consumption per capita is growing exponentially. Reducing our global footprint to sustainable levels while population grows and billions around the world legitimately aspire to rise out of poverty is the defining issue of our time.

Meeting the challenge requires rapid change and transformation throughout society. But how can such change be achieved? Here I offer a dynamic systems perspective to raise questions about the processes of change required, at multiple scales.

At the organizational level, firms are implementing improvement programs to cut energy and resource use, reduce waste generation, design more sustainable products and services, and so on, often with the expectation that they can do well by doing good: simultaneously reducing costs and environmental impact. Yet research shows that traditional process improvement initiatives directed at cost, quality, and productivity commonly fail. Sustainability initiatives share many of the same attributes. Why do so many such programs fail and what can be done to improve them?

At the industry level, many attempts to introduce radical new technologies, such as alternative fuel vehicles, exhibit "sizzle-and-fizzle" behavior. Why, and

---

[1] E.g., Wackernagel et al. (2002) (updated at <http://www.footprintnetwork.org> (accessed July 2014); Rockström et al. (2009); and Running (2012).

what can be done to create markets for radical new technologies that are sustainable not only ecologically but economically?

At the level of the economy, does it all add up? If firms are successful in "greening" their operations and products, if new, more sustainable industries arise, will they actually move our society towards sustainability, or will greater consumption overwhelm eco-efficiency?

Throughout, I draw on modern research to outline answers to these questions, provide examples showing how some managers have been able to improve the sustainability of their products and operations—often profitably—and suggest how organizations can move forward, individually and collectively, to help build a more sustainable world in which all can thrive.

Sustainability as product-and-process improvement

To begin, consider programs designed to promote sustainability within existing organizations. Nearly all firms now seek to reduce their GHGs, energy consumption, and waste generation in the name of sustainability. Initiatives to reduce a firm's environmental impact, improve labor practices and ethical sourcing, and develop more sustainable products and services can be usefully analyzed through the lens of process improvement programs. The primary difference is that traditional improvement initiatives are justified and marketed to employees, supply chain partners, customers, and investors as critical for competitive advantage, profitability, or firm survival—that is, they are seen as central to the core business—while sustainability initiatives are framed as (also) helping to heal the world.

Across nearly all industries, the unit costs of production, product capabilities, and other product-and-process attributes steadily improve through learning by doing, investment in R&D, responding to feedback from customers, and other means.[2] The rate of learning in any process can be characterized by its *improvement half-life*, the time required for defects in the process to be cut in half. The concept of "defects" includes any characteristics of a process that lead to waste or error, including product defects, safety incidents, unit costs, process cycle times, and other traditional business metrics, as well as energy consumption, pollution, solid waste generation, and other metrics relevant to sustainability. Figure 3.1 shows two examples with very different half-lives: the manufacturing cycle time for an electronics assembly plant at Ford Motor Company, and the number of traffic fatalities per vehicle mile traveled (VMT) in the US. After the plant initiated an improvement program, the manufacturing cycle time fell rapidly, from over 100 hours to about 16

---

[2] The literature is huge. See, e.g., Argote (2013) and Nagy et al. (2013).

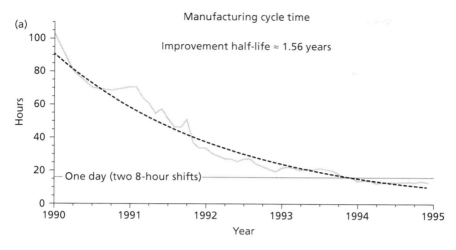

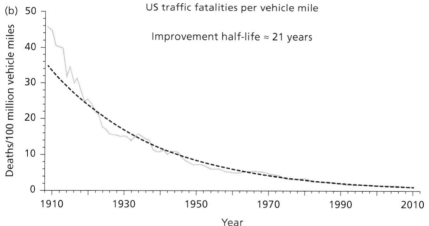

Figure 3.1. Improvement and improvement half-life in two processes. (a) Manufacturing cycle time in an electronics assembly plant

Source: Repenning 1996.

(b) US traffic fatalities per VMT. Note: solid line: data; dashed line: best-fit exponential decay at the estimated half-life.

Source: Historical Statistics of the United States, Table Df413-417 (1900–1995); NHTSA, <http://www-fars.nhtsa.dot.gov/Main/index.aspx> (1995–2010) (accessed July 2014).

(a single two-shift workday), with an average improvement half-life of only about 1.6 years. In contrast, US auto fatalities fell from a peak of 45 per 100 million vehicle miles traveled (VMT) in 1909 to about 1.1 per 100 million VMT by 2010, an average improvement half-life of about 21 years.

What accounts for the difference in improvement half-lives? Improvement arises from an iterative process in which workers search for and experiment with new ways of carrying out tasks, select and adopt the best ones, then search

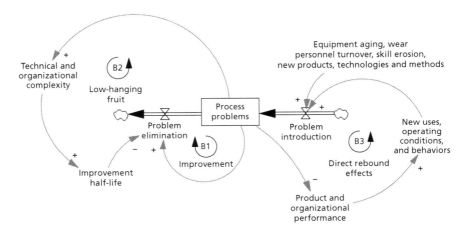

The stock of problems in any process represents the root causes of all sources of defects, waste and error. Process problems are eliminated by learning and process improvement. The stock of process problems, P, is governed by

$$dP/dt = Problem\ Introduction\ -Problem\ Elimination = Problem\ Introduction - \phi\ (P{-}P min)$$

where $P_{min} \geq 0$ is the minimum possible problem level and ϕ, the fractional improvement rate, is determined by the improvement half-life, $\phi = \ln(2)/t_h$. If the improvement half-life is constant, the level of process problems falls exponentially. Improvement will be slower than exponential when the improvement half-life rises with increasing process complexity, as shown by the balancing *Low Hanging Fruit* feedback B2.

Figure 3.2. Core feedback structure of process improvement

for additional improvements.[3] The iterative process of search, trial, evaluation, and adoption of improvements can be informal and tacit, or take place in the context of a formal improvement methodology such as Six Sigma.

Figure 3.2 shows the core feedback structure governing improvement processes. The stock of process problems—the total number of root causes generating defects, waste, or errors of any type—is decreased by improvement and increased as equipment ages and wears, as personnel turnover and skills are lost, and as new products, technologies, and methods are introduced. If problem elimination from improvement exceeds the creation of new problems, then the stock of process problems will fall, boosting the performance of the organization's products and processes. The larger the stock of process problems, the greater the effort to improve, forming the balancing (negative) *Improvement* feedback labeled B1 in Figure 3.2. How fast can that improvement occur? Whether formal or informal, the improvement half-life for any process is determined by the cycle time for each iteration of the learning cycle and the fractional improvement achieved per cycle. The faster the cycle time and the more learned per cycle, the shorter the improvement half-life.

---

[3] Sterman et al. (1997) develop and test a system dynamics model of process improvement. See also Zangwill and Kantor (1998) and Argote (2013) for theories of learning and improvement as an iterative cycle.

Improvement half-lives vary across processes and over time. Sterman et al., following Schneiderman,[4] argue that improvement half-lives increase with the technical and organizational complexity of the process. Technical complexity is straightforward: improvement will be faster for a simple milling machine than for the tooling used to fabricate the wing for the Boeing 787. Organizational complexity refers to the number of different personnel, organizational functions and levels, and organizations that must be involved to improve the process. Improving the milling machine requires only a few people—the operator, perhaps a mechanic—while improving the 787 wing requires the active participation of labor from multiple crafts, engineers from many different disciplines inside Boeing, and from its suppliers and tooling vendors, and the managers in each of those organizations required to coordinate the process. Improvement half-lives are on the order of a few months for processes with low technical and organizational complexity, but several years or more for processes with higher complexity, such as product development or vendor–supplier relationships.[5]

Considering the examples in Figure 3.1, the technical and organizational complexity of the electronics assembly plant is low: cutting the manufacturing cycle time involved improving the reliability and quality of relatively simple equipment and processes. Doing so required the participation of relatively few workers, engineers, and front-line managers, all from the same facility. In contrast, automobiles are technically complex, with tight couplings among major subsystems including drive train, brakes, suspension, sensors, and controls, and between the vehicle and driving environment, including road design, signage, traffic conditions, and driver skills. Organizational complexity is even higher: modern automobile product development involves hundreds of engineers from multiple backgrounds, along with people from marketing, production, procurement, finance, environment, legal, and other departments, and representatives of component suppliers from tires and glass to airbags and telematics. Coordination among auto companies also affects the pace of improvement. Working sometimes with, and sometimes in opposition to, their rivals, governments, the insurance industry, physicians, and citizen groups, automakers have shaped technology, regulations, and legislation affecting safety such as seat belts and air bags. Such high technical, organizational, and political complexity leads to a much longer improvement half-life for automotive safety compared to process improvement within a plant.

Figure 3.3 qualitatively maps different sustainability issues into the space of technical and organizational/political complexity. Many energy efficiency and waste reduction programs, for example, have very low complexity on both

---

[4] Schneiderman (1988) developed the concept of the improvement half-life and showed how these vary with technical and organizational complexity. Sterman et al. (1997) showed how differences in improvement half-lives in different processes, such as manufacturing and product development, led to stress, including lay offs at a major semiconductor firm. Repenning and Sterman (2002) showed how such mismatches undermined improvement programs in a major automaker.

[5] Schneiderman (1988).

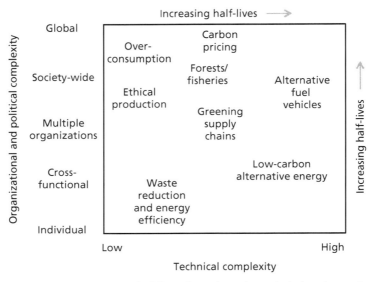

Figure 3.3. Process improvement half-lives depend on the technical and organizational/political complexity of the process. The complexity of illustrative sustainability issues is shown.

dimensions, and there are many such opportunities with very short payback times, high Return-on-Investment (ROI,) and positive net present value.[6] Alternative energy projects such as wind turbines and solar photovoltaics have higher technical and organizational complexity—insulating your attic is often a DIY project, while installing a solar PV array on your roof involves PV module suppliers, an architect or contractor, installers, and local governments who permit and inspect the work. Greening a firm's supply chain is technically challenging due to the need to consider life-cycle impacts of the entire process from raw materials to disposal/recycling, and organizationally challenging, as the focal firm must partner effectively with multiple tiers in increasingly global supply networks. Creating a low-carbon automobile fleet involves envelope-pushing technical complexity but also requires society-wide coordination among automakers and their supply chains, fuel providers, governments, and other actors required to build critical complementary assets, including fueling infrastructure, to develop consumer awareness and acceptance of new technologies, and so on. Ethical production, including decent wages and healthy, safe workplaces is technically simple—there is no technical challenge in providing fire alarms and emergency exits in garment factories—but involves coordination across retailers, suppliers, unions, labor activists, NGOs, governments, and others in a global economy.[7] Sustainable management

---

[6] See, e.g., Porter and Van der Linde (1995); McKinsey (2010); Lovins (2012); and and Lyneis and Sterman (2016).
[7] Amengual (2014) and Locke (2013).

of common pool resources such as forests, fisheries, and the climate involves moderate technical complexity, but very high organizational and political complexity, often requiring multi-scale, polycentric governance extending from the community level to the global level of international agreements and treaties.[8] Finally, reducing overconsumption is technically simple, but raises contentious social and political issues rooted in difficult questions about the meaning and purpose of our lives.

The implications for sustainability are clear. Within firms, we can expect that technically and organizationally simple actions, primarily around resource efficiency and waste generation, will yield large returns and rapid improvement, while programs to improve ethical production, labor standards, and the health, safety, and environmental sustainability of the supply chain will prove to be more difficult. Walmart provides a typical example: energy efficiency and waste reduction initiatives, where improvement half-lives are short, were notably successful. More complex supply chain initiatives had mixed outcomes, including some failures (organic cotton, sustainable seafood, RoHS-compliant electronics sourcing, e-waste take-backs), while Walmart chose not to address organizationally and politically complex issues such as ethical sourcing and working conditions,[9] and reportedly "played the lead role in blocking an effort to have global retailers pay more for apparel to help Bangladesh factories improve their electrical and fire safety," with fatal consequences for those who labored on its behalf.[10]

Improvement half-lives are not constant over time. Over time, improvement rates slow as performance approaches physical limits. Typically, as the easy improvements are made, the technical and organizational complexity of the next improvement effort increases, shown in Figure 3.2 as the balancing *low-hanging fruit* feedback, B2. Although the best fit to the US auto fatality data for the entire period from 1910 to 2010 yields an average improvement half-life of about 21 years, the estimated improvement half-life for the decade from 1910–1920 is just 12 years, while the best fit for the period 1990–2010 yields a half-life of 29 years. Safety-related innovations at the dawn of the auto age included such low-hanging fruit as brakes, headlights and taillights, windshields and windshield wipers, stop signs, and traffic laws. Recent innovations—air bags, antilock brakes, traction control, stronger social norms against drunk driving—involved far greater technical and especially organizational, political, and social complexity.

The rate of problem introduction is also at least partly endogenous. As the stock of process problems falls and the organization's products and processes improve, quality and functionality rise while costs fall. Better, less expensive products attract new customers and find new uses, creating new process problems. The balancing *rebound effects* feedbacks (B3 in Figure 3.2)

---

[8] Ostrom (2010).
[9] Plambeck and Denend (2010) and Humes (2011) discuss Walmart's sustainability programs.
[10] Greenhouse (2012).

undermine the benefits of improvement activity by introducing new process problems as a consequence of improvement itself. For example, as automobiles and roads became better, cheaper, and more widely available, driving increased. The growth in VMT per capita, together with population growth, caused total US VMT per year to grow explosively, from essentially zero in 1900 to 250 billion in 1945, to nearly 3 trillion in 2010, an increase of nearly a factor of 12 from 1945 to 2010. Further, as autos became safer, people drove faster and in more dangerous conditions, slowing the improvement in fatalities per VMT, an example of a rebound effect through risk homeostasis.[11] As a consequence, automobile fatalities in the US grew from 36 in 1900 to nearly 27,000 in 1945, and have exceeded 30,000 per year ever since, despite continued reductions in fatalities per VMT.

Sustainability programs are subject to similar rebound effects: reducing the waste and energy embedded in a product lowers costs and prices, stimulating demand for the more efficient product (the direct rebound effect) and increasing people's disposable income, so that overall consumption rises (the indirect rebound effect).[12] Population growth, rising incomes, and rebound effects can overwhelm even large improvements in eco-efficiency.

The implications for sustainability are clear: goals for reductions in resource use and waste generation must be framed in absolute terms. For example, limiting global warming to the internationally ratified goal of no more than 2°C above pre-industrial levels requires global CO_2 emissions to fall roughly 80 percent relative to 2005 by 2050. However, many firms and nations pledge only to reduce their CO_2 *intensity*, measured in CO_2 generated per unit produced or per dollar of revenue, because they expect and desire to grow. Thus, in 2009 China pledged to reduce the carbon intensity of its economy— CO_2 per unit of real gross domestic product—45 percent by 2020 relative to the year 2005. However, even if China's economy grew at a conservative rate of only 7 percent/year, its real GDP would grow over those 15 years by a factor of 2.9. Even if China achieves its intensity goal, its CO_2 emissions would rise by 57 percent. In fact, China's emissions have grown dramatically. Now the world's largest emitter, China generated more than 26 percent of world CO_2 emissions from fossil fuels in 2011.[13] Nature does not care about the CO_2 intensity of your factories or the concentration of carcinogens in your effluent stream. Total emissions accumulate in the atmosphere and total carcinogen emissions determine the risk borne by your workers, your neighbors, and yourself.

---

[11] See Wilde (2001) on risk homeostasis.
[12] On rebound effects in energy and sustainability, see Herring and Sorrell (2009) and Sorrell et al. (2009).
[13] Carbon Dioxide Information Analysis Center (2011). Available at: <http://cdiac.ornl.gov/> (accessed July 2014).

The capability trap

The model presented in the section "Sustainability as product-and-process improvement" suggests why improvement rates vary across industries and processes. However, in many situations improvement and learning are not taking place even at the potential rate. Numerous studies demonstrate that individuals and organizations have not taken advantage of opportunities to reduce their energy use and waste generation, even when these have positive net present value, high ROI, and short payback times, and involve ready-to-use, off-the-shelf technology. As Amory Lovins puts it, "the low-hanging fruit is mushing up around our ankles and spilling in over the tops of our waders while the innovation tree pelts our head with more fruit."[14] McKinsey,[15] for example, finds that more than 12 $GtCO_2e$/year of greenhouse gas emissions—nearly one-third of the global total in 2012—can be abated at negative cost using well-established technologies. While the existence of such win–win opportunities may seem like good news, it is actually a sign that the improvement process is failing: something has gone badly wrong when profitable opportunities to eliminate defects, cut energy use and waste, and improve sustainability go unimplemented.

Why are profitable improvement opportunities so often left on the table? Some economists argue that win–win investments must not exist because rational actors would have already made them, therefore studies reporting such opportunities either ignore other costs or inflate the benefits. Others acknowledge the existence of win–win investments and instead attribute underinvestment to market failures. Actors may lack access to the credit necessary to finance up-front investments. Information asymmetries and principal–agent problems such as the famous landlord–tenant problem may arise when actors making investments do not directly realize savings, or when sellers of a technology cannot credibly communicate future (unobservable) benefits.[16]

Other scholars stress the role of behavioral and organizational biases. People tend to evaluate projects from the parochial perspective of their organizational function rather than what's best for the organization as a whole, buy products with lower initial costs despite higher life-cycle costs, and resolve to go to the gym and start a diet.... tomorrow. And organizations often face market and stakeholder pressures to prioritize short-term results over longer-term investment.[17]

---

[14] Lovins is quoted in Olson and Fri (2008), p. 80. On low-hanging fruit, see Porter and Van der Linde (1995); Lovins (2012); and Lyneis and Sterman (2016).

[15] McKinsey & Company (2010).

[16] See, e.g., Jaffe and Stavins (1994); Howarth and Stanstad (1995); and Gillingham et al. (2009).

[17] Yates and Aronson (1983); Frederick et al. (2002) and Bazerman (2009) consider behavioral biases relevant to failures to implement profitable improvement opportunities at the individual and organizational levels. Repenning and Henderson (2010) and Rahmandad (2012) explore the self-reinforcing interactions of organizational short-termism and market pressures.

Certainly, the costs of some improvement opportunities are underestimated, and principal–agent problems, information asymmetries, management biases, and short-termism affect investment decisions in organizations. These phenomena don't merely afflict environmental, health, safety, and other pro-social improvement opportunities. Many, perhaps most, improvement programs fail. From airline kitchens to health care, similar firms in the same industry, units within the same firm, and even different floors of the same hospital exhibit persistent performance differences despite powerful financial incentives for improvement, market forces favoring high performers, and the wide availability of process improvement methods that should lead to widespread adoption of best practices.[18] For example, total factor productivity varies by about a factor of 2 between the 10th and 90th percentile firms in the same 4-digit SIC industries in the US, and by more than a factor of 5 in China and India.[19]

One common failure mode for process improvement is the *capability trap.*[20] Figure 3.4 augments the core structure of defect reduction with the feedback processes affecting the intensity and effectiveness of improvement activity.

Managers responsible for any process, whether production, product development, maintenance, human resources, or environmental quality, are responsible for the performance of that process against target or required performance. When performance falls short of the target, managers have two basic options to close the gap: working harder or working smarter. Working harder includes adding resources (hiring, capacity expansion), increasing work intensity (overtime, shorter breaks), and boosting output per person-hour by cutting corners (skipping steps, cutting testing, foregoing maintenance, failing to follow safety procedures). These activities form the balancing (negative) *work harder* feedback, B4: the performance gap leads to greater effort, longer hours, corner cutting, deferring maintenance, and other shortcuts that improve performance, thus helping to close the gap. Alternatively, managers can interpret the performance gap as a sign that the organization's capabilities are insufficient. They can seek to increase improvement activity designed to eliminate the root causes of poor performance, including improving the productivity and reliability of plant and equipment, and investing in the capabilities that make improvement effort effective, including improvements in physical equipment and in human capital that build people's skills and knowledge of best practices, enhance adherence to those practices, and build cooperation and trust. Investing in capability improvement forms the balancing *work smarter* feedback, B5.

---

[18] On failed improvement programs, see Beer et al. (1990), Easton and Jarrell (1998) and Repenning and Sterman (2002). On airline kitchens, see Chew et al. (1990); on medicine, Wennberg (2010). Gibbons and Henderson (2012, 2013) survey the empirical evidence and theory behind persistent performance differences in seemingly similar enterprises.

[19] Syverson (2011).

[20] Repenning and Sterman (2001, 2002) introduce and provide examples of the capability trap; also Keating et al. (1999).

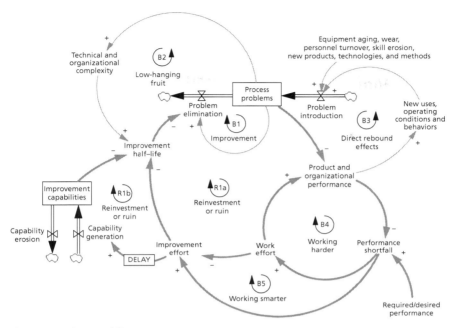

Figure 3.4. The capability trap: structure

Improvement half-lives therefore depend not only on the technical and organizational complexity of the process, but on the intensity and effectiveness of improvement effort.[21] The greater the effort devoted to improvement, and the greater the organization's improvement capabilities, the shorter the improvement half-life.

The organization's capabilities are shown as a stock: capabilities, from productive, well-maintained equipment, to skilled workers, to knowledge of improvement methodologies, to trust between workers and management and across organizational boundaries, are assets that build up as the result of investment and erode over time as equipment ages, employees leave, and by changes in the environment that render existing skills, knowledge, and relationships obsolete.

Working harder and working smarter interact because time is limited. When organizations are heavily loaded, increasing work effort comes at the expense of improvement, maintenance, learning, training, and other activities needed to preserve and enhance capabilities, as illustrated by the following comment of a manager in an electronics assembly plant:

... supervisors never had time to make improvements or do preventive maintenance on their lines ... they had to spend all their time just trying to keep the line going, but this meant it was always in a state of flux, which in turn, caused them to want to hold

---

[21] Sterman et al. (1997).

lots of protective inventory, because everything was so unpredictable. A quality problem might not be discovered until we had produced a pile of defective parts. This of course meant we didn't have time to figure out why the problem happened in the first place, since we were now really behind our production schedule. It was a kind of snowball effect that just kept getting worse.[22]

The result is the reinforcing feedbacks denoted *reinvestment or ruin* (R1a and R1b). As the name suggests, these feedbacks can operate either as virtuous cycles that cumulatively build capabilities and performance, or as vicious cycles that degrade both. An organization that increases the time and resources devoted to improvement will, after a lag, augment its capabilities and performance, easing the performance gap and yielding still more time and resources for further improvement in a virtuous cycle. In contrast, if managers respond to a performance gap by increasing pressure to boost output, the time spent on improvement falls, and the organization's improvement capabilities erode. Eventually, problem elimination falls below the rate at which new problems are introduced by changes in products, processes, personnel, and other conditions, increasing the throughput gap further and forcing ever-greater reliance on working harder. The vicious cycle quickly drives out any meaningful improvement activity, leading to low capabilities and poor performance, and, all too often, to major accidents, environmental harms, or organizational failure.

Many believe that an organization would never allow itself to fall into the capability trap: after all, doesn't everyone know that "an ounce of prevention is worth a pound of cure" and that "a stitch in time saves nine"? Since the quality revolution of the 1980s, businesses claim to understand that it is better to eliminate the root causes of defects than to fix defects later on. Consider, however, an organization facing a performance gap. Working harder is the fastest way to close the gap. Overtime, deferring maintenance, and cutting corners will quickly boost output. The results are highly observable, closely related in time and space, and quite certain: managers can be highly confident that a 10 percent increase in work hours will yield about 10 percent more throughput. However, there is a long lag between an increase in the time spent on improvement and the resulting increase in capabilities, and both the length of the lag and the yield to improvement effort are uncertain. Improvement experiments often fail; search takes time and may lead down some blind alleys. It takes time to develop the capabilities that make improvement effort productive, train people in improvement, develop norms that prevent corner cutting, and build new routines, networks of relationships, commitment, and trust. These features interact to bias many organizations towards working harder instead of working smarter, even when the payoff to working smarter is higher.

---

[22] Repenning and Sterman (2002), 282–3.

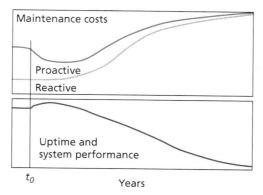

Figure 3.5. The capability trap: dynamics. Budget cuts at time t_0 force the organization to cut proactive maintenance and improvement effort. As organizational capabilities fall, defects increase, increasing reactive maintenance and forcing further reductions in proactive maintenance and process improvement.

Figure 3.5 illustrates using the example of maintenance in a manufacturing plant.[23] Initially, the plant is performing well, with high uptime, equipment reliability, product quality, and safety. The bulk of total maintenance spending is devoted to proactive maintenance and improvement. Now imagine a company-wide budget cut (due to recession, competitive pressures, or other causes). The maintenance manager must cut expenses. Reactive maintenance cannot be cut: when equipment fails it must be fixed, lest plant uptime falls and customer commitments cannot be met. Instead, proactive maintenance and improvement suffer, along with training, part quality, design improvement efforts, and, all too often, adherence to safety protocols. The first impact? Maintenance costs fall, closing the budget gap, and plant uptime rises, because operable equipment is no longer taken down for preventive/scheduled maintenance. Soon, however, the stock of latent defects starts to rise because the rate at which maintenance and process improvement eliminate defects falls below the rate at which aging and wear introduce new ones. The rate of breakdowns and failures grows, increasing the reactive maintenance workload and costs, forcing further reductions in proactive maintenance and improvement.

As rising breakdowns cut plant uptime and output, revenue falls and budgets are cut further. Squeezed between growing expenses and falling budgets, managers feel compelled to cut proactive maintenance and process improvement effort still further. The plant becomes trapped in a vicious cycle of increased breakdowns, higher costs for urgent repairs, lower uptime, greater production pressure, less improvement effort, still more breakdowns and still higher costs.

---

[23] Carroll et al. (1998) and Repenning and Sterman (2001, 2002) provide detailed examples.

Soon, the organization finds itself in a paradox: it pays more to maintain its plants than the industry average, yet gets less for it. Risks to the health and safety of employees and the community rise as the equipment deteriorates and production pressure leads to corner cutting.

The consequences are often tragic. Recent examples just from the US include the 2005 BP Texas City refinery explosion (15 dead), the 2007 collapse of the I-35 bridge in Minneapolis-St Paul (13 dead), the 2008 Imperial Sugar explosion (14 dead), the 2009 Massey Energy Upper Big Branch coal mine explosion (29 dead), and the 2010 Deepwater Horizon explosions and oil spill (11 dead). All resulted from capability trap dynamics, including inadequate inspections, maintenance and improvement activity, excessive cost and production pressure, and corner cutting. For example, the Chemical Safety Board's report on Imperial Sugar found:

Imperial Sugar and the granulated sugar refining and packaging industry have been aware of sugar dust explosion hazards as far back as 1925.... However, [plant] equipment was not designed or maintained to minimize the release of sugar and sugar dust into the work area.... Emergency evacuation plans were inadequate and the company did not conduct emergency evacuation drills.... The secondary dust explosions would have been highly unlikely had Imperial Sugar performed routine maintenance on sugar conveying and packaging equipment.... [The] resulting fatalities would likely not have occurred if Imperial Sugar had enforced routine housekeeping policies and procedures....[24]

The power of management pressure to work harder at the expense of improvement, maintenance, and safety is illustrated by a 2005 memo sent to all Massey Energy employees by then-CEO, Donald Blankenship:[25]

If any of you have been asked by your group presidents, your supervisors, engineers or anyone else to do anything other than run coal (i.e. build overcasts, do construction jobs, or whatever) you need to ignore them and run coal.... This memo is necessary only because we seem not to understand that the coal pays the bills.

The US Mine Safety and Health Administration report on the Upper Big Branch mine calamity documented the impact of that pressure, including "inadequate training," "failure to identify, report, and correct 'obvious hazards,'" and a "culture of intimidation," as illustrated by a miner's testimony:

... they (miners) were scared if they took the time to ventilate that way it should be [sic] ... they'd be fire [sic] or gotten rid of ... you knew that you better go ahead and

---

[24] US Chemical Safety and Hazard Investigation Board Report 2008-05-I-GA. Available at: http://www.csb.gov/assets/1/19/Imperial_Sugar_Report_Final_updated.pdf (accessed July 2014).

[25] Fisk et al. (2010). Available at: <http://www.bloomberg.com/news/2010-04-09/massey-s-blankenship-fought-regulators-town-as-coal-mine-operator-s-chief.html> (accessed July 2014).

mine the coal or—the atmosphere around Massey was, you know, you just keep your mouth shut and do it if you want to keep your job.[26]

If financial and production pressures cause managers and employees to violate federal law and cut corners in ways that obviously threaten their own lives, how often does more subtle pressure to serve customers or get the new product to market prevent people from working on improvement and sustainability initiatives, initiatives that they often view as peripheral to their jobs?

Now consider what happens when an organization seeks to escape the capability trap. Figure 3.6 shows the plant illustrated in Figure 3.5, now stuck in the trap, with high costs and low uptime, reliability, safety, and quality. At time t_1, the managers initiate an improvement program, focusing on proactive maintenance and improvement. The first impact? Costs rise while uptime and output fall.

Costs rise, of course, because the maintenance group must increase the level of preventive maintenance and improvement activity, while still carrying out reactive repair work at the same rate. Uptime and production fall because operable equipment must be taken offline to perform preventive maintenance and test improvement ideas. In many organizations, the next impact is the abandonment of the improvement initiative.

What happens, however, if the organization doesn't give up when costs rise and uptime falls? After a new improvement program is started (at time t_2 in the figure) the increased improvement effort and gradual growth in improvement capabilities eventually begin to eliminate process problems faster than

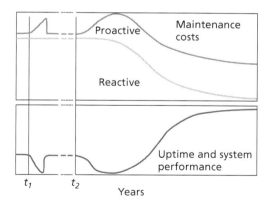

Figure 3.6. Escaping the capability trap: worse-before-better. Improvement effort is given priority at time t_1, but the increase in costs and drop in uptime causes the organization to abandon the effort. If a new effort begins (at time t_2) and is not abandoned, then the initial cost increase and performance drop eventually reverse, leading to lower costs and higher uptime, output, quality, reliability, and safety, in a worse-before-better pattern.

---

[26] UBB accident report, US Department of Labor (2010). Available at: <http://www.msha.gov/Fatals/2010/UBB/FTL10c0331noappx.pdf> (accessed July 2014).

new ones are introduced. Failures start to fall, uptime and output rise, and the burden of reactive maintenance eases, allowing resources to be reinvested in still more proactive maintenance and improvement, speeding defect reduction: the *reinvestment or ruin* feedbacks now operate as virtuous cycles, bootstrapping the plant to low costs and high performance. Note, however, that the system exhibits worse-before-better (WBB) behavior.

Once an organization has fallen into the capability trap, worse-before-better behavior is inevitable: to improve the organization's capabilities and reduce process problems requires either cutting output in the short run by reallocating existing resources from production to improvement, or increasing total costs so that improvement effort can rise while maintaining current output.

The depth and duration of the WBB behavior depends on two factors. First, organizational slack (or, since managers equate the term "slack" with "waste," a "strategic margin of reserve capacity") can decouple the working harder and working smarter processes to some extent. Slack allows an improvement program to be implemented without compromising work effort, limiting the performance drop and surge in production pressure that often quenches improvement effort before capabilities can improve and process problems can be eliminated. Slack can take a variety of forms, from financial reserves used to increase capacity and buffer earnings, to the high ratio of kaizen experts to front-line workers in Toyota plants, to a committed, well-rested workforce willing and able to work overtime when called upon, to excess production capacity or inventories that can be used to maintain shipments when operable equipment is taken off-line for maintenance and improvement or personnel are reallocated from production to improvement.

Second, the shorter the improvement half-life of the process, the shorter and milder the WBB behavior will be. In settings with very low technical and organizational complexity, performance can improve so quickly that the initial decline is negligible. Many energy efficiency, water use, and waste reduction programs fall into this category. MIT, for example, had gradually fallen into the capability trap, accumulating a backlog of deferred maintenance of about $2 billion, a largely reactive and overburdened maintenance organization, and high energy, water and other utility costs. As part of a campus-wide improvement program, the maintenance department implemented a continuous commissioning program. The biology building, a relatively new facility built in 1995, was one of the first projects. Defects had crept in to the equipment after years of mostly reactive maintenance. Sensors and controls had drifted so that the building was heating and cooling itself simultaneously.[27] Eliminating that waste, along with cleaning and repairs to other HVAC system elements, yielded immediate energy savings worth about $360,000 per year. The total

---

[27] Lyneis and Sterman (2016) detail the MIT case, develop a system dynamics model to evaluate policies for improvement, and describe how MIT is implementing these across the campus. Halber (2010) documents the biology building case.

cost of the program was about $150,000. The savings were so large and so immediate that there was essentially no WBB behavior.

In contrast, the long improvement half-life for technically and organizationally complex processes means a longer, deeper WBB period after improvement is initiated, and often thwarts successful implementation, or leads to unanticipated harms as different functions improve at different rates. For example, long-improvement half-lives for product development compared to manufacturing caused excess capacity and other unintended impacts of successful quality improvement at semiconductor firm Analog Devices, leading to a large drop in profits, the first lay offs in the history of the firm, and the collapse of the firm's quality improvement effort.[28]

The short- and long-run impacts of policies are often different[29] and manifest in many familiar settings: overtime boosts productivity today but leads to lower productivity, higher errors, and increased worker turnover later; credit card debt boosts consumption today but forces austerity when the bills come due. But WBB is particularly problematic in sustainability contexts because of the long time delays compared to many business processes. Restoring a depleted fishery requires cutting the catch long enough for stocks to recover; doing so may idle the fleet longer than the fishing community can survive. Converting a farm from conventional to organic production may increase costs and reduce output for several years until organic practices can restore the communities of bacteria, insects, and other organisms that rebuild soil fertility and provide natural protection from pests. Even longer lags arise in the response of the ozone hole to CFC production, the accumulation of long-lived toxins in the food chain and in our bodies, and in the response of the climate to changes in GHG emissions.

The implications for sustainability programs are clear.

First, few organizations today have much slack. Decades of downsizing, rightsizing, outsourcing, and cost reduction have increased the workload on front-line workers and managers alike. Many organizations are stuck in capability traps involving basic functions such as maintenance, customer satisfaction, and product development, and survive through continual firefighting.

Second, sustainability initiatives add to the existing workload on already-overloaded personnel. Many opportunities with high net present value and short payback times go unimplemented because the organizations lack the staff and budget to act on them, and the constant pressure to control costs means managers are often unwilling to add resources, even if the payoff is high. Most organizations view maintenance and operations as cost centers to be minimized, not profit centers.

Third, high work pressure, intense competition, and pressure from financial markets mean that initial improvements are often harvested through cost

---

[28] See Sterman et al. (1997); Repenning (2002).
[29] Forrester (1969); Sterman (2000); and Repenning and Sterman (2001).

cutting, weakening the reinvestment feedbacks so essential in building the capabilities and resources for continuous improvement.

Fourth, sustainability initiatives involving technically and organizationally complex processes are particularly vulnerable to the capability trap because they involve longer, deeper periods in which performance falls and/or costs rise before the benefits of improvement will manifest.

Fifth, the capabilities needed to address complex sustainability challenges will not develop if organizations believe that they cannot sustain the investments needed to succeed. A history of failed efforts can lead to a vicious cycle of eroding goals and low ambition seen today in widespread cynicism about the prospects to mitigate GHG emissions.[30]

Forward-thinking organizations address all of these barriers to escape the capability trap. They frame the resources needed to get started as investments, not costs. They use life-cycle costs instead of up-front costs to assess the return to proposed initiatives. They forge agreements with senior management to reinvest at least a portion of those savings in further improvement. They use the improvement half-life framework to gauge the complexity of their projects and set realistic goals for progress. They use the savings from initial programs with low-hanging fruit to begin work on the programs that may be more difficult and take longer but offer larger potential benefits. They build shared understanding of improvement dynamics, including worse-before-better, through training and interactive simulations. They reduce the bias towards working harder by changing incentives for all, from senior executives to front-line employees, to reward improvement and investments in capabilities. They are willing to fire those who cut corners, compromise safety, or otherwise undermine capabilities, even if those employees or managers deliver high throughput and profits. Box 3.1 lists a few examples.

Radical disruption: building new, sustainable industries

For the reasons articulated earlier, eco-efficiency, waste reduction, and other improvements to existing processes in existing organizations, although necessary in reducing the global ecological footprint of humanity down to a sustainable level, are not sufficient. Many pin their hopes on the creation of entirely new industries, built by new firms with intrinsically sustainable operations and

---

[30] The Climate Interactive Scoreboard (available at: <http://climatescoreboard.org> (accessed July 2014)) assesses the impact of the commitments individual nations have made under the voluntary Copenhagen Accord of 2009. As of 2013, total commitments, even if fully implemented, are grossly inadequate (see also UNEP, 2011). On ambition and aspirations for greenhouse gas mitigation, see <http://thinkprogress.org/climate/2013/07/05/2258731/adaptation-or-mitigation-lessons-from-aboli tion-in-the-battle-over-climate-policy> (accessed July 2014).

BOX 3.1 CREATIVE ORGANIZATIONS FIND WAYS TO SET APPROPRIATE GOALS, KICK-START IMPROVEMENT, REINVEST SAVINGS, AND OVERCOME THE CAPABILITY TRAP, FOR BOTH NORMAL OPERATIONS AND PROGRAMS IN SUSTAINABILITY

- Many organizations have established "revolving green loan funds" to finance sustainability programs, using the returns on those investments to finance still more improvement.[31]

- The facilities manager in a university without a green loan fund was denied the budget to implement energy retrofits, despite their high expected return. He went to the manager responsible for the fuel budget and "borrowed" the funds needed to implement the program. The energy savings "repaid" the "loan"—and then some—so quickly there was no negative impact on the fuel manager's budget.

- Many firms use "hackathons" in which employees can work on any projects they like to generate creative ideas for new products and processes, including sustainability programs.

- A product line manager in a corporation developed metrics to assess savings from improvement, then agreed to take the risk of funding the program in return for an agreement with senior management allowing the product group to retain most of the savings for further improvement.

- The sustainability manager for a major firm in the life sciences won approval to hire more staff by arguing that the savings generated would more than pay for the costs. In the first year alone, the new hires generated more than twice their fully loaded costs in documented savings.

- The product engineering group of a major manufacturer was told by senior management to cut warranty costs by 50 percent in three years. Working backwards, they determined that hitting that target given the product development cycle time required an improvement half-life of 6 months, far shorter than evidence suggested was possible. They used the improvement half-life framework to set more realistic goals, leading to higher morale, lower turnover, and faster progress.

- A large firm was using a rule of thumb requiring energy retrofit projects to yield payback times of 2 years or less, implying a simple ROI of 50 percent/year or higher. Managers argued that the hurdle rate for such investments should be the same as the much lower rate used for other capital budgeting decisions (or lower, given the lower risks of the retrofit projects).

- In partnership with the World Wildlife Fund, dozens of firms, including IBM, Johnson and Johnson, Sony, Sprint, and Volvo, have set goals for absolute reductions in their greenhouse gas emissions and other forms of waste, not goals for reductions in emissions per dollar of sales. The short half-lives for energy efficiency and waste reduction have led to large emissions reductions and significant financial savings.[32]

- Major firms in the chemical and oil industries, among others, use interactive role-play simulations and training in systems thinking to build shared understanding of the dynamics of maintenance and improvement, including how to manage the worse-before-better dynamic, generating billions in savings while improving safety and environmental quality.

- Managers at a major software developer are accountable not only for delivering projects on time and within budget but for adhering to the firm's development process. Those who cut corners can, and have been, fired even if they bring their projects in on time and under budget. Senior leadership believes corner cutting initiates the slippery slope of the capability trap and that

(continued)

---

[31] E.g., <http://www.greenbiz.com/blog/2013/06/07/are-green-revolving-funds-next-frontier-corporate-energy-efficiency> (accessed July 2014).

[32] Available at: <http://wwf.panda.org/what_we_do/how_we_work/businesses/climate/climate_savers/> (accessed July 2014).

BOX 3.1 (CONTINUED)

tolerating it would send a toxic message to all employees that corner cutting—and covering it up—is how to get ahead. By firing those who, as GE's Jack Welch put it, fail to "live the values" of the organization, no matter how large their apparent contribution to the bottom line, senior management not only encourages people to do the right thing but builds a high-capability organization filled with those motivated by a worthy mission, not short-term gain.

producing sustainable products. Solar, wind, and renewable energy sources will displace fossil fuels. Vehicles powered by renewable, low-carbon energy will displace internal combustion vehicles powered by fossil fuels. Organic, local, small-scale agriculture will displace monocultures and factory farms.

The history of such transitions is one of path dependence, false starts, and delays. Consider the transition to alternative-fuel vehicles (AFVs). There is no doubt that the current dominant design—internal-combustion-engine (ICE) vehicles powered by fossil fuels—cannot scale with current technology and patterns of use. If everyone drove the way those in the US do today, then in 2050 the projected population of 9.3 billion people would be driving 7.8 billion passenger vehicles, consuming 382 million barrels of oil per day (more than 5 times total world production today), emitting 60 billion tons of CO_2 per year (almost double total world emissions today), and taking up 143,000 sq. kilometers—an area the size of Bangladesh—just in parking spaces.[33]

A wide range of alternative drive train and fuel technologies are now contending to be the new dominant design, including electric, hydrogen fuel cells, internal combustion engines powered by hydrogen, ethanol, methanol, biofuel blends such as E85, compressed natural gas (CNG), or combinations thereof, including conventional and plug-in hybrids. The history of attempts to introduce AFVs can be characterized as "sizzle and fizzle" (Figure 3.7). Multiple attempts to (re)-introduce electric vehicles have failed. Brazil's first attempt at an ethanol-powered fleet failed, and initially promising programs to introduce natural gas vehicles stagnated in Italy and withered in Canada and New Zealand after initial subsidies ended.[34]

The failure of AFV programs to date is commonly attributed to high costs and immature technology. Certainly, the high cost and low functionality of AFVs compared to fossil-ICE limits their market potential today, particularly in nations like the US, where gasoline is priced far below the level that would reflect its environmental, climate, health, and other externalities. More subtly, the current low functionality and high cost of alternatives—and low gasoline taxes—are endogenous consequences of the dominance of the internal combustion engine and the petroleum industry, together with the transport networks, settlement patterns, technologies, and institutions with which they

---

[33] Projections based on US data for 2008.
[34] On sizzle and fizzle in alternative vehicles, see Hard and Knie (2001); Flynn (2002); and Struben and Sterman (2008).

Figure 3.7. Sizzle-and-fizzle behavior in the adoption of alternative-fuel vehicles (AFVs): Brazil (ethanol); New Zealand and Argentina (CNG).

Source: Struben (2008).

have coevolved. The dominance of internal combustion suppresses the emergence of alternatives, maintaining the dominance of fossil-ICE. These feedbacks mean that sustained AFV adoption would be difficult even if AFV performance equaled that of fossil-ICE today.[35]

The enormous scale of the automobile and oil industries and associated infrastructure creates a set of powerful positive feedback processes that confer substantial advantage to the incumbent fossil-ICE technology (Figure 3.8). First, AFVs including electrics, hydrogen, CNG, and biofuels require new fueling infrastructure incompatible with the existing fuel supply chain and retail distribution network. Drivers will not buy AFVs without ready access to fuel, parts, and repair services, but energy producers, automakers, and governments will not invest in AFV technology and infrastructure without the prospect of a large market—the so-called chicken and egg problem, shown in the figure as the *infrastructure* loop. Fuel availability also affects VMT per year for those early adopters who buy AFVs: without ubiquitous fueling infrastructure, early adopters will drive fewer miles and avoid areas in which fueling infrastructure is sparse, limiting AFV fuel demand and therefore the profitability and deployment of fueling infrastructure in those areas, further suppressing the use of the few AFVs that are purchased. AFV drivers, knowing that fuel is not readily available, will likely seek to maintain a large buffer, leading to topping-off behavior that reduces the effective range of the AFVs even further below the range of fossil-ICE vehicles, and may lead to congestion at the few fuel stations that are deployed. These behavioral effects cut both AFV miles driven and the attractiveness of AFVs to potential customers, suppressing the growth of the market (the *range anxiety* feedback).

---

[35] Struben and Sterman (2008).

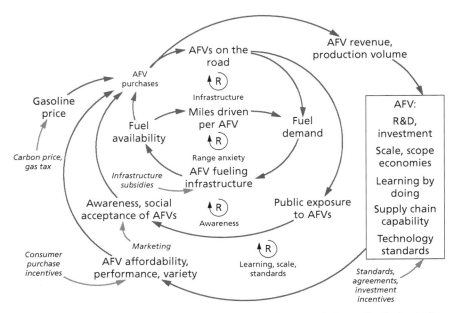

Figure 3.8. Reinforcing feedbacks conditioning the adoption of alternative-fuel vehicles (AFVs)

Demand for AFVs is significantly conditioned by word of mouth, social exposure to the vehicles, and other social processes. Keith[36] found that adoption of the Toyota Prius was powerfully driven by the installed base in a potential buyer's local region, with marketing far less effective. People need to become familiar with a new type of vehicle through multiple exposures, word of mouth, and other social network effects before they are willing to include it in their consideration set. Thus low initial awareness suppresses purchases, which limits the number of AFVs on the road and thus public exposure to and word of mouth about the AFV, further suppressing purchases (the *awareness* loop).

Even if potential customers were sufficiently familiar with AFVs to consider purchasing them, the utility of such vehicles is initially low because the current state of technology for many alternative drive trains means these vehicles are more expensive; offer lower performance, range, cabin and storage space; and are available in fewer makes and models than fossil-ICE vehicles. The lack of standards, both across and within AFV platforms, suppresses demand, as consumers delay purchases until they are sure that a particular platform will survive. For example, current battles over charging formats and plug shapes for electrics, such as SAE 1772 vs CHADeMO, confuse consumers and raise the costs and uncertainties facing infrastructure providers. Improvements in costs, performance, range, interior space, variety, and the emergence of standards are driven by scale economies, R&D, learning by doing, and field

---

[36]   Keith (2012).

experience, but these, in turn, are suppressed by low initial sales of any one AFV platform (the *learning, scale, and standards* loops).

Figure 3.8 also shows the principal policy levers available to industry actors and governments to stimulate the AFV market, including subsidies offered to consumers by either governments (tax credits, access to HOV—High Occupancy Vehicle [carpool] lanes or automakers setting prices below unit costs), subsidies to infrastructure providers or government installed fuel points, marketing (paid by either the industry or governments), and carbon prices or higher gasoline taxes. However, the network of reinforcing feedbacks above, and the dominant position of the fossil-ICE platform—full familiarity and acceptance, ubiquitous fueling, part, and repair infrastructure, a full range of makes and models, low costs, and high performance—mean any AFV faces a long uphill battle before it achieves the installed base, awareness, scale, and standardization to succeed. Simulations capturing these feedbacks show that crossing the tipping point to sustained success requires the early adoption of standards and much larger and longer marketing campaigns and subsidies for vehicles and infrastructure than is typical in most markets. Failure to provide such sustained, coordinated support leads to the sizzle-and-fizzle behavior observed in many markets.[37]

In terms of the improvement half-life framework, the AFV industry faces not only high technical complexity, but high organizational and political complexity: success will require coordination across automakers, infrastructure providers, the energy supply chain, local, state, and federal governments, and other actors. At the moment such coordination is weak.

Consumers can choose among conventional hybrid electrics, plug-in hybrids, pure battery electrics, clean diesel, E85, flex-fuel, CNG, and hydrogen-powered vehicles, and leading automakers including GM and Ford are pursuing an "all-of-the-above" strategy by promoting portfolios of different AFVs. But hedging bets due to the uncertainty over which technology will become the new dominant design limits the ability of any AFV to achieve the scale needed to succeed, increasing uncertainty and delaying the transition away from fossil-ICE that is so urgently needed.

Although the specifics will vary, similar reinforcing feedbacks exist around other core infrastructures of modern society, including agriculture, air transportation, public transit, the electric grid, and settlement patterns. All must be transformed away from their current unsustainable structures to new, low-carbon and low waste, sustainable systems. All face high tipping thresholds. Success will require overcoming the market failures created by these dynamics. Coordination is required among actors in these industries, including suppliers, complementors, consumers, and government. Achieving such coordination can be difficult. Yet organizations and governments have successfully coordinated to establish thousands of standards, overcome market failures, and preserve common pool resources in diverse settings, through both industry

---

[37] Struben and Sterman (2008); Keith (2012).

self-regulation and government regulation, from local laws to international agreements (Box 3.2).

Elinor Ostrom, who identified many such successes, articulated key principles for effective management of common pool resources such as fisheries, forests, fresh water, and the climate, and other settings where coordination is required to overcome market failures, such as provision of police and fire protection for communities. These principles include rules adapted to local conditions, inclusion of key parties in decision making, effective and independent monitoring, graduated sanctions to punish those who violate community rules, accessible, transparent conflict resolution processes, self-determination of communities respected by higher-level authorities, and, particularly for

---

BOX 3.2 EXAMPLES OF SUCCESSFUL COORDINATION ACROSS ORGANIZATIONAL AND POLITICAL BOUNDARIES TO MANAGE COMMON-POOL RESOURCES, SET STANDARDS, AND CERTIFY THE SUSTAINABILITY OF PRODUCTS AND PROCESSES

- Philips and Sony independently developed optical disc storage technology, then worked together to agree on standards for the discs and data storage protocols for them. The resulting open standards led to success of the compact disc for audio recordings and data storage, with hundreds of billions sold. The success of the open standards for CDs stands in stark contrast to format wars over videocassette standards (Sony Betamax vs Matshushita VHS) and high-definition DVDs (Sony Blu-Ray vs Toshiba HD-DVD). Importantly, although Blu-Ray ultimately prevailed, the delay created by the format war delayed the development of the market, which ultimately failed as consumers increasingly turned to digital downloads, rather than purchasing physical discs.

- The TCP/IP standard, arising out of US Government support through DARPA, became the standard for data transmission in computer networks, enabling the growth of the Internet.

- Industry groups have established thousands of standards, from USB, to shipping containers, to radio spectrum allocations.

- Since 1947, the International Organization for Standardization (ISO, <http://www.ISO.org>) has worked to create standards to certify process improvement and product integrity in areas including quality management, environment, food safety, energy, greenhouse gases, social responsibility, and others relevant to sustainability.

- The Marine Stewardship Council, Forest Stewardship Council, and similar multi-stakeholder NGOs work to certify resources that are harvested responsibly and managed sustainably.

- Dozens of NGOs and industry groups certify whether foods and other products adhere to "Fair Trade" principles including prices and wages, working conditions, worker rights, and environmental sustainability.

- The UN Convention on the Law of the Sea and the International Whaling Commission regulate and set standards for the use of marine resources.

- The 1987 Montreal Protocol provided coordinated standards to phase out CFCs and related compounds that catalyze the destruction of stratospheric ozone. The treaty, amended multiple times to capture evolving science, has been ratified by nearly all nations on Earth and is one of the most successful international agreements to protect a common pool resource. The success of the Montreal Protocol fostered similar negotiations to limit mercury emissions (the Minamata Convention of 2013) and the (so far less-than-successful) climate negotiations under the UN Framework Convention on Climate Change.

large-scale, common-pool resources, multiple, nested organizations and management processes (so-called polycentric governance).[38] These principles will also be needed to overcome many of the market failures that currently thwart or delay the development and deployment of the radical innovations needed to promote sustainability.

Overconsumption

Suppose, despite the barriers described earlier, that learning and improvement within incumbent organizations accelerate, and that the coordination and standards required to bootstrap new, sustainable technologies emerge quickly, disrupting and displacing legacy industries. Suppose that rebound effects are mild and that the market failures plaguing common pool resources, from forests and fisheries, to water and the climate, are resolved. Would we then be on the road to a sustainable society? Unfortunately the answer is no.

Humanity has already overshot the carrying capacity of the Earth. We are harvesting renewable resources faster than they regenerate, creating pollution and wastes faster than they can be rendered harmless or sequestered, and are overwhelmingly dependent on non-renewable resources.

Clearly, if innovation is too slow, if capability traps delay or thwart profitable improvements, if market failures prevent the emergence of new, sustainable products and industries, or if technological solutions to the sustainability challenge create harmful side effects, then the result will be overshoot and collapse: technological solutions will be too little, too late, or will actually worsen the problem.

More interesting, what happens if the impediments to learning and the creation of new industries discussed earlier are overcome, if markets work well, if the delays in innovation are short and unintended harms absent? By easing resource limitations and reducing the environmental degradation that threaten growth, successful improvement and sustainability initiatives enable population and economic output to grow still further. The result: society is once again pushed up against one environmental limit or another. If markets and technology again succeed in addressing those new limits, then human activity grows still further until a new limit and new problems arise.

As long as growth is the driving force, there can be no purely technological solution to the challenge of creating a sustainable society. The high leverage points lie elsewhere, in the forces that cause population and economic growth. Even with significant potential for new technical solutions, a prosperous and sustainable future can only be built if growth of both population and material throughput cease voluntarily, before growth is stopped involuntarily by

---

[38] Ostrom (2010).

scarcity or environmental degradation.[39] Population growth may end if the demographic transition continues, particularly in the developing world,[40] though the UN population program, despite assuming rapid fertility decline, projects more than 10 billion by 2100. More troubling is the growth in consumption per capita. The world economy has been growing at an average rate of about 3.5 percent/year (real), a doubling time of only 20 years, and growth is far faster in the emerging economies. Nearly every nation seeks to continue that growth indefinitely. People have strong preferences for growth in their incomes, to earn more than their colleagues and peers, to not only keep up with, but surpass the Joneses.[41] Since everyone cannot be richer than everyone else, the result is an unwinnable rat race.

Product-and-process innovation for sustainability, new business models, and other technical solutions are absolutely necessary to create a sustainable economy and society. Business firms have a vital role to play. They must—and many are—improving their processes and products, and developing the new technologies and industries that are essential in building a sustainable world. The unfolding transition from the unsustainable world of today to a sustainable, prosperous, and fulfilling world is, I believe, the greatest entrepreneurial opportunity since the industrial revolution.

But that is not sufficient. Until we learn to end the quest for more—more income, more wealth, more consumption, more than last year, more than our neighbors—then a healthy, prosperous, and sustainable society cannot be created no matter how clever our technology, how fast we learn, how quickly we can build new industries. Innovation simply lets us grow until one or another limit to growth becomes binding.

We cannot expect traditional business firms to promote policies that would cause their growth to stop, to cease the marketing and advertising campaigns that urge people to buy ever more, to unilaterally internalize environmental and social costs when their competitors do not. The leverage points for action on overconsumption do not lie within business organizations, but in the beliefs, goals, and values of the public, and in public policies that would both enact and reinforce those values. Yet we are not accustomed to asking "How much is enough?," uncomfortable connecting abstract debates about growth and scarcity with the way we live, with our personal responsibility to one another, and to future generations. We don't understand how the quest for more is not only destroying the ecosystems upon which all life, including ours, depend, but is not leading to fulfillment and well-being.[42] Research, teaching, and action to promote sustainability must grapple with these issues if we are to fulfill Gandhi's vision of a world in which "there is enough for everyone's need but not for everyone's greed."

---

[39] Daly (1991); Meadows et al. (2004); and Sterman (2012).
[40] Caldwell (2006). [41] Sterman (2012).
[42] See, e.g., Princen et al. (2002); Layard (2005); Whybrow (2005); Victor (2008); Easterlin et al. (2010, 2012); Schor (2010).

▨ ACKNOWLEDGMENTS

The material in this chapter was presented at the Change and Sustainability Conference, May 9–15, 2013, Harvard Business School.

I thank the participants and my colleagues Matt Amengual, Robert Gibbons, Ranjay Gulati, Rebecca Henderson, Jason Jay, David Keith, Andy King, John Lyneis, Nelson Repenning, Jeroen Struben, and Michael Tushman for helpful discussions and contributions to the ideas and examples contained here. Financial support was provided by the Project on Innovation in Markets and Organizations at the MIT Sloan School of Management.

▨ REFERENCES

Amengual, M. (2014) "Pathways to Enforcement: Labor Inspectors Leveraging Linkages with Society in Argentina," *Industrial and Labor Relations Review* 67 (1): 3–33.

Argote, L. (2013) *Organizational Learning: Creating, Retaining, and Transferring Knowledge*, 2nd edn. New York: Springer.

Bazerman, M. (2009) "Barriers to Acting in Time on Energy and Strategies for Overcoming Them," in K. Gallagher (ed.), *Acting in Time on Energy Policy*. Washington, D.C.: Brookings Institution Press, 162–81.

Beer, M., Spector, B., and Eisenstat, R. (1990) "Why Change Programs Don't Produce Change," *Harvard Business Review* Nov/Dec: 158–66.

Caldwell, J. (2006) *Demographic Transition Theory*. Dordrecht, Netherlands: Springer.

Carroll, J., Sterman, J., and Marcus, A. (1998) "Playing the Maintenance Game: How Mental Models Drive Organizational Decisions," in J. J. Halpern and R. N. Stern (eds), *Debating Rationality: Nonrational Elements of Organizational Decision Making*. Ithaca, NY, Cornell University Press, 99–121.

Chew, B., Clark, K., and Bresnahan, T. (1990) "Measurement, Coordination and Learning in a Multiplant Network," in Robert Kaplan (ed.), *Measures for Manufacturing Excellence*. Boston, MA: Harvard Business School Press, 129–62.

Daly, H. (1991) *Steady-State Economics*, 2nd edn. Washington, D. C.: Island Press.

Easterlin, R., McVey, L., Switek, M., Sawangfa, O., and Zweig, J. (2010) "The Happiness–Income Paradox Revisited," *PNAS* 107: 22463–8.

Easterlin, R., Morgan, R., Switek, M., and Wang, F. (2012) "China's Life Satisfaction, 1990–2010," *PNAS* 109 (25): 9775–80.

Easton, G. and Jarrell, S. (1998) "The Effects of Total Quality Management on Corporate Performance: An Empirical Investigation," *Journal of Business,* 71 (2): 253–307.

Flynn, P. (2002) "Commercializing an Alternate Vehicle Fuel: Lessons Learned from Natural Gas for Vehicles," *Energy Policy* 30: 613–19.

Forrester, J. W. (1969) *Urban Dynamics*. Waltham, MA: Pegasus Communications.

Frederick, S., Loewenstein, G., and O'Donoghue, T. (2002) "Time Discounting and Time Preference: A Critical Review," *Journal of Economic Literature* 40 (2): 351–401.

Gibbons, R. and Henderson, R. (2012) "Relational Contracts and Organizational Capabilities," *Organization Science* 23 (5): 1350–64.

Gibbons, R. and Henderson, R. (2013) "What Do Managers Do?," in R. Gibbons and J. Roberts (eds), *Handbook of Organizational Economics*. Princeton, NJ: Princeton University Press, 680–731.

Gillingham, K., Newell, R. G., and Palmer, K. (2009) *Energy Efficiency Economics and Policy*. Washington, D.C.: Resources for the Future. Available at: <http://www.nber.org/papers/w15031> (accessed July 2014).

Greenhouse, S. (2012) "Documents Indicate Walmart Blocked Safety Push in Bangladesh," *New York Times*, 5 December 2012. Available at: <http://www.nytimes.com/2012/12/06/world/asia/3-walmart-suppliers-made-goods-in-bangladeshi-factory-where-112-died-in-fire.html> (accessed July 2014).

Halber, D. (2010) "Gaining Visibility into Buildings' Real-Time Energy Performance." Available at: <http://mitei.mit.edu/news/gaining-visibility-buildings-real-time-energy-performance> (accessed July 2014).

Hard, M. and Knie, A. (2001) "The Cultural Dimension of Technology Management: Lessons from the History of the Automobile," *Technology Analysis and Strategic Management* 13: 91–103.

Herring, H. and Sorrell, S. (2009) *Energy Efficiency and Sustainable Consumption: The Rebound Effect*. London: Palgrave Macmillan.

Howarth, R. and Sanstad, A. (1995) "Discount Rates and Energy Efficiency," *Contemporary Economic Policy* 13 (3):101–9.

Humes, E. (2011) *Force of Nature: The Unlikely Story of Wal-Mart's Green Revolution*. New York: Harper-Collins.

Jaffe, A. and Stavins, R. (1994) "The Energy-Efficiency Gap. What Does It Mean?," *Energy Policy* 22 (10): 804–10.

Keating, E., Oliva, R., Repenning, N., Rockart, S., and Sterman, J. (1999) "Overcoming the Improvement Paradox," *European Management Journal* 17 (2): 120–34.

Keith, D. (2012) "Essays on the Dynamics of Alternative Fuel Vehicle Adoption: Insights from the Market for Hybrid–Electric Vehicles in the United States," Cambridge, MA, MIT Engineering Systems Division, Ph.D. dissertation.

Layard, R. (2005) *Happiness: Lessons from a New Science*. New York: Penguin Press.

Locke, R. (2013) *The Promise and Limits of Private Power: Promoting Labor Rights in a Global Economy*. New York: Cambridge University Press.

Lovins, A. (2012) *Reinventing Fire*. White River Junction, VT: Chelsea Green.

Lyneis, J. and Sterman, J. (2016) "How to Save a Leaky Ship: Capability Traps and the Failure of Win-Win Investments in Sustainability and Social Responsibility," *Academy of Management Discoveries*. doi: 10.5465/amd.2015.0006.

McKinsey & Company (2010). "Impact of the Financial Crisis on Carbon Economics. Version 2.1 of the Global Greenhouse Gas Abatement Cost Curve." Available at: <http://www.mckinsey.com/~/media/McKinsey/dotcom/client_service/Sustainability/cost%20curve%20PDFs/ImpactFinancialCrisisCarbonEconomicsGHGcostcurveV21.ashx> (accessed July 2014).

Meadows, D. L., Randers, J., and Meadows, D. H. (2004) *The Limits to Growth: The Thirty Year Update*. White River Junction VT: Chelsea Green.

Nagy, B., Farmer, J., Bui, Q., and Trancik, J. (2013) "Statistical Basis for Predicting Technological Progress, PLoS One." Available at: <http://www.plosone.org/article/info%3Adoi%2F10.1371%2Fjournal.pone.0052669> (accessed July 2014).

Olson, S. and Fri, R. (2008) *The National Academies Summit on America's Energy Future: Summary of a Meeting*. Washington, D.C.: National Academies Press.

Ostrom, E. (2010) "Beyond Markets and States: Polycentric Governance of Complex Economic Systems," *American Economic Review* 100: 641–72.

Plambeck, E. and Denend, L. (2010) "Walmart's Sustainability Strategy," Stanford Graduate School of Business Cases OIT-71A, OIT-71B, OIT-71C. Stanford, CA: Stanford Business School.

Porter, M. and van der Linde, C. (1995) "Toward a New Conception of the Environment–Competitiveness Relationship," *Journal of Economic Perspectives* 9 (4): 97–118.

Princen, T., Maniates, M., and Conca, K. (2002) *Confronting Consumption*. Cambridge, MA: MIT Press.

Rahmandad, H. (2012) "Impact of Growth Opportunities and Competition on Firm-Level Capability Development Trade-Offs," *Organization Science* 23 (1): 138–54.

Repenning, N. (1996) "Reducing Cycle and Development Time at Ford Electronics. Part I: Continuous Flow Manufacturing." Available at: <http://web.mit.edu/nelsonr/www/MCT_CASE.pdf> (accessed July 2014).

Repenning, N. (2002) "A Simulation-Based Approach to Understanding the Dynamics of Innovation Implementation," *Organization Science* 13 (2): 109–27.

Repenning, N. and Henderson, R. (2010) "Making the Numbers? 'Short Termism' and the Puzzle of Only Occasional Disaster," Harvard Business School Working Paper 11-033. Available at: <http://www.hbs.edu/faculty/Publication%20Files/11-033.pdf> (accessed July 2014).

Repenning, N. and Sterman, J. (2001) "Nobody Ever Gets Credit for Fixing Problems that Never Happened: Creating and Sustaining Process Improvement," *California Management Review* 43 (4): 64–88.

Repenning, N. and Sterman, J. (2002) "Capability Traps and Self-Confirming Attribution Errors in the Dynamics of Process Improvement," *Administrative Science Quarterly* 47 (2): 265–95.

Rockström J., Steffan, W., Noone, K. et al. (2009) "A Safe Operating Space for Humanity," *Nature* 461: 472–5.

Running, S. (2012) "A Measurable Planetary Boundary for the Biosphere," *Science* 337: 1458–9.

Schneiderman, A. (1988) "Setting Quality Goals," *Quality Progress* 21 (4): 51–7.

Schor, J. (2010) *Plenitude: The New Economics of True Wealth*. New York: Penguin Press.

Sorrell, S., Dimitropoulos, J., and Sommerville, M. (2009) "Empirical Estimates of the Direct Rebound Effect: A Review," *Energy Policy* 37: 1356–71.

Sterman, J. (2000) *Business Dynamics: Systems Thinking and Modeling for a Complex World*. New York: Irwin/McGraw-Hill.

Sterman, J. (2012) "Sustaining Sustainability: Creating a Systems Science in a Fragmented Academy and Polarized World," in M. Weinstein and R. E. Turner (eds), *Sustainability Science: The Emerging Paradigm and the Urban Environment*. New York: Springer: 21–58.

Sterman, J., Repenning, N., and Kofman, A. (1997) "Unanticipated Side Effects of Successful Quality Programs: Exploring a Paradox of Organizational Improvement," *Management Science* 43 (4): 501–21.

Struben, J. (2008) "The Diffusion of Complex Market Technologies: Multifaceted Dynamics for Alternative Fuel Vehicles," Industry Studies Association Working Paper Series WP-2008-29. Available at: <http://isapapers.pitt.edu/113/1/2008-29_ Struben.pdf> (accessed July 2014).

Struben, J. and Sterman, J. (2008) "Transition Challenges for Alternative Fuel Vehicle and Transportation Systems," *Environment and Planning B* 35: 1070–97.

Syverson, C. (2011) "What Determines Productivity?," *Journal of Economic Literature* 49: 326–65.

UNEP (2011) "Bridging the Emissions Gap. United Nations Environment Programme (UNEP)." Available at: <http://www.unep.org/publications/ebooks/bri dgingemissionsgap> (accessed July 2014).

Victor, P. (2008) *Managing Without Growth.* Cheltenham, UK: Edward Elgar.

Wackernagel, M., Schulz, N., Deumling, D. et al. (2002) "Tracking the ecological overshoot of the human economy," *PNAS* 99: 9266–71.

Wennberg, J. (2010) *Tracking Medicine: A Researcher's Quest to Understand Health Care.* New York: Oxford University Press.

Whybrow, P. (2005) *American Mania: When More is Not Enough.* New York: W. W. Norton.

Wilde, G. (2001) *Target Risk 2: A New Psychology of Safety and Health.* New York: PDE Publications.

Yates, S. and Aronson, E. (1983) "A Social Psychological Perspective on Energy Conservation in Residential Buildings," *American Psychologist* 38 (4): 435.

Zangwill, W. and Kantor, P. (1998) "Toward a Theory of Continuous Improvement and the Learning Curve," *Management Science* 44 (7): 910–20.

4 | From Periphery to Core

A Process Model for Embracing Sustainability

Luciana Silvestri and Ranjay Gulati

"Customers can have any vehicle they want, as long as it is green."
William Clay Ford, Jr, former chairman and current executive chairman
The Ford Motor Company. Press release October 21, 1999.

Introduction

Sustainability is, undoubtedly, one of the most powerful tenets of contemporary life. More than seven billion people now live on our planet. Given unprecedented demands on our ecosystem, society is increasingly valuing sustainable technologies, processes, and products. Sustainability is transforming the landscape in which we live and consequently changing the ways in which organizations operate. Many, if not all, industries today are being prompted in one way or another to embrace sustainability in a meaningful way (Delmas and Toffel, 2004, 2008; Short and Toffel, 2010).

Start-ups built on sustainability principles are burgeoning in many industries. A great number of established organizations, however, have found the promise of sustainability elusive. Only some have made serious commitments towards embracing sustainability at their core. Many still relegate sustainability to the periphery. A recent survey of top managers showed that more than 50 percent considered sustainability "very" or "extremely" important in a range of areas, including new-product development, reputation building, and overall corporate strategy. Yet only about 30 percent said their organizations actively sought opportunities to invest in sustainability or embed it in their business practices (Bonini et al., 2010).

In this chapter, we propose that moving sustainability from the organization's periphery into its core is a three-pronged endeavor; one that holistically addresses how the organization thinks about sustainability (i.e., how it weaves sustainability into its identity), how it plans for sustainability (i.e., how it generates an adequate sustainability strategy), and the actions it takes to bring its sustainability goals to life (i.e., how it configures its organizational design). Drawing inspiration from the efforts made by nearly 30 established organizations to embrace sustainability, we then develop a process model delineating how an established organization can bring sustainability into its core.[1] After describing our model, we showcase the journey of The Ford Motor Company as an illustrative case study. We chose Ford for several reasons. First, as a company whose lifespan extends for more than a century, Ford's journey provides something of an "extreme case": the organization had decade upon decade of inertia and complacency to overcome in order to embrace sustainability. Second, Ford's sustainability challenges mirror those faced by most large organizations and thus may prove relevant and informative beyond the automotive industry. Finally, Ford's journey is remarkably transparent: the organization has been candid about its victories and losses as it strives to bring sustainability into its core. Moreover, the amount of publicly available data on Ford's sustainability efforts made the organization an attractive candidate for an in-depth illustrative case study. Overall, the approach we follow in this chapter mirrors that of other studies in change management and organizational evolution in which a model is developed first, followed by a detailed illustrative case study (for example, Henderson and Clark, 1990; Siggelkow, 2001; O'Reilly et al., 2009).

The unfulfilled promise of sustainability

During an era in which sustainability is touted as the next frontier in innovation, it is rare to find an organization that openly rejects the concept. An overwhelming number of organizations (especially established organizations), however, maintain an arm's-length approach to it. In these organizations, sustainability lingers at the periphery, virtually divorced from what the organization is and does (Prahalad and Hamel, 1990; Gulati and Kletter, 2005). Indeed, organizations that keep sustainability at the periphery view it as an endeavor that does not lie fully within the organization's purview, and do not treat it as an integral aspect of the organization.

Many organizations that keep sustainability at the periphery do so out of aversion to challenging the status quo. While seeking to show stakeholders they are making efforts to embrace sustainability, they avoid taking bold steps, getting caught in a web of insufficient reflection, imprecise goals, and timid actions. At times, economic and technological conditions preclude

---

[1] Our review included organizations such as Altron, BMW, BP, CEMEX, Clorox, CLP, Conoco-Phillips, Dow Chemical, DuPont, Fiji Water, The Ford Motor Company, LG, Marks & Spencer, Nestlé, Nike, Patagonia, Petrobras, Procter & Gamble, Puma, Toys "R" Us, Unilever, and Walmart, among others. We looked at a broad sample of established organizations in order to assess both successes and pitfalls. While some of these organizations have succeeded in bringing sustainability into their core, others are making progress in distinct areas and a few are still struggling.

organizations from fully embracing sustainability. Some initiatives, while desirable, cannot be implemented because the associated costs could prove prohibitive both for the organization and its customers. Arguably, it is only once economic conditions are favorable that organizations can take action to bring sustainability into their core. While this is certainly true in some contexts, in others waiting for conditions to change may become a self-fulfilling prophecy. Through commitment and conviction, organizations can sometimes trigger the creativity required to turn the tide on the economic barriers that delay progress on making their businesses more sustainable. Hence, bringing sustainability into its core is not something an organization can do by adopting a "wait-and-see" attitude or by taking a collection of indecisive steps.

Organizations that truly embrace sustainability approach the journey from three mutually reinforcing perspectives: (1) how they think about sustainability (i.e., how they relate to sustainability as they define their organizational identity); (2) how they plan for it (i.e., how they relate to sustainability as they formulate strategies); and (3) how they act on it (i.e., how they relate to sustainability as they configure their organizational design). Table 4.1 summarizes our arguments; we expand on each issue in the following section.

Table 4.1 Organizational engagement with sustainability: Periphery versus core

	Sustainability at the periphery	Sustainability at the core
Identity		
Understanding of sustainability	Abstract and unclear: no definition, generic definition, or multiple competing definitions	Concrete: one definition acts as organizational north
Orientation towards sustainability	Focus on external image: gaining green credentials, enhancing reputation	Balanced focus on internal identity and external image
Strategy		
Sustainability planning	No formal plan, or existing plan detached from business strategy	Formal sustainability strategy integrated with business strategy
Sustainability initiatives	Piecemeal, incremental, functional: focused on eco-efficiency gains	Mutually reinforcing, radical, and generative: focused on innovation and growth, as well as eco-efficiency gains
Commitment to sustainability	Fickle investment; a luxury for good years	Constant investment, even in lean years
Sustainability performance	Not measured or selectively measured and communicated as an indicator of socially responsible behavior	Actively measured and communicated as an indicator of overall business value
Design		
Managerial involvement with sustainability	No specific office in charge of sustainability, or presence of sustainability manager without real empowerment	C-suite level executive in charge of sustainability, fully empowered
Employee involvement in sustainability	Sustainability function as an add-on to pre-existing structures; limited employee participation	Sustainability function woven into pre-existing activities; all employees participate
Board involvement in sustainability	No board members specifically selected for their knowledge and experience with sustainability	One or more board members specifically selected for their knowledge and experience with sustainability

IDENTITY: HOW WE THINK ABOUT SUSTAINABILITY

Organizations that keep sustainability at the periphery and those that embrace it at their core differ in the way they craft a perspective for the organization vis-à-vis sustainability; that is, they relate sustainability to their organizational identities differently. Organizational identity is the collection of attributes that defines what is central, distinctive, and enduring about an organization (Albert and Whetten, 1985). It explicitly articulates who the organization is and what it represents in the eyes of its members and its external stakeholders (Dutton and Dukerich, 1991; Gioia et al., 2010).

To the organization's members, organizational identity is their joint definition of the organization's central character; indeed, it is what they believe the organization stands for and embodies. Members who strongly identify with the organization's identity use this definition to refer not only to the organization but also to themselves. This creates a bond of identification between what they believe is core to the organization and core about them as individuals (Dutton et al., 1994). As such, organizational identity expresses members' personal and collective commitment to what the organization is and what it strives to become. Identity thus acts as the organization's highest-level compass, guiding members' thinking as they identify issues, make decisions, and take actions (Dutton and Dukerich, 1991; Gioia and Thomas, 1996). To external stakeholders, identity is the collection of claims the organization makes to portray itself as a legitimate member of a market category (Albert and Whetten, 1985; Glynn and Abzug, 2002). These claims help the organization communicate how it is similar to, yet distinct from, others, allowing stakeholders to classify it easily and to understand how they should relate to it (Zuckerman, 1999; Rao et al., 2003). In some cases, the definition of the organization's identity can contribute to setting a standard for its industry, prompting others to adopt similar identities (Albert and Whetten, 1985; Navis and Glynn, 2010).

A clearly defined organizational identity is therefore crucial to both providing an internal anchor with which members can identify and creating an external image that conforms to stakeholders' expectations. Hence, if sustainability is to be incorporated as a central attribute of the organization's identity, the organization's understanding of sustainability as it fits its identity must be clearly defined. Organizations that keep sustainability at the periphery of their identity, however, tend to think about sustainability in abstract terms (Marshall and Toffel, 2005). They speak about "being green" without truly understanding what the concept entails. In a recent survey of top managers, 20 percent of respondents said their organizations had no clear definition of sustainability, and 56 percent of respondents worked with two or more definitions at the same time (Bonini et al., 2010). Moreover, organizations that keep sustainability at the periphery are often more preoccupied with creating an external identity to communicate to stakeholders than engaging their members in making that identity meaningful internally. In the same survey, 72 percent of respondents said they considered sustainability "extremely" or "very important" for managing their organizations' corporate reputation and brands, and a staggering 36 percent conceded that building reputation was the top reason for addressing sustainability issues (Bonini et al., 2010). In short, organizations that keep sustainability at the periphery either avoid reflecting on sustainability in concrete terms or they focus disproportionately on producing externally valid definitions to the detriment of internal ones (Senge, 2010).

In contrast, organizations that bring sustainability into their core hold a concrete understanding of what sustainability means to them from both internal and external perspectives (Marshall and Toffel, 2005). Internally, they engage in deep reflection to revise members' collective understanding of "who we are." In so doing, they remain open to challenging their current identity attributes and redefining them if necessary. This produces an envisioned definition of "what we strive to become" that mentally aligns members behind sustainability values. Externally, they engage stakeholders that have conflicting expectations regarding the organization and work to establish an external image rooted in consistent sustainability claims. They may thereby contest widely accepted standards in their industry and prompt stakeholders to embrace new norms.

At DuPont, for example, continued reflection about "who we are" in regard to sustainability has led to different identity definitions over time, yet at each stage sustainability has meant something concrete and actionable for the organization. According to Linda Fischer, DuPont's Chief Sustainability Officer:

If you had talked to folks at DuPont in 1970 ... we focused on environmental compliance. By the '80s we were focusing on footprint reduction; in the '90s, energy efficiency ... More recently ... we've been looking at what our products can do to improve society's impact on the environment. So it's been 40 years of an evolving topic ... If you and I were sitting here in 10 years there probably would be a whole new wave of sustainability. (Colvin, 2009.)

Throughout the evolution of its identity, as sustainability migrated from DuPont's periphery into its core, the organization has become "much less of a chemical company than it used to be, having transformed itself over the past decade into a broad-based science company with an emphasis on biotech" (Colvin, 2009).

STRATEGY: HOW WE PLAN FOR SUSTAINABILITY

Organizations that keep sustainability at the periphery and those that embrace it at their core also differ in the way they engage with sustainability from a planning perspective; i.e., they approach formulating a bespoke sustainability strategy in different ways. An organization's sustainability strategy includes determining short-term and long-term sustainability goals and objectives, evaluating and adopting appropriate courses of action, allocating resources and responsibilities to carry out these goals, and designing adequate metrics to assess results (Chandler, 1962; Ansoff, 1965; Porter, 1996). Establishing a sustainability strategy may require challenging the traditional parameters of value creation and value capture of an organization in its industry. Indeed, it may force managers to revisit the assumptions they made about what business the organization is in and how it should compete (Gavetti and Rivkin, 2007).

Organizations that keep sustainability at the periphery are often non-programmatic about their sustainability efforts and lack a formal sustainability strategy (one that results from systematic strategic analysis). Returning to Bonini and Görner's 2011 McKinsey survey, we see that 57 percent of respondents' organizations fell into this situation. Some of these organizations eschew a formal sustainability plan because they hold a narrow view of sustainability: they see it as separate from the organization's business goals. This leads to a "do-what-we-can" approach, where they commit only marginally to sustainability, limiting their involvement to piecemeal and disjointed initiatives that run without a coherent strategic north (Lubin and Esty, 2010). Other organizations that keep sustainability at the periphery avoid formal planning for sustainability based on cost concerns. They overestimate the expenses of becoming green, while downplaying the benefits (Hart and Milstein, 2003; Nidumolu et al., 2009). A 2009 survey showed that whereas top managers tend to believe that environmental programs do create value, that value is, in their minds, too long-term, abstract, or indirect to measure (Bonini et al., 2009). Such organizations appear to mistrust sustainability's potential to create tangible value. This bias leads them to focus on deploying initiatives that target quick eco-efficiency gains but ignore more complex (and perhaps more rewarding) ways of creating sustainable value (Hart, 1997).

In contrast, organizations that bring sustainability into their core invariably have a formal and truly comprehensive sustainability strategy. This strategy contains a concert of mutually reinforcing initiatives that include, but extend beyond, short-term eco-efficiency gains to involve long-term gains derived from innovation, growth, and previously unrecognized opportunities (Dunphy et al., 2003). The sustainability strategy is integrated with the organization's business strategy so that value generated through sustainability initiatives has a direct impact on the organization's overall performance (Dunphy et al., 2003). These organizations see sustainability as a generative opportunity that has the potential to alter the organization's basis for competing and generating value in its industry (Hart, 1997; Sharma and Vredenburg, 1998).

For example, over the past 20 years, Du Pont has shifted its strategic focus from creating discrete chemical products to providing sustainable solutions that address large global issues associated with sustainability. The organization has three strategic priorities: agriculture and nutrition, bio-based industrials, and advanced materials (DuPont, 2013). DuPont's agricultural seeds and crop protection business, for instance, is geared towards serving a growing population that requires capabilities to produce increasing amounts of food from limited acreage. To this end, DuPont aims to make food "healthier and more nutritious, fresher longer, safer and more sustainable" (DuPont, 2013). The organization is investing "$3 million a day in research and development targeted toward the agriculture, nutrition, health and bio-based markets," a $1.2-billion-dollar commitment in a year (DuPont, 2013). Complementary to these goals, DuPont has created sustainability metrics directed at overseeing the organization's progress in food security matters, which include milestones for new product development, farmer training, and young people's education, among others.

ORGANIZATIONAL DESIGN: HOW WE ACT TOWARDS SUSTAINABILITY

Organizations that keep sustainability at the periphery and those that embrace it at their core also differ in the way they organize to take action to achieve their sustainability goals, i.e. in the way they create an appropriate organizational configuration. Two types of arrangements are needed to configure the organization so that it can embrace sustainability: (1) formal structure; and (2) collaborative agreements. Formal structure consists of the set of interdependent elements (for example, roles, units, and links) that specify how an organization operates (Galbraith, 1973; Mintzberg, 1979; Nadler and Tushman, 1997). Formal structure defines areas of accountability connected to specific rewards and incentives. In turn, collaborative agreements define the arrangements that underlie the organization's relationships with key external constituents, such as suppliers, distributors, customers, and alliance partners (Sytch and Gulati, 2008). Both formal structure and collaborative agreements provide a blueprint upon which the organization's processes run.

Organizations that keep sustainability at the periphery typically lack the structural arrangements that empower their members to embrace sustainability. They often fail to define a formal unit to drive and oversee the organization's sustainability efforts. Such a unit, if it exists, is either disconnected from the rest of the organization or is too low in the hierarchy to have material impact. Furthermore, the resources dedicated to sustainability are often insufficient for this unit to make a difference (Bonini and Görner, 2011). In a recent study, less than 13 percent of Russell 1000 companies (an index that measures the performance of large-capitalization US companies) reported having an executive-level committee responsible for sustainability efforts, and less than 6 percent had appointed a C-level executive to drive progress in this area (Sustainable Enterprise Institute, 2007). Moreover, the organizational units mandated to coordinate these initiatives tend not to support employee involvement, because too few individuals are charged formally with responsibility for sustainable practices (Bonini and Görner, 2011). Finally, at these organizations the board's support remains inconsistent due to lack of knowledgeable, steadfast members. As a result, sustainability initiatives are often discontinued in lean years, when early momentum has subsided and other pressing issues take priority.

Organizations that keep sustainability at the periphery also tend to lack a systematic approach to advancing their sustainability goals through collaborative agreements. Some organizations' relationships with supply-chain partners are purely transactional; that is, they focus on business matters without regard for other issues, let alone sustainability (Senge, 2010). Other firms unilaterally demand that their collaborators introduce green practices without contributing knowledge, support, or guidance (Lee, 2010). Moreover, relationships with external constituents beyond the value chain, such as non-governmental organizations (NGOs), tend to develop in an ad hoc fashion and do not yield actionable results to significantly alter the organizations' practices.

Organizations that incorporate sustainability into their core purposefully transform their internal processes and structures. These organizations often name a Chief Sustainability Officer (CSO) and appoint board members who are selected for their knowledge and experience with sustainability. Engagement, however, is not limited to a few key individuals. Employees spanning the organization's entire operations develop a sense that they own the sustainability mandate and are charged with questioning, challenging, and improving their daily activities to be greener (Dunphy et al., 2003). This allows sustainability initiatives to impact operations in fundamental ways, rather than manifest as marginal projects.

DuPont, the first organization to appoint a CSO in 2004, selected a true expert: Linda Fisher, a lawyer who served at the Environmental Protection Agency for 13 years. About her responsibilities as DuPont's CSO, she stated:

My responsibility has two parts . . . The first is keeping our operations in compliance and going beyond that to reduce our footprint. The second part is the growth piece, . . . to help tie our business strategies with [social] megatrends. (Colvin, 2009.)

Fisher is supported by a team that has deep roots in each of DuPont's business units. She explained:

At DuPont the CSO leads a team of people responsible for Government Affairs, Public Affairs, Regulatory Affairs, Safety, Health and Environment, and Sustainable Growth . . . We are structured so that each of our key 13 business units as well as other divisions within the company all have sustainability leaders and team members with sustainability as part of their job. These team members are tasked with looking holistically at sustainability and environmental impacts within their business, their product line, or their research and development techniques. (Arend, 2010.)

Furthermore, organizations that incorporate sustainability into their core spill the results of their initiatives over to their supply chain and non-market partners (such as universities, NGOs, and government agencies), creating a network of organizations that collaborate and hold themselves mutually accountable for making progress in sustainability matters (Hart and Milstein, 2003). These organizations invest in, discover, and jointly adopt new techniques, reinforcing everyone's commitment to sustainability (Lee, 2010). With sustainability at their core, such organizations see their investments following an upward trajectory that is not impacted by short-term economic shifts.

For example, in 2011, a group of apparel manufacturers and retailers (including Adidas, C&A, H&M, Inditex, Nike, and Puma) made a joint commitment to help lead the apparel and footwear industry towards zero discharge of hazardous chemicals for all products by 2020. Their "Joint Roadmap" provides an overview of the guiding principles and long-term vision of the group, articulates its goals, sets the standards for current and future actions, and establishes measurable milestones. Emphasizing the collaborative nature of the endeavor and the need for mutual accountability, the roadmap states:

To deliver the change we would like to see, all parts of the supply chain—brands, chemical suppliers, manufacturers and other intermediaries—must come work together to engage with concerned stakeholders, drive innovation and establish new ways of reducing and eliminating hazardous chemicals. Members must accept and share responsibility whilst maintaining individual accountability for both their actions and contributions to the delivery of the Joint Roadmap. (Zero Discharge of Hazardous Chemicals Programme, 2013.)

Besides their value-chain partners, the group reached out to other stakeholders, such as government agencies, NGOs, academic institutions, and advocacy groups for feedback and ideas on how to achieve their ultimate goal, and refined their commitments accordingly.

IN SEARCH OF A HOLISTIC VIEW

Why do established organizations find it so difficult to weave sustainability into their core? We contend that this difficulty stems from the organizations' inability to view the three factors discussed above—identity, strategy, and design—holistically. Organizations that successfully bring sustainability into their core consider each of these elements jointly, whereas organizations that keep sustainability at the periphery generally take a fragmented approach. Some jump on the sustainability bandwagon and attempt to green their operations without thinking about strategy or identity implications; others communicate a green identity before they can adequately support it operationally or strategically.

To a certain extent, prior research on organizations and sustainability mirrors this fragmented approach. Multiple studies have highlighted particular practices organizations have implemented to become more sustainable, but these practices are often highly operational and industry specific. They provide an inspiring message, but contribute little to creating actionable frameworks from which organizations can learn in order to incorporate sustainability into their core. More nuanced studies combine an operational and a strategic view of sustainability, but often fail to consider the need to revise the organization's identity. Indeed, studies exploring organizational identity in tandem with sustainability are rare (see Hamilton and Gioia, 2009 and Glynn et al., Chapter 6 (this volume) for two notable exceptions). In the next section, we present a process model that tackles identity, strategy, and design holistically and thus allows an organization to bring sustainability from the periphery to its core.

From periphery to core: a process model to embrace sustainability

Our process model lays the groundwork for bringing sustainability from the organization's periphery into its core. The model consists of four stages: (A) imagining; (B) experimenting; (C) planning; and (D) consolidating. Figure 4.1 illustrates this process.

We derived this model by combining existing theoretical knowledge in organizational change and sustainability and contrasting it with empirical evidence (see, for example, Siggelkow, 2001, 2007 for an exhaustive description of comparable methods). To this end, we reviewed the on-going change journeys of nearly 30 established organizations[2] and looked at patterns of identity, strategy, and organizational design change as they attempted to embrace sustainability. Some organizations that have succeeded in bringing sustainability into their core have followed similar paths to that presented here. We believe this process is non-trivial; valuable lessons can be extracted from mapping it and looking at each stage in detail.

STAGE 1: IMAGINING

In the journey to bring sustainability from the periphery to the core, the first step usually has little to do with operations or strategy, but with someone's hopes, dreams, and expectations for the organization. This key agent (a founder, the chief executive officer (CEO), a top manager, or someone in a position to disseminate the idea and convert others) plays a visionary role and mobilizes others towards a renewed organizational identity. The imagining stage begins when this person confronts the status quo and considers an organization built on sustainable principles. She starts by contrasting "who the organization is" and "what it stands for" with "who the organization should become" and "what it should commit to embodying" once it embraces sustainability. She plays with different conceptions of sustainability as an

---

[2] Details about these companies are presented in the introduction.

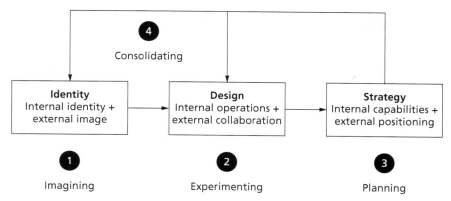

Figure 4.1. A process model for bringing sustainability from the organization's periphery into its core

identity attribute and evaluates how these relate to other, pre-existing identity attributes of the organization. In doing so, she treads the fine line of retaining the organization's traditional sense of self while incorporating the new sustainability ethos. She also considers what an organization built on sustainability principles would represent in its industry and beyond. She treads a second fine line here, because altering the organization's external narrative to include sustainability claims may affect the organization's degree of legitimacy in its institutional environment.

After this initial time of reflection, she makes aspirational claims for the organization, projecting an identity that does not yet exist but has the potential to come to life. Strategy and operations are not yet aligned to deliver on the promise of this new identity. Still, she plants the seeds of possibility, inspiring some and creating skepticism in others. She faces criticism but weathers the storm as internal and external stakeholders struggle to reconcile the proposed identity with what they know to be true about the organization. She works with stakeholders to move them past the ambiguity by retelling the organization's narrative in a way that links "who the organization was" to "who it is striving to become." She continues to speak of the organization in sustainable terms, even if some stakeholders choose to disengage.

The visioning and mobilizing inherent to imagining can be a solitary endeavor, especially in organizations in which skepticism is widespread. However, as the key agent's ideas take root, a new identity grows in the minds of the organization's members and stakeholders, where sustainability is featured as a core identity attribute.

STAGE 2: EXPERIMENTING

As the seeds of a new identity are planted, the second stage consists of experimenting with sustainability practices, selectively adapting the organizations' structure and processes to green endeavors. The key agents in this stage are pioneers willing to devote time, skills, and resources to discovering different ways to make the organization sustainable. These key agents may work at all levels in the organization, from top managers who grant resources to specific units with the mandate to explore, to middle managers who prompt their teams to undertake green projects, and to scientists, engineers, and other workers who devise opportunities to make the organization more sustainable. At this time, it is not uncommon to see a thousand flowers bloom: myriad sustainability initiatives surface, some with express support from top management and others spontaneously.

Despite this burgeoning activity, the organization's structures and processes may still support the organization's traditional ways of working. While processes may evolve organically to accommodate new sustainability-oriented activities, structures require formal definitions to adapt—definitions that the organization may not yet be ready to formulate. In this way, informal areas of responsibility may start emerging and roles may begin expanding in an ad hoc way to support specific initiatives. The organization, however, is still a long way from having a CSO or a fully fledged unit dedicated to driving and overseeing sustainability matters.

A similar effect is seen as the organization's collaborative agreements evolve. Although the organization's budding engagement with sustainability may lead members to reach out to external partners to exchange or coproduce ideas, at this stage the organization lacks a proven process and best practices for drafting green collaborative agreements. What the organization expects from these agreements and what the best structuring policy might be are likely still unclear. Moreover, even in the presence of clear sustainability goals for collaboration, stakeholders may not necessarily interpret or value sustainability to the same degree that the organization does. Members are therefore challenged to create dialogue between disparate institutional agents and to steer the conversation towards a joint understanding of sustainability and common goals before structuring an agreement.

Without an appropriate structure for its internal design and its collaborative agreements, the organization's sustainability initiatives at this stage typically lack cohesiveness; indeed, they often evolve in idiosyncratic and disjointed ways. As with all experimentation, the results can sometimes be haphazard. Some initiatives yield immediate results, others fail, and still others show potential but cannot yet be translated to processes and products. Despite mixed results, during this stage the kernels of sustainability are disseminated throughout the organization, as individuals at all levels of the hierarchy gain exposure to sustainability. This wave of experimentation, however, may still encounter a wave of resistance from those who are weary of risking the organization's resources for exploratory sustainability endeavors. Consequently, contention and dissent may still be present, and even peak, during this stage.

STAGE 3: PLANNING

At this stage, the organization's incipient commitment to sustainability through a newly imagined identity and experiment-laden structures and processes reaches a tipping point, which culminates in defining a formal sustainability strategy. Key agents at this stage are the organization's CEO and her top management team, who set an overarching plan which defines the organization's sustainability goals. The plan articulates a new strategic positioning for the organization by reformulating the parameters on which the organization competes in its market; identifies sustainability-specific capabilities and creates a map to allocate resources towards their development; appoints individuals and teams as responsible for concrete sustainability initiatives; and establishes meaningful metrics to track the organization's progress.

It is not uncommon at this stage for the CEO and other top managers to think of the organization's sustainability strategy and business strategy as two sides of the same coin. In doing so, some initiatives that sprang to life in the previous stage may be pruned and others enhanced, depending on their expected contribution to both the organization's sustainability and business goals. The intent is for the organization's sustainability endeavors to have a concrete impact on the organization's overall business performance. Once sustainability becomes an integral part of the organization's core strategy, those who have resisted the efforts to this point may either convert or leave the organization. The existence of a formal sustainability strategy tends to leave little room for the undecided.

STAGE 4: CONSOLIDATING

With a comprehensive plan for sustainability in place, the final stage includes revisiting the organization's identity and design in the light of the new strategy; i.e., of redefining, adjusting, or pruning the organization's pre-existing sense of self and supporting structures. At this stage, the organization can truly establish links between its identity claims regarding sustainability and its own operations, readying itself to "walk the talk." The key agents at this stage can be senior leaders such as the CEO, the CSO (a position that was either created with the plan or pre-existed, but had not yet been fully empowered), and top managers with special interests in the organization's sustainability and overall performance such as the Chief Operating Officer (COO).

At this stage, the organization refines its claims regarding its identity by crafting a formal and more nuanced notion of "who we are" than was achieved in the imagining stage. Formally defining the organization's identity serves both as a source of internal identification (so that employees see themselves and their work imbued with specific commitments to sustainability) and as a source of image, reputation, and credibility externally (so that external constituents such as analysts, activists, value-chain partners, and collaborators know what to expect from the organization in terms of sustainability). Any resistance encountered during the organization's attempted identity shift in the imagining stage yields to more widespread support from both members and stakeholders in the consolidating stage.

In terms of design, the organization makes changes to deliver operationally on its sustainability goals. Individuals become tasked formally with integrating sustainability into their roles so that they can identify concrete opportunities to contribute. The CSO is not only fully empowered, but a specific unit of the organization dedicated to sustainability coordinates the efforts and tracks performance against previously defined metrics. One or more board members may have been selected due to their knowledge and expertise regarding sustainability, and their recommendations trickle down to influence operations. Finally, collaborative agreements are formally in place and their endeavors are connected directly to the organization's sustainability goals. The organization actively challenges and supports its partners in moving forward with their own sustainability initiatives. Proven processes and best practices are formalized to guide the organization's future collaborative endeavors in this area.

While descriptively this stage seems to be an end-state, it is actually not: it lays the groundwork for the organization to kick-start future cycles of identity, design, and strategy redefinition to continually renew its sustainability goals. For many organizations—even those most successful in embracing sustainability at the core—the quest to become greener is an on-going process.

The Ford Motor Company: an illustrative case

In this section, we showcase Ford's journey towards sustainability through the lens of our process model. Ford is an emblematic organization in an industry that is considered to be one of the greatest polluters. With more than 100 years of business history and family tradition, Ford has made significant progress in switching from gas-guzzling trucks and SUVs to fuel-efficient, technology-laden smaller vehicles. Ford's experience richly illustrates our model, as it evidences some of the nuances and complexities of bringing sustainability from the periphery into an organization's core. Figure 4.2 shows a graphic representation of Ford's journey.

To build this illustrative case, we assembled a collection of about 180 articles from trade journals and the press that referenced Ford and its sustainability efforts. Articles mostly covered the period 1999 to the present (encompassing William Clay Ford, Jr's tenure as chairman, with three different CEOs, including himself) but selectively dated back to the 1980s and 1990s, when discrete sustainability initiatives and challenges occurred. We also worked with Ford Sustainability Reports for the past 10 years and Ford's Blueprint

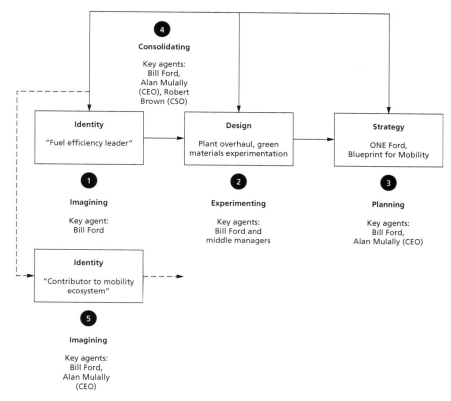

Figure 4.2. From periphery to core: Ford's engagement with sustainability

for Mobility, which establishes a foundation for the company's near-, mid-and long-term visions of the world's transportation landscape. Combining these data sources, we coded their contents for our three main constructs (identity, strategy, and design) and built a timeline of events. Our intent in showcasing Ford's experience is to add richness to our model by examining the ways in which Ford navigated each stage. This approach mirrors that of other studies in organizational change and evolution that showcase a case study to illustrate a previously derived model (for example, Henderson and Clark, 1990; Siggelkow, 2001; O'Reilly et al., 2009).

IDENTITY: IMAGINING A SUSTAINABLE FORD

It was business as usual in the late 1970s, when William Clay (Bill) Ford, Jr, Henry Ford's great-grandson, joined the ranks of the family firm. His ambition was to infuse The Ford Motor Company with sustainable principles and practices, an idea about which he had been passionate since his years as a student.

Bill was not the first Ford to think green. The seeds of sustainability at Ford were planted by founder Henry Ford himself. In 1922's *My Life and Work* he wrote:

We dig coal and ore and cut down trees. We use the coal and the ore and they are gone; the trees cannot be replaced within a lifetime. We shall someday harness the heat that is all about us and no longer depend on coal...As chemistry advances I feel quite certain that a method will be found to transform growing things into substances that will endure better than the metals...The spirit of true service will create for us. We have only each of us to do our parts sincerely.

Henry Ford is credited with advocating for ethanol, rather than lead, as the chemical that should be used to improve octane in gasoline (Ford Motor Company, 2012a). He is also credited with creating a car made from soybean fibers in 1941 (McCue, 2013). But ethanol lost the battle to lead and, due to the outbreak of World War II, the green vehicle was never produced. Sustainability thus remained at the periphery of the organization's vision for decades to come.

When Bill Ford entered the company, the board and top management regarded his ideas about sustainability with suspicion. In an interview, he recalled how difficult it was to diffuse his commitment to sustainability throughout the organization: "I was alone in my thinking in those days. Through the '80s, I tried to find kindred spirits within Ford. There were a few, but it was an uphill battle, particularly with top management, who thought I was probably a Bolshevik" (Bonini and Kaas, 2010).

Bill Ford joined the board of directors in 1988, started his tenure as chairman in 1999, and became CEO in 2001. At the turn of the century, the organization's highly successful product line included large, gas-guzzling vehicles, SUVs, and trucks. Oil prices were low (a gallon was retailing for less than a dollar) and neither the industry nor the company was preoccupied with sustainability. Yet Bill Ford began imagining a sustainable Ford Motor Company and began making bold declarations both to his employees and the market. In a 1999 press release, for example, he warned consumers they would be able to "have any vehicle they wanted, as long as it was green" (Segal, 2005), making a playful twist of the founder's famous line. At the time, Ford Motor Company's identity was oriented heavily towards attributes such as quality, endurance, and resistance. Bill Ford, however, desired that the quest for environmental leadership "become like quality—a prism through which we look when we make decisions. I want Ford to be recognized around the world as a company that does more than just make products," he said. Instead, he envisioned "a company that lends its strength to help solve some of society's problems" (Connelly, 1998).

Yet his imagined dream remained distant. For example, in the year 2000, The Ford Motor Company pledged it would increase the fuel economy of its SUVs by 25 percent within five years. This pledge was infused with Bill Ford's conviction that the organization needed to be greener and should take early action, before sustainability became an unavoidable issue. He stated, "There is a rising tide of environmental awareness and activism among consumers that is going to swell to undreamed-of heights in the 21st century... Smart companies will get ahead of that wave, and ride it to success and prosperity. Those that don't are headed for a wipeout" (Warner, 2008). Yet despite his conviction, the opportunity did not materialize. The costs involved in achieving that level of fuel efficiency were prohibitive. The technology had already been tested in the labs, but adding it to the vehicles would increase costs to a point where no consumer would pay for it.[3] Jim Schroer, Ford's global marketing chief at the time, maintained, "I'm sitting there, and I think, 'Oh boy, that's not going to happen... By anybody's financial present-value calculation, you'd be crazy to do it'" (Warner, 2008). Eventually, Ford was forced to backtrack from its pledge. Activist groups launched campaigns against the company and Bill Ford personally, labeling him "Pinocchio" and calling for a boycott of Ford vehicles. John DeCicco, a senior fellow with the Environmental Defense Fund, concluded, "The '25 by 5' pledge is a very instructive story because it really points out the inability of the individual corporate actor to go in a different direction from where the competitive marketplace wants to go" (Warner, 2008).

Bill Ford's tenure as CEO was marked by struggles to bring the organization back to profitability. Despite economic hardships, however, he continued to imagine a green Ford. Reflecting on this in an interview, he stated, "I have to look in the mirror every day... And to me, this commitment is not something new. It's not some PR person's dream. In fact, it's probably a PR person's nightmare" (Naughton, 2004).

DESIGN: EXPERIMENTING WITH SUSTAINABLE PRACTICES

Despite generalized internal opposition to his sustainability agenda, Ford's few followers managed to experiment with several sustainability initiatives. Although these initiatives grew in the absence of an appropriate structure dedicated to sustainability or a comprehensive sustainability strategy, they helped set early milestones for Ford's engagement with sustainability both internally and externally.

Internally, Bill Ford reportedly resisted heavy pressure from top management to discontinue several green projects at a time when the company was facing serious financial shortcomings. For example, he defended the construction of a $2 billion environmentally friendly factory and pushed for the iconic River Rouge plant to be overhauled. What was once a decaying enclave was now a test lab for sustainable manufacturing practices. To accomplish the

---

[3] Two other events further diminished Ford's sense of opportunity for fuel efficiency: the 2000 Firestone tire recall, which brought significant losses to the organization, and the September 11th attacks in 2001, which severely affected the automotive industry and the economy at large.

transformation, Ford hired the environmentally progressive architect William McDonough. Ford stated:

We took the world's largest brownfield site and made it into the world's greenest assembly plant. At Rouge, we're turning paint fumes into energy. We have grass roofs [that retain and cleanse rainwater and moderate the internal temperature of the building, saving energy]...We have permeable parking lots, so that storm waters aren't flushed but sink into the ground...We have a lot of technologies we're applying, some high tech, some low tech (Bonini and Kaas, 2010).

Such initiatives faced harsh criticism. Bill Ford reflected, "Many of my executives said, 'Hey, we've got to kill this. This is something we just can't afford' ...My rejoinder was: 'This is something we simply can't afford not to do'" (Naughton, 2004).

Other initiatives, however, could not be salvaged. When Debbie Mielewski, technical leader of Ford Plastics Research, pitched the possibility of using plants as car parts to executives, she faced nothing but rejection. She recalled:

It was a very tough sell...We would go into every conference room at Ford, and they would say, "If it is that green stuff, you can get up and go. We're not interested"...I thought if there were products available that were better for the environment and performed just as well, then why wouldn't we use them instead of using limited resources? (McCue, 2013.)

Externally, Ford began using meetings with high-profile NGOs, conference appearances, and interviews as opportunities for sustainability advocacy. Ford remembered:

Someone had to build a bridge between the environmental community and the business community—which, in that era, all through the '90s, were very much polarized. I think I was the first executive to ever speak at a Greenpeace business conference, in London in 2001. That didn't play well here at Ford, but I thought it was an important signal to send. (Bonini and Kaas, 2010.)

Finally, at the turn of the millennium, the company began issuing a sustainability report, a rare occurrence in the automotive industry. Reflecting on the consequences of introducing a practice that seemed outlandish at the time, Bill Ford stated:

When I first introduced that report—I think around 2000—I was blasted by the business press. They asked: Why would you criticize your own performance? We said in the report: Here's where we're falling short, here are the challenges ahead of us, and check in with us next year to see how we're progressing....It was very controversial when we did it. Now it's become much more widely accepted. (Bonini and Kaas, 2010.)

The report symbolized Ford's commitment to sustainability at a time when the organization still had a long way to go to make its products and operations green.

STRATEGY: PLANNING FOR SUSTAINABILITY

Bill Ford stepped down as CEO in 2006, but remained as executive chairman. His replacement, former Boeing senior executive Alan Mulally, was tasked with orchestrating the organization's financial and environmental turn-arounds. This would entail building a solid strategy based on Ford's feeble identity commitments toward sustainability and myriad disparate initiatives and practices that had blossomed under Bill Ford. The time was nigh, however. Oil prices were soaring, consumers were moving toward smaller, fuel-efficient cars, and the case for alternative modes of propulsion began to show signs of profitability.

As his tenure at Ford began, CEO Alan Mulally introduced an integrated strategic plan called ONE Ford. The plan articulated the company's overarching goals and included targets for business, environmental, and social matters with the goal of aligning efforts in these three areas towards a common definition of success. Metrics pointed to financial health, CO_2 emissions, water use, vehicle safety, supply-chain training, and employee health and safety. During his appearance at the 2012 Fortune Brainstorm GREEN conference, Mulally stated, "All the elements of the plan are on [the same] card...We don't have a different plan for sustainability or energy independence and security or environmental sustainability that's not on this plan...We just have one plan" (Mulally, 2012). According to the organization's *Sustainability Report Summary 2012/13*, metrics in most dimensions improved vis-à-vis the previous year, a handful remained level, and only one (related to employee safety) presented a "not-on-track" status (Ford Motor Company, 2012c).

Mulally also maintained and reinforced the company's commitment to alternate technologies. Bill Ford explained the organization's stance as follows:

For 100 years, pretty much all we had was the internal-combustion engine...Now we stand at the threshold of some real technological revolutions. And it's still unclear, ultimately, whether there will be one dominant form of propulsion or whether we will have a mix [but] we won't be the laggard. Whichever avenue proves to be the predominant one—whether it's electric or biofuels or hydrogen or diesel—we will be there with the hardware. (Bonini and Kaas, 2010.)

Ford learned the importance of investing in different technologies when the company's heavy bet on hybrids was crushed by the rise of ethanol-fueled cars. In 2006, the organization had to backtrack from a promise to build 250,000 hybrids by 2010. Bill Ford conceded: "When we looked at the hybrid market 18 months ago, we didn't see anything else out there that was going to be really viable. And I think this whole notion of biofuels has really come on strong ...In the past year there's been tremendous progress made on ethanol, both in terms of infrastructure and also availability. (Naughton, 2006.)

As part of the ONE Ford plan, Mulally also advocated rethinking the company's family of vehicles. He shifted the organization's focus to smaller, fuel-efficient cars, explaining:

You can imagine the transformation at Ford to...move from a truck and SUV company to a full family of vehicles dominated by smaller and midsized vehicles... Nearly 60 percent of the vehicles worldwide in the next few years are going to be B to C size like Fiestas and Focuses, about 25 percent will be C–D size like a Fusion, and about 15 percent will be larger vehicles like a Taurus and, of course, the bigger trucks and SUVs. (Mulally, 2012.)

IDENTITY AND DESIGN: CONSOLIDATING SUSTAINABILITY AT FORD

The ONE Ford plan impacted the way the company thought and acted regarding sustainability. In terms of identity, Ford chose fuel efficiency as its core identity attribute. Bill Ford explained: "Inside Ford...we don't use the term sustainability very much, because it lacks clarity. We talk about *being the fuel economy leader,* about which technology is going to drive that, and we talk about cleaning up our plants and about applying technology to our facilities to drive our carbon dioxide emissions out. It all adds up [to that fuel-efficiency goal]" (Bonini and Kaas, 2010; emphasis added). Ford believed that the organization was finally positioned to deliver on this claim:

With gas cheaper than bottled water, there really wasn't a great pull in the marketplace for fuel-efficient vehicles. [Also], fuel-efficient vehicles were seen as cheap and not fun to drive...Now fuel prices have risen, and the technology has developed to the point where we can give customers great fuel economy and a great driving experience; they don't have to make that trade-off anymore. So now we're at the point where we can say *we want to be the fuel economy leader in every segment we participate in*—and that statement does not scare people internally. They understand this is the right thing to do...In the past, they may have been sceptical. (Bonini and Kaas, 2010; emphasis added.)

Ford has taken several steps to reconvert its formal structure and processes to support its fuel-efficiency claims. Structurally, the organization created a board-level Sustainability Committee tasked with helping management formulate and implement policies, principles, and practices to foster the organization's sustainable growth. The Committee is also responsible for supporting management in responding to stakeholder concerns and government regulations regarding sustainability. To this end, the Committee periodically reviews new and innovative technologies, analyzes opportunities for partnerships and relationships, and evaluates Ford's communication and marketing strategies relating to sustainable growth (Ford Motor Company, 2008). At the executive team level, Ford created the highly visible position of Vice President of Sustainability, Environment and Safety Engineering, who reports directly to the CEO. Robert Brown, who has occupied that role since 2012, is responsible for the company's environment and safety strategy, policies, and performance, and assuring Ford meets or exceeds all safety and environmental regulations worldwide. Brown supervises teams operating on three continents that manage the relationships among the organization, the unions, the dealers, the community, and government in each location where Ford does business. The charge to these teams is to make joint progress toward the organization's social and environmental goals. In tandem, Ford has reviewed the content of certain core functions to make them accountable for specific sustainability issues. In this way, sustainability is not interpreted as the sole domain of the VP of Sustainability and his team, but recognized as an organization-wide endeavor. Groups such as Human Resources, Communications, Marketing, Product Development, Purchasing, Information Technology, and Manufacturing are adopting larger roles in the organization's sustainability efforts. Finally, Ford consolidated its R&D centers so that knowledge regarding sustainability could flow more efficiently. Bill Ford credits this particular instance of reorganization as a seminal event. He explained:

Derrick Kuzak, who is head of our global product development, took all of the disparate product development centers around the world and slammed them together. It was a huge management undertaking—these product development centers had grown up, over many years, as independent. Doing that allowed him to drive this sustainability philosophy through the whole product-development system, in a way that would have been impossible before. (Bonini and Kaas, 2010.)

Efforts extended to the individual level as well. Aiming to make sustainability every employee's responsibility, regardless of their position, personal sustainability goals and metrics were tied to compensation in different ways. Brown specified:

We develop business plans in five-year increments and establish sustainability targets based on an analysis of external factors that could impact the business and available resources. Each business unit and function leader has accountability for meeting the targets. Progress is reviewed . . . weekly at the highest level of the company. So virtually every function has some accountability for sustainability performance. In addition, each salaried Ford employee has individual metrics that are established with their supervisor; the metrics are based on the overall company business plan, which includes sustainability targets . . . Progress is reviewed against the metrics at least twice a year, and performance relative to the metrics is an important factor in determining merit salary increases. (Brown, 2012.)

From an operations perspective, Ford has redesigned plants, processes, and products. The organization has invested billions to reconvert its plants to lower CO_2 emissions, diminish water use, reduce landfill waste, and conserve energy. Each facility has a comprehensive set of environmental targets and uses a detailed scorecard for reporting so that further improvements can be planned. At the same time, Ford has made great efforts to streamline its product platforms and make them global. Traditionally, Ford offered different products built under different logics in each region of the world. Now building on common infrastructure, production plants have been outfitted with flexible systems and tools so they can build vehicles with a full array of powertrains on the same production line. Mulally noted: "We've moved to these global platforms...So, petrol, diesel, hybrid, plug-in hybrid, and all electric, not only are they [in] the same family, but they're on the same production line. So, no matter what vehicle you want that works for you, and we can't guess what the demand is going to be, but it's on the same line, 70 to 80 percent of the parts are the same, you can imagine the efficiencies and sustainability of that" (Mulally, 2012).

Auto parts were also made greener whenever possible. Susan Rokosz, Ford's principal environmental engineer, noted, "These days at Ford, we work to build sustainability into the DNA of our vehicles. We've incorporated a sustainable approach to the whole lifecycle of a vehicle, from the design, raw materials, and manufacturing to customer use and end-of-life" (Rokosz, 2012). For example, Ford's Plastic Research unit has long experimented with non-polluting materials to replace plastic- or fossil-fuel-based auto parts. Scientists have developed, tested, and whenever possible deployed seat cushions and seat backs made by combining soy-based foam, sugarcane-based plastic, and corn-based fabric; armrests and center consoles made from strains of hemp; air ducts and storage bins made of wheat straw; and coin trays made from shredded currency retired by the Federal Reserve. Some of these materials would otherwise go into landfills; others are burned by farmers because of their low economic value. "Ford's policy states that engineers must choose a sustainable material if it meets all performance and durability requirements at an equivalent cost...[Yet] a customer can't tell the difference," said Debbie Mielewski, technical leader of Ford Plastics Research. "Durability, rebound—everything is the same" (McCue, 2013).

Finally, Ford instituted a unified approach to supply-chain management. Rokosz (2012) explained, "Ford has been ISO 14001 certified for about 15 years, and we have been cascading the lessons learned to our suppliers." She further added: "The automotive supply chain is one of the most complex in all of industry, and our efforts to help our suppliers become more sustainable have far-reaching impacts...We are working with our suppliers to help them understand and improve their environmental footprints, especially in greenhouse gases." Ford regularly conducts supplier training, assessments, and remediation on sustainability matters, and works with partners to align approaches to issues ranging from labor rights to sourcing raw materials.

In the non-market space, Ford is working with a variety of NGOs such as Word Resources Institute, Ceres, Business for Social Responsibility, the Interfaith Center on Corporate Responsibility, the Union of Concerned Scientists, the Natural Resources Defense Council, and The Ecology Center (Rokosz, 2012). The company is also collaborating with for-profit organizations such as Coca-Cola, Nike, Procter & Gamble, and Heinz on developing bioplastics, and with the Oak Ridge National Laboratory and the Dow Chemical company on perfecting carbon fibers (Brown, 2012).

Overhauling the organization's collaborative endeavors with external partners stems from the indispensable acknowledgment that no organization can tackle sustainability on its own. Sustainability is too comprehensive and too expensive to pursue in isolation. Furthermore, best practices are not necessarily always created within the organization's boundaries. Bill Ford maintained:

We're doing a lot more collaboration with universities and with our suppliers because we don't have a monopoly, by any means, on good ideas. We need to stay humble, and by that I mean recognizing that good ideas are coming from everywhere. We need to embrace good ideas no matter where they come from ... The magnitude of what we've got ahead of us ... means we can't afford, either intellectually or monetarily, to be the sole investor. [Now we] have an early-warning system. If they start working on things we hadn't thought about, we're part of that. (Bonini and Kaas, 2010.)

BEYOND FUEL EFFICIENCY: IMAGINING AGAIN

Within the past few years, Ford's identity claims have gone beyond fuel efficiency. The seeds of a new identity have been planted. The organization no longer views itself as a vehicle manufacturer but as *a contributor to a larger mobility ecosystem*. Bill Ford explained:

There are about 1 billion vehicles on the road worldwide ... That number could grow to 4 billion by mid-century ... We need to view the automobile as one element of a much broader transportation ecosystem, and look for new ways to optimize the entire system ... We believe a truly sustainable long-term solution will require a global transportation network that enables wireless communication among vehicles and infrastructure. This system would use real-time data to [bring] all modes of travel into a single network that links together public and personal transportation. Pedestrian walkways, bicycles, buses, airplanes, trains, automobiles—in our vision of the future everything would be fully integrated to save time, conserve resources and lower emissions. (Ford, W.C., 2011.)

With a ceiling on the number of cars that can and will be sold over the next 20 years, Ford has started to explore opportunities for car sharing. The organization recently partnered with Zipcar to offer Ford cars on 250 college and university campuses in the United States. The agreement stipulates that Ford subsidizes part of the membership fee and the hourly rental rates for students (Vlasic, 2011). The company also created FORD2GO in Germany, with its network of dealers and DB Rent, the company behind Flinkster car sharing. It is the first manufacturer-backed, nationwide car-sharing program in Europe to incorporate dealerships (Ford Motor Company, 2013). These experiments are allowing Ford to gauge how the company can remain a central player when automotive industry's boundaries merge with those of other means of transportation and complementary technologies.

Bill Ford, Alan Mulally, and other top executives have been actively creating ties in different directions. Bill Ford delivered the keynote address at the 2012 Mobile World Congress, where he spoke to telecommunications executives about the need to collaborate with the automotive industry to build "a global transportation network that utilizes communication between vehicles, transport infrastructure and individual mobile devices" (Ford Motor Company, 2012b). He emphasized: "The telecommunications industry is critical in the creation of an inter-connected transportation system where cars are intelligent and can talk to one another as well as the infrastructure around them. Now is the time for us all to be looking at vehicles on the road the same way we look at smartphones, laptops and tablets; as pieces of a much bigger, richer network" (Ford Motor Company, 2012b). It was the first time an automotive industry executive had spoken at this leading annual telecommunications industry event. Yet despite these efforts, Ford's strategy, internal structure, and external collaborations still have a long way to go to bring the organization's mobility-oriented identity to life.

Discussion and conclusion

A growing number of social agents clamor for the adoption of sustainable principles and practices, yet many established organizations continue to struggle in their quest to embrace them. In this chapter, we analyzed how organizations that keep sustainability at the periphery and those that hold it at their core differ in their approaches to identity (how they think about sustainability), strategy (how they plan for sustainability), and design (how they act towards sustainability). In advocating a holistic approach, we presented a process model that showed, along four specific stages, how acting on these three elements may help organizations embrace sustainability. Subsequently, we illustrated the model through the experience of The Ford Motor Company.

Our work contributes to the literatures on organizational congruence and configuration, which posit that organizations are systems of interdependent choices (for example, Nadler and Tushman, 1997; Siggelkow, 2001). According to this view, changes to a specific choice are followed by adaptive changes in other choices which enable the organization to attain both internal fit (i.e., a coherent configuration of internal activities) and external fit (i.e., a configuration that proves adequate vis-à-vis the demands of the external environment). Configuration studies typically focus on an organization's choices related to activities, policies, structures, capabilities, and resources. Our model, however, emphasizes not only these lower-order organizational elements, but also higher-order ones, such as strategy and identity. Some organizational change processes (such as bringing sustainability from the periphery to the core) may be so overwhelming that they involve making interdependent choices that affect the entirety of organizational life—from the most mundane and simple elements to the most abstract and complex. At the same time, our process model stresses that while the organization is working to bring sustainability from the periphery into its core, a lack of fit both internally and externally may be evident for a considerable length of time. For example, in the imagining stage, the envisioned identity will be at odds with the organization's existing strategy and structure. Similarly, during the experimentation stage, both identity and design may collide with strategy and with external stakeholders' views and expectations regarding the organization. Given the intricacies and the timeframe involved, the organization may not regain fit among these three organizational elements until the consolidation stage.

The present work also contributes to the burgeoning literature on sustainability (for example, Sharma and Vredenburg, 1998; Dunphy et al., 2003; Hart and Milstein, 2003). Although sustainability scholars have tackled the issue of organizational change, many models focus on managers' roles in developing a sustainability strategy and designing structures and processes. However, these studies usually neglect the core task of reshaping the organization's identity. Embracing sustainability at the organization's core far exceeds planning and organizing. Although these actions are critical, sustainability will never truly permeate what the organization is and does unless the organization changes its self-concept. Indeed, the first stage in our model, the imagining stage, centers on recreating the organization's identity even before strategy and structure are addressed. The organization's capacity to imagine itself as an entity that embraces sustainable values later enables it to formulate an adequate strategy and operate sustainably. If the question of identity is not explored, sustainability may be strategically and operationally emphasized or de-emphasized in an ad hoc fashion. When sustainability becomes part of "who we are," however, it is crystallized as a permanent organizational tenet that can be recreated over time, but rarely abandoned. Notably, managers must be attuned to the challenges inherent to altering the organization's identity before they attempt to incorporate sustainability into the organization's strategy and design. Managers need to develop tools (concrete and symbolic) to address any backlash that surfaces when asking members and stakeholders to think of the organization in terms that vary from the norm.

In advocating a holistic view of identity, strategy, and design, we acknowledge that these three organizational elements cannot always be addressed effectively at the same time. The progression we present here—from identity, to design, to strategy, and back to identity and design—flows sequentially. The bases set in one dimension provide the catalyst to effect change in the next. The longitudinal nature of our model highlights the fact that bringing sustainability into the organization's core is a time-consuming endeavor, one that requires reflection and action in specific realms before progress can be made in another. As they tackle each organizational element at the appropriate time, managers must keep in mind what lies ahead and steer their organizations accordingly towards the next challenge.

Many established organizations continue to keep sustainability at the periphery because they do not develop the momentum to leave the imagining and experimenting stages behind. They continue to dream and make unsubstantiated claims, while wasting resources on myriad disjointed initiatives. Although these initial stages provide valuable lessons, the organization truly succeeds in bringing sustainability to its core during the planning and consolidating stages. To move the organization forward, managers must remain vocal about where the organization is positioned and provide a vision of what lies ahead. They must also be attuned to opportunities and threats that may directly impact the organization's ability to move from one stage to another.

It is worth noting that, whereas our process model touches on the identity, strategy, and design dilemmas that most (if not all) established organizations may face as they seek to bring sustainability from the periphery into their core, there may be alternative paths to resolving these issues. For example, our model combines emergent (bottom-up) and mandated (top-down) actions: the imagining and the planning stages require strong key agents to be set in motion, whereas the experimenting stage (and to a great extent the consolidating stage) allow for employee autonomy, empowerment, and self-directed action. Many models in the sustainability literature follow the top-down approach espoused by classic change-management frameworks (Lewin, 1947; Kotter, 1996). It would be interesting to establish under what conditions more or less emergent processes might occur that move sustainability from the organization's periphery to its core and what managers' roles might be in fostering more emergent actions regarding sustainability.

Our model is situated at the organizational level and the illustrative case covers a single organization's experience with sustainability over roughly two decades. Future research should investigate how a cluster of organizations in the same industry or ecosystem evolve their identities, strategies, and designs to pursue both individual and collective sustainability goals. For example, it would be interesting to explore how similar or dissimilar identity claims regarding sustainability might influence these organizations' abilities to garner member commitment and stakeholder allegiance. In other words, future research should assess to what extent identity uniqueness and distinctiveness as regards sustainability helps organizations establish themselves as leaders in their competitive space or sets them up for failure.

Finally, future research could take an intra-organizational perspective to examine how units within an organization respond during each stage of our model. While responses could certainly be somewhat uniform, one might expect certain units to embrace a sustainability-oriented identity or the opportunity to adapt their structures and processes to accommodate sustainability-oriented experimentation to a greater extent than others. Future studies could look at synergies that may arise from mutually reinforcing initiatives across units and the processes whereby more sustainability-inclined units influence others units to embrace it.

Embracing sustainability is a complex and far-reaching challenge; the kind that organizations encounter a handful of times in their lifespan. Our process model highlights the nuances of taking on a truly transformative journey, one that redefines the organization's way of thinking and acting through a non-trivial sequence of imagining, experimenting, planning, and consolidating. The challenge of bringing sustainability into the organization's core perhaps mirrors the nuances of other complex organizational challenges. A similar process could apply, for example, to an organization's journey towards ensuring total quality or committing to diversity. Further research is required to assert whether the lessons we have learned here regarding sustainability can illuminate the path towards making other outstanding challenges core to our organizations.

■ ACKNOWLEDGMENTS

The authors gratefully acknowledge the insightful comments and ideas of Rebecca Henderson, Chris Marquis, William Ocasio, Melissa Paschall, George Serafeim, Mike Toffel, and Mike Tushman. The Division of Research of Harvard Business School generously provided funding.

■ REFERENCES

Albert, S. and Whetten, D. A. (1985) "Organizational Identity," in L. L. Cummings and B. M. Staw (eds), *Research in Organizational Behavior*, Vol. 7. Greenwich, CT: JAI Press, 263–95.

Ansoff, H. I. (1965) *Corporate Strategy: An Analytic Approach to Business Policy for Growth and Expansion.* New York: McGraw-Hill.

Arend, M. (2010) "C-Suites Add Sustainability Chiefs: Is Real Estate on their Minds?," *Site Selection Magazine.* Available at: <http://www.siteselection.com/issues/2010/jul/gg-c-suites.cfm> (accessed July 2014).

Bonini, S. and Görner, S. (2011) *McKinsey Global Survey Results: The Business of Sustainability.* New York: McKinsey and Company. Available at: <http://www.mckinsey.com/insights/energy_resources_materials/the_business_of_sustainability_mckinsey_global_survey_results> (accessed July 2014).

Bonini, S. and Kaas, H. W. (2010) "Building a Sustainable Ford Motor Company: An Interview with Bill Ford," *McKinsey Quarterly* January. Available at: <http://www.mckinsey.com/insights/sustainability/building_a_sustainable_ford_motor_company_an_interview_with_bill_ford> (accessed July 2014).

Bonini, S., Brun, N., and Rosenthal, M. (2009) *McKinsey Global Survey Results: Valuing Corporate Social Responsibility.* New York: McKinsey and Company. Available at: <http://www.mckinsey.com/insights/corporate_finance/valuing_corporate_social_responsibility_mckinsey_global_survey_results> (accessed July 2014).

Bonini, S., Görner, S., and Jones, A. (2010) *McKinsey Global Survey Results: How Companies Manage Sustainability.* New York: McKinsey and Company. Available at: <http://www.mckinsey.com/insights/sustainability/how_companies_manage_sustainability_mckinsey_global_survey_results> (accessed July 2014).

Brown, R. (2012) "Letter from Robert Brown. Ford Motor Company Sustainability 2012/13." Available at: <http://corporate.ford.com/microsites/sustainability-report-2012-13/review-letter-brown> (accessed July 2014).

Chandler, A. D. (1962) *Strategy and Structure*. New York: Doubleday.

Colvin, G. (2009) "Linda Fisher." Fortune 160 (10): 45–50

Connelly, M. (1998) "Ford: New Leaders Share a Vision," *Automotive News* 73 (5784): 1.

Delmas, M. and Toffel, M. W. (2004) "Stakeholders and Environmental Management Practices: An Institutional Framework," *Business Strategy and the Environment* 13 (4): 209–22.

Delmas, M. A. and Toffel, M. W. (2008) "Organizational Responses to Environmental Demands: Opening the Black Box," *Strategic Management Journal* 29 (10): 1027–55.

Dunphy, D., Benn, S., and Griffiths, A. (2003) *Organizational Change for Corporate Sustainability*. London: Routledge, 695–8.

DuPont. (2013) *Dupont 2013 Sustainability Progress Report*. Available at: <http://www.dupont.com/contentdam/assets/corporate-functions/our-approach.sustainability/documents/2013DuPont%20Sustainability%20Report_web.pdf> (accessed July 2014).

Dutton, J. E. and Dukerich, J. M. (1991) "Keeping an Eye on the Mirror: Image and Identity in Organizational Adaptation," *Academy of Management Journal* 34: 517–54.

Dutton, J. E., Dukerich, J. M., and Harquail, C. V. (1994) "Organizational Images and Member Identification," *Administrative Science Quarterly* 29: 239–63.

Ford, H. and Crowder, S. (1922) *My Life and Work*. New York: Doubleday.

Ford Motor Company. (2008) "Charter of the Sustainability Committee of the Board of Directors." Available from: <http://corporate.ford.com/doc/corpgov_sustainability_committee_charter.pdf> (accessed July 2014).

Ford Motor Company. (2012a) "@fordonline: Q&A with Robert Brown on Ford's Sustainability Report." Available at: <http://corporate.ford.com/annual-report-2012/better-world-blueprint-for-mobility.html> (accessed July 2014).

Ford Motor Company. (2012b) *Bill Ford Outlines Blueprint for Mobility" Vision: Calls on Mobile Industry to Help Develop Transportation Solutions* (press release). Available at: <http://www.ford.co.uk/experience-ford/AboutFord/News/CompanyNews/2012/Bill-Ford-Outlines-Blueprint> (accessed July 2014).

Ford Motor Company. (2012c) *Sustainability Report Summary 2012/13*. Available at: <https://www.google.com/#q=Sustainability+Report+Summary+2012%2F13> (accessed July 2014).

Ford Motor Company. (2013) *Ford Launches Pioneering FORD2GO Car Sharing Program with German Dealer Network* (press release). Available at: <http://corporate.ford.com/news-center/press-releases-detail/pr-ford-launches-pioneering-ford2go-37770> (accessed July 2014).

Ford, W. C. (2011) "Letter from William Clay Ford. Ford Motor Company Sustainability 2012/13." Available at: <http://corporate.ford.com/microsites/sustainability-report-2012-13/review-letter-ford> (accessed July 2014).

Galbraith, J. R. (1973) *Designing Complex Organizations*. Boston, MA: Addison-Wesley Longman.

Gavetti, G. and Rivkin, J. W. (2007) "On the Origin of Strategy: Action and Cognition Over Time," *Organization Science* 18 (3): 420–39.

Gioia, D. A. and Thomas, J. B. (1996) "Identity, Image, and Issue Interpretation: Sensemaking During Strategic Change in Academia," *Administrative Science Quarterly* 41: 370–403.

Gioia, D. A., Price, K. N., Hamilton, A. L., and Thomas, J. B. (2010) "Forging an Identity: An Insider–Outsider Study of Processes Involved in the Formation of Organizational Identity," *Administrative Science Quarterly* 55 (1): 1–46.

Glynn, M. A. and Abzug, R. (2002) "Institutionalizing Identity: Symbolic Isomorphism and Organizational Names," *Academy of Management Journal* 45 (1): 267–80.

Glynn, M. A., Lockwood, C., and Raffaelli, R. (2015) "Staying the Same While Changing: Organizational Identity in the Face of Environmental Challenges," in Henderson, R., Gulati, R., and Tushman, M. (eds), *Leading Sustainable Change: An Organizational Perspective*. Oxford: Oxford University Press.

Gulati, R. and Kletter, D. (2005) "Shrinking Core, Expanding Periphery: The Relational Architecture of High-Performing Organizations," *California Management Review* 47 (3): 77–103.

Hamilton, A. and Gioia, D. (2009) "Fostering Sustainability-Focused Organizational Identities," in L. M. Roberts and J. E. Dutton (eds), *Exploring Positive Identities and Organizations: Building a Theoretical and Research Foundation*. New York: Routledge, 435–60.

Hart, S. (1997) "Beyond Greening: Strategies for a Sustainable World," *Harvard Business Review* (January–February): 66–76.

Hart, S. L. and Milstein, M. B. (2003) "Creating Sustainable Value," *Academy of Management Executive* 17 (2): 56–67.

Henderson, R. M. and Clark, K. B. (1990) "Architectural Innovation: The Reconfiguration of Existing Product Technologies and the Failure of Established Firms," *Administrative Science Quarterly* 35 (1): 9–30.

Kotter, J. P. (1996) *Leading Change*. Boston, MA: Harvard Business School Press.

Lee, H. (2010) "Don't Tweak Your Supply Chain—Rethink It End to End," *Harvard Business Review* (October): 62–9.

Lewin, K. (1947) "Frontiers in Group Dynamics: Concept, Method and Reality in Social Science; Social Equilibria and Social Change," *Human Relations* (June): 5–41.

Lubin, D. A. and Esty, D. C. (2010) "The Sustainability Imperative," *Harvard Business Review* (May): 42–50.

Marshall, J. D. and Toffel, M. W. (2005) "Framing the Elusive Concept of Sustainability: A Sustainability Hierarchy," *Environmental Science & Technology* 39 (3): 673–82.

McCue, M. (2013) "The Greening of Auto Parts," *American Way*. Fort Worth, TX: AA Publishing. Available at: <http://hub.aa.com/en/aw/greening-auto-plants-car-parts> (accessed July 2014).

Mintzberg, H. (1979) "The Structuring of Organizations: A Synthesis of the Research," *University of Illinois at Urbana—Champaign's Academy for Entrepreneurial Leadership Historical Research Reference in Entrepreneurship*. Available at: <http://ssrn.com/abstract=1496182> (accessed July 2014).

Mulally, Alan. (2012) "Brainstorm Green: Ford's Alan Mulally," unedited transcript of presentation at the Fortune's Brainstorm GREEN Conference, Laguna Niguel, CA, April 16–18, 2012. Available at: <http://tech.fortune.cnn.com/2012/04/17/ford-alan-mulally-transcript/> (accessed July 2014).

Nadler, D. and Tushman, M. (1997) *Competing by Design: The Power of Organizational Architecture*. New York: Oxford University Press.

Naughton, K. (2004) "Seeing Green," *Newsweek* 144 (24): 40–2.

Naughton, K. (2006) "Average Joes are Going Green," *Newsweek* 148 (25): E12–13.

Navis, C. and Glynn, M. A. (2010) "How New Market Categories Emerge: Temporal Dynamics of Legitimacy, Identity, and Entrepreneurship in Satellite Radio, 1990–2005," *Administrative Science Quarterly* 55 (3): 439–71.

Nidumolu, R., Prahalad, C. K., and Rangaswami, M. R. (2009) "Why Sustainability is Now the Key Driver of Innovation," *Harvard Business Review* 87 (9): 56–64.

O'Reilly, C., Tushman, M., and Harreld, J. B. (2009) "Organizational Ambidexterity: IBM and Emerging Business Opportunities," *California Management Review* 51 (4): 75–99.

Porter, M. E. (1996) "What is Strategy?," *Harvard Business Review* (November–December): 61–78.

Prahalad, C. K. and Hamel, G. (1990) "The Core Competence of the Corporation," *Harvard Business Review* (May–June): 79–91.

Rao, H., Monin, P., and Durand, R. (2003) "Institutional Change in Toque Ville: Nouvelle Cuisine as an Identity Movement in French Gastronomy," *American Journal of Sociology* 108 (4): 795–843.

Rokosz, S. (2012) "Sustainability: A Strategic Imperative at Ford. TriplePundit." Available at: <http://www.triplepundit.com/2012/07/sustainability-strategic-impera tive-ford/> (accessed July 2014).

Segal, H. P. (2005) *Henry Ford's Village Industries: Recasting the Machine Age.* Amherst, MA: University of Massachusetts.

Senge, P. (2010) "The Sustainable Supply Chain," *Harvard Business Review* (October): 70–2.

Sharma, S. and Vredenburg, H. (1998) "Proactive Corporate Environmental Strategy and the Development of Competitively Valuable Organizational Capabilities," *Strategic Management Journal* 19 (8): 729–53.

Short, J. L. and Toffel, M. W. (2010) "Making Self-Regulation More Than Merely Symbolic: The Critical Role of the Legal Environment," *Administrative Science Quarterly* 55 (3): 361–96.

Siggelkow, N. (2001) "Change in the Presence of Fit: The Rise, the Fall, and the Renaissance of Liz Claiborne," *Academy of Management Journal* 44 (4): 838–57.

Siggelkow, N. (2007) "Persuasion with Case Studies," *Academy of Management Journal* 50 (1): 20–4.

Sustainable Enterprise Institute. (2007) *The Road Not Yet Taken: The State of US Corporate Environmental Policy and Management.* Vienna, VA: Soyka & Company. Available at: <http://www.soykaandcompany.com/The_Road_Not_Yet_Taken_FINAL_2009_08.pdf> (accessed July 2014).

Sytch, M. and Gulati, R. "Creating Value Together." Business Intelligence. MIT Sloan Management Review 50, no. 1 (fall 2008): 12–13.

Vlasic, B. (2011) "Via Zipcar, Ford Seeks Young Fans," *New York Times*, Available at: <http://www.nytimes.com/2011/08/31/business/ford-and-zipcar-join-forces.html?_r=0> (accessed July 2014).

Walmart. (2013) *2013 Global Responsibility Report.* Available at: <http://corporate. walmart.com/microsites/global-responsibility-report-2013/> (accessed July 2014).

Warner, F. (2008) "How Ford Lost its Focus," *Mother Jones* (November–December). Available at: <http://www.motherjones.com/environment/2008/11/how-ford-lost-focus> (accessed July 2014).

Zero Discharge of Hazardous Chemicals Programme. (2013) "Joint Roadmap: Version 2." Available at: <http://www.roadmaptozero.com/joint-roadmap.php> (accessed July 2014).

Zuckerman, E. W. (1999) "The Categorical Imperative: Securities Analysts and the Illegitimacy Discount," *American Journal of Sociology* 104 (5): 1398–438.

5 | How Purpose-Based Companies Master Change for Sustainability

A Systemic Approach to Global Social Change

Rosabeth Moss Kanter

Introduction

Organizational change for sustainability can emanate from unexpected places. Consider the Cemex example.

Cemex, headquartered in Mexico, is a global giant in a highly polluting industry. Yet Cemex cleaned up a newly acquired cement factory in Rugby, England—a plant that the BBC had designated the worst in the nation—in a mere three months after taking over the former operation. Its values-based culture and emphasis on innovation led Cemex to win global environmental awards for such developments as anti-bacterial cement for hospitals, financing for the poor to replace unhealthy dirt floors with cement floors, and highway road beds made of recycled rubber tires. But it would be misleading to view Cemex only through such practices, as though these practices were an end in themselves. Through acquisitions, Cemex grew to become one of the top two building materials companies in the world by deliberately engineering a strong culture that would integrate diverse country units and create standardized operations for efficiency and profitability.[1]

The experience of Cemex, and that of other purpose-based vanguard companies to be discussed in this chapter, shows how organizations can change in sustainable directions and impact the society and ecosystem around them. My empirical findings suggest normative possibilities for new models of market capitalism.

In recent decades, a social logic stressing purpose, values, and long-term institution building has become a contrasting strategic theme in some progressive

---

[1] Kanter et al. (2007a, 2007b, 2007c). See also Kanter (2009), 25, 33, 37, 43, 68–71, 87–90, 114–15, 131–9, 140–8, 156, 161, 171, 182, 199, 204, 210, 226, 230–2, 243, 246–7, 250, 258, 277, 301–2, 304, 308, 311, 315, 317.

companies in many parts of the world, balancing the financial logic that had come to dominate Western business corporations in the last quarter of the twentieth century.[2] That social logic defines a company or similar organization in terms of its connection to society at large and obligations as a member of society—an institution infused with meaning beyond its economic transactions—while also acknowledging the necessity for financial success in order to carry out its commitments to society.[3]

More recently, that social logic has come to explicitly include the term 'sustainability,' with its environmental implications (impact on natural resources and climate) as well as its organizational implications (continuity and endurance over time). The two are linked, even though the former appears to be more outward-facing and suggestive of public goods and the latter more inward-facing and suggestive of management excellence in developing and executing strategies that ensure favorable relationships with customers, suppliers, employees, and the public. This is made clear through in-depth examination of the practices of purpose-based companies around the world.

This chapter seeks to learn from companies that are prominent among those adopting this perspective and undertaking activities that go beyond passive conformity to societal standards by actively seeking positive societal outcomes. When companies in the vanguard of change internalize a societal perspective, which itself is dynamic and changing, and seek to add a social logic to financial logic in their strategies and decision making, they must reframe guiding themes and undertake new actions. I will explore the impetus for change, the change process, and the elements sustaining change. The framework I offer for conceptualizing organizational change is widely applicable.

At the same time, there can be a gap between units or levels of change, as organizational change and sustainability does not automatically equate to societal change and environmental sustainability. Hence, I will explore another issue: a framework for seeing where organizational change fits into the development of societal or ecosystem change—which I call Even Bigger Change (EBC). Ecosystem change—for example, effective action to mitigate climate change and its consequences—occurs at the societal level, not the organizational level. It requires more than good works by any one organization, which is why environmentalists are skeptical of corporate actions and sometimes label them "greenwashing," a way of getting credit for good works while not having much impact. Furthermore, in these volatile times, with high rates of mergers and acquisitions, companies come and go, join and separate, and practices come and go with them.

Even so, I show that purpose-based companies have a role to play in wider ecosystem change.

[2] Kanter (2011a).
[3] The growing literature includes: Makower (2008) and Jackson and Nelson (2004).

Purpose-based companies and the impetus for change

Starting in the mid-2000s, I undertook a set of field studies ultimately comprising 18 major global or regional companies headquartered on five continents, with 10 of them studied in depth in multiple locations, and others continuously added. This was an opportunistic sample, with access an important criterion, but all companies were among the most respected in their countries of origin. (Due to charters, the banks tended to be national or regional in scope.) These companies sought reputations as leaders in corporate citizenship and issued public statements of their aspiration. Many of them were part of an IBM-initiated global leadership network of a small set of companies seeking to share best practices and find common metrics. I was interested in how these companies adopted global frameworks and how those frameworks were translated and utilized on the ground.

My research group and I ultimately conducted nearly 400 interviews with top leaders, middle managers, professionals, and employees across functions in 23 countries, examining how their functions operated and how they applied global prescriptions to national/local considerations, including global social and environmental goals. We produced comprehensive case studies of the main companies, including IBM (USA),[4] Procter & Gamble (USA),[5] Cemex (Mexico),[6] Banco Real (Brazil)[7] and its (changing) European parents, Shinhan Financial Group (South Korea),[8] Omron (Japan),[9] MTN (South Africa), Diageo (UK),[10] and Publicis Groupe (France).[11] I analyzed the patterns in this first set of companies for my book *SuperCorp*,[12] identifying how vanguard companies created innovation, profits, growth, and social good together. I later added others, such as PepsiCo (with HBS colleagues Rakesh Khurana and Rajiv Lal) in the US, Peru, and India;[13] Verizon (USA);[14] Desjardins (Canada);[15] and Grupo ABC (Brazil).[16]

The first set was chosen in 2005; by January 2009, during the depths of the aftermath of the financial markets crash, most of them had exceeded industry peers in financial performance. A notable exception was Cemex, the global cement and building materials company headquartered in Mexico, which had taken on debt to make a major acquisition as part of growth to #1 or #2 in

---

[4] Kanter, Rosabeth M. (2008a, 2008b, 2008c). IBM is featured throughout *SuperCorp*. There are also earlier cases on IBM, a company I have engaged with since 1997.

[5] Kanter, Rosabeth M., and Matthew Bird. (2008a, 2008b, 2008c, 2008d, 2008e).

[6] See Kanter et al. (2007a, 2007b, 2007c).   [7] Kanter and Reisen de Pinho (2005).

[8] Kanter and Raffaelli. (2005a); Kanter and Morgan (2008).

[9] Kanter and Bernstein (2008).   [10] Kanter and Bird (2009a).

[11] Kanter and Bird (2009b); Kanter and Raffaelli (2005b). There are also earlier cases on Publicis and its growing network; Publicis is a company I have engaged with since 1992.

[12] Kanter (2009).   [13] Kanter and Bird (2011a); Kanter et al. (2011a, 2011b).

[14] Kanter et al. (2004); Kanter and Bird (2011b).

[15] Kanter and Malone (2013a).   [16] Kanter et al. (2013).

industry size in the world. But even in Cemex's case, the sources of sustainability were in place. Like most of the other vanguard companies in the midst of volatility and multiple mergers, Cemex was the acquirer and brought its targets into its system, thus making possible organizational sustainability to further its environmental sustainability goals.

The company set included three main organizational types: (a) companies with a strong values-legacy that decided to refresh their values to gain coherence as they entered more countries and globalized some processes (IBM, P&G, Omron); (b) companies that used purpose and values as sources of integration and identity following a merger (Banco Real, Diageo, P&G); and (c) emerging companies that put purpose and values in the forefront to create a culture permitting growth (Cemex, Grupo ABC, Shinhan) or established companies seeking growth into new business areas (PepsiCo).

A combination of factors led these companies to make deliberate choices to emphasize sustainability. First, leaders sought organizational coherence in order to manage integration of diverse entities; they wanted to shape a culture that permitted decision speed and communication across boundaries with a common set of principles.[17] This was the result of globalization and the actual or anticipated additions of new people and new geographies, as well as technologies and country regulatory changes that enabled borderless operations. Purpose and values were emphasized after major expansions or strategic shifts, with deliberate culture building at the center. Cemex developed the Cemex Way after its first major acquisitions in Spain, realizing that despite a common language, Mexico and Spain were very different. CEO Lorenzo Zambrano did not want country subsidiaries that operated independently. His mantra was One Cemex. Similarly, IBM refreshed its values at the same time that CEO Samuel Palmisano heralded the coming of the Globally Integrated Enterprise, a sort of borderless IBM.

Second, for these companies the business strategy involved emerging markets, including new geographies or new products tapping emerging consumer desires.[18] Showing societal responsibility and investing in public good was a way to signal future intentions as well as to build immediate goodwill and relationships. To gain these benefits, it was important that social logic dominate financial logic. Good citizenship had to come first, because commercial motives would create suspicion and opposition. But at the same time, the approach had to support business strategy, to lay the foundation for future business advantage, including market entry and market building.

A third factor also greatly influenced the direction of business goals and the content of new values—the public agenda, including social movement pressures. There were three subsets here too: (a) companies originating in a nation that put social and environmental themes on the public agenda, making it an

---

[17] The literature on organizational identity is applicable. i.e. Glynn (2000): 285–98; Navis and Glynn (2010): 439–71; Raffaelli (2013).

[18] Khanna and Palepu (2006, 2011: 18–20); Khanna et al. (2006): 69–90.

imperative for public legitimacy and customer and employee good will (Banco Real and its original Dutch parent); (b) companies seeking growth in nations where social and environmental responsibility would result in public approval and favorable positioning with public officials (IBM, Diageo, P&G, MTN) (in less-developed countries, where social needs were high, serving society was also a way to improve the ecosystem for doing business, partnering with or propelling the public sector through innovations (IBM's KidSmart workstations donated to public schools in India and South Africa)); and (c) companies in an industry leadership position with high visibility that made them potential targets for activist non-governmental organizations (NGOs) (Banco Real) or that built on a long tradition of serving society which created momentum as well as pressure to continue (IBM). Clearly, the external context is a highly significant force in internal organizational change.

Thus, three big forces were aligned in the companies I studied—*leadership for organizational identity/coherence, business growth strategies, and public pressure*. When these forces push in a similar direction, the combination raises organizational aspirations and provides an impetus for change. If they are decoupled, the drive for change is weakened. For example:

- Public pressure without a business growth target can result in piecemeal concessions from companies to comply with external demands—for example, paying a fine after an oil spill or adjusting an internal practice, as might happen after communities protest the presence of toxic waste or after a company is found to violate a labor practice.

- Growth strategies without leadership to define values that provide continuity and coherence in the face of market or cultural differences will not necessarily succeed because they might result in applying obsolete home-country-based ideas of conduct that will not address the new constituencies that growth requires.

- A statement of organizational purpose without pressure to live up to it, perhaps because it is not on the public agenda, will weaken its application in any domain—for example, if climate change remains low on the public agenda in a nation, then even purpose-based companies seeking an identity through their values might choose to put their societal emphasis elsewhere.

For these reasons, it's important to remember that organizational change is not just driven internally but requires an external context that includes both threats and opportunities. Threats take the form of public pressure, actual or implied (as in publicity for a failure to act on a company's values) and opportunities involve a pathway to growth by realizing the values, whether in existing markets or entering new ones.

The external context combines with company situation and leadership desires to propel the companies I studied to align internal practices with a societal purpose to produce sustainable organizations that innovate to remain sustainable and also begin to help move society in a sustainable direction.

Positive, transformational change is most likely when the impetus for change results in all forces being reflected in a new system default position that supports sustainability.

Action on goals: how organizations change

By going deeply inside the vanguard companies, I could learn exactly how they put actions in place to support their business and societal goals. This can be summarized using a framework I call the Change Wheel (Figure 5.1). It arrays ten key elements of change in a dynamic model that shows the interconnections between and among them as they mutually reinforce (or fail to reinforce) the state of the system.

Getting in gear to get change rolling requires more than announcing a strategic decision. To support the decision, a culture for change needs to be programmed into an organization's (or a wider system's) method of operating. Without fundamental systemic change, organizations will always revert to their basic pattern, like the default position on a computer program. Leaders must thus reset the organization's default position; they must change the template and get to the underlying code (which some call the organization's

Figure 5.1. The Change Wheel

Source: Rosabeth Moss Kanter, Harvard Business School.

DNA). A single intervention in a dysfunctional system won't change outcomes unless the underlying design is addressed.

Before applying the Wheel to the change process, I will describe what it adds to theories of organizational change. The model is complementary to existing theories of change management and builds on many of them, while suggesting a useful new approach. It looks at systemic, or more holistic, organizational change, rather than episodes of change, which is more common in the research literature. The model presented here also identifies in more detail the elements that enable structure and behavior to change, encompassing many parts of an organization and many forms of action. It belongs in the tradition of organization coherence and the fit among parts of a system. It has echoes of Tushman's and Romanelli's punctuated equilibrium theory[19] in that it posits a set of mutually reinforcing elements that can lock a system in place, until natural evolution produces revolution and a new equilibrium point. In previous studies, I have shown that deviant, incongruent elements (departures from tradition) gradually appear and accumulate to make revolutionary change—that is, bottoms-up or grass-roots innovations become the basis for strategic change announced by organizational officials.[20]

The Change Wheel also echoes organizational fitness or coherence models in which culture, structure, task, or technology must be aligned for organizations to be well functioning, or must be adjusted to increase the ability to accomplish important goals.[21] There are useful attempts to identify the elements of overall organizational change in the study of overall performance improvements[22] or organizational turnarounds.[23] The literature on CEO leadership, particularly the accounts by CEOs about how they have led change and transformation, sometimes co-written with academics, also tends to consider the whole system, rather than parts.

However, most scholarly theories of change focus on episodes—how a particular practice is adopted—rather than whole organizations. And despite frequent invocations of the garbage can model[24] or the serendipitous, unplanned nature of change,[25] many theories still tend to be top-driven, deliberate, and sequential, identifying phases or stages in change processes led by sentient agentic actors. Most are variations on Kurt Lewin's classic tripartite framework of unfreezing, moving, and refreezing. This was expanded by John Kotter and others to include a sense of urgency that begins the change process, a vision for change, engagement and enlistment of a set of actors to drive change, and new organizational routines that make changes stick.[26] While useful, it is also general and favors process over substance. This does not guide either practitioners or scholars to the key substantive areas— the elements of a system—that provide the content of change, nor does it

[19] Tushman and Romanelli 1994.   [20] Kanter (1983).
[21] Tushman et al., Chapter 10 Leading Proactive Punctuated Change (this volume).
[22] Jim Collins 2001.   [23] Kanter (2004).   [24] March 1972.
[25] Weick 2012.   [26] Kotter 2007.

always help leaders see how to mobilize for change in the entire organizational system when action must take place on many fronts simultaneously.

There are numerous studies of problems with change, including the problem of innovating in established organizations or developing new ventures to take them in new directions.[27] These help inform the current model by indicating the ways promising experiments and new ideas cannot gain traction as isolated activities without the elements of systemic change aligned with them, as will be shown later. The literature on diffusion of innovation also provides some useful insights, including the role of opinion leaders (related to the champions of sponsors of change in my model) and the identification of the importance of early adopters. The purpose-led vanguard companies in my study tended, in general, to be early adopters of socially and environmentally friendly practices, although they were not necessarily first movers.

There is also a recent wave of interest in applying social movement theory to change within organizations,[28] which is an antidote to both top-down planned change models and models that imply that organizations are bounded systems not particularly responsive to the societal context (both of which are rejected here). In the US, the study of organizational change in response to pressure groups or issue advocates, always more prominent in political science than organizational behavior, declined in the face of several historical phenomena: a reduction in labor organizing in the US and the "freedom" of management from organized countervailing pressure with legal claims; a growth in MBA programs led by economists, which saw organizations as economic black boxes run by technocrats for purely "rational" financial ends, as Rakesh Khurana's work has shown;[29] and the popularity in the late 1980s through the global financial crisis of 2008 of the concept of "shareholder value." The social movements being studied in organizations today, in the Western world and particularly the US, are more likely to be oriented toward modification of practices, rather than claiming decision rights and financial spoils. Still, the social movements literature can explain how environmental issues come to be on the change agenda of leading "early-adopter" companies, such as the purpose-based companies described here.

The Change Wheel model used here can advance understanding of organizational change for sustainability and contribute to research and theory about organizational change in several ways:

- It is empirically grounded. The model was built from field observations of entire companies, operating in diverse contexts. It is thus less culturally biased than frameworks based on single cultures or countries.

- The model acknowledges the complexity of large multi-business, multi-divisional organizations, while defining common elements that reinforce the status quo or can produce new behavior of the organization and members.

---

[27] Christensen1997; see also Kanter 1997.   [28] Zald 1977.   [29] Khurana 2010.

- The Change Wheel combines both the "hard" (structures and processes) and "soft" (human actions) side of organizational systems.
- The Wheel offers a dynamic view of change that does not depend on any particular sequence of change, while reflecting the connections among elements, making certain logical sequences more likely.
- This model allows room for bottom-up or middle-out as well as top-down change, and indicates the importance of leadership at many levels and in many functions of organizations.

The interconnections among the elements of change and the organic nature of the model are described in further detail elsewhere.[30] In this chapter, the Change Wheel model is applied to identify the ways that purpose-based companies move from their sustainability theme to action that produces new practices, behaviors, and organizational outcomes.

The Change Wheel in motion: momentum for systemic change

Ten major elements either lock a system in place or contribute to systemic change. These elements can be arrayed on a diagnostic tool and planning guide, the Change Wheel[31] (Figure 5.1). Taken one by one, some of these could seem like management basics, yet they are often neglected or worse, they are not aligned with the change goal and thus undermine the effort. Their importance lies in their connections with other spokes of the wheel. These propellants of change are key to the success of the purpose-based companies I studied—their ability to be financially sustainable and support social and environmental sustainability.

Each element is defined and illustrated by examples from the vanguard companies study.

COMMON PURPOSE, COMMON THEME, SHARED VISION

The change message must be well and widely understood. It can be crafted by a top leader or small group, but it becomes truly shared—internalized—as it is used by large numbers of people. Initially, spreading the message is a matter of articulating it well and broadcasting it to many audiences on many occasions. Repetition and redundancy help get attention in a noisy world of too much information. Themes by themselves do not produce change, and they can be written off by skeptics as marketing slogans, but without a

---

[30] Kanter (2011).
[31] Kanter (2011). For another narrative view of the Wheel, see Kanter (2001), ch. 10.

common guiding theme, it is impossible to gain organizational coherence. The theme provides a general ballpark for numerous independent actions without prescribing any particular actions, which would be impossible anyway. When the theme is uplifting and states a purpose of serving society, not just making a profit or dominating a market, then the way is paved for the use of social/institutional logic.

It is striking that all the vanguard companies defined or redefined a set of values in the period just before the study began in the early twenty-first century, as a result of the impetus for change described earlier. Omron restated principles laid down by the founder and reinforced the purpose, sensing societal needs and finding solutions. Diageo and Banco Real, formed from mergers, created new statements. Banco Real called itself the bank of values and chose social and environmental responsibility as its differentiator in the marketplace. P&G took a similar path using already-created purpose and values. When A. G. Lafley became CEO of P&G in 2001, he re-emphasized the purpose, values, and principles (PVP) which had been made explicit a dozen years earlier after an acquisition (Richardson-Vicks) that brought a flood of new people to P&G. The PVP began with the stated purpose of improving the lives of the world's consumers, now and for generations to come. He and top executives, one of whom became his successor, took time to teach the PVP to leadership development sessions throughout the company and took the message on the road. Categories restated their mission in societal terms, so that baby care became dedicated to helping babies thrive, not merely selling diapers—a nobler purpose (which, of course, is a condition for a strong market for diapers and is thus a sustainability goal). In Nigeria, one of P&G's growth markets, this goal led to a successful initiative to combat high rates of infant mortality by sending mobile clinics with a physician, two nurses, and medical equipment (and a few Pampers samples) to areas without access to health care.

Sam Palmisano, CEO of IBM from 2002 to 2011, made refreshing IBM values a priority, as he took the business strategy in new directions in a world of rapidly changing technology and the opening of emerging markets. IBM's actions went farther than other companies to ensure that the values would be shared by involving the entire IBM community in the process. Palmisano led the creation of a Values Jam, a three-day web chat in which any IBM employee and selected partners could comment about the values. Approximately 140,000 people did. A team refined the comments and articulated three values—dedication to every client's success, innovation that matters for clients and the world, and respect for individuals and individual responsibility. In my visits to IBM facilities in a dozen countries, interviewees often pointed to the values in explaining their actions, especially innovation that matters for the world. Those words opened the door to thinking about societal needs, which was one of the impetuses for managers in the UK to look at IBM's environmental performance and begin a green initiative.

Palmisano also offered two grand themes that oriented IBM actions, one internally focused, one externally focused. The globally integrated enterprise was an organizational aspiration, reflected in a range of actions on other spokes of the Wheel, including moving global procurement to China, reducing regional headquarters staff, and changing the role of country general managers. Smarter Planet was a broad business theme, defining IBM to its clients, as well as indicating that IBM wanted to offer solutions, not merely just to provide hardware and software. Articulation of this theme made it easier to explain the rationale for divesting the PC business.

SYMBOLS AND SIGNALS

The next question is whether leadership actions match the message. People are always examining leader actions, looking for signs of whether the change is serious and how it will feel. Small symbols can have big consequences, and they become stories that organization members tell one another. The right early signals can show people what the change will mean for them. (Eliminating reserved parking is how some companies signal a reduction of hierarchy.) Leaders are scrutinized for the consistency between their message and their model—what they say versus what they do. Change leaders in particular will gain or lose credibility based on whether their actions seem authentic. They need to send signals that they mean it. Symbols and signals become iconic stories frequently repeated—defining moments that shape a narrative.

For Banco Real, one of the iconic stories that symbolized the bank's commitment to environmental responsibility involved a trash-filled, crime-ridden alley next to bank headquarters. It was frequent discussion of Banco Real's purpose and values that made executives more conscious of the alley and led them to mount a clean-up campaign to make it a safe public park meeting high environmental standards. Later, Banco Real developed green lending product (for solar panels or retrofitting cars), created an environmental screening process for customers, enlisted suppliers in green initiatives, took leadership roles in the national banking federation and encouraged adoption of similar practices, and became the first bank in the region to trade carbon credits.

Palmisano became a symbol of change at IBM when he announced the results of a global Innovation Jam (similar to the Values Jam but voting on IBM innovation priorities for the next decade) in Beijing showing his avatar entering Forbidden City. IBM's disaster relief efforts also sent a powerful signal about the company's commitment to society. IBMers were fast on the ground to deploy technology after disasters in Kosovo, New Orleans (Hurricane Katrina), and the Asian tsunami to locate supplies and people. It was the highest use of technology, not lowest-common-denominator donations, and became embodied in a kit developed with a Swedish NGO, Sahana. Professionals at IBM India volunteered extra hours to create solutions for government officials on the ground, also rallying partners. Although IBM was 37th on the list of companies by cash donation, IBM received the Indian government's highest award—resulting in another iconic story.

P&G sent a powerful signal about the seriousness of its commitment to the PVP when facing the choice about whether to continue producing a water purification powder, then known as PuR, which was especially important for places without access to clean, safe drinking water but was also unprofitable, soaking up investment needed by profitable growth categories. Applying a social logic to override the financial logic (but without jeopardizing financial performance), P&G set up a non-profit organization, Children's Safe Drinking Water, in collaboration with NGOs and government entities, to which PuR could be donated. P&G kept making it, and society kept benefiting from it. Note that a secondary signal in such efforts is that vanguard companies build coalitions outside the company for their societal efforts and enlist partners to fulfill the mission.

GOVERNANCE AND ACCOUNTABILITY STRUCTURE

Change needs someone at the controls, even if ultimately everyone has to get involved in change. And there needs to be a process for steering it in the right direction. This involves the nuts and bolts of project management, on a large scale. Assigning accountability for the big picture—the overview of all the elements of change—is an important step. For large-scale transformations, the governance mechanism might overlap with existing formal groups, such as the board or top management group. But often another group is formed specifically to oversee and guide the change, which might require special attention and a different kind of accountability.

Shinhan, created from a merger, developed a set of integration management teams with equal representation from both legacy companies. The financial group also sorted change activities into three buckets—dual bank, one bank, and new bank. Management teams and employee task forces tackled specific issues. This elaborate structure resulted in widespread participation and assurance that the change process was on track.

The vanguard companies often combined an executive in charge of change with an internal board. Banco Real established a sustainability directorate under a top leader and created a cross-sectional management committee for oversight, guidance, and participation. Desjardins designated a top executive as change leader, reporting to the CEO and executive team, and used teams for change efforts, such as a youth task force creating green initiatives. At IBM, Integration and Values Teams (IVT) of 300 top executives were formed, from a subset of the full population at the senior executive level, to work on and oversee company-wide change. IVT5, for example, was focused on how IBM could develop global leaders faster and more cost-effectively.

EDUCATION, TRAINING, ACTION TOOLS

How do people know what to do to make the change operational, to make it real in their activities? The same words can be understood differently by each part of the organization as interpreted from their own perspectives. Therefore education is necessary to communicate the why, what, and how of change. (The why can sometimes be more important than the what or how; once people understand the goal and its rationale, they are better able to envision and carry out new actions.) Training is also necessary for people to become adept at the new behavior implied by the change. And action tools help people relate the change to their own day-to-day work by giving them models or templates. This element is critical to shape and guide behavior. Change is sometimes difficult not because of resistance, but because people simply don't know what to do or how they should act differently.

All of the vanguard companies made large investments in providing training and tools. Even though the study did not include comparisons with peer companies, there is suggestive evidence of their distinctiveness in the fact that IBM and P&G were regularly placed at the top of lists of the best companies for developing leaders, for which training expenditures were a factor. Banco Real ran cascading programs about its purpose and values, including NGO leaders discussing environmental issues and how they applied to the bank. Employees also took advantage of online resources. Shinhan would not disclose figures, but the group invested heavily in unusually large conferences discussing strategy and values, starting with 1,500 top managers at a 3-day retreat followed by extensive sessions throughout the ranks, called Sing Sing Together and Run Run Together (in English translation). Cemex used its post-merger integration teams as a primary training vehicle, deploying hundreds of people on assignments ranging from 3 months to 2 years to work with acquired facilities to teach the values and processes, and guide change. IBM has its own education center and is education-rich enough to be a university. It is also rich in online tools for nearly every process, and especially collaboration tools. (IBM's top leadership forums, which give managers change tools while producing innovation, are described by Michael Tushman and Bruce Harreld.[32])

CHAMPIONS AND SPONSORS

Changes need people who become passionate about seeing that they take place. Champions are the activists and cheerleaders for change, the leaders of new initiatives who argue for change and develop mini change projects themselves. Sponsors are more senior people who make sure that the change has the backing of those with the power to fight for it. In some organizations or

---

[32] See Tushman et al., Chapter 10 Leading Proactive Punctuated Change (this volume).

systems, these are formal roles or assignments that go beyond the actual job (for example, change agent programs at various companies, with identified change agents for particular initiatives and assigned sponsors); in other cases, they are volunteers who take on self-organizing tasks because of a belief in the vision and find their own top-level sponsors.

Champions in the vanguard companies led numerous projects supporting social impact and sustainability goals that created new products and services and had direct or indirect impact on the business. It is an important component of this set of companies that social logic is not an afterthought or a nice-to-have. It tends to be linked to how people think about developing the business. For example, they might consider how their products can meet social needs. At Omron, the US division head championed a heart monitor for women, succeeding when he found a sponsor in Japan, where executives were not accustomed to thinking in gender terms. Professionals in Spain observed solar panels and championed the development of sensors to improve their energy efficiency.

At IBM, the executive in charge of corporate citizenship, Stanley Litow, was adept at championing projects for which he found sponsors in the business, including the CEO, because the efforts were business strategic. World Community Grid, for example, was a non-profit project established and powered by IBM that could demonstrate IBM's prowess in grid computing—aggregating the computing power from computers that are on but not being used—by applying it to some of the world's biggest and most significant scientific problems that require the power of a supercomputer, such as curing heart disease or mapping rivers. Almost immediately after IBM's research labs had the breakthrough, Litow sold the idea to Palmisano as a better form of demonstration for clients in retailing or banking, and a way to engage IBM partners, since anyone could donate unused computing power. The buzz went around the world. Other Litow initiatives, such as cultural heritage projects, built and showcased new IBM capabilities as societal gifts that later attracted new paid projects.

Leadership permission and encouragement can help potential innovators surface in many places. A young PepsiCo headquarters employee decided on her own to argue for a rooftop garden, and succeeded. Sometimes the champion has been waiting for the right moment. For a PepsiCo manager in Latin America, the wait was ten years, while he and two colleagues were moved throughout the region, to get support for his idea that PepsiCo should have a second potato research center in Peru, the home of the potato (the first and then only was in Rhinebeck, Wisconsin). The right moment came when CEO Indra Nooyi announced the environmental pillar and her desire to empower employees to find new ideas. For Banco Real, energizing the organization and empowering staff to develop initiatives of their own was considered so important that the CEO defined success of his change efforts, he said, when sustainability initiatives popped up with which he had nothing to do and heard about after the fact.

QUICK WINS AND LOCAL INNOVATION

The theme does not become common, the purpose, values, and vision not fully shared until it is reflected in actions throughout the organization, on the ground and at the grass roots. Omron's CEO suggested this when he said in an interview that the 35,000 Omron employees might have 35,000 different interpretations of the Omron principles, but the important thing was that they discussed and used the principles.

Early successes (quick wins) show that change is possible and indicate what the change means in practice.[33] Champions and sponsors take the lead in showing results from action on the change goals on the ground, in the grass roots of the organization. Proof of concept through a robust demonstration is essential to overcome inertia and get anyone to believe that change is possible. In fact, systemic change sometimes occurs as emergent change, from the ground up, when local units or change champions depart from tradition and innovate towards new models. When change is an official process, it is important to get the grass roots involved in shaping change by picking projects that particular units can tackle. This is improvisational theater at its best—a clear overall direction, but details created as units take hold of the change and make it their own, in a form of rapid prototyping familiar in the technology world. Small wins give people the confidence to embrace the change and try even bolder innovations over time, and local action initiates innovations that support the overall goals while shaping the specifics.

In the vanguard companies, numerous local initiatives reflected the values and demonstrated the change goals in action, showing what they could mean concretely, while at the same time producing both financial and social benefits for the company and becoming models that could spread elsewhere. These initiatives made the guiding theme, the purpose and values, real to everyone and were critical in shaping the culture. P&G Brazil turned around the country unit, which had been badly lagging, through a series of incremental product innovations known as basico (meaning essential in Portuguese), which would enhance the value to low- and middle-income consumers while continuing to meet high standards. The innovation for laundry detergent also made the product greener and its effect smoother on the hands for those without washing machines. The basico idea, which was initially a difficult sell to global brand managers focused on premium products, was a hit that spread around the world in other developing countries. PepsiCo Peru, inspired by the company's environmental responsibility pillar and the permission it gave for innovation, created a new potato chip offering with a biodiversity theme, drawing from the wide variety of potatoes grown in the mountains and supporting small farmers. The products were a big hit and contributed to

---

[33] Quick wins or small wins are also highly motivating. See Amabile and Kramer (2011). This point was also made in Kanter (2004).

PepsiCo's decision to establish the environmentally friendly potato research center for Southern climates.

COMMUNICATIONS, BEST PRACTICE EXCHANGE

Change requires much more communication than routine activities. Top leaders need to know what's happening in the field so they can make adjustments to support it or steer it in a different direction. Local units need role models to learn from the experience of their peers, to see what's possible, and to be spurred to new heights. Change can be chaotic without a way to communicate what's happening everywhere so that anyone can see the context, know the full array of actions, and can modify their own plans accordingly. New media multiply communication channels and open possibilities for posting, networking, alerting, and reflecting. Self-organized communities of practice also constitute a new channel for spreading ideas.

External communication is critical for companies to derive the value from their investments and tell a story that builds the business (and that others might adapt). Smarter Planet is a marketing initiative for IBM, but the stories of accomplishments in smart grids that save energy or congestion pricing that cuts down on traffic pollution are important to show what is possible. Significant achievements set new norms and educate the public. IBM added a series of corporate citizenship donations, the Smarter Cities Challenge Grants, to deploy IBM teams to work pro bono with cities on sustainability initiatives. A summit was convened after the first 100 grants, in which mayors and others told the stories of change in their cities.

POLICY, PROCEDURES, STRUCTURE ALIGNMENT

Every organizational rule, routine, job description, requirement, or procedure can either reinforce or undermine the desired change: the formal organization chart or division of powers, human resource systems (hiring criteria, promotion criteria, compensation policy), policies about who gets to talk to customers or to the press, and, of course, within organizations, the organization structure itself—the groupings of people, tasks, business units, etc. Rules and processes need to be reassessed and adjusted to support the new direction. Organization structures and reporting relationships need to be modified to support the change goal. All of the companies mounted reorganizations to better support their goals and developed processes that would permit new ideas to surface. IBM encouraged self-organizing and created a process by which groups of employees with a business idea could apply to become an emerging business opportunity. This is how IBM got into the new field of virtualization, which later became an emerging business opportunity and one of the ten priorities emanating from the Innovation Jam mentioned earlier.

MEASURES, MILESTONES, AND FEEDBACK

It is important to know whether the change is on track. Establishing measures of progress is important, especially for softer changes (such as shift of culture) or ones that will not show up in conventional financial results. Dividing big changes into small increments with clear milestones is helpful for measurement and morale; each milestone successfully passed is a cause for celebration, or each one missed a cause for readjustment. There needs to be a feedback loop based on agreed-upon measures of progress, which reinforces the "education and training" element just across the Wheel. And accountability for performance is essential for achieving any goal, whether winning a game in a team sport or transforming a health-care system; metrics that permit peer comparison and self-adjustment can be powerful levers. The purpose-based companies were leaders in reporting on their own social and environmental responsibility.

REWARDS AND RECOGNITION

A system's carrots and sticks combine with its publicity engine to create heroes of the revolution or enemies of the change. Who gets rewarded and for what reason is an essential component of change. Financial incentives are considered by economists to be essential to motivate and direct behavior, and indeed, compensation schemes can be powerful. At the same time, non-financial rewards, such as recognition (an often under-utilized tool that is abundant and free) can tell people what the system's leaders think is valuable and also offer emotional rewards. But unless the behavior targeted for reward is consistent with the goal, change will be stymied. Climbing out of the global financial crisis was made more difficult when under-performing, even failing, companies paid big bonuses to executives—in that case, why should anything change? The purpose-led vanguard companies had multiple forms of recognition for those who were exemplars of the values.

Organizations cannot always do everything at the same time, and what happens within one element of change influences others. So there is logic to the order in which I've presented the spokes of the Wheel. These shouldn't be thought of as steps, because many of them need to be done together, and there is a risk to leaving some spokes until later—like riding a broken bicycle. But it is possible to think of planned systemic change as unfolding clockwise around the Change Wheel, starting with a theme or vision. However, planned change that begins with leaders defining and disseminating a common theme/shared vision is not the only way that the action begins. In fact, grass-roots innovation or departures from tradition—actions led by people in so-called "middle," "lower," or "local" positions—often precedes official statements of the change leaders seek and might even become the model for larger change, when crisis or threat dictates a search for a better systems model.

The ten elements fall into two large segments of the Wheel, one involving people and culture,[34] the other involving formal mechanics/engineering. These are sometimes (unfairly) characterized as "soft" and "hard." Some companies fail to create sustainable change because managers lean towards one half or the other. A lopsided wheel can't roll forward. Failures at major transformation are common because of this. Some companies restructure, change processes, add metrics, and change incentives on the mechanics or engineering side, but do little or nothing to frame a vision, symbolize it through leadership actions, offer training, and empower champions for local innovations on the people and culture side.

The people/culture and formal mechanics/engineering sides of the Change Wheel are connected via the various spokes of the Wheel. Spokes reinforce one another across the Change Wheel. And each spoke has more strength when its counterpart directly opposite on the Wheel is also moving in the same direction. For example, a common theme or vision can't be fully shared unless local innovations/quick wins are in motion. It's not clear what the vision means until there are concrete demonstrations of new possibilities. Local or grass-roots innovations seem like random deviations without a guiding theme or vision. Similarly, education, training, and action tools require feedback mechanisms, including metrics and measurements—otherwise, how can those guiding the system know whether the training is effective, the tools put in use? At the same time, the use of appropriate metrics of performance and timely feedback indicates where the shortfalls are that can be overcome by training and new tools for action. Champions of change who lead initiatives, and the sponsors that support them, might not perform the extra work of change without rewards and recognition.

The Change Wheel is moved by human agency, by people who put their own passion and brainpower into the effort of change. To sustain change, there must be momentum that propels the organization closer to the goal, despite setbacks, sidetracks, and obstacles. Momentum occurs when (a) a culture is in effect that blurs the distinctions between external and internal dimensions, or social good/CSR and business strategies; (b) activities are undertaken across a range of business functions; and (c) organization leaders articulate and promulgate well-understood connections to ensure consistency across functions. Ultimately, sustainability comes not just from the social or institutional logic by which top leaders make decisions, but by the desire of units and individuals to reach the purpose-based aspirations in their own work. The Omron CEO's comment about 35,000 who might have 35,000 discussable interpretations of the Omron principles is in this spirit.

---

[34] For more information, see Kanter (2011b).

From organizational change to societal change

Purpose-based companies in the vanguard serve society by producing innovations, changing their practices, engaging in direct action in communities, and shifting industry norms. Certainly, companies make a contribution when they reduce their carbon footprint and influence their suppliers and customers to do the same, clean up polluting cement factories and create cleaner ones, or produce technologies for energy saving or safer drinking water. It is worthwhile to encourage more companies to join them, and more action to result. But even if companies adopt sustainability goals and master the change process, this is only a step towards sustainability in the external sense, and by itself does not necessarily aggregate to produce significant societal change.

The magnitude of some problems cannot be addressed by companies acting alone. NGOs often have deeper knowledge of particular societal issues because of their singular focus, and they can be social movement leaders pressing for changing the law. The public sector sets rules and provides a regulatory framework. Governments manage public goods with taxation power and potentially larger resources overall than even the largest individual companies.

An ecosystem, in contrast to an organizational system, has a diverse set of organizational actors that are loosely coupled, loosely organized, and independent.[35] Issues such as eradicating disease or addressing climate change are characterized by having multiple stakeholders with conflicting goals, lack of a clear pathway for action, and no single entity in charge.

Change in non-bounded or less-bounded systems—such as communities, nations, health-care systems, etc., in contrast to specific organizations or companies—often resembles social movements more than it resembles all-knowing leaders creating a great strategy and expecting its execution. Addressing environmental sustainability requires action on many fronts by many types of actors pursuing many paths.

There are five major areas of linkage between internal change in organizations and societal or ecosystem change.

First, the biggest impact of organizations on society comes through their products and services. As companies link their societal purpose to their products, they change the context for consumers and the public, as P&G Brazil did in translating the company's common corporate theme of improving lives to developing a "green" laundry detergent that was also soft enough for the hand-washing performed by lower-income people who did not use machines. If products embodying purpose are successful, they compel encouragement in the infrastructure context to support them—just as electric vehicles require plug-in stations. The healthy beer produced by Diageo's East Africa Brewing subsidiary using clean water saved the eyesight and productivity of more people in Kenya than all of the company's philanthropic

---

[35] Kanter and Khurana (2010) and Kanter (2012).

efforts around village water systems. Thus, the primary contribution of van-guard companies to ecosystem change is through their own innovation. Innovations serve as demonstrations of new possibilities. Cemex's develop-ment of antibacterial cement became a model for construction of hospitals or schools in new ways.

Second, the innovations developed by purpose-based companies have implications for their immediate business partnerships. Innovations require the companies to set new requirements for change and adjustment in their own specific ecosystem of suppliers and distributors. Banco Real sought to become the Bank of Values not only through internal practices but by mobil-izing suppliers to pledge with them to consider high environmental and social standards. The bank screened customers for environmental risk factors (for example, a real estate development near the rain forest that would destroy eucalyptus forests) and helped them modify their practices to be more envir-onmentally friendly (working with local farmers to set aside land parcels). These actions are direct contributions to sustainability, but also ripple out into the wider ecosystem. Alliances forged across the supply chain and with strategic partners can be complex to manage, as Ranjay Gulati has shown,[36] but they provide a platform for action that many companies undertake, thus multiplying impact.

Third, their success encourages competition and imitation, producing institutional isomorphism.[37] In many cases, vanguard companies actively seek imitation, for any of several reasons: for example, they believe in their values and thus feel an obligation to spread them. External imitation is the flattery that reinforces internal motivation. Also, they don't want to be out there alone; if more companies have new requirements, then the cost of higher standards will be lowered—the reason Banco Real wanted other Brazilian banks to "demand" green products. Thus, IBM regularly includes groups of its best suppliers and customers in innovations that have a societal dimension, such as Supplier Connection; Federal Express employees joined IBM Corporate Service Corps teams in Smarter Cities Challenge programs, many with environmental themes.

Fourth, they spread the message in communications and convenings aimed both internally and externally. This goes beyond advertising and PR. They often convene actors across sectors to put issues on the public agenda and share the responsibility for solving problems through ad hoc coalitions or new umbrella organizations. When P&G became committed to clean drinking water as an expression of company values, especially for children whose well-being was a business and social focus, the company realized the necessity of working through a variety of NGO's such as Population International and Save the Children to reach consumers with their water-purification powder.

---

[36] Gulati 2009.   [37] DiMaggio and Powell 1983.

P&G's CEO led the internal sponsors for this external commitment and reflected it in public forums, such as pledges at the Clinton Global Initiative, thereby publicizing the importance of the issue. IBM convened three national summits in the US, attended by the CEOs of leading companies as well as the Governors of every state and Presidents of the US to agree on standards for accountability in public K-12 education. This led to legislation in many states and influenced national policy.

Fifth, communication and convening can lead to explicit cross-sector coalitions and the creation of new stand-alone organizations dedicated to action, supported by the founding organizations, but operating independently. Spinoffs can more readily focus on specific social or environmental change goals. P&G founded a new non-profit organization, Children's Safe Drinking Water, to which P&G could donate its water-purification powder but with the non-profit and its governing board as the distribution arm, especially for disaster relief and education of the public. After the first IBM National Education Summit, the company supported the creation of a new non-profit called Achieve, which could work with states to get accountability on the legislative agenda. These new organizations can become vehicles for influencing change in ways that would not be possible for a for-profit company.

In general, purpose-based organizations manage ecosystem relationships in integrated ways, linking their business purpose and financial goals with their societal engagement. In run-of-the-mill companies, societal or ecosystem issues would be dealt with by detached government affairs or corporate citizenship/CSR functions, and those would also have lobbying or PR responsibilities. But for purpose-based companies, their internal transformation makes it more likely that such external societal actions will be more powerful. Following the spokes of the Change Wheel, the actions of purpose-led companies are more likely to be guided by the common theme as articulated by the CEO and top leaders; reflected in leadership gestures that signal their importance; part of the governance discussion; highlighted in training programs; championed by a variety of managers and advocates; echoed in innovative actions; spread through company communications; reflected in altered processes (for example, supply chain standards); measured and reported (for example, social and environmental reports); and the basis for rewards and recognition. Thus, ecosystem change is propelled by internal organizational change, by a reset that gives meaning and legitimacy to external actions to change society.

It is also important to note the other link between internal transformation and external societal impact. As indicated in the Diageo example earlier, the purpose-based companies I studied tended to have their greatest impact when they used their own organizational capabilities to produce change, rather than acting through philanthropy. They shift the emphasis from "spare change"— giving away a portion of profits as an afterthought, without commitment to results—to "real change"—an alignment of the organization with external stakeholders to take action with impact goals in mind. In this way, social and

Action vehicle

Target	Use existing org'n	Create new org'n	Work thru coalition of org'ns	Ad hoc convening of org'ns	Individual action
Policy (advocacy)					
Rules, resources					
Programs (delivery/ modeling)					
Services, innovation					
People and culture (mobilization/ empowerment)					
Awareness, tools for action					

Figure 5.2. Even Bigger Change framework

Source: Rosabeth Moss Kanter, Harvard Business School.

environmental issues become internalized as a kind of beta site for business innovation.[38] Indeed, IBM's corporate foundation stopped giving cash grants in favor of providing company capabilities through employee teams that would contribute their talent and also learn and bond in the process.

In short, by innovating in products or services, enlisting and engaging business partners, convening actors across sectors, crafting coalitions or umbrella organizations, and starting new stand-alone entities, single organizations can demonstrate change, put issues on the public policy agenda, and raise the consciousness of the general public.

It is possible to map the terrain of organizational involvement in societal change—or what I call Even Bigger Change (EBC).[39] The vanguard companies' actions just described can be conceptualized and arrayed along two axes of a matrix: Targets of Change (policies, programs, or people) along one, and Action Vehicles along the other (see Figure 5.2). The policy level involves the legal and resource allocation context—what the laws say, and where the money goes. The program level involves enterprises, ventures, and specific programs; new services or products (tools, technologies) are an important part of societal change. Public opinion is also a target, through consciousness raising, mass marketing, or mass mobilization. Change agents can act through an established entity, start a new one, build a coalition, convene others on an ad hoc basis, or engage in individual advocacy. Some involve depth, others

[38] Kanter (1999).   [39] Kanter (2005).

involve breadth of involvement, and all are necessary. Societal change or ecosystem change occurs as all cells of the EBC matrix are filled with roughly aligned actions pushing in the same direction, reinforcing new policies, enterprises/programs, and behavior.

The vanguard companies I studied carried out actions in many cells for the issues on which they were interested parties. Individual advocacy was the least used and was generally aimed at influencing industry practice, such as Fabio Barbosa's attempt to establish sustainability as the norm when he was an officer of the Brazilian banking federation. There was also evidence of big companies setting up independent non-profits to pursue social goals, Both P&G and IBM created new non-profit organizations to operate socially oriented activities that could not be pursued profitably within the company or would achieve their goals more effectively without (P&G's Children's Safe Drinking Water or IBM's World Community Grid) because competitors could also join.

But for the most part, the impact of purpose-based companies on EBC came from two kinds of action: innovation that demonstrated a model in depth, and coalition building that built broad support for a change effort.

IBM's efforts to reinvent education provide a telling example. IBM is not in the business of running public schools, but as part of a turnaround beginning under CEO Louis Gerstner, education became a central arena for strategic societal action (with little commercial motivation) occurring worldwide, as governments everywhere grappled with education for the less advantaged. In the US, IBM impacted education policy and national and state laws through convening three national summits—examples of ad hoc convening—and spinning off an independent organization, Achieve, to push for greater outcome accountability on behalf of a coalition of companies. In 2011, IBM initiated a high school innovation in partnership with the New York City K-12 school board and the City University of New York community college system, a 6-year grade 14 high school called P-TECH (Pathways in Technology Early College High School). This model proved so successful and promising in its first year in Brooklyn that Chicago Mayor Emanuel opened five high schools the following year, one in partnership with IBM and the others with other companies providing the mentors and job interviews (for example, Microsoft and Intel). New York State Governor Cuomo created 16 the year after, and President Obama mentioned emulating the model in his 2013 State of the Union address. To support the idea behind P-TECH, that students should get useful skills and a free education for the first two years of college, IBM worked with the US Department of Education on behalf of the reauthorization of the Perkins Act, national legislation and funds for new models of vocational education.[40]

---

[40] Kanter and Malone (2013b, 2013c).

Many of the purpose-based vanguard companies create or participate in coalitions well beyond industry associations with narrow commercial interests. Cross-sector alliances are a relatively new mode growing in importance for those companies that actively seek societal change. Large cross-sector coalitions can help align disparate efforts for greater cumulative impact. Former US Secretary of State Hillary Clinton led an enhanced Global Partnership Initiative at the State Department to create an Alliance for Clean Cook Stoves that included numerous companies, key NGOs, and numerous national governments, including China, to solve an environmental, health, and women's economic problem. Cooking on open fires is a major cause of death for women in impoverished areas and a major environmental polluter, while stripping forests.[41] The problem had been known for a long time, and there were many isolated attempts to deal with it. The formation of a global alliance made it possible to align and accelerate efforts, sign up national governments, and gain critical mass to develop an affordable cook stove industry.

Limits, gaps, and possibilities

Although the purpose-based vanguard companies that I researched are widely admired, there are no perfect companies.[42] They have flaws, and they stumble. The goals of purpose-based companies are aspirations, but not necessarily achieved. They cannot always satisfy activists on any one issue or maximize the satisfaction of every stakeholder. As companies face a multitude of societal issues, some are more immediately strategic than others. For some companies, mitigating climate change might be a lower priority than improving health, education, or poverty. And only a subset of companies is in the business of dealing with any particular societal issue as its main business purpose, its core technology or products and services.

Companies are living systems operating in volatile circumstances, steering the Change Wheel over rocky terrain. Mergers, acquisitions, divestitures, opening product lines, closing product lines, restructuring in size or layers, employee turnover, leadership succession—all mean that continuity is difficult. Although Banco Real operated as a publicly traded company in Brazil, it was the subsidiary of a European company; when the parent company was sold to another bank, the CEO in Brazil could no longer maintain the same emphasis on sustainability. Even without change in control, business portfolios change, and culture must be renewed. IBM was rescued from financial peril 20 years ago and recently celebrated its 100th anniversary, but it is not in

---

[41] Kanter and Malone (2012).   [42] This point is documented in Kanter (2009), ch. 10.

the same sets of businesses. Is it the same company?[43] And new people, who never shared in disaster relief or participated in a Values Jam, might not understand the purpose and values.

A social logic can accompany a financial logic, but financial logic cannot be abandoned. Financial performance is essential to the ability of investor-owned companies to deploy resources to serve society. When short-term performance is in jeopardy, long-term considerations cannot always take precedence. Indeed, A. G. Lafley's successor as P&G CEO was attacked by an activist investor for not acting faster to cut costs (financial logic) while over-emphasizing emerging markets (which required a social logic).

There are also limits to what even the best companies can do in terms of industry leadership. Companies are responders, rather than activists. They do not want to get too far ahead of their customers or engage in controversial action. To propel them to operate differently requires change in laws and regulations. Public sentiment must also shift, to both propel public policy changes which force change in companies and also provide favorable consumer opinion for company action.

Still, this analysis makes clear that there is a role for business organizations in social and environmental sustainability writ large as well as their own sustainability, and the two might be intertwined—a better society and ecosystem can produce better companies, and better companies can have a positive impact on society. Progressive companies such as the vanguard set referenced in this chapter can be players in societal change when they take the lead to form coalitions that can change norms and policies, or when they develop innovations/demonstrations that help diffuse new practices.

Conclusion

This chapter shows how purpose-driven companies that internalize societal needs and apply a social, institutional logic alongside a financial logic can change themselves and the societal context around them to be more sustainable.

The frameworks presented here conceptualize the empirical findings from in-depth study of major companies around the world. Use of these frameworks can be prescriptive as well as descriptive; they can also serve as tools for assessing and guiding change in directions that leaders seek. The examples from companies in the vanguard of change can inspire others to adopt, build on, and improve practices that combine innovation, profits, growth, and social good.

---

[43] See literature on Organizational Identity: Glynn (2000); Navis and Glynn (2010); Rafaelli (2013).

▇ REFERENCES

Amabile, Teresa M. and Kramer, Steve J. (2011) *The Progress Principle: Using Small Wins to Ignite Joy, Engagement, and Creativity at Work.* Boston, MA: Harvard Business School Press.

Christensen, Clayton. (1997) "The Innovator's Dilemma." Boston, MA: Harvard Business School Press.

Collins, Jim. (2001) "Good to Great: Why Some Companies Make the Leap and Others Don't." New York, NY: Harper Business.

DiMaggio, Paul and Powell, Walter. (1983) "The Iron Cage Revisited: Institutional Isomorphism and Collective Rationality in Organizational Fields," *American Sociological Review* 48 (2) (April): 147–60.

Glynn, Mary Ann. (2000) "When Cymbals Become Symbols: Conflict Over Organizational Identity Within a Symphony Orchestra," *Organization Science* 11 (3): 285–98. Special Issue: Cultural Industries: Learning from Evolving Organizational Practices.

Gulati, Ranjay, Lavie, D., and Singh, H. (2009) "The Nature of Partnering Experience and the Gains from Alliances," *Strategic Management Journal* 30 (11): 1213–33.

Jackson, I. R. A. and Nelson, Jane. (2004) *Profits with Principles: Seven Strategies for Delivering Value with Values.* New York: Currency/Doubleday.

Kanter, Rosabeth M. (1983) *The Change Masters.* New York: Simon & Schuster.

Kanter, Rosabeth M. (1989) *When Giants Learn to Dance.* New York: Simon & Schuster.

Kanter, Rosabeth M. (1999) "From Spare Change to Real Change: The Social Sector as a Beta Site for Business Innovation," *Harvard Business Review* (May–June): 123–32.

Kanter, Rosalind M. (2001) *Evolve!: Succeeding in the Digital Culture of Tomorrow.* Boston, MA: Harvard Business School Press, ch. 10.

Kanter, Rosabeth M. (2004) Confidence: How Winning Streaks and Losing Streaks Begin and End. New York: Crown Business.

Kanter, Rosabeth M. (2005) "Even Bigger Change: A Framework for Getting Started at Changing the World," Harvard Business School Background Note 305-099. (Revised May 2005.) Boston, MA: Harvard Business School Press.

Kanter, Rosabeth M. (2008a) "IBM Values and Corporate Citizenship," Harvard Business School Case 308-106. (Revised December 2011.) Boston, MA: Harvard Business School Press.

Kanter, Rosabeth M. (2008b) "IBM in the 21st Century: The Coming of the Globally Integrated Enterprise," Harvard Business School Case 308-105. (Revised October 2009.) Boston, MA: Harvard Business School Press.

Kanter, Rosabeth M. (2008c) "IBM's Dynamic Workplace," Harvard Business School Case 308-107. (Revised September 2009.) Boston, MA: Harvard Business School Press.

Kanter, Rosabeth M. (2009) *SuperCorp: How Vanguard Companies Create Opportunity, Profits, Growth, and Social Good.* New York: Crown Business, 25, 33, 37, 43, 68–71, 87–90, 114–15, 131–9, 140–8, 156, 161, 171, 182, 199, 204, 210, 226, 230–2, 243, 246–7, 250, 258, 277, 301–2, 304, 308, 311, 315, 317.

Kanter, Rosabeth M. (2011a) "How Great Companies Think Differently," *Harvard Business Review* 89 (11): 66–78.

Kanter, Rosabeth M. (2011b) "The Change Wheel: Elements of Systemic Change and How to Get Change Rolling," Harvard Business School Background Note 312-083. Boston, MA: Harvard Business School Press.

Kanter, Rosabeth M. (2012) "Enriching the Ecosystem," *Harvard Business Review* 90 (3): 140–7.

Kanter, Rosabeth M. and Bernstein, Ethan S. (2008) "Omron: Sensing Society," Harvard Business School Case 309-066. (Revised February 2009.) Boston, MA: Harvard Business School Press.

Kanter, Rosabeth M. and Bird, Matthew. (2008a) "Procter & Gamble Brazil (A): 2 1/2 Turnarounds," Harvard Business School Case 308-081. Boston, MA: Harvard Business School Press.

Kanter, Rosabeth M. and Bird, Matthew. (2008b) "Procter & Gamble Brazil (B): Turning to Success," Harvard Business School Supplement 308-083. Boston, MA: Harvard Business School Press.

Kanter, Rosabeth M. and Bird, Matthew. (2008c) "Procter & Gamble in the 21st Century (A): Becoming Truly Global," Harvard Business School Case 309-030. (Revised September 2009.) Boston, MA: Harvard Business School Press.

Kanter, Rosabeth M. and Bird, Matthew. (2008d) "Procter & Gamble in the 21st Century (B): Welcoming Gillette," Harvard Business School Supplement 309-031. (Revised September 2009.) Boston, MA: Harvard Business School Press.

Kanter, Rosabeth M. and Bird, Matthem. (2008e) "Procter & Gamble in the 21st Century (C): Integrating Gillette," Harvard Business School Supplement 309-032. (Revised September 2009.) Boston, MA: Harvard Business School Press.

Kanter, Rosabeth M. and Bird, Matthew. (2009a) "Diageo and East African Breweries Ltd.: Tapping New Markets for Social Good," Harvard Business School Case 310-010. (Revised December 2009.) Boston, MA: Harvard Business School Press.

Kanter, Rosabeth M. and Bird, Matthew. (2009b) "Publicis Groupe 2009: Toward a Digital Transformation," Harvard Business School Case 309-085. (Revised March 2009.) Boston, MA: Harvard Business School Press.

Kanter, Rosabeth M. and Bird, Matthew. (2011a) "PepsiCo Peru Foods: More than Small Potatoes," Harvard Business School Case 311-083. Boston, MA: Harvard Business School Press.

Kanter, Rosabeth M. and Bird, Matthew. (2011b) "Transforming Verizon: A Platform for Change," Harvard Business School Case 312-082. (Revised April 2012.) Boston, MA: Harvard Business School Press.

Kanter, Rosabeth M. and Khurana, Rakesh. (2010) "Advanced Leadership Note: An Institutional Perspective and Framework for Managing and Leading," Harvard Business School Background Note 410-076. (Revised August 2010.) Boston, MA: Harvard Business School Press.

Kanter, Rosabeth M. and Malone, Ai-Ling Jamila. (2012) "Hillary Clinton & Partners: Leading Global Social Change from the U.S. State Department," Harvard Business School Case 313-086. Boston, MA: Harvard Business School Press.

Kanter, Rosabeth M. and Malone, Ai-Ling Jamilla. (2013a) "Monique Leroux: Leading Change at Desjardins," Harvard Business School Case 313-107. (Revised April 2013.) Boston, MA: Harvard Business School Press.

Kanter, Rosabeth M. and Malone, Ai-Ling Jamila. (2013b) "IBM and the Reinvention of High School (A): Proving the P-TECH Concept," Harvard Business School Case 314-049. Boston, MA: Harvard Business School Press.

Kanter, Rosabeth M. and Malone, Ai-Ling Jamila. (2013c) "IBM and the Reinvention of High School (B): Replicating & Scaling P-TECH and Partners," Harvard Business School Case 314-050. Boston, MA: Harvard Business School Press.

Kanter, Rosabeth M. and Morgan, Matthew J. (2008) "Shinhan Financial Group (B)," Harvard Business School Supplement 308-095. Boston, MA: Harvard Business School Press.

Kanter, Rosabeth M. and Raffaelli, Ryan Leo. (2005a) "Shinhan Financial Group (A)," Harvard Business School Case 305-075. (Revised March 2008.) Boston, MA: Harvard Business School Press.

Kanter, Rosabeth M. and Raffaelli, Ryan Leo. (2005b) "Publicis Groupe: Leading Creative Acquisitions." Harvard Business School Case 506-010. (Revised February 2009.) Boston, MA: Harvard Business School Press.

Kanter, Rosabeth M. and Reisen de Pinho, Ricardo. (2005) "Banco Real: Banking on Sustainability," Harvard Business School Case 305-100. (Revised November 2008.) Boston, MA: Harvard Business School Press.

Kanter, Rosabeth M., Raymond, Douglas A., and Raffaelli, Ryan Leo. (2004) "The Making of Verizon," Harvard Business School Case 303-131. Boston, MA: Harvard Business School Press.

Kanter, Rosabeth M., Yatsko, Pamela, and Raffaelli, Ryan Leo. (2007a) "CEMEX (A): Building the Global Framework (1985–2004)," Harvard Business School Case 308-022. (Revised September 2009). Boston, MA: Harvard Business School Press.

Kanter, Rosabeth M., Yatsoko, Pamela, and Rafaelli, Ryan Leo. (2007b) "CEMEX (B): Cementing Relationships (2004–2007)," Harvard Business School Supplement 308-023. (Revised September 2009.) Boston, MA: Harvard Business School Press.

Kanter, Rosabeth M., Yatsoko, Pamela, and Rafaelli, Ryan Leo. (2007c) "CEMEX's Foundations for Sustainability," Harvard Business School Case 308-024. (Revised September 2009.) Boston, MA: Harvard Business School Press.

Kanter, Rosabeth M., Khurana, Rakesh, Lal, Rajiv, and Baldwin, Eric. (2011a) "Pepsi Co, Performance with Purpose, Achieving the Right Global Balance," Harvard Business School Case 412-079. (Revised January 2012.) Boston, MA: Harvard Business School Press.

Kanter, Rosabeth M., Khurana, Rakesh, Lal, Rajiv, and Kindred, Natalie. (2011b) "PepsiCo India: Performance with Purpose," Harvard Business School Case 512-041. Boston, MA: Harvard Business School Press.

Kanter, Rosabeth M., Herrero, Gustavo, and Reisen De Pinho, Ricardo. (2013) "Grupo ABC and Nizan Guanaes's Path from Brazil to the World," Harvard Business School Case 313-095. Boston, MA: Harvard Business School Press.

Khanna, Tarun and Palepu, Krishna G. (2006) "Emerging Giants: Building World-Class Companies in Developing Countries," *Harvard Business Review* 84 (10): 66–9.

Khanna, Tarun and Palepu, Krishna G. (2011) "Winning in Emerging Markets: Spotting and Responding to Institutional Voids," *World Financial Review* (May–June): 18–20.

Khanna, Tarun, Kogan, Joe, and Palepu, Krishna G. (2006) "Globalization and Similarities in Corporate Governance: A Cross-Country Analysis," *Review of Economics and Statistics* 88 (1): 69–90.

Khurana, Rakesh. (2010) *From Higher Aims to Hired Hands*. Princeton, NJ: Princeton University Press.

Kotter, John. (2007) "Why Transformation Efforts Fail," *Harvard Business Review* 85 (10): 96–103.

Makower, Joel. (2008) *Strategies for the Green Economy.* New York: McGraw-Hill.

March, James. (1972) "A Garbage Can Model of Organizational Choice," *Administrative Science Quarterly*, 17 (1) (March): 1–75.

Marquis, Christopher and Kanter, Rosabeth M. (2009) "IBM: The Corporate Service Corps," Harvard Business School Case 409-106. (Revised July 2010.) Boston, MA: Harvard Business School Press.

Navis, C. and Glynn, Mary Ann. (2010) "How New Market Categories Emerge: Temporal Dynamics of Legitmacy, Identity, and Entrepreneurship in Satellite Radio, 1990-2005," *Administrative Science Quarterly* 55 (3): 439–71.

Paine, Lynn Sharpe. (2004) *Values Shift: Why Companies Must Merge Social and Financial Imperatives to Achieve Superior Performance.* New York: McGraw Hill.

Raffaelli, Ryan. (2013) "Mechanisms of Technology Re-Emergence and Identity Change in a Mature Field: Swiss Watchmaking, 1970–2008," Harvard Business School Working Paper, No. 14-048. Boston, MA: Harvard Business School Press.

Tushman, Michael, O'Reilly, Charles, and Harreld, Bruce. (2015) "Leading Proactive Punctuated Change," in Rebecca Henderson, Ranjay Gulati, and Michael Tushman (eds), *Leading Sustainable Change: An Organizational Perspective.* Oxford: Oxford University Press.

Tushman, Michael and Romanelli, Elaine (1994) "Organization Transformation as Punctuated Equilibrium: An Empirical Test," *Academy of Management Journal* (with E. Romanelli) 34: 1141–66.

Weick, Karl. (2012) *Making Sense of the Organization: Vol. 2: The Impermanent Organization.* London: Wiley.

Zald, Meyer and McCarthy, John (1977) "Resource Mobilization and Social Movements, A Partial Theory," *American Journal of Sociology* 82 (6): 1212–41.

Part III
The Role of the Senior Team

6 Staying the Same While Changing

Organizational Identity in the Face
of Environmental Challenges

Mary Ann Glynn, Christi Lockwood, and Ryan Raffaelli

Change has always been a challenge for organizations. Weick (1979) succinctly explains the organizational dilemma in his statement that "adaptation precludes adaptability:" as an organization becomes well fitted to—and successful in—a particular environmental context, it can find it increasingly difficult to change when that context changes. Adapting to new environmental realities often necessitates innovation, which can involve a departure from organizational tradition or the adoption of new practices, all of which can be enabled or frustrated by the organization's identity (for example, Tripsas, 2009; Raffaelli and Glynn, 2014).

Identity, the organization's self-description of "who we are" and "what we do" (Navis and Glynn, 2010), serves a number of important organizational functions affecting organizational survival and performance, including: filtering managers' understanding of the organization's capabilities and resources; framing strategic problems and solutions; enabling positive valuations of organizational worth; serving as a touchstone for stakeholders' connection to, or identification with, the organization; and facilitating wealth creation (Lounsbury and Glynn, 2001; for a review, see also Corley et al., 2006). Given its centrality to the organization, identity can be remarkably resilient, its durability (for example, Albert and Whetten, 1985) sometimes thwarting change (for example, Tripsas, 2009). And, paradoxically, identity can also enable change by serving as a springboard for new organizational strategies and practices (for example, Glynn, 2000; Navis and Glynn, 2010; 2011; Glynn and Rafaelli, 2013).

In this chapter, we explore the role of the organization's identity in the adoption of new sustainability practices, examining how identity functions as a driver of (or sometimes a drag on) organizational shifts to sustainability. Our identity-oriented approach directs attention to how sustainability becomes not only "what we do" as an organizational practice but also "who we are" as an organization, in terms of its central, distinctive, and enduring attributes, values, or beliefs (Albert and Whetten, 1985).

Sustainability involves the organizational adoption of those practices that are considered environmentally or socially responsible. Becoming sustainable, however, is neither straightforward nor simple for organizations: "Sustainability is a multifaceted concept that presumes a dynamic balance among economic, environmental, and social goals... *an enduring shift toward sustainable organizational practice requires that sustainability become a fundamental, indispensable part of an organization's identity*" (Hamilton and Gioia, 2009: 436, emphasis added). In for-profit organizations, the logic of sustainability typically sits beside the logic of the market, each logic associated with a specific constellation of practices (Thornton et al., 2012). When there is alignment between the two logic–practice constellations, we see the probability of the organizational adoption of sustainable practices as high, as the rationale for the practice is supported (and even amplified) by both logics. An example where a sustainability effort is supported by both logics is the organizational practice of replacing traditional incandescent light bulbs with energy-efficient LED bulbs; here, cost savings and environmental responsibility go hand in hand. One manager described the mutual payoff: sustainability is "the right thing to do from our standpoint and the right thing to do from the consumer's standpoint" (Bansal and Roth, 2000: 728). However, when a practice conflicts with one logic, as for instance when the costs of green construction efforts threaten profitability, contestation ensues and the implementation of sustainability practices is typically sacrificed for economic considerations (Davis, 2009; Battilana and Dorado, 2010).

Sustainability initiatives thus require organizational managers to attend to a complex set of logics, practices, and identities and to secure their alignment. Typically, this tasks organizations to come up with innovative ways of changing to become more sustainable while simultaneously preserving core identity elements and capabilities. This is acknowledged by The Clorox Company (2013), recipient of the Most Innovative Corporate Social Responsibility (CSR) Disclosure Policy Award by Corporate Secretary magazine, in their claim that "Shrinking our environmental footprint while growing our business" requires us to "Think Outside the Bottle".[1] Moreover, to be effective, the adoption of sustainable practices cannot be mere "window dressing". Rather, as organizations strive to be seen as authentically committed to sustainability, they must integrate sustainability practices with the values, beliefs, and identity of the organization. As the eco-friendly Lenox Hotel in Boston, Massachusetts, puts it: "Green is in our roots—not only in the leaves that you see" (Hopps, 2012).

Researchers have shown how organizations are more likely to be responsible to their stakeholders when they work to solve some of world's most difficult social challenges, including that of environmental sustainability (for example, Hillman and Keim, 2001; Margolis and Walsh, 2003). Organizations

---

[1] Available at: <http://www.csrhub.com/SCR_and_sustainability_information/The-Clorax-Company/> (accessed July 2014).

that engage in sustainability practices not only benefit society, but also themselves, as they are able to market solutions that can drive the future growth and performance of the company (Marquis et al., 2007), through strategy, change, and leadership efforts (for example, Kanter, 2009). Scholars have shown that organizations with strong corporate social responsibility (CSR) programs face lower capital constraints; these firms gain easier access to financial resources due to better stakeholder engagement and enhanced transparency through CSR reporting (Cheng et al., 2014). Related work indicates that high-sustainability firms, i.e., companies with comprehensive sustainability programs, consistently outpace low-sustainability ones, both in terms of stock market performance and accounting performance (Eccles et al., 2014). Our perspective, focusing on the role of organizational identity, is intended to complement extant organizational scholarship on sustainability that has highlighted stakeholder management and firm performance; we seek to explore the role that organizational identity may play to help (or hinder) sustainability initiatives.

We believe that our work can make several contributions to understanding organizational sustainability. First, our perspective affords a counterpoint to the dominant rationale focused on the value proposition of the "triple bottom line," which encompasses environmental, social, and economic performance (for example, Elkington, 1997; Waddock, 2000, 2004). An identity perspective highlights how sustainability practices are not only "what we do" as an organization, which is often defined in service of the market and profitability, but also "who we are" as an organization, in service of the values, ideological beliefs or central character of the firm (Navis and Glynn, 2010). An identity approach emphasizes how sustainability mirrors the value proposition of the organization. For example, the Lenox Hotel claims that "Green is in our roots" (Hopps, 2012).

Second, identity serves as a touchstone for sustainability that can endure over time, conjoining a sustainable future to the organization's historical legacy (Walsh and Glynn, 2008); this occurs when organizations interpret (or reinterpret) their identity as being sustainable. For instance, Martha Stewart Living Omnimedia, self-described as "a leading provider of original 'how-to' information, inspiring and engaging consumers with unique lifestyle content and beautifully designed, high-quality products"[2], relates lifestyle issues, long a part of the organization's identity, to that of food sustainability. In the October 29, 2012 airing of The Martha Stewart Show, author Michael Pollan advised viewers that "What you choose to eat not only affects your health, but also the health of the planet...And one ingredient that has absolutely infiltrated our diets, to the detriment of both our bodies and our ecosystem, is corn".[3] To promote sustainability, viewers were urged to change

---

[2] Available at: <http://phx.corporate-ir.net/phoenix.zhtml?c=96022&p=irol-irhome, retrieved 8/28/2013> (accessed July 2014).
[3] Available at: <http://www.marthastewart.com/268706/food-sustainability-with-michael-pollan, retrieved 8/28/2013> (accessed July 2014).

not only their own eating habits but the food industry as well, transforming it by "voting with our forks". Thus, Martha Stewart Living Omnimedia used organizational identity to direct its efforts to make sustainability a part of its own—and its viewers'—ongoing lifestyle practices. The identity-oriented approach we adopt in this chapter points more broadly to the role that identity may play for a range of organizations in selecting and implementing efforts to become sustainable.

Finally, because identity sits at the interface between internal organizational members and external audiences (Navis and Glynn, 2010), it can be a point where the organization connects to key stakeholders and their interests. Organizations' relations with stakeholders "constitute a prominent feature of organizational identity" and are perceived to be "tightly coupled" (Brickson, 2005). Waldron et al. (2013) elaborate this relationship in the context of organizational responses to activism. They suggest that activists exert pressure to influence external stakeholders' perceptions of the identity of the target firm; in turn, managers in these firms assess the activists' campaigns in relation to internal perceptions of organizational identity. When activist efforts are seen to threaten target firms' identities or fiscal positions, managers change practices to assuage the activists' concerns: internal and external stakeholder assessments are, indeed, intimately linked. We seek to explain how organizational identity influences a range of stakeholders and directs decisions around sustainability in a similar fashion.

We explore organizational sustainability using the US hotel industry as an illustration, with a discussion of two hotels for which organizational identity played very different roles in their sustainability efforts: the Lenox Hotel (Boston, MA), a century-old historic hotel that incorporated sustainability into its identity as a provider of luxury accommodations, and the Element Hotel (Lexington, MA), a new venture founded with sustainability as its core identity. Hoteliers as a collective (at the industry level) offer a telling illustration of the interplay between sustainability and identity. We find that similar dynamics also play out at the firm level as organizations try to integrate sustainability into their organizational identity. Over the past three decades, the hotel industry has changed significantly in its orientation to, and practices of, sustainability, such that today sustainability initiatives are core to the hotel business and to numerous individual hotels.

Our chapter, investigating the interplay between organizational identity and sustainability practices, unfolds as follows. We first review the relevant literature on sustainability and organizational identity, focusing on insights about the diffusion and adoption of sustainability practices gleaned from theories of identity and institutionalism. Next, we illustrate these ideas in a brief narrative history of sustainability in the hotel industry. Then, we turn to examine how the industry dynamics played out in the sustainability efforts of two very different hotels, the century-old Lenox Hotel and the newly founded Element Hotel; we use the former to show how sustainability became integrated into a legacy organizational identity and the latter to show how sustainability defined the organizational identity from the founding. We discuss similarities and differences between the two hotels to draw out the dynamics of becoming sustainable organizations. We close with a discussion of the implications for theory and managerial practices of an identity-oriented perspective on sustainability.

Sustainability and organizational identity

Broadly speaking, organizational sustainability refers to "a company's activities, voluntary by definition, demonstrating the inclusion of social and environmental concerns in business operations and in interactions with stakeholders" (van Marrewijk, 2003). The World Commission on Environment and Development (WCED) defines sustainability as "development that meets the needs of the present without compromising the ability of future generations to meet their own needs" (World Commission on Environment and Development, 1987: 43). Focusing explicitly on the organizational level, Hamilton and Gioia (2009: 437) argue that sustainability involves "achieving a balance among environmental responsibility, social equity, and economic capability." Generally speaking, the corporation of the twenty-first century is one that serves society as well as rewards shareholders and employees (Kanter, 2009). The notion of organizational sustainability seems to have an affinity with organizational identity (for example, Corley et al., 2006), as both sustainability and identity are concerned not only with the practices enacted, but also the values symbolized.

Although identity has a long and lively intellectual history in several different domains of scholarship, inquiry into organizational identity was launched with vigor in 1985 when Albert and Whetten published their influential article in *Research in Organizational Behavior*. Albert and Whetten (1985) conceptualized organizational identity as those organizational claims to its core, distinctive, and enduring character. They defined these elements as follows: *core* consists of the "claimed central character" of the organization (making its central beliefs, values, and character evident); *distinctive* refers to those identity elements that differentiate the organization from other organizations (making it unique); and *enduring* is a "degree of sameness or continuity over time" (making it stable over time; Albert and Whetten, 1985: 265). Evident in this conceptualization of organization identity is an embedded tension between the sameness of identity, particularly over time, and differences in identity, making a particular organization distinct from others. Applying these ideas to sustainability suggests that, when organizations adopt new practices that are environmentally or socially friendly, it is important to emphasize not only the new direction the organization takes in becoming sustainable, but also the consistency of this direction with its past. For example, as the Lenox Hotel became a leader in sustainability through adoption of new environmentally friendly practices, it worked simultaneously to maintain its longstanding identity as a historic luxury hotel. Thus, in becoming sustainable, organizations confront the challenge suggested in the title: staying the same while changing.

Subsequent research, drawing more heavily from sociological traditions, reinforced this sameness–difference tension, but at a higher level of analysis. Organizations are embedded in industries or market categories that extend beyond the individual organizational identity; accordingly, identity serves as a claim to their position in this social space (for example, Glynn, 2008). To make their identity understandable to both their internal employees and external audiences, organizations focus on explaining "who they are" and manage outsiders' expectations of "what they do" (Navis and Glynn, 2010, 2011). Organizations accomplish this by balancing sameness and difference: sameness, in terms of resembling other organizations in their category (so as to garner categorical membership and legitimacy); difference, in terms of making them distinctive from other organizations within the category (to lend competitive advantage; for example, Glynn and Abzug, 2002). Managing these tensions can make organizations "legitimately distinctive" (Navis and Glynn, 2011) which, in turn, enables survival, strategic advantage, and performance.

Sociological perspectives on organizational identity bring in the audience, along with the organizations' management of their perceptions and evaluations (for example, Hsu and Hannan, 2005; Hsu, 2006; Hannan et al., 2007; Hsu et al., 2009; Navis and Glynn, 2010). Organizational identity is not only about the claims made by organizations, but also the granting of those claims by influential audiences (for example, Glynn, 2008). Consistent with this view, Albert and Whetten (1985) observed how identity stands at the interface between the claims made by its internal members (employees) and the claims granted by external audiences (stakeholders); this inside–outside differentiation is evident across theoretical variants of organizational identity (for example, Gioia et al., 2013). More generally, organizational identity functions to define and prioritize what the organization stands for, in terms of a constellation of values, beliefs, or norms (Albert and Whetten, 1985), and the practices it engages in as a social actor (Whetten and Mackey, 2002).

As organizations adopt sustainability practices, the importance of aligning new sustainability initiatives with internal and external perceptions of the organization's identity becomes evident. Although organizations may make claims to sustainability, it is how internal and external audiences react to these claims that can make them seem valid, legitimate, or authentic to the organization. Without alignment between the organization's claims to sustainability and audience perceptions of sustainability, organizations may be met with skepticism or doubt—from employees and consumers alike—as to whether they are truly sustainable. We believe that organizations are more likely to be perceived as legitimately sustainable when their sustainability claims align with their identity, such as when an eco-friendly grocery store (like Whole Foods) primarily sells food items that are locally sourced and organic.

Organizational identity can affect the adoption of sustainability practices, but it is not the only driver. Organizations also look to their industry peers and to networks of like-minded practitioners in making adoption decisions (Raffaelli and Glynn, 2014). The diffusion of practices within these fields affects the adoption of sustainability initiatives by individual organizations (for example, Utterback, 1971; Leblebici et al., 1991; Scott, 2001). Organizations adopt innovations already used by other focal organizations to obtain legitimacy (Meyer and Rowan, 1977; Westphal et al., 1997) or to protect or increase their reputation (Zucker, 1987), often without regard to efficiency gains (for example, Tolbert and Zucker, 1983; Baron et al., 1986; Westphal et al., 1997). As innovations become more prevalent, taken-for-granted, and therefore, more broadly institutionalized, the decision to adopt is often based on the organization's goal to avoid illegitimacy within the field (Tolbert and Zucker, 1983). More generally, organizations tend to succumb to isomorphic pressures to adopt institutionalized practices within their field (Marquis et al., 2007). All in all, our review of the relevant literature suggests that organizational sustainability will likely be affected by a set of factors that arise at the level of the firm and its identity, and at the level of the industry and its diffusion of sustainability practices. We now turn to examining these dynamics, using the illustrative example of the hotel industry and its efforts to become more sustainable. We first offer a narrative overview of sustainability in the US hotel industry. We then examine sustainability in two firms within the industry that differed in their approaches to becoming sustainable.

Sustainability in the US hotel industry

The topics of environmental preservation and stewardship have been part of public discourse in the US since the early 1960s, following the rise of American consumerism post World War II and the release of Rachel Carson's popular book, *Silent Spring* (1962). In the early 1970s, environmentalism began to reflect a broad concern for sustainability, influenced in part by the 1972 UN Stockholm Conference on the Human Environment, widely viewed as the first international conference on sustainability (Houdré, 2008), which closely connected environmental issues with economic priorities. With the release of influential publications, such as the Brundtland Commission's *Our Common Future* in 1987, which outlined the core tenets of sustainable development, and Agenda 21, which listed recommendations for sustainable development in 1992, as well as summits across sectors and industries (Houdré, 2008; Ing, 1995), sustainability became a regular topic of discussion.

Since the 1990s, a range of international players has taken steps to push sustainable development forward, particularly through the establishment of reporting methods and vehicles for investment in sustainable firms. In 1999, the Global Reporting Initiative (GRI) introduced what has become a very successful voluntary worldwide sustainability reporting system. In addition, the Leadership in Energy and Environmental Design (LEED) designation was introduced in 2000, serving as a third-party certification system for assessing high-performance green buildings and their sustainability around human health and environmental factors (Butler, 2008). Most recently, the Sustainable Stock Exchanges (SSE) was introduced, partnering with eight exchanges, including NYSE Euronext and NASDAQ, to promote corporate transparency around sustainability and encourage responsible investing.

SUSTAINABILITY PRACTICES IN THE US HOTEL INDUSTRY

Although the public push for sustainable development began in the 1970s, concern for sustainability among mainstream hoteliers did not take hold until about twenty years later. Responding to increasing calls for sustainable practices by regulatory and non-governmental organizations (NGOs) worldwide, international hospitality leaders issued their own guidelines for sustainability in 1995, developing the Charter for Sustainable Tourism (Ing, 1995). The Charter formalized the industry's commitment to protecting the environment and supporting long-term economic development and the cultural preservation of communities worldwide.

Initially, hoteliers' sustainability efforts focused on environmental preservation and consisted of incremental changes to existing operations, such as using low-flow showerheads and recycling and linen reuse programs. Typically, these programs operated largely behind the scenes, somewhat invisible to guests so as to prevent disrupting their stays. Sustainability-related changes were often driven primarily by increasingly stringent governmental policies related to environmental impact (Butler, 2008) and by potential cost savings realized by reducing energy consumption, waste disposal needs, water usage, and more (Enz and Siguaw, 1999). Accordingly, the hotel industry's early sustainability efforts remained primarily limited to "what we do" in organizations, impacting operations without substantially affecting organizational identity claims. Moreover, they introduced practices that were both fiscally and environmentally sound, thereby integrating the logic of sustainability with that of the market.

As travelers grew increasingly attuned to sustainability, formerly cutting-edge practices, like towel reuse programs and guestroom recycling bins, became more widely diffused throughout the industry, taking hold first in Europe and later, in the United States (Bohdanowicz, 2005; White, 2007). Hoteliers quickly recognized the need to invest in more extensive sustainability efforts, which they expected would reduce operating costs and entice new types of guests (Butler, 2008); here again, they sought to conjoin the sustainability logic to that of the market.

The 2006 introduction of Starwood's Element hotel brand, a line of extended-stay hotels for which sustainability is central to organizational identity, spoke to the strength of this industry shift. At this time, numerous independent hotels had adopted a "green mission", but the introduction of a sustainability-focused brand identity by a major industry player spurred the expansion of sustainability-related marketing and communication programs across the industry (for example, Jameson and Brownell, 2012). Sustainability began to shift from organizational practices ("what we do") to core identity claims about "who we are". However, organizational claims to a sustainability identity were not always granted by interested audiences. Industry wide, claims of sustainability and greenness were sometimes met with skepticism; many hotels were accused of "greenwashing", or exaggerating descriptions of their sustainability programs in an effort to enhance their images and attract more guests (White, 2007; Margulis, 2010).

The buzz about sustainability had reached a near-fever pitch when the 2008 economic recession hit, turning attention away from environmental preservation and refocusing it on self-preservation, for consumers and hoteliers alike (White, 2010). The economic downturn drove hotel occupancy rates to an historic low (Beehner, 2010) and slashed hotel revenues to near-unsustainable levels. As a result, many hotels found "that their environmental ambitions [ran] headlong into the harsh realities of the recession" (White, 2010: B5[L]). Market logic—and organizational survival—overshadowed sustainability logic. Moreover, doubts arose about the authenticity and legitimacy of organizations' identity claims to sustainability; an increasing number of hotels were accused of "greenwashing", rather than truly investing in sustainability. Hoteliers recognized the need to avoid appearing disingenuous: "I want to be a trend-setter and be eco-conscious. But I'm careful how I phrase it. There's so much greenwashing...I never want to be labeled as that" (Margulis, 2010: 4[L]).

At the same time, the travel industry came under increased scrutiny after insurance giant AIG sponsored a retreat at a Ritz-Carlton resort immediately after its government bail-out (White, 2011). In a concerted effort to "look like good corporate citizens" (White, 2010: B5[L]), companies from a range of sectors began to review hotels' green credentials and demand sustainability practices for their travel partners. Consumers and regulators called for hoteliers to adopt more measurable, balanced practices. The result of such stakeholder demands was to propel the diffusion of sustainability practices despite the economic crisis. Hotels across the industry stepped up their efforts to become sustainable, mostly through environmental practices. This time, however, they did so cautiously and selectively. "Lacking the capital to sink into big expensive retrofits, hotels [turned] to small-scale conservation programs [to] satisfy corporate buyers" (White, 2010: B5[L]). In effect, pressures for corporate responsibility and environmental stewardship fueled the institutionalization of sustainability efforts in the hotel industry. In 2009, sustainability was on the agenda of the Cornell Hospitality Research Summit, in which hotel leaders, academics, and industry consultants participated; this reinforced the important role of sustainability in the industry's strategic planning and recovery efforts.

Today, the hotel industry has rebounded from the economic recession, with occupancy and revenue expected to surpass record-setting pre-recession levels (HNN Newswire, 2013). As the economy has recovered, expectations about sustainability have expanded. "A few years ago, it was enough not to wash the towels every day. But it takes much more for hotels to earn their green stripes these days" (Zissu, 2010: 72[L]). Importantly, a broadened definition of sustainability was accompanied by the realization—among hoteliers and consumers—that sustainability efforts are diverse and scalable. As a result, the practices became more legitimated within the industry and benchmarks for sustainability grew, as hoteliers recognized the range of possibilities and, perhaps more importantly, their impact on hotels' operations and bottom lines (Withiam, 2013).

With the widespread diffusion of sustainable practices, most of the larger hotels took at least small steps towards going green by offering programs like recycling and towel reuse. Basic sustainability efforts have become so institutionalized as to be taken for granted and comparable across hotels; consumers generally do not pay a premium for such efforts because they expect them to be part of their hotel experience (Zhang et al., 2012). *Not* adopting the sustainability practices that dominated the industry could risk the hotel's reputation and attractiveness to guests. Accordingly, hoteliers sought distinctiveness from their peers with additional "green" features, investing carefully in operational and design upgrades that could be created with existing assets, supply chain constraints, customer preferences, location, and more (Butler, 2008; Ricaurte et al., 2012). Moreover, different from earlier efforts that tried to simply add on eco-friendly programs, hotels now emphasized the importance of an integrated sustainability program (Withiam, 2011). For many hoteliers, sustainability should "become the DNA in corporate culture, values, and strategy" (Withiam, 2011: 7), central to both identity claims and practices. This fully integrated approach is slowly taking hold in some segments of the industry, particularly in upscale and luxury hotels, where sustainability efforts are now coming to be seen as "adding to the authenticity and charm" of hotel stays (Conlin, 2008: 7[L]).

Over the past 25 years, evolving competitive pressures, governmental mandates, hoteliers' interests, and stakeholder demands have established sustainability as the "new normal" in hospitality (Ricaurte et al., 2012), constituting both the identity claims of organizations and the expectations of relevant audiences. Our brief recounting of the history of sustainability in the hotel industry generated several insights on the relationship between sustainability and organizational identity that, we believe, extend beyond this particular context.

Overall, the narrative exposes how sustainability practices moved from the periphery of the hotel industry, as incremental changes to practices and identities, to the core, becoming a taken-for-granted and integral aspect of both practices and identities. Early hotel adopters of sustainability practices borrowed from the behavior of a broader set of extra-industry organizations that carried the logic of sustainability and constituted what could be called a community of practice (for example, Raffaelli and Glynn, 2014) or an issue-based field, where concerns about sustainability drew together a varied set of actors (Hoffman, 1999). These early practices were largely easy-to-implement, off-the-shelf, turnkey practices that required little tailoring by the adopting organization (Raffaelli and Glynn, 2014); they were tweaks to existing organizational systems such as recycling bins or linen reuse. At this point, organizational identity functioned largely as a filter that regulated the decision of whether or not to adopt any type of sustainability practice (Greenwood et al., 2011).

As more hotels adopted sustainability practices—and practice diffusion took the shape of the familiar S-curve of innovation (Rogers, 1962)—hotels experienced mounting isomorphic pressure to conform and be similar to other "sustainable" hotels, but did this in ways that differentiated them from their counterparts in the industry. Sustainable practices became tailored to the organization's particular identity, in ways that redounded to its historical legacy, or came to define new ventures founded explicitly with an identity of sustainability. At this stage, the logic of the market and competitive advantage shaped the kinds of sustainability practices that organizations adopted. In effect, as basic sustainability practices became more prevalent, hotels that differentiated themselves from the rest of the field based on a sustainability identity were required to adopt even more innovative practices. For example, as towel and linen reuse became common in the hotel industry, some sustainability-focused hotels moved to also using organic linens and natural detergents to further ensure that laundry was eco-friendly. In extending their green practices beyond the most common industry practices, such hotels maintained a distinctive identity as a sustainable hotel.

We graph these industry-level dynamics in Figure 6.1, showing how the relationship between the issue-based logic of sustainability and the market-based logic of efficiency shifted over time. Individual hotels responded to forces arising from the diffusion and institutionalization of sustainability practices, but did so in different ways. Over time, the rationale for adoption of sustainable practices shifted from one based on efficiency gains to one based on enhancing legitimacy. Next, we show how two very different hotels responded to the institutionalization of sustainability practices: the historical incumbent, the Lenox Hotel, and the entrepreneurial Element hotel. In both illustrative cases, the hoteliers were successful in adopting sustainability practices that were perceived to be legitimate and authentic to their identity; they did this by balancing identity continuity with efforts to change to become more sustainable.

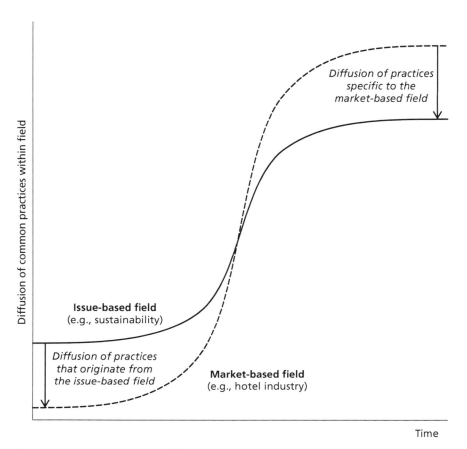

Figure 6.1. Stylized pattern of diffusion of sustainability practices in the US hotel industry

Sustainability and identity in two "green" hotels: the Lenox Hotel and the Element

The sustainability programs at both the Lenox and Element hotels have been widely recognized as industry leading. However, their approaches to sustainability are quite distinct, reflecting how variation can still exist at the organization level in spite of industry-level pressures that often drive organizations towards isomorphism and conformity. The Lenox, a century-old hotel, was an early player in hotel sustainability, pioneering now commonplace practices that were incremental relative to its well-established, legacy identity. By contrast, the Element, a 2008 entrant to the hotel field, was founded on an identity of sustainability; as such, it implemented a broad range of sustainability practices from the outset. In this section we describe sustainability at these two hotels, focusing on "who we are" and "what we do" and the linkages these hotels made between the two. To develop these illustrations, one of the authors interviewed five experts on the sustainability programs at the two hotel firms; visited the hotels on site to observe their sustainability practices; and collected archival data on the hotels. We use these illustrative examples to draw out lessons on identity sameness and difference and how sustainability enables "changing while staying the same" (or sometimes the reverse).

THE LENOX HOTEL: STAYING THE SAME WHILE CHANGING

The Lenox Hotel in Boston, MA first opened its doors in 1901, briefly claiming the title of Boston's tallest building at a towering eleven stories. The hotel quickly gained a reputation as the "Waldorf Astoria" of Boston, a nod to the other hotel owned by Lucius Boomer. Lavishly appointed and centrally located in the city's desirable Back Bay neighborhood, near to Copley Square and only a stone's throw from the boutiques and restaurants of Newbury Street, the Lenox Hotel has played host to innumerable celebrity guests, ranging from Judy Garland to George W. Bush.

Identity claims: who we are

As Albert and Whetten (1985) might predict, the Lenox's identity has been enduring over time, with its "century-old reputation for excellence...long justified and steeped in tradition".[4] Throughout its storied history, the Lenox has enjoyed a reputation as one of the city's original and best small, luxury hotels, providing guests with lavish accommodations, upscale amenities, and tailored service. Today, the hotel touts itself as "the original boutique" hotel, highlighting its longstanding place as a niche player in the luxury market.

Interestingly, despite the hotel's clear and enduring focus on delivering luxury to guests, the Lenox succeeded in expanding its identity to include eco-friendly elements, as well, by "preserving the past [and] protecting the future".[5] By expanding ideas about "who we are", the Lenox now makes claims to being not only a luxury hotel, but also a pioneer in "green". For the Lenox, sustainability and luxury are two sides of the same identity coin and are held in a productive but dynamic tension. "It's a good tension to have because we want to achieve both" (personal interview with sustainability manager, Lenox Hotel, August 29, 2013). Upholding both the luxury and sustainability elements of the organizational identity is a key objective: "We're still going to have world-class service and amenities, and we're still being responsible and being true to ourselves from a sustainability standpoint. One can't undermine the other in either direction" (personal interview with sustainability manager, Lenox Hotel, August 29, 2013).

---

[4] Available at: <http://www.lenoxhotel.com/boston-hotels-our-story/> (accessed July 2014).
[5] Available at: <http://www.saundershotelgroup.net/hotel-management-services.php> (accessed July 2014).

Importantly, although the Lenox makes claims to both sustainability and luxury, the hotel is clear that its enduring luxury focus is foremost in its identity and in the experience it provides to guests. When possible, sustainability programs are implemented with an eye to enhancing the luxury guest experience: "It's something that really strengthens our relationship and builds that bond with the customer, in the same way that service and location and the quality of the operation do" (personal interview with sustainability officer, Lenox Hotel, August 29, 2013). When the two identity components conflict, sustainability is explicitly subordinated to luxury; the Lenox focuses on "non-intrusive, awareness-building initiatives to strengthen our sustainability while providing the high level experience our guests have come to expect".[6] Guest feedback reflects the Lenox's focus on luxury: recent traveler comments on TripAdvisor, a user-generated travel review website, praise the Lenox's great location, well-appointed rooms, and other amenities, but virtually no guests comment on the hotel's sustainability efforts.[7] Although the hotel is deeply committed to sustainability, "we don't do anything that would compromise the quality or the service; the comfort or the sense of luxury that we're offering here" (personal interview with sustainability officer, Lenox Hotel, August 29, 2013). The Lenox's "green" organizational identity integrates the logics of sustainability and the market; however, practices tend to prioritize the market (in this case, through a focus on luxury) over that of sustainability. At the Lenox Hotel, sustainability decisions are made in a manner that preserves luxury, upholding the hotel's enduring identity while expanding it to include aspects of sustainability.

Practices: what we do

Although the Lenox Hotel tends to focus on identity claims related to luxury, its sustainability program is industry leading. The hotel's efforts to become more sustainable began with incremental changes in operations in the late 1980s and shifted, over the following years, to implementing increasingly larger changes throughout the hotel. Today, the Lenox is recognized as one of the world's "ultimate green hotels",[8] with a range of practices that support its sustainability-related identity claims. According to Scot Hopps, Director of Sustainability at the Lenox, "Green is definitely the term du jour, but the duration and scope of what we are doing is more about sustainability and a long-term scope that encompasses not just the environment, but also a dedication to community, service, health, and business" (Hopps, quoted in

---

[6] Available at: <http://www.lenoxhotel.com/boston-hotels-our-story/our-commitment/> (accessed July 2014).

[7] Available at: <http://www.tripadvisor.com/Hotel_Review-g60745-d114134-Reviews-The_Lenox_Hotel-Boston_Massachusetts.html> (accessed July 2014).

[8] Available at:<http://www.travelandleisure.com/articles/the-ultimate-green-hotel-august-2006/2> (accessed July 2014).

Atoji Keene, 2013: G2). Sustainability-related changes to organizational practices, in other words, have been wide-ranging, affecting everything from linen selection to the long-range plan for the hotel (personal interview, Lenox Hotel, August 29, 2013).

As the Lenox has made changes to its practices and expanded its identity to include sustainability-related claims over the past 25 years, leaders have worked diligently to uphold the standards of luxury for which the Lenox has long been known. Recognizing the need to reduce its environmental footprint while continuing to deliver the level of service guests demand, the Lenox designed sustainability initiatives to operate unobtrusively or completely behind the scenes. For example, the Lenox offsets 100 percent of its energy use by purchasing renewable energy credits and carbon offsets—an investment of which most guests are unaware. As well, hotel staff members are involved in discreet on-site sustainability initiatives; all housekeeping employees wear uniforms made from recycled material, for instance. The hotel saves an estimated 110,000 paper cups annually by providing reusable mugs to all staff for employee dining facilities. Each department in the hotel holds regular eco-meetings, and weekly "green" tips are sent to all employees.

In guest spaces, sustainability-related changes are implemented only after thorough consideration and, sometimes, debate: "We may be pushing for something that is pretty aggressive on the sustainability front, and the general manager [focused on luxury] will say, 'I'm not comfortable with that,' [and we re-think it]" (personal interview with sustainability officer, Lenox Hotel, August 29, 2013). Sustainability changes to the guest experience that are implemented are designed to be as unobtrusive as possible. Traditional bulbs used in chandeliers and in the Lenox's iconic sign have been replaced with low-energy LED lights. The hotel uses waterless urinals, low-flow showerheads, and earth-friendly in-room materials, including paint and flooring. Guests are also given the option to contribute to some of the hotel's sustainability efforts by using recycling receptacles and opting out of daily linen and towel changes, a practice that the Lenox pioneered. High-end bath products are in recyclable bottles, and filtered water and ice stations are available on each floor to eliminate the need for in-room bottled water.

Over time, sustainability has become an important aspect of "what we do" at the Lenox, expanding to also involve fostering social good in the local community. "It's absolutely about doing the right thing, serving others" (personal interview with sustainability officer, Lenox Hotel, August 29, 2013). The most dramatic example of this commitment to service is the Lenox's response to the April 15, 2013 Boston Marathon Bombings. Located just steps from the site where one of the bombs detonated, the Lenox welcomed medical staff, investigators, police officers, and other government officials, allowing them to use the hotel as a makeshift headquarters (Alcindor, 2013). Over the ensuing eight days, the hotel provided accommodations, meals, and spaces for officials. The efforts emptied the hotel's pantries and refrigerators; however, with assistance from other local businesses, the

Lenox served up an estimated 1,500 meals each day at no charge. About 70 Lenox employees and managers volunteered their time, cooking, changing sheets, washing towels, restocking amenities, and ensuring that the hotel "guests" were comfortable and rested. "The environmental program [and] the reaction to the Boston Marathon Bombing are outgrowths of the ethics and the values that are at the heart of the company" (personal interview with sustainability officer, Lenox Hotel, August 29, 2013). Paraphrasing the Director of Sustainability at the Lenox, sustainability has truly taken "taken root" at the Boston hotel, changing practices while upholding the organization's enduring luxury identity and the values that have long been central to the Lenox.

Over time, the Lenox Hotel has remained the same, continuing to define its identity as a luxury hotel, while changing to integrate sustainability-related claims and practices that fit with the hotel's history, values, and longstanding identity claims. Although "what we do" as a hotel is continuously updated to remain similar to other sustainability leaders in the hotel industry and in other fields, "who we are"—a luxury hotel—endures as a core aspect of the Lenox Hotel's identity.

THE ELEMENT HOTEL: CHANGING TO BE THE SAME

Inspired by the growing interest in sustainability across the industry, the Element was launched as part of the Starwood Hotels and Resorts collection, which includes the Sheraton, W Hotels, Westin, and The Luxury Collection, among others. Inspired by the successful Westin brand,[9] the Element targets the eco-friendly niche developing in the business travel market; its name reflects its connection with the environment as well as its broader efforts to make guests feel at home or "in their element" at the hotel. The first Element Hotel opened its doors to guests in 2008 in Lexington, MA. Since that time, the Element concept has grown into a larger hotel brand (i.e., a chain of hotels that are held to similar design and service standards). The Element brand serves as "Starwood's green trailblazer" (HNN Newswire, 2008), a testing ground for a variety of earth-friendly initiatives and a player in the growing niche focused on sustainability. Today, there are 11 Element hotels, mainly in the US, with about ten additional hotels planned domestically and internationally in coming years.

Identity claims: who we are

Sustainability—or more specifically, environmental responsibility—is central to the identity of the Element. The Element prides itself on being "green from the ground up", built in accord with LEED standards, designed to make "green

---

[9] Available at: <http://www.starwoodhotels.com/element/about/index.html> (accessed July 2014).

choices easy for our guests without compromising a great experience" (Starwood Hotels and Resorts Worldwide, Inc., 2008a: 3) and delivering "guest experiences through the lens of environmental responsibility" (Frits van Paasschen, Starwood CEO, in Starwood Hotels and Resorts Worldwide, Inc., 2008b). A sustainable identity underpins nearly all aspects of the Element's approach to engaging employees and serving guests: "We have to be true to our roots [in sustainability] and have integrity with that" (personal interview with guest experience manager, Element Hotel, September 16, 2013).

The theme of environmental preservation is core: "Element is grounded by smart thinking, a natural sense of balance and an optimistic energy that's alive and vibrant, all of which is reflected in our programs, services and communications" (Starwood Hotels and Resorts Worldwide, Inc., 2008a: 2). Being an eco-friendly hotel also affects material decisions that shape the guest experience: "Element's key green features are cleverly designed to be as appealing aesthetically as they are eco-friendly, so travelers never compromise on style and comfort" (Starwood Hotels and Resorts Worldwide, Inc., 2008b). Moving forward, company executives intend for the Element to serve as the birthplace of a range of company- and industry-leading eco-innovations (Starwood Hotels and Resorts Worldwide, Inc., 2008b). Sustainability, in other words, is an essential component of the Element's identity claims and market position, and it directs virtually all of what the Element does. The Element is "a new kind of hotel",[10] where sustainability is central to who they are and what they do. "It's not that if you're going to be green, you're going to give something up at the Element. It's simply who we've been from the beginning" (personal interview with guest experience manager, Element Hotel, September 16, 2013).

Practices: what we do

For the Element, sustainability is largely about responsibility to the natural environment. Different from sustainability-related changes at the Lenox, which focused on organizational identity stability and used an incremental approach to becoming sustainable, the Element's approach to change is more radical, and it centers on differentiation from competitors by adopting extensive sustainability practices that surpass the industry norm (see Figure 6.1). A break from the status quo is literally built into the Element Lexington: distinct from many competitors that integrate sustainability into existing operations, the Element in Lexington was built new, allowing sustainable practices to be implemented from the ground up. Element is the first major hotel brand that requires all its hotels to pursue LEED Certification. The Lexington Element Hotel achieved LEED Gold Certification, the second-

---

[10] Available at: <http://www.starwoodhotels.com/element/experience/index.html> (accessed July 2014).

highest level of certification, shortly after its opening in 2008. At present, it is the only hotel in Massachusetts with this level of LEED certification; it serves as the prototype for new Element properties in other locations. Different from most other hotels that have adopted sustainability, eco-friendliness is also central to the Element's value proposition for guests: "Our prices are higher because of the various [sustainable] things that are a part of who we are... For us, it works really well" (personal interview with supervisor, Element Hotel, September 6, 2013).

Unlike the Lenox Hotel, which tends to subordinate sustainability to luxury, the Element's sustainable organizational identity drives the practices it implements in the hotel: "At Element, being green from the ground up is one of those founding fundamentals that's something that we need to be true to... if we're adding something, it's making sure it's compatible with that 'green from the ground up'" (personal interview with guest experience manager, Element Hotel, September 16, 2013). Inside and around the Element Lexington, an eco-friendly identity is reflected in a wide range of design and service-related choices. The hotel parking lot is small, preserving as much of the local environment as possible, and it includes preferred parking spots for guests' hybrid vehicles. The hotel makes bicycles available for guests and staff, and public transit routes are nearby. All of the hotel's public spaces, from guest meeting rooms to employee break rooms, are designed to maximize exposure to the outdoors; natural light fills the lobby, pouring in through energy-efficient glass walls. Guest rooms are outfitted with "green" basics, such as recycling bins and LED lighting, as well as additional earth-friendly features, like energy-efficient appliances, low-flow showerheads, and mounted dispensers for bath amenities. Standard services—room cleaning and linen changes—occur once every three days, rather than daily, as is the norm in most hotels. Even paints and flooring materials are selected with eco-friendliness in mind: the Element uses green and recycled materials whenever possible.

The theme of earth-friendliness and balance is evident in additional programs and initiatives, as well. Monday through Thursday evenings, the hotel promotes personal balance and relaxation by sponsoring a happy hour with complimentary snacks, drinks, and smoothies for guests to enjoy. Fully equipped workout spaces are open 24 hours daily to encourage guests to take time to get moving, and the hotel features a saline pool, rather than a chlorinated one. The Element offers guests complimentary breakfast that includes organic and natural foods, an on-site "pantry" sells a range of healthy foods, and grocery delivery is available, making it easy for guests to make smart and personally sustainable eating choices. Taken together, the Element Lexington's practices support a uniquely green identity, manifest in all that the Element does. "The sustainability initiatives all kind of flow into each other and it creates this ambience that makes us who we are. And that's a neat thing... The whole is definitely stronger than each of its individual parts" (personal interview with supervisor, Element Hotel, September 6, 2013).

The Element hotel focuses on identity differentiation as it pursues sustainability in a field where these practices are common. Entering the hotel market about 20 years after sustainability gained notice in the industry, the Element claimed a unique identity in an effort to differentiate itself from other sustainable hotels. The Element's organizational identity, focused expressly on environmental balance and stewardship, drove its adoption of innovative practices that highlighted its break from the status quo in sustainability. In a market where sustainability practices had diffused and basic environmental programs had become taken for granted, the Element used claims about "who we are" to direct practices that guests and peers considered unique.

SUSTAINABILITY AND IDENTITY AT THE LENOX AND ELEMENT HOTELS

The sustainability programs at the Lenox and Element hotels illustrate the organizational-level identity dynamics that underpin the broad diffusion of practices across the industry. As sustainability practices became commonplace and institutionalized, organizations moved from focusing on similarity with their "green" peers that might legitimate their "green" identities, to differentiating themselves from their peers to gain competitive advantage. As they did, the relationship between the organizational identity claims of "who we are" and the practices comprising "what we do" changed accordingly.

Before sustainability practices became widespread in the industry, hotels tended to adopt those practices that aligned them with other organizations perceived to be sustainable, regardless of their industry. For example, leaders at the Lenox judge their sustainability program "against best-of-class, and we judge ourselves against other industries. I hold us up, in terms of standards, to a Timberland or a Patagonia or Stonyfield or Aveda...that category of companies that are fully-integrated, enterprise-wide sustainability programs" (personal interview with sustainability officer, Lenox Hotel, August 29, 2013). The Lenox, like other early adopters, looked to the communities of sustainable practices and, particularly early-on, adopted initiatives that were turnkey or less tailored to their particular organization (Raffaelli and Glynn, 2014). At this point in time, hotels pursued a strategy of "sameness"—or comparability with other sustainable organizations—to legitimate their identity as sustainable. For early adopters, as sustainable practices became increasingly central to "what we do" as an organization, they drove updates and expansions to "who we are", as the example of the Lenox Hotel illustrated.

With the taken-for-granted establishment of sustainability with the hotel industry, organizations turned to differentiating their offerings (Navis and Glynn, 2010) from hotel industry peers. Rather than looking outside the industry, later adopters focus on differentiating themselves from others within the hotel industry, as did the Element, which considers other extended-stay hotels to be its peers (personal interview, Element Hotel, September 6, 2013).

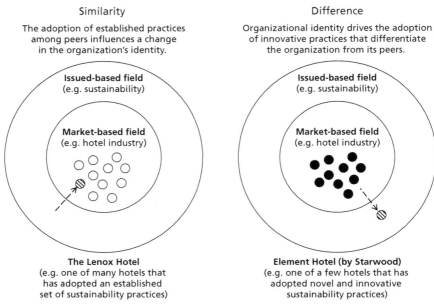

Figure 6.2. Comparison between incumbent and new entrant in organizational identity similarity and differentiation

In order to clearly differentiate themselves from others, later adopters' organizational identities tend to be more explicitly focused on sustainability as a unique identity claim, one that drives the practices that comprise "what we do" as an organization. Thus, the organizational identity dynamics of similarity and differentiation were related to, and shifted with, the institutionalization of sustainability practices in the industry. For example, as sustainability practices were introduced to the industry, early adopters, such as the Lenox Hotel, tended to adopt turnkey practices, like towel and linen reuse, and integrate these with their legacy identity. As these practices came to be expected in the industry, later adopters, such as the Element, tended to tailor their sustainability practices to their particular organization (installing in-room Energy Star washing machines for their extended-stay guests, for example) so as to differentiate themselves from their industry peers through claims of a distinctive identity. We depict these identity claims in Figure 6.2.

Discussion and conclusions

In this chapter, we sought to understand the relationship between the organizational adoption of sustainable practices—going "green"—and the organizational identity, with its constellation of central, distinctive, and enduring attributes. Our theorization of this interplay, along with industry and case illustrations from the hotel industry, revealed how becoming sustainable relies on a complex interchange between the diffusion and adoption of sustainability practices at the level of the industry or community of practice (see Figure 6.1) and the identity of the individual organization (see Figure 6.2). Moreover, we see how these dynamics shift as conditions at the organizational level and the industry shift. We draw out the implications of our exploration into organizational sustainability for the development of future theory and for managerial practices that support sustainability.

Theoretically, our work can help to develop a finer-grained understanding of sustainable organizational identities and to extend existing scholarship in these areas. Two perspectives that might usefully elaborate our work are those focusing on identity hybridicity (Albert and Whetten, 1985; Battilana and Dorado, 2010) and identity ambidexterity (Raffaelli, 2013; Raffaelli et al., 2013). Both of these theoretical perspectives permit us to consider how sustainability might render organizational identities as pluralistic, having multiple identity elements.

Identity hybridicity occurs when an organization embeds two identity elements that do not necessarily go together (Albert and Whetten, 1985). In thinking about sustainability, this may be an approach of high interest (Haigh and Hoffman, 2012); in fact, organizational hybridicity has been offered as a lens for understanding how the logic of sustainability might productively exist side-by-side with the logic of the market in an organization (for example, Battilana and Dorado, 2010). The two logics are associated with different (and potentially conflicting) identity elements and organizational practices (Battilana and Dorado, 2010; Thornton et al., 2012). Specifically, the logic of *sustainability* is associated with social and environmental responsibility, while the logic of *market* is associated with profitability, sometimes at the expense of social or environmental responsibility (Davis, 2009). At times, the two logics can converge harmoniously in sustainability practices, as we saw with energy efficiencies, recycling, and linen reuse in hotels. At other times, however, the logics can clash, as was evident in the 2008 economic recession when hotels pulled back from sustainability initiatives for the sake of economic survival. Thus, conflict can emerge as organizations try to balance sustainability and market orientations and the associated hybridicity in identity.

An alternative theoretical perspective—that of identity ambidexterity—may better explain the approaches adopted by the focal hotels in our illustrative cases; moreover, we suggest that this perspective might help to conceptualize organizational sustainability more fully. Organizational ambidexterity refers to the work of O'Reilly and Tushman (2008: 200) that shows how leaders reconfigure competing assets and competencies to promote growth and adaptation. Identity ambidexterity refers to an organization's ability to exploit past and present identities while simultaneously integrating elements of a new (or future) organizational identity (Raffaelli, 2013; Raffaelli et al., 2013). For example, identity ambidexterity is evident in the case of the Lenox Hotel: the organization maintained its longstanding luxury identity while also developing, slowly and over time, elements of a sustainability identity. At the Element, too, identity ambidexterity has been important to the organization's success. Being relatively new, the Element used aspects of the longstanding upscale, customer-centric identity of its sister brand, the Westin; however, it expanded this identity to focus more centrally on eco-friendliness and balance. Rather than treating the two central aspects of their identities—upscale or luxury hotel and sustainability pioneer—as conflicting or incompatible (characteristic of a hybrid organizational identity), the Lenox and Element treat them as largely complementary, distinguishing the two from similar hotels and likely helping to ensure their financial sustainability over the longer term.

Theorizing organizational sustainability in terms of identity ambidexterity focuses on how organizations like the Lenox and the Element ably switch between sustainable practices and market-oriented practices, over time, to meet environmental needs. Whereas identity hybridity accounts for multiple identities housed within one organization, identity ambidexterity also acknowledges the importance of temporality to organizational identity (for example, Schultz and Hernes, 2013), highlighting the organization's capacity to update and expand identity, aligning past and present identity aspects to meet anticipated future demands. Identity ambidexterity places a special emphasis on how organizations manage *current* identity attributes (for example, a luxury hotel), but it also accounts for how an organization goes about assimilating additional identity elements that are deemed critical to the organization's *future* survival and legitimacy (for example, an environmentally friendly hotel). Future research on sustainability could benefit by more fully exploring the role of organizational identity ambidexterity in the organization's pursuit of a robust triple bottom line.

Managerially, our work highlights a number of likely issues that organizational executives may confront in making their firms more sustainable. First, we highlight the important role that the organizational identity plays, both as an independent variable, filtering potential practices for adoption (as at the Lenox Hotel), and as a dependent variable, the outgrowth of the practices of being a sustainable organization (the Element Hotel). In the former instance, managers need to be vigilant about how identity can bias decisions (for example, Tripsas, 2009) around common sustainability practices to adopt. In the latter, managers need to be prepared for articulating the sustainable identity, not only in terms of "what we do" but also "who we are," as the firm implements new sustainability practices that may be less common in the industry.

Second, we illustrate how organizational sustainability does not occur in a vacuum, but rather in an organizational field or industry; as such, organizational executives need to look beyond their organization to broader fields that might include their industry, the community of sustainability practitioners, or the broader social contexts that can shape stakeholders' expectations. Changes in these wider fields or environments affect the adoption of sustainability practices (see Figure 6.1) and how the organization casts these adoptions (see Figure 6.2). Early adopters differ from later ones; the nature of sustainability practices adopted—turnkey or tailored (Raffaelli and Glynn, 2014)—and their impact—legitimation or strategic (Navis and Glynn, 2010)—shifts with the degree of diffusion and institutionalization of sustainability practices. Savvy managers would do well to appreciate the broader context in which sustainable practices are adopted.

Finally, we suggest that organizational sustainability has implications for organizational design. Given the potentially conflictual tension between the orientations to sustainability and the market, executives might consider how these logics are structured in the formal and informal systems in the organization. Often, sustainability and market orientations are present but partitioned in organizations, associated with different structures (for example, the core business and the corporate foundation) and personnel (for example, administrators and professionals). When both of these work in concert, they can be potent and effective ways of enacting a sustainability identity; however, when their boundaries are breached, conflict can rupture and disable the organization (for example, Glynn, 2000; Battilana and Dorado, 2010). Santos and Eisenhardt (2005: 501) note that organizations need to continually manage vertical and horizontal identity boundaries that determine "how members perceive what is appropriate for the organization ... [and] guides decisions regarding the value-chain activities to incorporate or product/market domains to enter". In this scenario, managerial work would simultaneously attend to compartmentalizing and coordinating the sustainability and market functions, logics and identities in the organization. The illustrative examples of the Lenox Hotel and the Element suggest that, with careful management of identity claims and practices to coordinate sustainability and market functions, both century-old and relatively new organizations can resolve conflict between these elements; the result would be to hold them in dynamic tension, facilitating ambidexterity in identity and in organizational capabilities. By considering sustainability in organizational design decisions both at organizational founding (as in the case of the Element) and continuously over time (as in the case of the Lenox), managers might best balance potentially competing logics and identities.

To conclude, we see our chapter as an initial foray into examining the linkages between sustainability and organizational identity. We hope we have provided a foundation rich enough for future researchers to continue to explore this terrain.

▓ ACKNOWLEDGMENTS

We gratefully acknowledge the helpful comments on earlier drafts by Mary Benner, Mike Tushman, and participants at the Change and Sustainability Conference at the Harvard Business School in May 2013. We also appreciate the generous support of the Joseph F. Cotter Professorship and the Winston Center for Leadership and Ethics at Boston College.

■ REFERENCES

Albert, S. and Whetten, D. A. (1985) "Organizational Identity," in L. L. Cummings and B. M. Staw (eds), *Research in Organizational Behavior* vol. 7. Greenwich, CT: JAI Press, 163–95.

Alcindor, Y. (2013) "Boston Hotel has Unique Role in Aftermath of Blasts," *USA Today* April 25, 4A.

Atoji Keen, C. (2013) "Proving Luxury Hotels can be Green," *Boston Globe*, January 20, G2.

Bansal, P. and Roth, K. (2000) "Why Companies Go Green: A Model of Ecological Responsiveness," *Academy of Management Journal* 43 (4): 717–36.

Baron, J. N., Dobbin, F. R., and Jennings, P. D. (1986) "War and Peace: The Evolution of Modern Personnel Administration in US Industry," *American Journal of Sociology* 92 (2): 350–83.

Battilana, J. and Dorado, S. (2010) "Building Sustainable Hybrid Organizations: The Case of Commercial Microfinance Organizations," *Academy of Management Journal* 53 (6): 1419–40.

Beehner, L. (2010) "Consumer Reports Passes Along Hotel Tips," *New York Times*, May 16, 2(L).

Bohdanowicz, P. (2005) "European Hoteliers' Environmental Attitudes Greening the Business," *Cornell Hotel and Restaurant Administration Quarterly* 46 (2): 188–204.

Brickson, S. L. (2005) "Organizational Identity Orientation: Forging a Link Between Organizational Identity and Organizations' Relations with Stakeholders," *Administrative Science Quarterly* 50 (4): 576–609.

Butler, J. (2008) "The Compelling 'Hard Case' for 'Green' Hotel Development," *Cornell Hospitality Quarterly* 49 (3): 234–44.

Carson, R. (1962) *Silent Spring*. Boston, MA: Houghton Mifflin.

Cheng, B., Ioannou, I., and Serafeim, G. (2014) "Corporate Social Responsibility and Access to Finance," *Strategic Management Journal* 35 (1): 1–23.

Conlin, J. (2008) "Eco-Tourism Moves Out of the Wilderness," *New York Times*, March 16, 7(L).

Corley, K. G., Harquail, C. V., Pratt, M. G., Glynn, M. A., Fiol, C. M., and Hatch, M. J. (2006) "Guiding Organizational Identity Through Aged Adolescence," *Journal of Management Inquiry* 15 (2): 85–99.

Davis, G. F. (2009) *Managed by the Markets: How Finance Re-Shaped America*. Oxford: Oxford University Press.

Eccles, R. G., Ioannou, I., and Serafeim, G. (2014) "The Impact of a Corporate Culture of Sustainability on Organizational Processes and Performance," *Management Science* (forthcoming).

Elkington, J. (1997) *Cannibals with Forks: The Triple Bottom Line of Twenty First Century Business*. Mankato, MN: Capstone.

Enz, C. A. and Siguaw, J. A. (1999) "Best Hotel Environmental Practices," *The Cornell Hotel and Restaurant Administration Quarterly* 40 (5): 72–5.

Gioia, D. A., Patvardhan, S. D., Hamilton, A. L., and Corley, K. G. (2013) "Organizational Identity Formation and Change," *The Academy of Management Annals* 7 (1): 123–92.

Glynn, M. A. (2000) "When Cymbals Become Symbols: Conflict Over Organizational Identity Within a Symphony Orchestra," *Organization Science* 11 (3): 285–98. Special Issue: Cultural Industries: Learning from Evolving Organizational Practices.

Glynn, M. A. (2008) "Beyond Constraint: How Institutions Enable Identities," in R. Greenwood, C. Oliver, K. Sahlin, and R. Suddaby (eds), *The Sage Handbook of Organizational Institutionalism*. Thousand Oaks, CA: Sage Publications, 413–30.

Glynn, M. A. and Abzug, R. (2002) "Institutionalizing Identity: Symbolic Isomorphism and Organizational Names," *Academy of Management Journal* 45 (1): 267–80.

Glynn, M. A. and Raffaelli, R. (2013) "Logic Pluralism, Organizational Design, and Practice Adoption: The Structural Embeddedness of CSR Programs." In Lounsbury, M. and Boxenbaum, E. (eds), *Institutional Logics in Action: Research in the Sociology of Organizations*. Bingley, UK: Emerald Publishing, 39B: 175–98.

Greenwood, R., Raynard, M., Kodeih, F., Micelotta, E. R., and Lounsbury, M. (2011) "Institutional Complexity and Organizational Responses," *Academy of Management Annals* 5: 317–71.

Guest Experience Manager. (2013) *The Element Hotel, Starwood Hotels and Resorts Worldwide*. Stamford, CT. Personal interview, September 6.

Haigh, N. and Hoffman, A. J. (2012) "Hybrid Organizations: The Next Chapter of Sustainable Business," *Organizational Dynamics* 41 (2): 126–34.

Hamilton, A. and Gioia, D. (2009) "Fostering Sustainability-Focused Organizational Identities," in L. M. Roberts and J. E. Dutton (eds), *Exploring Positive Identities and Organizations: Building a Theoretical and Research Foundation*. New York: Routledge, 435–60.

Hannan, M. T., Pólos, L., and Carroll, G. R. (2007) *Logics of Organization Theory: Audiences, Codes, and Ecologies*. Princeton, N.J.: Princeton University Press.

Hillman, A. J. and Keim, G. D. (2001) "Shareholder Value, Stakeholder Management, and Social Issues: What's the Bottom Line?," *Strategic Management Journal* 22 (2): 125–39.

HNN Newswire. (2008) "Starwood's Element gets Gold Certification," in *Hotel News Now*. Available at: <http://hotelnewsnow.com/Article/435/Starwoods-element-gets-gold-certification> (accessed July 2014).

HNN Newswire. (2013) "STR Releases Updated 2013, 2014 Forecasts," in *Hotel News Now*. Available at: <http://hotelnewsnow.com/Article/9764/STR-releases-updated-2013-2014-forecasts> (accessed July 2014).

Hoffman, A. J. (1999) "Institutional Evolution and Change: Environmentalism and the US Chemical Industry," *Academy of Management Journal* 42 (4): 351–71.

Hopps, S. (2012) *Green is in Our Roots*. Available at: <http://blog.greenpromotionalitems.com/featured-client-lenox-hotel-green-is-in-our-roots/> (accessed July 2014).

Houdré, H. (2008) *Sustainable Hospitality: Sustainable Development in the Hotel Industry*. Ithaca, NY: Cornell University, School of Hotel Administration, The Center for Hospitality Research.

Hsu, G. (2006) "Jacks of all Trades and Masters of None: Audiences' Reactions to Spanning Genres in Feature Film Production," *Administrative Science Quarterly* 51 (3): 420–50.

Hsu, G. and Hannan, M. T. (2005) "Identities, Genres, and Organizational Forms," *Organization Science* 16 (5): 474–90.

Hsu, G., Hannan, M. T., and Koçak, Ö. (2009) "Multiple Category Memberships in Markets: An Integrative Theory and Two Empirical Tests," *American Sociological Review* 74 (1): 150–69.

Ing, D. (1995) "Sustainable Tourism Charter Issued," *Hotel & Motel Management* 210 (10): 4.

Jameson, D. and Brownell, J. (2012) "Telling your Hotel's 'Green' Story: Developing an Effective Communication Strategy to Convey Environmental Values," *Cornell Hospitality Tools* (2): 1–20.

Kanter, R. M. (2009) *SuperCorp: How Vanguard Companies Create Innovation, Profits, Growth, and Social Good*. New York: Crown Business.

Leblebici, H., Salancik, G. R., Copay, A., and King, T. (1991) "Institutional Change and the Transformation of Interorganizational Fields: An Organizational History of the U.S. Radio Broadcasting Industry," *Administrative Science Quarterly* 36 (3): 333–63.

Lounsbury, M. and Glynn, M. A. (2001) "Cultural Entrepreneurship: Stories, Legitimacy, and the Acquisition of Resources," *Strategic Management Journal* 22 (6): 545.

Margolis, J. D. and Walsh, J. P. (2003) "Misery Loves Companies: Rethinking Social Initiatives by Business," *Administrative Science Quarterly* 48 (2): 268–305.

Margulis, J. (2010) "Northwest Hotels Go Eco-Plus," *New York Times*, October 13, 4(L).

Marquis, C., Glynn, M. A., and Davis, G. F. (2007) "Community Isomorphism and Corporate Social Action," *Academy of Management Review* 32 (3): 925–45.

Meyer, J. W. and Rowan, B. (1977) "Institutionalized Organizations: Formal Structure as Myth and Ceremony," *American Journal of Sociology* 83 (2): 340–63.

Navis, C. and Glynn, M. A. (2010) "How New Market Categories Emerge: Temporal Dynamics of Legitimacy, Identity, and Entrepreneurship in Satellite Radio, 1990–2005," *Administrative Science Quarterly* 55 (3): 439–71.

Navis, C. and Glynn, M. A. (2011) "Legitimate Distinctiveness and the Entrepreneurial Identity: Influence on Investor Judgments of New Venture Plausibility," *Academy of Management Review* 36 (3): 479–99.

O'Reilly III, C. A. and Tushman, M. L. (2008) "Ambidexterity as a Dynamic Capability: Resolving the Innovator's Dilemma," *Research in Organizational Behavior* 28: 185–206.

Raffaelli, R. (2013) *Identity and Institutional Change in a Mature Field: The Re-Emergence of the Swiss Watchmaking Industry, 1970–2008*. Chestnut Hill, MA: Boston College.

Raffaelli, R. and Glynn, M. A. (2014) "Turnkey or Tailored? Relational Pluralism, Institutional Complexity, and the Organizational Adoption of More or Less Customized Practices," *Academy of Management Journal* 57 (2): 541–62.

Raffaelli, R., Glynn, M. A., and Tushman, M. L. (2014) "Organizational Identity as a Strategic Resource: Building Dynamic Capabilities for Innovation," Harvard Business School Working Paper.

Ricaurte, E., Verma, R., and Withiam, G. (2012) "Hospitality Sustainability Reporting: Slow, Steady Progress," *Cornell Hospitality Proceedings* 4 (8): 1–22.

Rogers, E. M. (1962) *Diffusion of Innovations*. New York: Free Press.

Santos, F. M. and Eisenhardt, K. M. (2005) "Organizational Boundaries and Theories of Organization," *Organization Science* 16 (5): 491–508.

Schultz, M. and Hernes, T. (2013) "A Temporal Perspective on Organizational Identity," *Organization Science* 24 (1): 1–21.

Scott, W. R. (2001) *Institutions and Organizations: Ideas and Interests*. Thousand Oaks, CA: Sage Publications.

Starwood Hotels and Resorts Worldwide, Inc. (2008a) *Element Hotels: Find Your Own Space*. [Brochure]. Available at: <http://development.starwoodhotels.com/writable/resources/element_hotels.pdf> (accessed July 2014).

Starwood Hotels and Resorts Worldwide, Inc. (2008b) "Starwood Hotels' Element Brand to Mandate Leed Certification in All Hotels Brand-Wide" [Press Release]. Available at: <http://www.starwoodhotels.com/en_US/Media/Graphics/Microsites/Promotions/EL_LEED/ELM_PR_LEEDS.pdf> (accessed July 2014).

Supervisor, Element Hotel, Lexington, MA. (2013) Personal, September 6.

Sustainability Manager, Lenox Hotel, Boston, MA. (2013) Personal Interview, August 29.

Sustainability Officer, Lenox Hotel, Boston, MA. (2013) Personal Interview, August 29.

Thornton, P. H., Ocasio, W., and Lounsbury, M. (2012) *The Institutional Logics Perspective: A New Approach to Culture, Structure, and Process*. Oxford: Oxford University Press.

Tolbert, P. S. and Zucker, L. G. (1983) "Institutional Sources of Change in the Formal Structure of Organizations: The Diffusion of Civil Service Reform, 1880–1935," *Administrative Science Quarterly* 28 (1): 22–39.

Tripsas, M. (2009) "Technology, Identity, and Inertia Through the Lens of 'The Digital Photography Company'," *Organization Science* 20 (2): 441–60.

Utterback, J. M. (1971) "The Process of Technological Innovation Within the Firm," *Academy of Management Journal* 14 (1): 75–88.

Van Marrewijk, M. (2003) "Concepts and Definitions of CSR and Corporate Sustainability: Between Agency and Communion," *Journal of Business Ethics* 44 (2–3): 95–105.

Waddock, S. (2000) "The Multiple Bottom Lines of Corporate Citizenship: Social Investing, Reputation, and Responsibility Audits," *Business & Society Review* 105 (3): 323.

Waddock, S. (2004) "Creating Corporate Accountability: Foundational Principles to Make Corporate Citizenship Real," *Journal of Business Ethics* 50 (4): 313–27.

Waldron, T. L., Navis, C., and Fisher, G. (2013) "Explaining Differences in Firms' Responses to Activism," *Academy of Management Review*, 38 (3): 397–417.

Walsh, I. J. and Glynn, M. A. (2008) "The Way We Were: Legacy Organizational Identity and the Role of Leadership," *Corporate Reputation Review* 11 (3): 262–76.

Weick, K. E. (1979) *The Social Psychology of Organizing*. Reading, MA: Addison-Wesley.

Westphal, J. D., Gulati, R., and Shortell, S. M. (1997) "Customization or Conformity? An Institutional and Network Perspective on the Content and Consequences of TQM Adoption," *Administrative Science Quarterly* 42(2): 366–94.

Whetten, D. A. and Godfrey, P. C. (1998) *Identity in Organizations: Building Theory Through Conversations*, London: Sage Publications.

Whetten, D. A. and Mackey, A. (2002) "A Social Actor Conception of Organizational Identity and its Implications for the Study of Organizational Reputation," *Business & Society* 41 (4): 393–414.

White, M. (2007) "Enjoy Your Green Stay," *New York Times*, June 26, C6.

White, M. C. (2010) "Going Green, Gradually," *New York Times*, August 17, B5(L).

White, M. C. (2011) "A Stigma Lifts For Luxury Hotels," *New York Times*, August 29, B6(L).

Withiam, G. (2011) "The Challenge of Hotel and Restaurant Sustainability: Finding Profit in 'Being green'," *Cornell Hospitality Proceedings* 3 (2): 1–16.

Withiam, G. (2013) "Cornell Hospitality Research Summit 2012: Toward Sustainable Hotel and Restaurant Operations," *Cornell Hospitality Proceedings* 5 (4): 1–14.

World Commission on Environment and Development. (1987) *Our Common Future.* Oxford: Oxford University Press.

Zhang, J. J., Joglekar, N. R., and Verma, R. (2012) "Exploring Resource Efficiency Benchmarks for Environmental Sustainability in Hotels," *Cornell Hospitality Quarterly* 53 (3): 229–41.

Zissu, A. (2010) "The Dream Team," *New York Times*, March 28, 72(L).

Zucker, L. G. (1987) "Institutional Theories of Organization," *Annual Review of Sociology* 13: 443–64.

7 Two Tales of One City

Samsung, Daewoo, and Lessons on Large-Scale Transformation

Donald Sull

As the evidence of climate change has grown overwhelmingly, many senior executives have embraced sustainability as a strategic imperative.[1] For most of these companies, delivering on the promise of sustainability will require large-scale organizational change.[2] In a 2013 survey of nearly 200 global corporations, changing the company's core business operations to integrate sustainable practices was cited as the single greatest obstacle to sustainability.[3] The same survey revealed that only one-fifth of companies in the sample were close to fully integrating sustainable practices in their operations, with the rest in the midst of transformation, or just getting started.

For decades, scholars have studied why existing organizations struggle to adapt to environmental shifts including globalization, increased competition on quality, and disruptive technology. A vast body of research has pinpointed several discrete obstacles to corporate change. These impediments include the tendency of core capabilities to harden into core rigidities;[4] the difficulty of reversing investments in specialized resources;[5] constraints imposed by institutions outside the boundaries of the firm; cognitive frames that lock organizations into an historical worldview;[6] the correspondence between a firm's organization and product architecture;[7] and high levels of past performance.[8] Other scholars have taken a more holistic view and shown how an organization's constellation of interrelated practices, resources, and values (for example, deep structure, archetype, quantum organization) impede change.[9]

Given the myriad obstacles, some scholars have concluded that organizational change is virtually impossible and that environmental selection rather than

---

[1] Kiron et al. (2012): 69–74.   [2] Dunphy et al. (2003).
[3] BSR (2013).   [4] Leonard-Barton (1992): 111–25.
[5] Tripsas (1997): 119; Ghemawat (2002): 37–74.
[6] Tripsas and Gavetti (2000): 1147–61; Benner and Tripsas (2012): 277–302.
[7] Henderson and Clark (1990): 9–30.
[8] Milliken and Lant (1991): 129–56 and Greve (1998): 58–86.
[9] Scholars use different terms to describe an organization's bundle of interdependent activities, resources, and values, including "quantum organization," see Miller and Friesen (1984); "deep structure," see Tushman and Romanelli (1985): 171–222 and Gersick (1991): 10–36; "archetypes," see Greenwood and Hinings (1993): 1052–81; and "institution," see Meyer and Rowan (1977): 340–63.

internal transformation explains how populations of organizations change over time.[10] Despite the well-documented impediments, however, some established enterprises *have* successfully transformed themselves. Well-known examples include Apple, IBM, Disney, and Lego. A growing body of research documents how change emerges from agency by individual agents,[11] institutional entrepreneurship,[12] and reorganization of the formal organization.[13]

Transformation in the face of daunting obstacles raises several questions for leaders attempting to embed sustainability in their organizations. How can leaders frame the change process in a way that acknowledges barriers to change while admitting the possibility of effective action? What concrete steps can they take to successfully lead a large-scale transformation? In particular, what role should top leaders play? To address these practical questions, this chapter introduces a framework that builds on and extends the existing literature on organizational inertia and change.

The model's key construct is managerial commitments—such as investments in specialized resources, relationships with stakeholders, and choice of cognitive frames—that channel an organization's future trajectory. Commitments represent a powerful tool, which helps managers to achieve desired results, but also constrains behavior in the future. Commitments are a double-edged sword, which both empower leaders and limit their ability to adapt. This chapter will use the lens of managerial commitments to examine how early decisions define an organization, how these commitments can harden over time, and how some leaders remake their organizations' bundle of commitments to break free of inertia.

A comparative case study of Samsung and Daewoo—two Korean *chaebol* that initiated similar change initiatives with very different results—will illustrate the model.[14] By way of background, these two *chaebol* (family-controlled confederations of diverse operating businesses) evolved over parallel histories and forged similar sets of commitments. Samsung and Daewoo both relied on close relationships with the government for funding and protection in the Korean market. In their early years, both groups focused on achieving scale through low prices, rather than quality or innovation.

As recently as 1993, Samsung and Daewoo were comparable along key dimensions. Of Samsung's 18 major lines of business, 14 overlapped with Daewoo's portfolio companies, including construction, shipbuilding, telecommunication devices, consumer electronics, and display devices. When the results of their major businesses were consolidated, the two groups were comparable in terms of assets ($26 billion for Samsung, $25 billion for

---

[10] Hannan and Freeman (1989); Hannan et al. (2007).
[11] Battilana et al. (2009); Kellogg (2009): 657–711; Beer et al. (2011); Battilana and Casciaro (2012): 381–98, 819–36.
[12] Greenwood and Hinings (1996): 1022–54; Greenwood and Suddaby (2006): 27–48; Hinings (2010): 659–75.
[13] Gulati and Puranam (2009): 422–40.
[14] The comparative case study in this chapter draws extensively on Sull et al. (2004).

Daewoo), book equity ($7 billion for both groups), and profitability ($345 million for Samsung and $289 million for Daewoo).

The chairmen of both groups launched ambitious attempts to transform their organizations within a few months of one another. In March 1993, Daewoo chairman Woo-Choong Kim launched the group's "Global Management Initiative," which set out the group's aggressive plan to expand abroad. In June of that year, Chairman Kun Hee Lee unveiled his vision of "New Management" in a meeting of Samsung's top executives in Frankfurt, Germany. Both leaders articulated a vision for transforming their respective groups to global leadership. Over the following years, both groups aggressively implemented their change initiatives.

Despite the similar beginnings, the Daewoo and Samsung stories had very different endings. Daewoo did expand globally, but did so without transforming the bundle of commitments that had enabled its historical success. Daewoo accumulated massive operating losses, which it covered with short- and long-term debt. By 1998, Daewoo's interest burden was twice its operating profits, and the next year the group was declared insolvent, creditors dismantled the conglomerate, and the chairman fled the country to avoid arrest.[15]

As the Daewoo empire collapsed, Samsung's flagship electronics business was emerging as an unequivocal global leader. By 2003, the Samsung brand was among the 25 most valuable brands in the world (ahead of Dell and Nike). Samsung Electronics was at the cutting edge of such leading technologies as flat panel displays, semiconductors, and cellular phones, and was fourth among all companies in the world in patents granted in the US. The combined revenues of the Samsung Group's affiliated companies exceeded $100 billion, and the group's listed subsidiaries accounted for over one-quarter of the total market capitalization of the Seoul stock exchange.

An analysis based on two observations cannot, of course, test the validity of the managerial commitment model against alternative explanations, and that is not the aim of this chapter. Rather, the comparative case provides a basis to elucidate the commitment framework and explore the differences between the two *chaebol* that help to explain their differential outcomes. This chapter will focus in particular on how top leaders can drive large-scale transformation. A long-standing debate in organizational studies questions the extent to which top executives shape organizational outcomes, and if they do whether their impact is positive or negative.[16] This chapter builds on recent research that argues top executives can play an important and positive role in driving large-scale organizational change.[17] The chapter compares how the leaders of Daewoo and Samsung attempted to reshape their organization's commitments, and derives six lessons on large-scale transformation that this comparative case study illustrates.

---

[15] For a discussion in more detail, see Ihlwan (2001) and Kraar (2003).

[16] Pfeffer (1981): 1–52; Finkelstein and Hambrick (1996): chs 1 and 2; Chatterjee and Hambrick (2007): 351–86; Eggers and Kaplan (2009): 461–77.

[17] Smith and Tushman (2005): 522–36.

While this chapter focuses on a specific context—the globalization of Korean *chaebol*—the lens of managerial commitments can provide a more general framework for executives trying to understand the obstacles to sustainability in their own organization. The lessons on successful large-scale change, moreover, provide guidance for leaders trying to translate the promise of sustainability into reality.

Managerial commitments and initial success at Daewoo and Samsung

The starting point of this analysis is a "managerial commitment," defined as any action that an entrepreneur or manager takes in the present that binds her organization to specific behaviors in the future.[18] Not all managerial actions qualify as commitments. A CEO's decision to build a war chest of cash, for instance, is not binding because it does not commit the business to a particular course of action—the cash remains available for any kind of investment. If, in contrast, the cash had gone towards erecting a specialized factory or building a brand, the company would have been making a commitment. An action becomes a commitment, in other words, if it restricts a company's future options in a way that would be costly to reverse.

Commitments are often associated with "big bets," such as infrequent and lumpy investments in specialized assets, such as factories or airplanes, which are difficult to reverse or redeploy to other uses.[19] The construct of managerial commitments also includes incremental decisions that cumulatively bind an organization to a course of action. Managerial commitments, as I use the term, entail actions such as public statements, personnel decisions, and forging relationships with resource providers extending beyond financial investments and disinvestments.

Of all the actions managers can take, commitments that fall into five categories—strategic frames, processes, resources, relationships, and values—are particularly likely set an organization on a future trajectory. Strategic frames are the shared cognitive models that help organization members interpret new data, measure success, and define how to compete. Processes are the recurrent procedures used to get work done, including both informal and formal routines. Resources refer to tangible and intangible assets that create economic value, such as brand, technology, real estate, expertise, etc. Relationships are the enduring associations forged with external individuals and organizations, including customers, regulators, suppliers, distributors,

---

[18] The notion of commitments as a mechanism of binding future action, is based on the construct of "pre-commitment" defined in Elster (1979): 36–111.

[19] Ghemawat (2001).

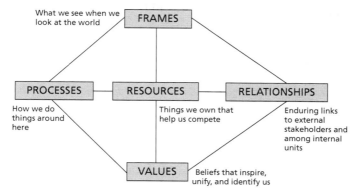

Figure 7.1. Five categories of managerial commitments

and other partners, who contribute to an organization's success. Values are the shared norms that inspire and unify employees and constitute the core of its corporate culture. (Figure 7.1 summarizes these commitments.)

These managerial commitments are particularly binding in the early years of an organization, when they imprint a way of operating on the fledgling organization.[20]

A set of distinct and strong commitments confers several advantages early in the organizational lifecycle. Clear strategic frames, for example, focus employees on what matters most and minimize distractions on peripheral concerns. Committing to a specific processes confers efficiency, enables cumulative learning, and greater consistency. By committing to long-term relationships with customers, distributors, investors, or suppliers, managers can induce firm-specific investment and attract resources required for future success. Daewoo and Samsung, as we will see later, forged a similar set of commitments that served both *chaebol* well for decades.

The founding of Daewoo illustrates how early managerial commitments imprint an organization and set it on a future trajectory. Woo-Choong Kim founded Daewoo Industrial in 1967 with only five employees, but had great aspirations for his enterprise from the start. The name Daewoo means "great universe" in Korean. Within 15 years of its founding, Daewoo had fulfilled its founder's grand ambitions. By the early 1980s, Daewoo had emerged as one of the four largest *chaebol* measured by assets and revenues. Samsung and Daewoo—as the second- and third-largest *chaebol*, respectively—were frequently compared to one another by the business press and government agencies such as Korea's Fair Trade Commission.

---

[20] Philip Selznick uses the term "character-defining commitment" to describe decisions that affect a company's capacity to control its future behavior. See Selznick (1957), 35 and 55. Although Selznick's treatment is very brief, he seems to imply that these commitments can occur at any stage in an organization's existence (p. 35) and that they refer primarily to decisions on values (p. 55). See also the literature on organizational identity (Albert and Whetten, 1985, and Gioia et al., 2000: 63–81).

Daewoo's dramatic rise began in 1970, when Kim—through sheer persistence—convinced major US retailers, including Sears, J. C. Penney, and Montgomery Ward, to purchase low-quality, but inexpensive textiles from his firm. While calling on his new American customers, Kim learned that the US government was planning to establish a quota for textile imports and would likely set percentage allocations for foreign suppliers based on their recent market shares. Kim bet all of Daewoo's limited resources on an effort to increase its share of US textile imports, sacrificing product quality and profits in his quest for volume. When quotas were set in 1972, Daewoo was allocated nearly one-third of South Korea's share. This quota, maintained by the Korean government, provided a steady cash flow to fund future growth. Daewoo's success as an exporter also qualified it for subsidized financing, bank loans, and permits for capacity expansion from the South Korean government.

In these early years, Kim established the key commitments that defined the group. In terms of strategic frames, Daewoo emphasized quantity over quality and measured success in terms of market share growth, rather than profitability. Consistent with this strategy, Daewoo avoided investments in brand, technology, or other specialized resources that might have increased customers' willingness to pay. When developing new products, the group relied on a process of backward engineering products produced by Japanese, American, or European companies. And Kim's personal values—relentless perseverance and fearless risk taking—permeated Daewoo's corporate culture.

Commitments to relationships with Korean government officials helped Daewoo to secure cheap funds, export quotas, and protection from competitors in its domestic market. Kim benefited in this regard from his personal ties with South Korea's ruler, General Chung Hee Park, who had been a student of Kim's father. In addition to his personal relationship with General Park, Kim forged close ties with the government by hiring former government officials and state bankers as executives. He also hired heavily from Kyunggi High School and Seoul National University, which had historically produced most of Korea's government officials. In the late 1980s, for example, 13 of South Korea's 17 governmental ministers were graduates of Seoul National University, and 7 were alumni of Kyunggi High School.

Kim's close relationship with the Korean government paid handsome dividends. General Park's government provided Daewoo with loans at 6–9 percent annual interest during a period when inflation ranged between 8 percent and 42 percent annually and private banks (which were, along with government-controlled banks, major sources of financial resources for Korean firms) charged interest rates exceeding 40 percent for corporate borrowers. Kim used the profits from textile exports and access to subsidized capital to expand rapidly during the 1970s through acquisitions.

Throughout the 1970s and 1980s, Kim fortified Daewoo's commitments. In exchange for favorable subsidies and permits from Park, Daewoo invested in industries the government targeted for growth in its five-year plans for economic development, including heavy machinery, shipbuilding, chemicals, automotive parts, and consumer electronics. Daewoo expanded aggressively in each industry, competing through high-volume production, rather than leadership in brand, quality, or technology. General Park provided Kim with access to potential acquisition candidates and, in some cases, urged Daewoo to acquire ailing companies over Kim's objections. Success was measured in terms of revenue growth, not profits.

During the 1980s, Daewoo's success began to attract attention in Korea and abroad. During the mid-1980s, Kim won a Global Business Award from the International Chamber of Commerce, received an honorary doctorate from two prestigious Korean universities, and was listed as one of the 50 most fascinating global business leaders by *Fortune* magazine. In 1989, Kim published *Every Street is Paved with Gold*, a book that codified Daewoo's commitments and advised other managers to follow a similar path.[21] Sales of Kim's book surpassed the 1 million mark in record time, earning the book a place in Korea's *Guinness Book of Records* for the shortest time to sell a million copies. Two years later, Kim donated the royalties from his book sales to construct a building bearing his name at the College of Business and Economics of Yonsei University, from which he had graduated.

Samsung's origins were, in many respects, remarkably similar to Daewoo's. Lee Byung Chull founded Samsung in 1938 to export dried fish and produce to China. When North Korean troops invaded in 1950, Lee was forced to abandon his operations in Seoul for the duration of the war. After the war ended in 1953, Lee rebuilt his company virtually from scratch and by 1959, Samsung had emerged as one of the largest business groups in South Korea. When General Park came to power in 1961, he charged Lee and 10 other prominent businessmen with treason for allegedly bribing officials in the preceding administration—a charge that carried the death penalty.

Lee escaped execution, however, by winning an audience with Park and convincing him that Samsung and the other *chaebol* could help rebuild Korea's economy. Along with Daewoo's Kim and a dozen other prominent executives, Lee cofounded the Federation of Korean Industries in 1961 and served as its first chairman. The federation members worked closely with government officials to develop the country's five-year economic plans. Lee and the chairmen of the other leading *chaebol*, in turn, followed the government's lead in their strategic planning. In 1967, Samsung introduced its first "five-year management plan," which targeted the same industries supported by the government's economic planners.

Like Daewoo, Samsung grew rapidly throughout the following decades. The group entered a variety of unrelated businesses including advertising, resorts, shipbuilding, life insurance, and petrochemicals. Samsung executives focused throughout this period on revenue growth, rather than profits. This focus on size made sense, since larger *chaebol* (as measured by revenues and assets)

---

[21] Woo-Choong (1992).

were more likely to receive government support for subsequent expansion, and government-subsidized financing reduced the need to generate operating cash flow to fund investments and acquisitions.

Employees often referred to the groups' shared set of values as "the Samsung spirit." Chairman Lee believed that Samsung existed to help Korea recover after the war. Well into the 1960s, Lee attended the final round of interviews for all candidates for managerial positions to determine whether they shared the values of helping Korea recover. Lee also emphasized an ethic of persevering against all odds and often rallied employees with the phrase "the only way is forward," a value that echoed Kim's emphasis on persistence against all odds.

Active inertia at Daewoo and Samsung

Managerial commitments can confer many advantages, as the Daewoo and Samsung examples illustrate. They also limit an organization's ability to adapt to shifts in the environment. When organizations face new circumstances, such as a disruptive technology in their core market or global climate change, existing commitments tend to channel their response into historical grooves for several reasons. Commitments, by their very nature, enable some behaviors by constraining or precluding others. Employees and managers are familiar with existing ways of doing things, which increases the odds they will resist change. To the extent historical commitments continue to work, employees will be reluctant to fix a system that is not viewed as broken, especially if the alternative is unclear or risky. Established commitments continue to confer efficiency and the legitimacy of conforming to historical industry norms. The interdependency among component commitments renders piecemeal change difficult and systemic transformation daunting. Finally, executives are reluctant to reverse historical commitments to the extent that such reversals might be construed as an admission that they were wrong in the past.

Rather than re-examine and transform their organization's bundle of commitments in response to new realities, executives often fall prey to active inertia, the tendency of firms to respond to different market conditions by persisting in, or even accelerating, activities that worked in the past.[22] Inertia is often equated with delayed or half-hearted changes. Companies suffering from active inertia, however, often respond quickly and vigorously to new circumstances, unleashing a flurry of initiatives. Their frenetic activity is not adaptive, however, because it is constrained by hardened commitments that are no longer appropriate to the market conditions.

---

[22] Sull (2005).

Korea's *chaebol* faced a set of major changes in 1979. General Park was assassinated that year, and his death set in motion a series of major shifts in the political and regulatory climate that threatened their position in Korea. Subsequent governments opened South Korea's product and capital markets to the outside world and withdrew much of the support for the *chaebol*. It soon became clear that two decades of heavy investment by the leading *chaebol* had resulted in significant overcapacity in many domestic industries. At the same time, the *chaebol* found themselves caught in a competitive vise. Chinese exporters were undercutting them on price, while Japanese firms leveraged brand strength and technological superiority to win share in high-end markets. As market conditions changed around them, both Daewoo and Samsung initially fell prey to active inertia.

Daewoo executives saw these market shifts—the developments were impossible to miss—but responded by accelerating actions consistent with their historical commitments. The group chose to globalize, but did so in a way consistent with how it had competed in South Korea. In March 1993, chairman Kim launched Daewoo's "Global Management Initiative," which set out the group's aggressive plan to expand abroad. In selecting which markets to enter, Kim sought countries with limited domestic production and relatively unsophisticated demand in terms of product quality and technology. Kim continued to believe that Daewoo could grow by targeting countries, like Korea in earlier decades, which did not value high-quality products. Kim observed:

It is not true that only those firms having globally first-class products will survive in global markets. America and Europe are not the only markets. In fact, there are a lot of countries in the world where firms can dominate the markets with products of less technical sophistication. With Daewoo's current level of technology, we can make at least 70% of the products that are globally traded.[23]

Daewoo did not completely ignore the importance of quality. The *chaebol* launched a series of initiatives that yielded impressive initial results. Defect rates at Daewoo Shipbuilding, for example, dropped by 80 percent in the first two years of the program. The group-level program ended two years later, before the initiatives were embedded more widely throughout the organization. In August 1993, Kim announced a plan to achieve world-class product technology by building a group-level research center and employing over 600 Ph.D.s by 1995 and 2,000 by the year 2000. Daewoo did build an Institute for Advanced Engineering in 1995, but never employed more than 200 researchers with Ph.D.s. Samsung Electronics, in contrast, had 598 researchers with doctoral degrees, LG Group had 536, and Hyundai Group had 356 in their respective research institutes.[24]

---

[23] Choi and Park (1997) (in Korean).   [24] Korea Industrial Technology Association.

Kim and his management team prioritized markets, including Vietnam, China, India, Poland, Romania, the Sudan, and Kazakhstan, in which the government played an active role in economic policy, much as Korea's military leaders had in earlier decades.[25] Kim personally participated in negotiations with government officials in every country Daewoo entered. In Uzbekistan, for example, Daewoo agreed in 1993 to build a green-field automobile factory and export half its production. The Uzbekistan government, in exchange, provided a free factory site, eliminated tariffs on manufacturing equipment, invested in necessary infrastructure, guaranteed Daewoo's loans, and imposed tariffs on imported automobiles. The close relationship between Daewoo and the government caused some commentators to joke that the country should be renamed "Daewooistan."[26] Critics argued that Daewoo's global management constituted "a global diffusion of an undesirable tradition of Korea, the cozy relationship between business and government."[27]

As he had in the past, Kim continued to set aggressive growth targets as part of Daewoo's global management initiative and measure success in terms of number of operations and sales growth, rather than profit. The total number of global "networks" was planned to grow from 175 in 1993 to 650 by the year 2000. (Global networks referred to all branch offices, research institutes, and construction sites, as well as foreign subsidiaries.)[28] Daewoo planned to expand the number of countries in which the group operated from 70 in 1993 to approximately 150 by 2000. Kim also set the goal of increasing the group's revenues from 26 trillion won (including foreign subsidiaries' 6 trillion won of revenues) in 1993 to 138 trillion won (including 57 trillion won of foreign subsidiaries) by 2000.

Kim continued to rely on debt to fund growth. Daewoo borrowed as much as $47 billion to fund the investments, in many cases securing loans from governments in the countries where they established operations. But while local governments could guarantee loans, they couldn't guarantee consumer demand for Daewoo's products. By the mid-1990s, several of Daewoo's operations were running well below capacity. In the wake of the IMF bailout of South Korea in 1997, Daewoo, like the other *chaebol*, faced a sharp increase in interest rates and the cost of servicing dollar-denominated debt.

In the wake of Korea's economic crisis, Kim resisted calls to decrease the Daewoo debt by selling off assets. Rather, he viewed the financial crisis as an opportunity to acquire distressed companies, including Hankook Electric Glass and Ssangyong Motors, both of which faced bankruptcy. Daewoo also increased its foreign direct investment during the crisis. Domestic banks were reluctant to lend to fuel Daewoo's expansion. As a result, Daewoo's affiliate companies turned to global capital markets, issuing corporate bonds and short-term commercial paper to fund its expansion. Daewoo's interest

---

[25] Choi and Park (1997) (in Korean).   [26] Schuman and Lee (1999).   [27] (1999).
[28] The number of global networks exceeded the number of affiliates because each affiliate could have multiple subsidiaries, foreign subsidiaries, and so on.

expenses increased from 3 trillion won in 1997 to 6 trillion won in 1998, nearly double its 1998 operating income of 3 trillion won; by June 1999, the group was insolvent.

Chairman Kim cannot be accused of inaction. He saw the changes impacting Daewoo in the Korean market and initiated a large-scale change initiative to compete in global markets. Unfortunately, his actions to take Daewoo global were channeled by the group's existing commitments into well-worn grooves. As the group expanded abroad, Daewoo forged relationships with government officials in the host countries; pursued a strategy of low-quality, low-price products; measured success in terms of revenue growth; failed to invest in the resources, such as technology or brand, that would have increased customers' willingness to pay; continued to diversify; and valued risk taking and persistence above all else. While these commitments had served Daewoo well for decades in Korea, they were poorly suited to the new situation.

Samsung faced the same market changes that Daewoo did. When Samsung founder Lee Byung Chull died in 1987, his third-born son, Lee Kun Hee, succeeded him as chairman. The 45-year-old (hereafter referred to as Lee) had studied business at Japan's Waseda University and received his MBA from George Washington University in Washington, D.C. Four months after succeeding his father as chairman, Lee declared Samsung's "Second Foundation," a sweeping change initiative intended to transform the group into a global leader. Lee pledged to restructure Samsung's portfolio to focus exclusively on businesses capable of producing world-class products by the twenty-first century. In 1991, Lee announced that Samsung would divest its profitable department store and paper businesses because they could not compete globally.

Lee publicly committed to establishing Samsung as one of the world's top five electronics firms. To gain scale in that sector, Lee merged Samsung's electronic, semiconductor, and telecommunications affiliates to create Samsung Electronics in November 1988. Samsung also sharply increased spending in electronics research and development and opened the group's Advanced Technology Research Center. In 1992, Lee announced Samsung's intention to produce automobiles within six years. Lee viewed automobiles as a logical extension of the group's focus on electronics and noted that electrical and electronic parts were forecast to constitute 60–70 percent of a car's total value by 2010.

In 1993, it appeared that Samsung, like Daewoo, might fall prey to active inertia. In the early 1990s, Lee grew increasingly worried that Samsung was not making the fundamental changes required to compete in global markets. In an essay distributed to all employees, Lee later recalled:

I had emphasized the necessity of change and innovation since my inauguration. Although some years had passed, nothing had changed. The inertia of the 50 long years of Samsung history was too hard to break. I often felt cold chills from my premonition of crisis, suffered from insomnia, and lost 25 pounds between the summer and winter of 1992. I felt that the entire Samsung Group—not just a few affiliates—would disappear if nothing changed.[29]

Lessons from Samsung's transformation

The Daewoo story is a cautionary tale of active inertia. Chairman Kim attempted to transform the group he founded by expanding the activities that had worked in the past without critically examining the commitments that had contributed to Daewoo's historical success. In the end, Kim's inability or unwillingness to change the commitments that enabled Daewoo's historical success undid the group. Samsung too, initially struggled to adapt to changing market circumstances. A visitor to Korea in 1993 might very well have predicted that Samsung would follow the same trajectory as Daewoo. But Samsung broke free of active inertia, despite sharing a similar history, set of commitments, and institutional context with Daewoo.

To successfully transform their organizations, leaders must evaluate whether the set of interwoven commitments that enabled their historical success will work in the future. If the answer is no, they should actively unpick historical commitments hindering adaptation, reinforce those commitments essential to future success, and make new commitments when necessary. Here is where the similarities between the two *chaebol* end.

The impetus to transform an organization's existing commitments can come from several sources. Transformation can be imposed by powerful external stakeholders such as governments or institutional investors who insist on change, or spread through an organization's informal networks in a manner akin to a social movement. In the case of Samsung and Daewoo, the change was driven top-down by the chairmen of the two groups, and the remainder of this chapter will focus on their respective roles in leading fundamental transformation of their organizations' historical commitments and discussing the implications for leaders attempting to embed sustainability in their organizations.

INSIDE-OUTSIDER LEADER AT THE TOP

The selection of which type of executive is best suited to lead large-scale transformation is often framed as a choice between elevating an insider and bringing in someone from outside. Insiders have the benefit of understanding an organization's historical commitments and first-hand knowledge of which commitments are retarding progress, which remain critical to future success, and which new commitments are necessary. Insiders also have deep

---

[29] Hee (1997) (in Korean).

experience with leaders throughout the organization, and can assess their commitment to the new direction and their appetite for change. Finally, they have credibility with employees and managers, which can help them to implement change. Outsiders, in contrast, bring a fresh perspective and freedom from historical commitments.

The insider/outsider dichotomy masks a subtle but important distinction between leaders that helps us to understand the different fates of Daewoo and Samsung. Both Kim and Lee were insiders in the sense that both spent their entire careers in the same organization. But they varied in their personal relationship to the organization's historical commitments. As the founder, Kim had personally made many of the commitments that defined Daewoo's business model, while Lee had inherited Samsung's commitments from his father. Kim had spent his entire business career in Korea, in contrast to Lee, who had studied in Japan and the US before returning to Seoul.

Lee's background qualifies him as an "inside-outsider," which I define as an executive who combines a deep familiarity with an organization's commitments with sufficient distance to evaluate them critically.[30] Lee grew up in the business, but because he had not personally made the decisions that defined the group and had extensive experience outside the Korean business environment, he was better positioned to understand both the advantages and limitations of the group's commitments. Wed to the historical choices that he had made and lacking a clear view of alternatives, Kim found it much harder to transform Daewoo's commitments.

Inside-outsiders have led some of the most successful transformations over the past few decades, including at General Electric, Asahi Breweries, and Apple. Leaders can gain intimate knowledge of an organization's commitments while retaining critical distance in a number of ways. They can, like Jack Welch, who ran General Electric's plastics business, rise through an organization outside its traditional core businesses. The combination of profit-and-loss responsibility with distance from headquarters creates fertile conditions for experimenting with alternative sets of commitments. A company's international division breeds inside-outsiders and tests leaders' ability to adapt to unfamiliar market conditions. International postings can expose managers to the world's best competitors before they hit the home market.

Inside-outsiders can be drawn from a company's lead bank. Hirotaro Higuchi joined Asahi Breweries from Sumitomo, the brewer's lead bank. Corporate bankers often combine in-depth understanding of the company's business with a banker's disciplined perspective. Sometimes managers who leave a company and return later can serve as inside-outsiders. As a cofounder, Steve Jobs knows Apple intimately; however, his time away from the company allowed him to gain perspective before returning to turn it around. All these

---

[30] Sull (2005), ch. 6.

paths to top leadership share a common feature—they provide familiarity with key commitments with critical distance.

To drive change, an organization's board of directors can actively seek out inside-outsiders committed to sustainability, and promote them to senior executive positions. Directors can, for example, look to business units outside the company's traditional core for middle managers who have pushed sustainability in their businesses or been active in environmental non-profits such as the Environmental Defense Fund or the Nature Conservancy. Another source of inside-outsiders is long-term employees who have worked in countries, such as Sweden, Switzerland, and Denmark, which rank highly in terms of sustainability.[31]

DEVELOP A COHORT OF LEADERS IN KEY POSITIONS TO SUPPORT THE TRANSFORMATION

Just because the impetus for change comes from the top does not mean that top leaders accomplish the transformation single-handedly. Instead, it is crucial for top leaders to build a cohort of leaders in key positions throughout the organization to help drive change at all levels in the organization.

Lee was disappointed by the results of his initial attempt at transformation, the "New Foundation" initiative launched in 1987. In 1990, Lee discharged So Beung-Hae, who had served as his father's closest advisor for 17 years, and replaced him with an executive noted for his participatory management style and willingness to experiment with new approaches. Lee also promoted a large number of young managers (68 in 1990, 82 in 1991, and 101 in 1992) to executive positions, bypassing the traditional approach of promotions based strictly on seniority within the firm. The number significantly exceeded the rate of promotions when Lee's father was chairman, which averaged about 40 executives per year. The most striking difference, however, was not the number of promotions but Lee's insistence that advancement be based on managers' willingness to challenge current practices and their personal commitment to competing globally.

Lee continued to promote promising young managers, who shared a commitment to transforming Samsung, over the heads of more senior colleagues. In November 1993, Samsung announced major changes in the composition of the top executives at the group and major affiliates. Five of Samsung's presidents and four vice presidents were relieved of operational authority and placed in advisory positions. In that same year, 136 managers were promoted ahead of more senior executives, and 129 young managers were newly promoted to executive positions. The promotion was the largest in a single year since the beginning of the group. Samsung employees were surprised by the personnel decisions, particularly by the loss of authority among well-respected

---

[31] Robeco (2013).

executives who had contributed to the group's success in the past. Daewoo, in contrast, continued to promote managers based primarily on their seniority.

To embed sustainability throughout an organization, it is critical for the board and top team to ensure that leaders in critical positions are committed to the company's agenda and values. The impetus and strategy for change can emerge from the top, but cannot succeed unless a cohort of like-minded executives translates the aspiration into reality on the ground.

MOVE BEYOND ABSTRACTIONS TO VISCERAL UNDERSTANDING OF WHAT VISION MEANS

Research on organizational change emphasizes the importance of a compelling vision or "picture of the future that is relatively easy to communicate and appeals to customers, stockholders, and employees."[32] Vision alone, however, does not account for the differential outcomes at Samsung and Daewoo. Lee announced Samsung's "New Management," his vision for globalization, within a few months of Kim's launch of Daewoo's "Global Management Initiative." Both chairmen laid out clear and compelling aspirations for their groups to compete on the global stage.

Visions fail to galvanize transformation, in part, because they never move beyond abstract aspirations, such as "globalization," "excellence," "innovation," or "sustainability." Many Korean executives agreed with the importance of globalization in theory, but their worldview remained intensely local. Their mindset was captured by the route maps found in the in-flight magazine of Korean Air, which showed Seoul as the center of the globe with routes extending outward in all directions. The problem, of course, was that only a small fraction of the planet's population saw the world the same way.

To motivate and guide action, a vision must move beyond the abstract and resonate for leaders at a visceral level. An intuitive understanding of the gap between where a company is and where it wants to be provides the motivation for change. A visceral understanding of what global (or innovative or sustainable) looks like in practice informs leaders' judgment in prioritizing activities and allocating resources to make progress in achieving the vision. Finally, a gut-level understanding of what the aspiration would mean concretely helps managers to communicate what the company is trying to achieve, and why it matters.

Lee had a deeply ingrained understanding of global markets and competition, based on his personal experience of studying in Japan and the US, travelling widely, and managing Samsung's entry into the intensely global semiconductor industry. Kim, in contrast, had studied and spent the vast majority of his professional career in Korea. When Lee talked about the importance of globalization, he spoke from a deep well of experience and

---

[32] Kotter (1995): 63.

personal conviction. For Kim, in contrast, globalization remained an abstraction divorced from his own experience.

For a transformation to gain traction, it is not sufficient that a few leaders at the top possess a visceral understanding of the company's overarching vision. It is equally important that the middle managers charged with translating that vision into reality share a similar assessment of the situation. Lee wanted to ensure that his key leaders shared his visceral understanding of what global competition entailed, and the gap between Samsung and global leaders. He orchestrated a series of meetings that provided middle managers with first-hand experience of what customers outside of Korea expected, and what the best global rivals had to offer.

In early 1993, Lee convened a meeting of 23 senior executives of Samsung Electronics in Los Angeles, their first meeting outside of Seoul. Before the meeting began, Lee took the managers to visit local electronics retailers, where they were dismayed to find their products stacked in corners gathering dust, while market leaders like Sony enjoyed prominent position and commanded a price premium. Dismayed by the disparity between their self-image and how American consumers perceived their products, the Samsung executives realized, based on first-hand experience, the gap between their products and the world's best in terms of quality, technology, and brand. In the next seven months, Lee arranged similar meetings for Samsung's top 1,800 executives in Japan, Europe, and the US so they too could see Samsung as others saw them. The visits to foreign electronics retailers helped jolt Samsung executives out of their parochial mindset, and instilled a deep global perspective throughout the ranks.

New metrics can also reinforce a visceral understanding of what a company's vision really means. At Samsung, Lee insisted that managers stop benchmarking their division's performance against other South Korean companies like Daewoo and Hyundai. Instead, performance was measured against the world's best performers in each segment. To deepen managers' understanding of what it took to compete globally, Lee not only shifted who was benchmarked, but also what metrics would measure success. To emphasize the innovation and quality necessary to compete against the world's best players, the metrics used to evaluate Samsung managers were shifted from unit volumes and sales growth, to proxies for innovation (for example, percentage of revenues from new products, patents applications filed, patents granted) and product quality (for example, defect rates, product recall rates).

Gaining a visceral understanding of what global (or sustainable) means in practice generally represents a rude awakening to local leaders. They must grapple with the magnitude of the gap between where they are and where they aspire to be. They must also acknowledge the scope of activities necessary to close that gap. In going global, for example, Samsung needs to be competitive not only in product markets, but also in markets for assets, talent, capital, technology, and raw materials, and across a range of competencies including operations, governance, post-merger integration, and information technology.

How can leaders move beyond abstractions to instill a visceral understanding of what sustainability means for leaders throughout their organization? One approach might be to visit firms at the leading edge of sustainability globally, much as manufacturing firms visit Toyota to see what lean manufacturing entails. Companies like Novo Nordisk in Healthcare, Natura in cosmetics, and Statoil in energy exemplify best practices in sustainability in very different industries.[33]

LINK VISION TO DRIVERS OF ECONOMIC VALUE CREATION

Transformation attempts are often framed in terms of visions that are appealing and exciting. Unless these visions are linked to the drivers of economic value creation, however, they are unlikely to be sustained, at least in for-profit companies. Chairman Kim's strategy for globalization had, at best, a tenuous link to economic value creation. Daewoo sacrificed profits for volume, while failing to capture potential economies of scale because production, marketing, and distribution were fragmented globally. Measuring success in terms of unit and revenue growth, rather than cash-flow generation, masked the group's value destruction, which was funded by short- and long-term debt. Kim's vision was truly global—within a few years Daewoo had operations in more than a dozen countries around the world—but it was unmoored from value creation.

Forging a clear linkage between the transformational vision and the drivers of value creation is critical for three reasons. First, a hard-nosed focus on economic value creation provides the cash required to cover the costs of transformation, which include disinvestment from profitable operations that do not support the vision and investments that will only pay off in the future. Second, anchoring a vision in terms of how a company will increase customers' willingness to pay or cut comparative costs makes it easier to sell within the organization. Finally, translating vision into measurable drivers of value creation provides clear criteria for prioritizing activities and allocating scarce resources.

Samsung's strategy to globalize was clearly linked to the drivers of economic value creation in their target industries. Lee commissioned studies to evaluate what was required to compete globally in each of the group's major businesses. In late 1993, Lee announced that Samsung would merge or divest more than a dozen companies deemed incapable of producing world-class products or services. Among the divested companies was Cheiljedang, the sugar-manufacturing business that was one of the first Samsung companies and had been closely associated with the group and Lee family for 40 years. Lee divested other profitable ventures including paper, textiles, department stores, amusement parks and a mining venture in Alaska, where Samsung lacked the competencies, resources, or market position to compete on the global stage.

[33] Smith (2012).

Lee decided to focus Samsung on technology-intensive business including displays, consumer electronics, and semiconductors. Through extensive analysis, as well as first-hand research, Samsung's consumer electronics team learned that customers' willingness to pay a premium for these goods depended on high quality, a strong brand, and a constant flow of technological improvements. Beginning in 2003, Lee declared the key objectives for Samsung Electronics to be improving product quality to world-class standards, building a global brand, and leading in relevant technology. These were ambitious objectives given where Samsung started, but they were also clearly linked to the drivers of customers' willingness to pay, and hence economic value creation.

Leaders attempting to enhance sustainability must likewise consider the linkage between this strategic imperative and their firm's ability to create, capture, and sustain economic value. A study of 180 companies found that firms which implemented progressive environmental policies outperformed comparable peers by both shareholder return and accounting measures of financial performance.[34] High-sustainability firms, in this study, were most likely to outperform peers in industries where customer willingness to pay was driven by a firm's brand, or in extractive industries—such as mining or oil—where periodic breaches in environmental policy can destroy significant economic value.

Transformation poses not only strategic and organizational challenges, but also thorny financing issues. Focusing on the soft side of transformation—the cultural and behavioral aspects—while ignoring the financial implications can derail an otherwise sound change effort. When he could no longer secure government funding, Kim issued over $10 billion in high-yield bonds to finance his global expansion, leaving his company vulnerable when expected profits failed to materialize. The finance function in Samsung, in contrast, was tenacious in asking the hard questions, dislodging necessary cash, and lining up sources of financing matched to the time horizon and risk profile of the group's transformation. A firm's commitment to corporate social responsibility can increase access to financing by improving engagement with stakeholders and increasing transparency.[35]

MAKE TRANSFORMING COMMITMENTS

Transforming commitments are binding actions, such as capital expenditure, disinvestment, or personnel decisions, which remake an organization by increasing the cost (or eliminating the possibility) of persisting in the status quo. An entrepreneur's early commitments define an organization's success formula, and later investments can reinforce the business model, but transforming commitments explicitly aim at remaking the bundle of interconnected frames, processes, resources, relationships, and values that shape behavior within an organization.

---

[34] Eccles et al. (2013).   [35] Cheng et al. (forthcoming).

In established organizations, change initiatives are often viewed as a passing fad. Middle managers pay lip service to the new vision, avoid changes in behavior, and hope that the initiative will pass. Daewoo initiated programs to increase product quality and research, but both efforts ran out of steam within a few years. Absent decisive actions by leaders, the gravitational pull of an organization's historical commitments will drag the company back into the status quo. Decisive actions not only convince employees and external stakeholders that top executives mean business, they also serve as a wake-up call that signals not only the company is in a crisis, but also that management has a way forward.

To pull employees out of active inertia, leaders need to make irreversible commitments to the transformational vision and the drivers of economic value creation that support that vision. Samsung's Lee took a series of quick and decisive actions that forced Samsung forward and prevented it from sliding back into the comfort of familiar activities. After divesting legacy companies that could not compete globally, Lee made large and sustained investments to achieve the company's objectives of building a global brand and world-class technology. Samsung's annual spending on global advertising increased more than fivefold between 1993 and 1999. Annual investments in research and development increased threefold over that same time period. Samsung funded much of this increased spending with the proceeds from asset disposals. Taken together these bold actions signaled to the organization that Lee meant business. Sticking to business as usual or waiting for the new initiatives to blow over was not an option.

Leaders aspiring to sustainability must consider how they can credibly commit to their vision in a way that will prevent the organization from slipping back into active inertia. Options include committing to public reporting of sustainability data, partnering with environmental non-profits, inviting environmental advocates to join the board of directors, exiting profitable businesses that are not sustainable, or firing executives who achieve their financial objectives but lack a commitment to sustainability.

MAINTAIN TRANSFORMATION MOMENTUM

A large-scale transformation typically can take up to a decade to complete. Transforming an organization's historical commitments is difficult, frustrating, and stressful for the managers who must lead the charge. Sustaining effort would be easier if progress was steady and even, but it rarely is. In the Samsung case, for instance, Lee believed that Samsung had little to show in the first six years after the "New Foundation," his initial attempt at launching corporate change.

Even after making transforming commitments beginning in 1993, the relationship between effort put towards transformation and results was not linear. Samsung began its heavy investment in research and development in 1993, but innovation (measured by the number of US patents granted) did not increase significantly until six years later. Nor was progress smooth. Group level net income trended upwards throughout the 1990s, but experienced volatility driven in large part by the prices of semiconductors.

The loss of momentum has a differential impact on employees, depending on their level of enthusiasm for change. In most organizations, a small minority—10–15 percent—will wholeheartedly embrace change, while a comparably sized minority will vehemently oppose new practices. The majority of employees will sit on the fence, and wait to see how events unfold. If initial change initiatives falter, the advocates will lose credibility and confidence, and may leave the organization. Opponents of change, in contrast, will be emboldened and may grow more obstreperous. After witnessing the failure of one transformation initiative, the silent majority will increase the threshold required for them to personally commit to change. A loss of momentum not only delays transformation, it makes change harder to accomplish at all.

One way to maintain momentum is by plotting progress over time. Achieving global leadership required hundreds of changes—large and small—Samsung's historical commitments. The new product development process, for example, was shifted from backward engineering and copying existing products to designing cutting-edge products superior to rivals' offerings. Manufacturing processes were improved through quality programs, including a "line stop program" in which any employee could stop the entire production line when they discovered a product defect, and the line could not be restarted until the source of the defect was identified and eliminated.

No company can, or should, try to change all their commitments simultaneously. Rather, they should prioritize the most important changes, make those, then move on to others. Samsung did just this. As importantly, the leadership communicated these changes in a consistent manner over time. Every year, senior leaders would show a chart divided into three columns. The left-most column listed changes the company had successfully made, the middle column highlighted the initiatives prioritized for that calendar year, and the right-most column laid out important changes that the company would tackle in the future. This simple graphic helped managers and employees recognize progress and better understand how the distinct initiatives fit into the big picture.

Leaders can also use external crises to maintain or accelerate momentum. The Korean won crisis of 1997 hit Samsung hard. The group's consolidated debt was approximately $38 billion at then-current exchange rates, $28 billion of which was classified as current, and the debt-to-book equity ratio stood at 366 percent at year end. While his counterparts at other *chaebol* saw the crisis as a disaster, Lee saw it as an opportunity to accelerate changes within Samsung. He explained to executives in December 1997: "So far, I have strongly appealed that we need to change. But we haven't changed enough because we didn't share a sense of crisis. Now everyone feels that the crisis has come, and we have a good chance to use the crisis to improve our competitiveness."[36]

Lee used the financial crisis to driver a series of hard decisions. In 1998, he reduced the size of the secretary's office from 250 to 150 employees to enhance the autonomy of the four sectors and the affiliated companies. Between April 1998 and April 2000, Samsung divested affiliated businesses from 61 to 45. Divestments included Samsung's sale of its construction machinery division to Volvo, the forklift business to Clark, and the Bucheon memory chip fabrication plant to Fairchild, which Lee himself had acquired in 1974. Samsung reduced the number of employees from 267,000 in 1997 to 161,000 in late 1999 through disposal of affiliates, downsizing, and outsourcing. Samsung eliminated transfer prices across affiliates and required them to buy and sell at market prices. Debt guarantees across affiliates were completely eliminated by April 2000.

To maintain momentum as they lead their organizations towards greater sustainability, executives can, like Lee, plot progress against the most important metrics over time.[37] Leaders can also take advantage of exogenous events, such as extreme weather or environmental disasters like the Deepwater Horizon oil spill, which increase the salience of sustainability in the minds of employees and other stakeholders. These events provide windows of opportunity where leaders can push through changes in the face of reduced resistance and apathy.

Conclusion: lessons on large-scale transformation

Man-made climate change presents a fundamental change in the context for major global corporations. Faced with such fundamental shifts, some leaders ignore the changes, deny their importance, or respond in a slow or half-hearted manner. The Samsung and Daewoo examples, however, illustrate a more nuanced dynamic that can undermine large-scale organizational change. Both Lee and Kim saw the changes in their competitive and institutional context, formulated a vision to respond, and aggressively put their plan into action. In both cases, their response was not inaction but active inertia—the *chaebol* responded to very different conditions by accelerating activities that had worked in the past. Managers who understand this dynamic are better positioned to notice if active inertia is undercutting their own organization's attempts to become more sustainable.

Large-scale organizational change can be daunting, even for the most talented and energetic executives. Managerial commitments provide a useful lens for understanding the sources of organizational inertia. Rather than

---

[36] *The Monthly Chosun*, July 2000.   [37] Eccles and Serafeim (2013): 50–60.

isolating a single obstacle to change, the framework discussed in this chapter encompasses the strategic frames, processes, tangible and intangible resources, enduring relationships with external stakeholders, and values that together shape behavior. This comprehensive model depicted in Figure 7.1 can help managers take a comprehensive inventory of their organization's current commitments. Once critical commitments have been surfaced, they can be sorted into obstacles that must be overcome, sources of historical strength that should be leveraged in the future, commitments that don't matter much one way or the other, and new commitments that will be necessary to achieve sustainability.

The managerial commitment framework provides not only a snapshot of the key commitments at a point of time, but also a script of how those commitments often evolve over time. Commitments are necessary for initial success, but tend to harden over time. When hardened commitments encounter changed circumstances, organizations struggle to adapt. This narrative helps leaders understand and communicate why change is so difficult. It also provides a rationale for change without losing face. Change is easier to accept when it is framed not as a corrective for historical mistakes, but as part of the inevitable co-evolution of organizations and dynamic environments.

The managerial commitment framework provides a lens to help recognize active inertia, understand its sources, and communicate the need for change to others. Managerial commitments are not just a lens, however, they are also a tool. Top leaders who understand the power of transforming commitments can help their organization break free of active inertia and avoid relapsing into the status quo. They can place a cohort of likeminded leaders in critical positions throughout the organization, and ensure that they share a common understanding of the vision and the gap that must be closed to achieve it. They can ensure that their commitments support not only their vision but also the competitive imperative of creating and capturing economic value over the long run. Boards that recognize the crucial importance of commitments can use their insight to select executives who achieve the right balance between familiarity with and distance from the bundle of commitments that enabled the organization to succeed in the past.

▦ REFERENCES

Albert, Stuart and Whetten, David A. (1985) "Organizational Identity," *Research in Organizational Behavior* 7: 263–95.

Battilana, J. and Casciaro, T. (2012) "Change Agents, Networks, and Institutions: A Contingency Theory of Organizational Change," *Academy of Management Journal* 55 (2): 381–98, 819–36.

Battilana, J., Leca, B., and Boxenbaum, E. (2009) "2 How Actors Change Institutions: Towards a Theory of Institutional Entrepreneurship." *The Academy of Management Annals* 3 (1): 65–107.

Beer, Michael, Eisenstat, Russell A., Foote, Nathanial, Fredberg, Tobias, and Norgreen, Flemming. (2011) *Higher Ambition: How Great Leaders Create Economic and Social Value*. Boston, MA: Harvard Business School Press.

Benner, M. J. and Tripsas, M. (2012) "The Influence of Prior Industry Affiliation on Framing in Nascent Industries: The Evolution of Digital Cameras," *Strategic Management Journal* 33 (3): 277–302.

BSR. (2013) *State of Sustainable Business Survey 2013*. New York: BSR.

Chatterjee, A. and Hambrick, D. C. (2007) "It's All about Me: Narcissistic Chief Executive Officers and Their Effects on Company Strategy and Performance," *Administrative Science Quarterly* 52 (3): 351–86.

Cheng, Beiting, Ioannou, Ioannis, and Serafeim, George. (2014) "Corporate Social Responsibility and Access to Financing," *Strategic Management Journal* 35 (1): 1–23.

Choi, Dosung and Park, Choelsoon. (1997) "Daewoo's Strategy in the Emerging Markets: Entry into the Eastern European Markets," *The Practice of Management* 31 (2):19–27 (in Korean).

Dunphy, Dexter, Benn, Suzanne, and Griffiths, Andrew. (2003) *Organizational Change for Corporate Sustainability*. London: Routledge.

Eccles, Robert G. and Serafeim, George. (2013) "The Performance Frontier: Innovating for Sustainable Strategy," *Harvard Business Review* (May): 50–60.

Eccles, Robert G., Ioannou, Ioannis, and Serafeim, George. (2013) "The Impact of Corporate Sustainability on Organizational Processes and Practices," Harvard Business School Working Paper 12-035. Boston, MA: Harvard Business School Press.

Elster, Jon. (1979) *Ulysses and the Sirens: Studies in Rationality and Irrationality*. Cambridge: Cambridge University Press, 36–111.

Eggers, J. P. and Kaplan, S. (2009) "Cognition and Renewal: Comparing CEO and Organizational Effects on Incumbent Adaptation to Technical Change," *Organization Science* 20 (2): 461–77.

Finkelstein, S. and Hambrick, D. C. (1996) *Strategic Leadership: Top Executives and their Effects on Organizations*. Minneapolis/St Paul: West Pub. Co., chs 1 and 2.

Gersick, Connie J. G. (1991) "Revolutionary Change Theories: A Multilevel Exploration of the Punctuated Equilibrium Paradigm," *Academy of Management Review* 16 (1): 10–36.

Ghemawat, Pankaj. (2001) *Strategy and the Business Landscape*. Upper Saddle River, N.J.: Prentice Hall.

Ghemawat, Pankaj. (2002) "Competition and Business Strategy in Historical Perspective," *Business History Review* 76 (Spring): 37–74.

Gioia, Dennis A., Schultz, Majken, and Corley, Kevin G. (2000) "Organizational Identity, Image, and Adaptive Instability," *Academy of Management Review* 25 (1): 63–81.

Greenwood, Royston and Hinings, Christopher R. (1993) "Understanding Strategic Change: The Contribution of Archetypes," *Academy of Management Journal* 36 (5): 1052–81.

Greenwood, Royston and Hinings, Christopher R. (2006) "Understanding Radical Organizational Change: Bringing Together the Old and the New Institutionalism," *Academy of Management Review* 21 (4): 1022–54.

Greenwood, R. and Suddaby, R. (2006) "Institutional Entrepreneurship in Mature Fields: The Big Five Accounting Firms," *Academy of Management Journal* 49 (1): 27–48.

Greve, Henrich R. (1998) "Performance Aspirations and Risky Organizational Change," *Administrative Science Quarterly* 43: 58–86.

Gulati, R. and Puranam, P. (2009) "Renewal Through Reorganization: The Value of Inconsistencies Between Formal and Informal Organization," *Organization Science* 20 (2): 422–40.

Hannan, Michael T. and Freeman, James. (1989) *Organizational Ecology*. Cambridge, MA: Harvard University Press.

Hannan, Michael T., Polos, L., and Carroll, G. R. (2007) *Logics of Organization Theory: Audiences, Code, and Ecologies*. Princeton, N.J.: Princeton University Press.

Hee, Lee Kun. (1997) *Read the World with Your Own Thinking*. Seoul: The Dong-a Ilbo (in Korean).

Henderson, Rebecca and Clark, Kim B. (1990) "Architectural Innovation: The Reconfiguration of Existing Systems and the Failure of Established Firms," *Administrative Science Quarterly* 35 (1): 9–30.

Hinings, C. R. (2010) "Thirty Years of Organization Studies: Enduring Themes in a Changing Institutional Field," *Organization Studies* 31 (6): 659–75.

Ihlwan, Moon. (2001) "Kim's Fall from Grace at Daewoo," *BusinessWeek*, February 19.

Kellogg, Katherine C. (2009) Operating Room: Relational Spaces and Microinstitutional Change in Surgery," *American Journal of Sociology* 115 (3): 657–711.

Kiron, D., Kruschwitz, N., Haanaes, K., and von Streng Velken, I. (2012) "Sustainability Nears a Tipping Point," *MIT Sloan Management Review* 53 (2): 69–74.

Kotter, John. (1995) "Leading Change: Why Transformation Efforts Fail," *Harvard Business Review* (March–April): 63.

Kraar, Louis. (2003) "Wanted: Kim Woo Choong," *Fortune,* January 22.

Lee, J. W. (2000) *The Monthly Chosun* (July).

Leonard-Barton, Dorothy A. (1992) "Core Capabilities and Core Rigidities: A Paradox in Managing New Product Development," *Strategic Management Journal* 13: 111–25.

Meyer, John W. and Rowan, Brian. (1977) "Institutionalized Organizations: Formal Structure as Myth and Ceremony," *American Journal of Sociology* 83: 340–63.

Miller, Danny and Friesen, Peter H. (1984) *Organizations: A Quantum View*. Englewood Cliffs, N.J.: Prentice Hall.

Milliken, Frances J. and Lant, Theresa K. (1991) "The Effect of an Organization's Recent Performance History on Strategic Persistence and Change: The Role of Managerial Interpretations," in P. Shrivastava, A. Huff, and J. E. Dutton (eds), *Advances in Strategic Management*, Vol. 7. Greenwich, CT: JAI Press, 129–56.

Pfeffer, J. (1981) "Management as Symbolic Action: The Creation and Maintenance of Organizational Paradigms," in L. Cummings and B. Straw (eds), *Research in Organizational Behavior*, Vol. 3. Greenwich, Conn.: JAI Press, 1–52.

Robeco. (2013) Country Sustainability Ranking, August. Zurich: RobecoSAM.AG.

Schuman, Michael and Lee, Jane L. (1999) "Won World: Dismantling of Daewoo Shows How Radically Korea is Changing," *The Wall Street Journal*, August 17.

Selznick, Philip. (1957) *Leadership in Administration*. Evanston, IL: Row, Peterson, 35 and 55.

Smith, Jacquelyn. (2012) "Ranking the World's Most Sustainable Companies," *Forbes* (January): 24.

Smith, W. K. and Tushman, M. L. (2005) "Managing Strategic Contradictions: A Top Management Model for Managing Innovation Streams," *Organization Science* 16 (5): 522–36.

Sull, Donald, Park, Choelsoon, and Kim, Seonghoon. (2004) *Samsung and Daewoo: Two Tales of One City*, Harvard Business School Case Study 804-055. Boston, MA: Harvard Business School Press.

Sull, Donald. (2005) *Why Good Companies Go Bad and How Great Managers Remake Them*. Boston, MA: Harvard Business School Press.

Tripsas, M. (1997) "Unraveling the Process of Creative Destruction: Complementary Assets and Incumbent Survival in the Typesetter Industry," *Strategic Management Journal* 18 (Summer Special Issue): 119.

Tripsas, Mary and Gavetti, Giovanni. (2000) "Capabilities, Cognition and Inertia: Evidence from Digital Imaging," *Strategic Management Journal* 21: 1147–61.

Tushman, Michael L. and Romanelli, Elaine. (1985) "Organizational Evolution: A Metamorphosis Model of Convergence and Reorientation," in L. L. Cummings and Barry M. Staw (eds), *Research in Organizational Behavior*. Greenwich, CT: JAI Press, 171–222.

Woo-Choong, Kim. (1992) *Every Street is Paved with Gold*. New York: William Morrow.

8 Chief Sustainability Officers

Who Are They and What Do They Do?

Kathleen Miller Perkins and George Serafeim

Introduction to Chief Sustainability Officers

Over the past few years, an increasing number of companies have engaged in some form of activity regarding sustainability.[1] Their approaches vary widely from activities related to regulatory compliance to transforming the corporate identity. A review of the literature suggests that firms frequently go through stages starting with simple, easy-to-implement actions and progressing towards more complex and potentially rewarding approaches (Mirvis and Googins, 2009; Hoffman and Bansal, 2012). While the studies and resulting models differ in the number and nature of the stages, most suggest that nearly all companies first engage with sustainability by focusing on compliance. Their actions are neither coordinated nor strategic. Many companies eventually evolve to a more strategic sustainability approach that centers on increasing efficiencies and impacting the companies' bottom lines. For example, they may look for ways to cut their energy or water usage. At this point, strategies tend to be characterized by transitional change aimed at improving existing organizational practices or moving from an existing practice to a new one. Some companies move beyond transitional adjustments to transformational change, in which they focus on innovation and reframe their corporate identities. It is at this point that sustainability tends to be integrated into the core business strategies and is no longer positioned as a "bolt-on" activity only marginally, if at all, related to the companies' business models (Eccles and Serafeim, 2013).

The literature indicates that CEO commitment is critical to successful implementation of sustainability strategies (Eccles et al., 2012). However, there is little research exploring how companies plot a course and transition from one stage to another. One recent trend has been the increasing appointment of Chief Sustainability Officers (CSOs) to drive the formulation and

---

[1] Sustainability is the ability to endure. From a societal perspective, sustainability means meeting the current needs of our society in ways that enable future generations to meet their own needs. Therefore, corporate sustainability is defined as a system of corporate strategy, business model, and operations that integrate economic, environmental, social, and governance factors to create and deliver products and services.

execution of an organization's sustainability strategy. The number of CSOs has grown substantially over the past few years, and while the growth has leveled off, companies are continuing to create and fill these positions. The number of companies with a full-time sustainability officer doubled between 1995 and 2003, and doubled again between 2003 and 2008 (Greenbiz 2013). We draw on a review of the literature on CSOs as well as our own study of CSOs to examine how the authority and responsibilities of CSOs differ across sustainability stages.

We begin by conducting a short review of the literature on the stages of change towards sustainability. We refer to theories from institutional and other organizational change research to address the question of what catalyzes organizations to move beyond compliance into more complex and strategic stages. After that, we narrow our focus to the role of the CSO in leading change. We discuss what previous research has shown concerning the roles and characteristics of CSOs, followed by a description of our own research of CSOs and other managers with primary responsibility for sustainability. In addition, we examine the mechanisms that CSOs employ to lead change. Finally, we include suggestions from CSOs on practices that have been successful in embedding sustainability in organizations, with specific examples for illustration. We conclude by summarizing the relationship of our findings to the broader field of research on sustainability and organizational change.

While our data do not allow us to make any definitive claims about how the CSO, as a change agent, affects the financial performance of an organization, we use our survey and interview data to advance hypotheses about the role of the CSO in leading change. Our first main finding suggests that a CSO decentralizes decision rights and allocates responsibilities as the organization increases its commitment to sustainability (the first stage being *Compliance*, second *Efficiency*, and third *Innovation*). In other words, one could say that the CSO, although she gains more authority, becomes *less* central in later stages of sustainability. Our second main finding relates to why this is the case. We advance a hypothesis and present field data that are consistent with the hypothesis that a firm's sustainability strategy becomes significantly more idiosyncratic in the later stages of sustainability. While most companies have fairly generic sustainability strategies in the initial stages (*Compliance* and *Efficiency*), in the latter *Innovation* stage the sustainability strategy is more customized to the needs of different organizations and driven by the demands of the markets where an organization has a presence or plans to expand in the future.

Our analyses suggest that in terms of formal authority, the likelihood that the manager with primary responsibility for sustainability has the title of a CSO versus a lower-level title increases monotonically as companies move through the stages of commitment to sustainability. Likewise, the probability that she reports to the CEO or the Board of Directors increases for companies that are in the later stages of sustainability commitment, suggesting higher CSO authority. In the *Innovation* stage, the frequency with which ultimate responsibility for sustainability rests with the CEO or the Board decreases significantly, further reflecting that the role of the CSO has matured at this stage. The probability of the Board having a separate sustainability committee is significantly higher in the *Innovation* stage. We interpret this finding as further evidence of increased authority, as now the CSO has the assistance and also supervision of the Board.

In terms of responsibilities, we find that almost all CSOs in the first two stages (*Compliance* and *Efficiency*) perform a generic set of activities such as formulating and executing a sustainability strategy, identifying material sustainability issues, learning from external sources, reporting sustainability data, managing stakeholder relations, and educating employees about sustainability. In contrast, in the *Innovation* stage we find a significantly lower frequency of CSOs engaging in most of those activities. We turn to our interview data to understand why and we find that this could be attributed to organizational needs becoming more idiosyncratic and CSOs decentralizing activities and decision rights.

Finally, the factors that affect the decision of where in the organization to locate the person who holds the primary responsibility for sustainability differs across the stages. We find that the importance of the location of sustainability champions and the type of sustainability strategy of each organization increases monotonically across stages. This last finding is consistent with the observation that organizational needs become idiosyncratic in later stages. As a result, sustainability strategies also become more idiosyncratic, thereby influencing more where to locate authority on sustainability issues.

With this study, we make a contribution to the literature on corporate sustainability by describing the evolving responsibilities and authority of a potentially key change agent in the firm, the CSO. While a number of studies have identified country, industry, and firm characteristics that are associated with corporate commitment to sustainability (McWilliams and Siegel, 2001; Campbell, 2007; Ioannou and Serafeim, 2012), none of the studies has examined how CSO characteristics relate to the stage of sustainability of different organizations. With this study, we attempt to provide preliminary evidence to shed light on what CSOs are doing in the different stages of sustainability. We view this as a first step towards understanding better how CSOs enable the change process inside organizations.

Stages of sustainability: literature review

While the terminology and details vary, much of the literature on corporate sustainability refers to a series of sequenced stages that companies traverse (for example, Nidumolu et al., 2009; Arbogast and Thornton, 2012; Willard, 2012; Dyllick and Muff, 2013). As companies move through the stages, they increase their interactions with stakeholders, assume more complex responsibilities, and attempt to align their business model with sustainability goals. Moreover, the stages represent the degree to which sustainability is strategic and central to the organization. First companies initiate activities that are related to compliance with an evolving set of regulations. During this stage, company efforts are rarely connected to business strategy or coordinated centrally. Subsequently, companies begin to become more strategic by seeking ways to achieve organizational efficiencies that will impact their bottom line. To accomplish these goals, they begin to build the business case to legitimize their efforts. While some companies never move beyond their focus on efficiencies, others shift to a more advanced transformative and innovative stage by integrating sustainability into the core of the business. As company efforts become more strategic, leaders create systems, business models, operations, and procedures that seek to maximize long-term profitability while tackling societal problems and minimizing negative externalities. Company leaders claim that their impact on society increases in this stage, as do the benefits and returns to the company, although rigorous empirical evidence is still lacking to prove this point.

Eccles et al. (2012) suggest that endogenous or exogenous forces, or a combination of both, can lead to sustainability-related change. Using survey data, they showed that the initial stimulus tends to come from two elements that are closely related: a strong conviction from the leadership of the organization, usually the CEO (endogenous change) and/or external engagement, sometimes in the form of external activism or pressure from shareholders (exogenous change). When leadership commitment drives the process, it usually comes from the personal resolution of a CEO. When external engagement drives the process, it is often in the form of societal activism or pressure from stakeholders. For example, public upheaval about enzymes transformed the corporate culture of Novo Nordisk and made the company an example of one that balances all stakeholder interests. Likewise, accusations about violations of human rights led Nike to transform itself into a business that takes stakeholder accountability very seriously. As a result, Nike strives to operate responsibly in its supply chain. These findings are consistent with the literature on institutional and organizational change, which indicates that the impetus for change can come from exogenous events or endogenous pressures (Meyer, 1982).

Once the CEO initiates a sustainability-related change, whether due to endogenous or exogenous forces, she seeks assistance from others. Some scholars argue that a leader alone cannot create change. Rather, they posit that organizational change occurs through social exchanges. Thornton et al. (2012) state that "social interactions provide the key motor that reproduces, alters, or transforms practices and organizational identities." While a CEO may initiate change by creating a new vision, it is the social interactions that create the common understanding and shared vision that predicate action (Demers, 2007). Often the rationale of a CSO appointment is that while the CEO can retain sponsorship of the change, a CSO in a centralized position can oversee the development and implementation of the strategies that will carry the company through the more complex stages of change. As early as 2007, the *New York Times* recognized this trend: "These are not simple environmental watchdogs there to keep operations and regulators at bay. The new environmental chiefs are helping companies profit from the push to go green."[2]

To understand how companies move from one stage to another, we need to better understand who the CSO is and what she does. As a leader of change towards sustainability, her responsibilities and organizational authority and relations with the ultimate centers of decision making in a company (CEO and Board of Directors) are important factors to consider in assessing her ability to be effective. Organizational research suggests that not all actors are equally successful in implementing change. The change agent's expertise, experiences, location in the structure of an organization, and organizational responsibilities are important factors in her success (Kellogg, 2011). For example, Lounsbury (2001) found that universities that made a greater commitment to waste recycling were the ones that employed staff with the relevant expertise and who had the commitment to develop and advocate for the introduction of new, more sustainable practices. The question then is whether the CSO can be a successful change agent. Perhaps her appointment is merely a symbolic action representing potential isomorphism. Under this scenario, the CSO has little power to affect the organization. Our survey data, explained in the section "CSO literature review," show that organizations differ in where they place the CSO in the corporate hierarchy, a frequently used measure of power within an organization. In some organizations, CSOs report directly to the CEO or the board of directors. In other organizations, they are two or three steps removed from the CEO. This suggests differences in the power that CSOs wield across organizations.

CSO literature review

Senior corporate executive positions are often created in response to significant opportunities and risks emerging from technological or social disruptions. Examples represent the creation of Chief Technology Officers (CTOs), Chief Information Officers (CIOs), Chief Quality Officers (CQOs), Chief Financial Officers (CFO) and, more recently, CSOs. Another example that emerged in the late nineteenth century is the Chief Electricity Officer in response to the invention and commercialization of electricity.

Similar to other relatively new C-suite positions, such as Chief Technology Officers (CTOs), and Chief Information Officers (CIOs), the CSO role is

---

[2] See Deutsch (2007). Available at: <http://www.nytimes.com/2007/07/03/business/03sustain. html?pagewanted= all.> (accessed July 2014).

evolving.[3] For example, the CIO position used to be viewed as primarily a support function. Computing was initially seen as a back-office tool for automating accounting and other financial matters. Later, when computers became more sophisticated and took on additional tasks throughout businesses, the title changed to Director of Management Information Systems. The breakthrough came in the mid-1980s, when chief executives increasingly invited their IT professionals to sit at the table with other C-suite executives.[4] The role of the CIO is now more integrated into the innovation and transformation parts of the business.[5] With technology embedded in every facet of business, and data becoming a necessary asset in order to obtain a competitive advantage, the CIO's role is more necessary to a business today than ever before.

Similarly, the role of the CFO has been evolving. While CFOs used to be viewed as bean counters, over time their scope has broadened to include an involvement in compliance, technology, and external reporting. The history of CFOs indicates that as the number of company stakeholders increased, the scope and significance of the CFO's job also increased. Now the function involves preserving the reputation of the business, risk management, and support for decision making. Changes to the structure and demands placed on finance teams are transforming career paths and core capabilities needed by finance professionals.[6] Their more prominent role in management is leading to a move away from basic processing and control, towards greater involvement in development and execution of business strategies.

Research on CSOs is currently limited. While there are a few practitioner survey studies examining their backgrounds and their roles, the samples in these studies tend to vary greatly. Nevertheless, a few patterns emerge that are worth our consideration, as they are relevant to our understanding of a CSO's role and how they lead change. We note that later we refer to CSOs as all people with primary responsibility for sustainability in an organization, even if their title is not CSO but a vice president or a director.

In terms of professional background, surveys suggest that more than half of those filling the CSO position moved from other positions inside their companies (Greenbiz, 55 percent; Weinreb Group, 86 percent). Most had been employed for an average of 15–20 years (Acre, 2012) and moved from departments such as External Affairs, Operations, Research, Marketing

---

[3] National Association of Corporate Directors (2013). Available at: <http://www.nacdonline.org/files/FileDownloads/PDF/C-Suite%20Expectations_1364247261983_2.pdf> (accessed July 2014).

[4] See IBM (2011). Available at: <http://www-03.ibm.com/ibm/history/ibm100/us/en/icons/emergenceofcio/> (accessed July 2014).

[5] Ernst & Young (2012). Available at: <http://www.ey.com/GL/en/Services/Advisory/The-DNA-of-the-CIO> (accessed July 2014).

[6] PwC (2013). Available at: <http://pwc.com.au/consulting/assets/publications/Evolution-CFO-Jul13.pdf> (accessed July 2014).

(Weinreb Group, 2011) or Environment, Health and Safety (EHS) (Greenbiz, 2013). Footprint Talent and WAP (2011) surveyed a group of 254 business professionals including CEOs, COOs, VPs, and HR executives about their perceptions of the necessary education for being a CSO. Fifty percent indicated that a business and financial background was required. Thirty-six percent reported the need for an MBA, 30 percent said a communications background, and 31 percent said engineering. The same study reports that when asked about desired previous experience, 53 percent said operations background, 43 percent said a science background, and 44 percent said product development.

In terms of authority inside the organization, the evidence is conflicting. Some surveys suggest that approximately 30 percent report to the CEO (Weinreb Graye, 2011; Acre, 2012). Other surveys indicate that less than 10 percent of CSOs report to the CEO (PwC 2012; Greenbiz 2013). In these studies, the largest percentage of CSOs (13–30 percent) reports to External Affairs.

Almost all of the studies cited here indicate that strategy development is a key responsibility of the CSOs. However, the additional responsibilities reported in these studies were not consistent. Some of these additional responsibilities included reporting, internal engagement, and external engagement. Twenty-three percent of the respondents included developing the business case as a key CSO responsibility currently and 30 percent reported that this would be a key responsibility over the next five years (PwC 2012).

In sum, the literature reveals inconsistencies in the role of CSOs. Titles and responsibilities of those who are primarily responsible for sustainability vary considerably across companies. However, a few patterns did emerge. Most CSOs are assigned to this role while being with the company already and have limited backgrounds in sustainability before their appointments to this position. Almost all of the CSOs have responsibility for sustainability strategy; however, their additional responsibilities vary.

Importantly, while existing CSO studies yield some insights, they do not shed light on how the CSO position differs across the different stages of sustainability. Specifically, none of the previous studies analyzed how titles, responsibilities, and organizational characteristics related to the different stages of sustainability. Analyzing these factors allows us to better understand how the role of the CSO evolves as organizations move from one stage to another.

Methods

RATIONALE

We used two interrelated methodologies to gather data on CSOs. First, we conducted an on-line survey to establish the general framework of who they are, where they come from, and what they do at varying stages of companies' sustainability commitments. Subsequently, we used the framework that we were able to establish through the results of our survey to craft interview questions that would allow us to paint a more detailed and clearer picture of how they actually function in companies known for their leadership in sustainability.

We emphasize that we do not suggest that the elements described here causally relate to the stage of sustainability. On the one hand, the role of the CSO is likely to evolve and adapt to serve the organization's needs. On the other hand, the evolving role of the CSO might lead the firm to move from one stage to the next. Or both the CSO and the firm adapt to each stage and guide movement from one stage to the next. Our results suggest correlation, rather than causality. Nevertheless, they provide insights into what a CSO does and how she does it inside organizations that are in different stages of the sustainability journey.

METHODOLOGY

Survey methods

We announced the survey on the Bloomberg Sustainability website and invited CSOs (or their equivalents, defined as those who have primary responsibility for sustainability within their organizations) to participate. While we broadly use the word CSO throughout the chapter, many respondents in our survey with primary responsibility for sustainability have different titles. In addition, we announced the survey to LinkedIn CSO-related groups and sent out invitations to individuals in all of our sustainability-related networks. The survey was conducted over a 6-week period from the end of October to early December, 2013. The survey consisted of 17 questions pertaining to roles and responsibilities for sustainability, involvement of the Board and the CEO, how and by whom the CSOs were chosen for their positions, and the nature of their reporting relationships. One-hundred-and-thirty CSOs or their equivalents with different titles completed the survey. Sixty-six of those who responded had primary responsibility for sustainability in the organization and completed the whole survey, providing us with the data we needed. We analyzed only these responses for two reasons. First, we were not sure whether more junior employees would have the necessary information to answer the questions, as many are strategic in nature. Second, requiring that all respondents have primary responsibility ensured a higher level of cross-firm comparability in respondents.

The participants in the survey (66 respondents) represented 27 industries with Professional Services comprising 20 percent, Financial Services 14 percent, Consumer Goods 13 percent, Energy 12 percent, Construction 12 percent, Technology and Communications 8 percent, Agriculture, Mining, and Water 6 percent, and other industries the remaining 15 percent. The majority of participants came from companies that had at least ten thousand employees, so our sample mainly represents very large companies. Companies with under five hundred employees comprised 23 percent of the sample, those with five hundred to a thousand 6 percent, those between one thousand and ten thousand 26 percent, and those with over ten thousand employees 46 percent. The respondents represented organizations that had operations in Australia–New Zealand 32 percent, North America 25 percent, Global 24 percent, Europe 21 percent, Asia Pacific 18 percent, Latin America 10 percent, and Africa–Middle East 10 percent.

In the survey, we asked participants to identify the organization's primary approach to sustainability. We provided three choices: *Compliance* with regulations and securing license to operate; *Efficiency* and focus on the bottom line; and *Innovation* and exploitation of opportunities for growth. The three stages are broadly consistent with the stages of sustainability we reviewed in the section "Stages of sustainability: literature review." We kept responses anonymous so as to avoid respondents overestimating the sustainability stage of their organization. The equal split between respondents across the three stages, twenty-two each, suggests that there is no obvious tendency of respondents to overestimate their organization's stage; something that would be apparent if we had received a very low number of respondents identifying their organization at the *Compliance* stage. That being said, we have no way to completely rule out the possibility that some respondents misclassified their organizations, adding noise to our results.

Interview methods

We conducted a series of interviews to complement our survey data. Our intention was to gain a better understanding of how the CSO impacts the transition of an organization from one stage to the next. In addition, we wanted to explore whether the CSOs see themselves as leaders of change, and if so, how they approach this responsibility. In choosing who to interview, we focused on companies that appeared to be either at the *Efficiency* or *Innovation* stage. Our reasoning was that we wanted to gather more detail about the nature of their experiences in each stage and learn about the steps that their companies had taken as they moved through the initial stages. We based our criteria for selection on whether the company was integrating sustainability-related elements into their products or services based on disclosures made by the company. Most of our interviewees came from large, global companies, although a few were from not-for-profit organizations both large and small. We asked them to describe how their companies first got involved in sustainability, including what motivated them and what approach they took in the beginning. Then we asked them to describe what had happened between that initial involvement and the current company status. We inquired about when and how a business case had been developed and what their role in the development had been. We questioned them about when their position had been created and why. We obtained detail on their roles in the past and in the present, and what their role would be in the projected future. Finally, we asked them whether they considered themselves to be change leaders, and if so, what approach they were taking. Interviews were done by phone between January 7 and 21. Each interview lasted approximately 45 minutes. In total, we interviewed twelve CSOs.

Most of the interviewees had served as the CSO for four years or less. They indicated that this is a typical CSO tenure currently. Consistent with what we found in our literature review, most had been in other positions within their companies before being appointed as the CSO. While those in this group of internal appointees had not been in formal positions related to sustainability, several had been involved with sustainability-related activities as either volunteers or in some other peripheral capacity within their companies. Their prior work included positions in areas such as marketing, human resources, plant engineering, compliance, procurement, IT, printing, and production management. Most were not formally educated in sustainability-related fields. Rather, their educational credentials included fields such as architecture, biology, and engineering, among others. The Board or the CEO had appointed all of them, and most of them reported to one or the other.

The profiles of those few who were hired from outside of the company differed from those who were appointed from within. They had educational credentials and previous experience in sustainability-related fields. Even though their backgrounds differed from internally appointed CSOs, the Board or the CEO of the hiring company chose them as well. Steve Howard, the CSO of Ikea, a Swedish company that sells home furnishings, appliances, and accessories, told us that the role of the CSO is evolving as companies' sustainability strategies are evolving. Similar to the Chief Information Officer (CIO) or Chief Risk Officer (CRO), over time, the role is becoming more "professionalized."[7] Howard suggested that as companies begin to take on more complex issues and integrate sustainability into the core of the business, a CSO with the related education and experience is a better fit for the position. He suggested that the trend is now moving in the direction of hiring CSOs who are able to take an informed approach to sustainability strategies as a result of their prior education and experience.

Upon hearing details from those we interviewed, we determined that the companies they represented ranged from the high end of the mid-level stages i.e. *Efficiencies* and building their business case, up through the highest stages involving *Innovation* and transformation for solving world problems. This is by construction, since we screened companies to interview based on their integration of sustainability factors in their products and services. All of the CSOs were responsible for at least assisting with, if not wholly owning, the

[7] See Spitze (2012), discussing the professionalization of the CIO; available at: <http://blogs.wsj.com/cio/2012/08/01/how-to-unlock-the-power-of-the-cio/> (accessed July 2014).

development of the sustainability strategy. All were accountable for overseeing the integration of sustainability into the organization, with some playing a more hands-on role than others. All see themselves as change leaders. Most are in influential positions, in which they report to the CEO and or the Board of Directors, and most sit on the Executive Committee.

Results

COMPLIANCE STAGE

The *Compliance* stage represents the point when most companies first engage with sustainability. Thirty-three percent of our survey sample indicated that their companies were in this stage. Very few of the respondents have the title of CSO in this *Compliance* stage (14 percent), far fewer than in the next two stages (*Efficiency* 27 percent; *Innovation* 36 percent). All results are reported in Table 8.1. The largest percentage have the title of Director of Sustainability (27 percent), indicating either that a lower-level title such as Director is more likely in this stage or, alternatively, more of those who fall into this category with the title of Director versus Chief chose to participate in the survey. Nevertheless, no matter what their title, when CSOs are appointed in this early stage, as opposed to the later stages, they have a greater positive influence on the involvement of the CEO. The likelihood that the appointment of a CSO will increase CEO involvement in sustainability declines monotonically as they move from the *Compliance* stage to *Efficiency* and then to *Innovation*. Most likely, the CEO of a company in the later stages is already very involved in the sustainability strategies and as a result the appointment of a CSO is unlikely to increase their commitment.

Table 8.1 also reports that although in most cases (77 percent) the CEO or the Board made the decision of where to position the CSO or equivalent, only 32 percent report to the Board or the CEO. In this stage, almost all CSOs are responsible for developing strategy, reporting sustainability-related data, embedding sustainability into the organization, determining the material sustainability issues, and learning about sustainability from other companies. Based on these findings, we conclude that during the *Compliance* stage, those primarily responsible for sustainability have a wide range of responsibilities but are not positioned for high levels of authority.

Our interview data corroborated that their companies began their involvement in sustainability through regulatory compliance. They confirmed that the activities were neither strategic nor centralized. Some reported that in addition to compliance, voluntary employee initiatives such as recycling projects or green teams also appeared during this stage. However, these activities were not seen as strategic and were rarely coordinated centrally.

Table 8.1 The role of the CSO

	Stage of sustainability		
Categories	Compliance	Efficiency	Innovation
CSO Authority			
Person with primary responsibility for sustainability has the title of CSO	14%	27%	36%
CSO reports to CEO or Board of Directors	32%	41%	41%
Organizational characteristics related to sustainability			
CEO or Board of Directors ultimately responsible for sustainability	73%	86%	59%
Board Sustainability Committee	32%	27%	64%
CSO responsibilities			
Sustainability strategy development	91%	91%	86%
Embedding sustainability strategy in the organization	91%	95%	86%
Reporting sustainability data	95%	100%	75%
Managing stakeholder relations	82%	82%	68%
Employee education around sustainability	82%	86%	73%
Facilities management	5%	45%	18%
Learning from external sources	91%	91%	64%
Determining material sustainability issues	86%	86%	77%
Impact on CEO involvement in sustainability from CSO appointment			
Change in CEO involvement in sustainability from CSO appointment	2.72	2.62	2.50
Who decides where to locate primary responsibility and which factors affect the decision			
CEO or Board of Directors decide where to locate primary responsibility for sustainability	77%	64%	77%
Breadth of organizational commitment to sustainability	55%	68%	55%
Where champions of sustainability are located	18%	23%	36%
Level of commitment of organization to sustainability	64%	68%	55%
Sustainability strategy of the organization	41%	55%	64%

Source: Authors' research. Results from a survey with 66 respondents. The *Compliance, Efficiency*, and *Innovation* stages have the same number of respondents, 22 each. The table reports frequency of survey participants that respond "Yes" to a question. For "Change in CEO involvement in sustainability from CSO appointment" the average of responses is reported where 3 is "CEO involvement has increased," 2 is "CEO involvement has stayed the same," and 1 is "CEO involvement has decreased." Bold numbers represent the most significant differences across stages.

Most of the CSOs we interviewed had some role in the company's sustainability activities during the *Compliance* stage, even though they did not hold the title of CSO. In some instances, the activities were voluntary and outside of their formal job responsibilities, while in other cases these tasks were part of a formal role that encompassed other related activities. For example, John Edelman, the CSO for Edelman, the largest PR firm in the world, reported that during their initial stage of engagement with sustainability much of the activity was through employee volunteer efforts. However, he said that the initiatives were not coordinated, and no one in the organization had knowledge regarding all of the activities. Edelman, as with most of those we interviewed, became an advocate for centralizing and coordinating the oversight of the sustainability initiatives. He also assisted in the creation of the CSO job and was subsequently appointed to it in order to spearhead the company's movement from compliance to efficiency. One of his highest priorities during his first year as CSO was to take an inventory of the sustainability-related activities and to create a global framework for central oversight with local execution as they moved into the *Efficiency* stage of sustainability.

On the other hand, Dave Keppler, the CSO for Dow, was the senior executive for EHS and Corporate Social Responsibility before he became the CSO. He too became an advocate for the position and helped design it before being appointed to it. These advocates helped move the company to a higher level of commitment. Thus they were leaders in assisting the company in transitioning from *Compliance* to the *Efficiency* stage. Then, as the companies began to move towards *Innovation*, they helped develop the CSO position and were appointed to it. Interestingly, our interviewees often already had a relationship with the CEO and/or the senior leaders even before they became CSO. Even though some were in higher levels of authority than were others, it is possible that their existing relationship with the CEO allowed them greater credibility as advocates.

In summary, our data validate the hypothesis that most companies at the *Compliance* stage do not have a formal CSO position. Our survey data suggest that if they have anyone at all who is dedicated to sustainability, the role tends to be a lower-level position not reporting directly to the CEO or the Board of Directors. We recognize that our interview data is not robust enough for definitive conclusions. However, our limited data do reveal a consistent pattern that can be tested in future studies. In most cases, a leader within the organization, often without the title of CSO, becomes the advocate for the company's increased commitment to sustainability. In general, this person has already engaged in some sustainability-related projects in the company, either outside of her formal position or as a small part of it. They also appear to have had a relatively strong connection with the CEO during this early stage. Thus the advocate is credible and well positioned to drive the change successfully. Our survey data seems to corroborate this conclusion in that when a company does have a CSO (or someone with equivalent responsibilities), she is likely to have a positive influence on the CEO's involvement in sustainability as the company moves from the *Compliance stage* to the *Efficiency* stage.

EFFICIENCY STAGE

In this stage, companies begin to move to a more strategic approach to sustainability. They begin to focus on how they can respond to stakeholder pressures and at the same time impact the company's bottom line through actions such as reducing waste and increasing resource efficiency. They also begin the process of sustainability legitimization by building the business case and engaging internal stakeholders in the interactions that lead to common understanding. Hans Wegner, the CSO of National Geographic, one of the world's largest non-profit scientific and educational institutions, explained in our interview how the organization entered the second stage of sustainability. National Geographic was reporting on climate and social crises around the world, and yet as an organization they were not doing much themselves to address the issues. These endogenous tensions led Wegner to push the organization for a greater commitment to sustainability. At the time, his job was to oversee production of the magazine, including its printing, publishing, and distribution. He organized a group of volunteers around the company to design and assist with a variety of sustainability-related projects. He led the volunteers in the development of a sustainability vision and acquired the sign-off of the CEO. It was at this point that National Geographic pursued a new goal of becoming a triple-bottom-line company. Subsequently, they have set targets to become carbon neutral and are moving towards zero waste with projects such as magazine life-cycle analysis. They are also focusing on policies and practices that would enable them to improve their resource efficiency and address employee health. These goals and actions place them squarely in the *Efficiency* stage, which they entered due to endogenous pressures. Wegner, the current CSO, was instrumental in moving the company from *Compliance* to *Efficiency* through his advocacy and organizing work.

Table 8.1 shows that 33 percent of our sample falls in this stage. Those who have the title of CSO rose to 27 percent in this stage, which is almost equal to the percentage that has the title of Director of Sustainability (31 percent). The Board and/or CEO places a lower percentage of CSOs on the organizational chart in this stage compared with both of the other two stages (64 vs 71 percent). They are more likely to base the positioning of the CSO on the breadth of the company's involvement with sustainability compared with the other two stages. And they are more likely to position the CSO to report to the CEO or the Board in this stage versus the *Compliance* stage (41 percent vs 32 percent). While the appointment of the CSO is less likely to increase the involvement of the CEO in this stage, the ultimate responsibility for sustainability is more likely to be attributed to the CEO than in either of the other two stages (86 percent vs 73 percent in the *Compliance* stage and 59 percent in the *Innovation* stage).

Similar to the *Compliance* stage, almost all CSOs are responsible for developing strategy, reporting sustainability-related data, embedding sustainability into the organization, determining the material sustainability issues, and learning about sustainability from other companies. In addition, they are likely to be involved in educating employees about sustainability. Even though the categorical responsibilities resemble those of the persons responsible for sustainability in the *Compliance* stage, the nature of the tasks attached to these responsibilities are likely to shift in this second stage. In the *Compliance* stage, the responsibilities primarily tend to center on how to comply with environmental regulations, while in the *Efficiency* stage the same responsibilities are more likely to be on how to address a variety of stakeholder concerns, how to protect or enhance the company reputation, and how to impact the company's bottom line through reducing waste and increasing efficiencies in the use of resources.

We interpret the findings around the increased authority of the person primarily responsible for sustainability as evidence that companies are evolving to become more strategic throughout the second stage. The CEO, along with the senior leadership team, is already involved in sustainability, and the CEO has already taken the lead when the CSO is appointed. Thus, the CEO continues to work in partnership with the new CSO. In cases where the person who is appointed to the position of CSO is already playing a leadership role in the company, as were most of our interviewees, this partnership is a natural extension from the earlier stage. Since the company is most likely in the initial phases of developing the business case and crafting its strategy, it makes sense that the positioning of the CSO would be based on the breadth of the company's commitment to sustainability at this point. Undoubtedly, the breadth of their commitment varies at this stage from company to company as company leaders sort out what should be included in the strategy. In contrast, the importance of where champions of sustainability exist in the organization and the nature of the sustainability strategy of the organization increases in importance for positioning the CSO as the stages progress from *Compliance* to *Efficiency* to *Innovation*.

Consistent with these survey results, our interview data indicate that it is in this stage that the companies are most likely to hire or appoint a CSO. For example, Peter Graf, the CSO of SAP, the world's largest inter-enterprise software company, told us that in 2008 he proposed to the CEO and the Board that SAP make a stronger and more strategic commitment to sustainability. He made the case based on the Return-on-Investment (ROI) of increasing efficiencies. At the time, he was the Executive Director of Marketing. He said that the leadership accepted his proposal quickly. He was appointed to the newly created position of the CSO within a few months and assisted the company in moving from *Compliance* to *Efficiency*. Upon his appointment, he was instrumental in developing the business case and communicating it to the appropriate stakeholders in order to legitimize sustainability endeavors. With his background in marketing, he was in a good position to advocate for moving the company into the *Innovation* stage. Graf said that as the company moved into a market-driven and *Innovation* stage, he was once again responsible for crafting the business case and tailoring how it was communicated to various stakeholders. The move from *Efficiency* to *Innovation* was a natural and quick process for SAP, according to Graf. SAP found that the technologies they developed to reduce their own footprint in the *Efficiency* stage were also attractive to their customers. Therefore, they took the opportunity to commercialize and readily moved into the *Innovation* stage.

INNOVATION STAGE

As companies move into the *Innovation* stage, they begin to take a proactive and transformational approach to sustainability, rather than the more reactive approaches that characterize the first two stages. The strategies become market driven, with a focus on innovation and often addressing societal problems, such as climate change, water management, and obesity.

Table 8.1 shows that 33 percent of our sample falls into the *Innovation* stage. Just as the number of people with the title of CSO increases from the *Compliance* to the *Efficiency* stage, it increases again from the *Efficiency* to *Innovation* stage (27 percent to 36 percent). The frequency of the CEO being named as holding the ultimate responsibility for sustainability drops in this stage to 59 percent (compared to 73 percent in *Compliance* and 86 percent in the *Efficiency* stage). We believe that this finding implies that the CSO role has evolved and matured in this stage, and that the ultimate responsibility shifts from the CEO to the CSO accordingly. Certain factors that affect where to locate primary responsibility for sustainability within an organization are more prominent in the later stages. In the *Innovation* stage, 36 percent thought the location of sustainability champions had an effect (compared to 18 percent in the *Compliance* stage and 23 percent in the *Efficiency* stage) and 64 percent thought the organization's sustainability strategy had an effect (compared to 41 percent in the *Compliance* stage and 55 percent in the *Efficiency* stage). The incidence of the Board having a special committee on sustainability increases dramatically in the *Innovation* stage (64 percent vs 32 percent in *Compliance* and 27 percent in the *Efficiency* stage). These findings imply that sustainability has achieved a new level of strategic focus and that its importance has become significant enough to warrant increased discussion by the Board.

Interestingly, the responsibilities of the CSO are quite different in this stage. Their duties of embedding sustainability, attending to stakeholder relations, and educating employees are less visible. Indicatively, we report that while in the *Compliance* and *Efficiency* stages responsibility over reporting sustainability data is assumed by almost 100 percent of the CSOs, the respective number is only 75 percent in the *Innovation* stage. An explanation of this finding is that as companies integrate sustainability with the core of their business they also move from sustainability reporting to integrated reporting. As a result, reporting of sustainability data now becomes a responsibility of the CFO, rather than the CSO. Similarly, the number of CSOs reporting that part of their responsibilities includes educating employees, learning from external sources, and managing stakeholder relations declines significantly. This decline is probably a result of the CSO delegating authority and decision rights to functional departments and local business units. While in the *Efficiency* stage the CSO manages and sometimes carries out all of these processes, in the *Innovation* stage the CSO allocates these responsibilities to champions of sustainability throughout the organization. This explanation is consistent with the increasing importance of where champions of sustainability are located as a criterion in where to locate primary responsibility for sustainability. The question then becomes what is the role of the CSO in the *Innovation* stage. Our interview data shed light on this question.

According to the interviewees, the primary responsibility of the CSO in the *Innovation* stage is to assist with the development of the sustainability strategy as it evolves into the third stage and to develop the change strategy to support it. For example, when Steve Howard, the CSO for IKEA was hired, the first thing he did was to review the company's sustainability strategy. With a Ph.D. in environmental physics and his experience in running The Climate Group, an NGO focused on climate change, he was determined to take the IKEA sustainability strategy to a new level. He said that he did not think that their strategy was visionary enough and that it did not clearly connect back to the business. Howard moved IKEA into the *Innovation* stage by pulling together the senior leadership at IKEA to discuss how the company could be prepared for long-term world changes. This discussion led to the company's new strategy, as well as a framework for the business case.

During this third stage, our interview data suggest that the CSOs also have a significant role in assisting with the companies' innovation strategies. Dave Keppler, the CSO of Dow Chemical, said that senior leadership had been involved with environmental sustainability for many years. He assumed the position of CSO as the company shifted from primarily managing its footprint (*Efficiency* stage) to becoming market driven in its approach to sustainability (*Innovation* stage). The CEO, with the Board's support, appointed him because they wanted someone who could facilitate the company's innovation while also engaging the business in the process. At the time, he was the CIO and he had previously been in charge of the safety strategy when it was transformed. It was a natural transition for him to assume the responsibilities of the CSO position, since the facilitation expertise for it resembled the skills he mastered in his other roles. Since his passion and experience were in the area of transformation, he was a natural candidate for the job.

The interviewees highlighted that for sustainability strategies to take hold, they must be legitimized with stakeholders. The business case is a key element of the legitimization process. If this case is weak and the vision is not legitimized, the CSO is less likely to successfully carry out his or her other primary role of driving change through the organization. One of the opportunities and challenges for market-driven sustainability is that as the strategy evolves, so must the business case. According to Peter Graf, CSO of SAP, to continuously legitimize the strategy as it evolves often means developing more than one business case. The CSOs own the process of what they call the never-ending evolution of the business case(s).

As the strategy is legitimized, the CSO cultivates a sophisticated plan to bring about transformational change. Some organizational change scholars refer to this plan as a blueprint for creating the organization of the future (Nadler et al., 1995.) The CSO is situated to play a key role in this process by working with local leaders to create the blueprint that takes into account their circumstances, as well as their necessary contributions to the transformation. The CSO is in the position to ensure organizational alignment across both functions and geographies.

Scholars have debated whether organizations are monolithic with one strong culture or pluralistic. Those who support a pluralistic view argue that organizations are usually not composed of one unified culture, but rather of many distinct subcultures. This view suggests that catalysts for change can have localized impacts on the various subcultures such as functions, hierarchies, and occupational groups, even when all are embedded in an overarching dominant culture (Demers, 2007). The implication for CSOs is that their change strategy must take into account these subcultures. Research shows that even in the most committed companies the process of transformation will move through the various parts of the companies at different rates (Miller Perkins, 2013). This can perhaps be explained by the theory that most organizations are fragmented, with several subcultures within the dominant culture. Each of the subcultures is likely to have its own collective identity, defined as the cognitive, normative, and emotional connection experienced by members of a social group because of their perceived common status (Thornton and Ocasio, 2008). Logics, i.e. belief systems that shape the cognitions and behaviors of actors, emerge from these collective identities. Therefore, the process of driving change must take into account the multiple subcultures and their own logics and identities. SAP's CSO, Peter Graf, holds the pluralistic view of culture when he argues that SAP has many groups with varying perspectives. He claims that the strategies and messaging must be customized to the subcultures.

Elizabeth Heider, the recently appointed CSO for Skanska USA, among the largest construction and development companies in the US, says that one of her main priorities is to work in partnership with the CEO, Mike McNally, to drive transformation through the multiple businesses and parts of the company. Skanska is recognized as an industry leader in constructing sustainable buildings.[8] She says that continuing to expand their leadership is a business imperative. To prove her point, she explained that during the Great Recession, the construction companies that were leaders in "green building" were the only ones to continue to grow.[9] Before her appointment to the CSO position, Heider spearheaded Skanska USA Building's green building initiatives. She has been working internally to pull together the company's green initiatives since 2005. When asked why the CEO created the CSO position and promoted her into it, she said that the time was right for a more centralized and concentrated approach, since the US is a growth market for Skanska. Now

---

[8] Skanska. "Green Building." Available at: <http://www.usa.skanska.com/Markets/Green-building/> (accessed July 2014).

[9] McGraw-Hill (2010). Available at: <http://www.construction.com/AboutUs/2010/1112pr.asp> (accessed July 2014).

her role is to work alongside McNally and provide support and a vision across all four business units to elevate their performance across the company. Heider explains that Skanska USA was created through acquisitions, ending up with what she refers to as a confederation of legacy companies, each with its own culture. She has been tasked with developing a strategy for moving the company from a confederacy to a union in the sustainability realm. And yet she explains that construction is a local activity, and that while some markets are progressive, others lag behind. In addition, her strategy is to support the civil construction business unit, where their sustainability story is untold. She said, "We have an opportunity to raise all ships by also bringing along our subcontractors."

John Mandyck, the CSO of UTC Building and Industrial Systems, described how his organization grew through the addition of other businesses, with sustainability becoming a unifier of the legacy companies. The organization is very diverse and includes elevators and escalators, refrigeration, heating and air conditioning, fire safety, and security. Moreover it carries more than 80 brands. Mandyck emphasized how sustainability can be used as the platform to unify the various groups by highlighting the sustainability aspects of each product line in a vertical. Thus all of the products in a vertical are branded with sustainability. The interaction of sustainability with the presence of subcultures is complex. While CSOs can devise a sustainability strategy that takes into account all of the many subcultures, they can also use the sustainability platform to unify these subcultures.

In summary, the CSO role often carries significantly more authority during the *Innovation* stage. The responsibilities may shift from tactical to strategic. The CSOs may not only help develop visionary, market-driven sustainability strategies, they also must devise one or more business cases as the strategies evolve. They craft an approach to legitimizing the strategies with stakeholders and devise a sophisticated plan for driving the transformational change to support the strategies through the company. These responsibilities seem to require the increased authority that the position appears to hold in this stage.

Conclusion and lessons learned

Our research shows that the role of the CSO changes as companies transition through the stages. In the first stage, *Compliance*, very few companies have a person holding the title of CSO or the equivalent. Those CSOs that are in place in the first stage tend to have relatively low levels of authority. It is in the second and third stages (*Efficiency* and *Innovation*) that companies begin to create the CSO position with more elevated authority. Nevertheless, many of those who were later assigned to the CSO position were already taking a strong leadership role in pushing the company from *Compliance* to *Efficiency*. Thus many of the individuals who now hold the CSO title were actively involved in every stage. However, their roles and responsibilities, as well as their titles, varied across the stages.

In this section we will present some of the specific lessons learned by the CSOs we interviewed. We will present an overview of what the CSOs who participated in our interviews recommend for all of the stages, and will summarize how they carry out their roles in helping their companies transition through the stages. We note that we do not have any evidence that their recommendations will improve the competitiveness of other organizations or that they have improved the competitiveness of their own organizations. However, we also note that their organizations are ranked by independent providers as leaders in sustainability, and each organization has made the business case for sustainability, showing that their sustainability initiatives have been financially beneficial.

RECOMMENDATIONS FOR ALL STAGES

Our interviewees suggested that CSOs in every stage are more successful in changing the organization when they locate themselves as close as possible to areas where sustainability can produce value for the company. In the first stage, CSOs, or those who will eventually gain that title, need to stay close to those who oversee compliance and risk for the company. However, as companies move through the second stage and into the third stage, the areas where sustainability will produce value will vary from company to company, depending on their business and the nature of their strategy. Therefore, a CSO must assess what is significant and relevant to the company where she is employed and build the sustainability strategy accordingly. As the CSO moves through the second to the third stage, he gains authority. Thus he is critical to the successful development and communication of the business case(s) to expanded groups of stakeholders.

Those we interviewed argue that CSOs should not get too hung up on naming their company's stage or on labeling the kind of change that they are leading. Peter Graf, CSO of SAP, stated that what is compliance for one group may be a transformation for another. He suggested that CSOs keep this in mind when they are developing their action plans. Graf's point is corroborated by scholars who study the social dynamics of change. They assert that organizational change cannot be imposed in a monolithic fashion by management. Rather, cultural change emerges from the interactions of the local subcultures. Thus while some subcultures may view the change as transformational, others may see it as merely transitional. As a result, the effect of the subcultures on overall organizational change is likely to be achieved in increments (Myerson and Martin, 1987), with long-term change being evolutionary (Warglein 2002).

Steve Howard, CSO of IKEA, also discussed the significance of diagnosing the culture before planning a change strategy. However, unlike Graf's and Heider's descriptions of their companies' pluralistic cultures, Howard describes the IKEA culture as unified and cohesive in supporting company strategy. He suggests that a successful approach to change in a strong, centralized culture will differ from strategies that will succeed in a less centralized, pluralistic company. According to Beth Heider, CSO of Skanska, in a decentralized culture the CSO should think of the company as an organism with moving parts. Some parts of the culture will be more mature than others and may be related to the markets that each serves. Thus the CSO must gauge her strategy on a granular level. In a more cohesive culture such as IKEA's, the CSO can take a more monolithic versus a pluralistic approach to the change strategy.

Almost all of the CSOs we interviewed stressed the importance of focusing on a manageable set of sustainability-related issues each year. John Edelman, CSO of Edelman, referred to his approach as "evolutionary, not revolutionary." Steve Howard agrees. "You can't transform everything at once," said Howard. "The hardest thing about leading the change is managing the complexity, especially in a company like IKEA where the public is interested and watching our actions." Beth Heider stated that it is important to understand that this is not a "once-and-done" process. It will continue to morph and change. She suggests staying focused and managing the complexity.

EFFICIENCY AND *INNOVATION* STAGE

The CSOs recommended that their counterparts in other companies get a baseline of what the company may already be doing when they first assume the role. It is important to focus on a few core issues in the beginning of this stage. And while some say that the CSO should develop a common language, others argued that it is important to learn to speak many languages—or the lexicons of a variety of stakeholder groups—in order to make the business case and strategy understandable and relevant to each. One of the most difficult challenges facing the CSO in this stage is to push the company leaders and investors to get out of the "trade-off" mentality. The CSO needs to be able to discuss the sustainability strategy of the firm with investors by using the language of the capital markets.

Our interviewees recommended that as a company moves through the *Efficiency* stage towards the *Innovation* stage, the CSO should work to engage as many people and groups as possible. For example, Scott Wicker, CSO of UPS, a package delivery company and provider of specialized transportation and logistics services, described their strategy committee and working committee. Through these committees, the CSO can help leaders and others in the organization think about the changes through their own area's lens. Edelman recommends working from the top down and the bottom up in this phase, since employees like to get involved.

INNOVATION STAGE

It is in this stage that the role of the CSO tends to gain an increasing level of authority. Our interviewees assert that the CSO should report to the CEO and should sit on the executive team. This positioning gives the CSO not only legitimacy, but also access to the decision makers, so that she can be an advocate for sustainability in the decision-making process and can provide input on market-driven strategies. Steve Howard advocates putting the CSO on the executive team because her physical presence makes a difference in the conversation. He asserts that without this presence, sustainability goals would slip down the agenda. These recommendations are consistent with the literature on institutional entrepreneurs, which suggests that those change leaders with high social positioning and power are more likely to be effective (Battilana 2007).

Many of the CSOs we interviewed take the lead in formulating vision and strategy in this stage. Several, including Steve Howard from IKEA and Alexandra Palt from L'Oreal, said that the best way to create the vision is to identify the company's unique position with respect to future global challenges. Palt argued that this is the only way to ensure that the company stays relevant and survives for the next 100 years.

Our CSO interviewees suggest bringing together executives, internal experts, opinion leaders, and even NGOs to assist with the strategy. For example, Palt said that when she was coordinating the process for setting L'Oreal's goals for 2020, she traveled around the world to meet with NGOs so that they could provide input and challenge L'Oreal's policies and strategies. Likewise, Dave Keppler, from Dow, described their close involvement with NGOs such as the Nature Conservancy. Dow leaders also expect their NGO partners to challenge them and push them to improve their internal processes.

The CSOs recommend carefully considering how to discuss vision and strategies with stakeholder groups. Beth Heider, from Skanska, suggested that communications focus on creating a positive future, for example by creating a better world for children. Similarly, Palt suggested that the communication strategy focus on how the actions and commitments can improve people's lives, rather than focusing on stimulating fear and guilt.

When asked about the knowledge, skills, and qualities that a CSO should possess to drive the change during this third stage, most agreed that a keen sense of the culture is critical, as is a sophistication in both understanding and implementing change through a complex organization. This is consistent with most CSOs being internally appointed to this position. However, when asked whether a person who has been with the company a long time is better equipped for the position than an external person with education and experience in fields related to sustainability, the interviewees were divided in their opinions. By and large they see this as a trade-off. On the one hand, those who are internal have a familiarity with the culture, understanding of the business, and credibility with the leaders. On the other hand, an external person with content expertise has a pair of fresh eyes to use in advancing the company and the knowledge to deal with the very complex issues pertaining to sustainability.

CONCLUDING REMARKS

We believe that our results open up a number of avenues for future research. Having documented the increased authority that CSOs have in companies that are in more advanced stages of sustainability, future research could explore how CSO incentives evolve as a result. First, for example, is it the case that as organizations advance through sustainability changes, the CSO is provided incentives on organization-level success metrics, such as the stock price and accounting profitability, versus more sustainability-specific metrics? And what is the relative effectiveness of the two compensation strategies? Answering these questions could enhance our understanding about the incentives of CSOs in different stages and their effectiveness as change agents.

Second, we have documented that the Board of Directors is more likely to have a sustainability committee in the third stage, *Innovation*. We still know very little about what this committee does and how it informs decision making inside the company. Nor do we know which members serve on this committee or, importantly, how the CSO interacts with its members. Collecting and analyzing data that help to answer these questions would contribute to the literature on corporate governance.

A third question relates to the potentially puzzling results regarding the responsibilities of CSOs in the third stage, *Innovation*. While we find that CSO responsibilities are similar in the first two stages, *Compliance* and *Efficiency*, and that CSOs perform a wide variety of tasks, in the *Innovation* stage fewer CSOs perform all these tasks. Our interview data suggest that their responsibility evolves to tasks that relate to forging a strong culture and unifying the different subcultures inside the firm. Future research could explore what is the most effective strategy for achieving this and what are the consequences of these actions for organizational performance. Having documented the importance of sustainability champions in the third stage as a factor for locating primary responsibility for sustainability, future research could study the location of sustainability champions as a possible mechanism for the unification of subcultures inside the firm.

Finally, future research could try to understand how CSOs interact with institutional investors as their authority and responsibility evolve. Presumably, by the third stage institutional investors are aware of the increasing decision rights and influence of the CSO inside the organization. Is it the case that the CSO becomes part of the conversation between senior management and investors in these later stages? How do different types of investors, short-term and long-term oriented, react to the business case made by the CSO? How does the CSO work with the CFO, the other C-level executive apart from the CEO, who is in charge of the discussion with investors? Shedding light on these phenomena would contribute to the literature on sustainability and integrated reporting and the literature that documents capital market benefits from enhanced communication of sustainability information.

We believe that our study also suggests some interesting avenues for future research on change, at the institutional, organizational, and individual levels. In a recent article, Binns et al. (2014) argued that organizations need to find a way to initiate transformation proactively. What is needed is a way to change before a crisis pushes the organization to transform out of fear. They suggest that companies should create growth-related goals that connect with the positive emotions of individuals and the sense of the company's identity. We propose that our interview data exhibits some evidence that endogenous tensions can create growth-related, proactive transformation related to sustainability. Our CSOs recounted how their advocacy, as well as the CEO's vision for becoming a sustainable company, precipitated the process of change. Beer and Walton (1987) suggested that as the leader's vision creates and structures the cognitive world of those connected to the organization, that vision becomes a logic that precipitates change in ideas, values, and behaviors. Perhaps future research could more systematically analyze the process by which a CEO develops this vision.

Another area for future research is what specifically happens in the *Compliance* stage that enables the company to ultimately move to *Efficiency* and possibly *Innovation*. Edelman and Suchman (1997) argue that regulations often have greater effects on organizations through the normative and cognitive processes that they set in motion than by their coercive mechanisms. They assert that constituency statute legislation gave firms the right to take stakeholder interests other than shareholders into account when making decisions. They also mention that legislative statutes are loose and that people collectively construct what it means to be in compliance. Therefore even in this first stage institutional logics are contested, as organizations coalesce into fields to construct meaning. Thus the process of change most likely begins in this stage and is probably emergent, rather than intentional. More exploration of the nature of these processes and possible role that they play in enabling transition to the higher stages would greatly improve our understanding in this field.

■ ACKNOWLEDGMENTS

George Serafeim acknowledges financial support from the Division of Faculty and Research Development of Harvard Business School. We are grateful to Robert Eccles, Ranjay Gulati, and Rebecca Henderson for many helpful discussions and comments. We thank Andy Knauer for providing excellent research assistance.

▪ REFERENCES

Acre, Aconas, Ethical Performance, Flag. (2012) "The CR and Sustainability Salary Survey." Available at: <http://crsalarysurvey.com/_media/documents/survey12.pdf>.

Arbogast and Thornton. (2012) "A Global Corporate Sustainability Model," *Journal of Sustainability and Green Business* (April).

Battilana, Julie. (2007) "Initiating Divergent Organizational Change: The Enabling Role of Actor's Social Position," *Academy of Management Annual Meeting Proceedings* 1: 1–6.

Beer, Michael and Walton, Anna. (1989) "Organizational Change and Development: New Arenas for Inquiry and Action," *Journal of Management* 15: 205–28.

Binns, Andy, Harreld, J. Bruce, O'Reilly, Charles A., and Tushman, Michael L. (2014) "The Art of Strategic Renewal," *MIT Sloan Management Review* 55 (2): 21–3.

Campbell, John. (2007) "Why Would Corporations Behave in Socially Responsible Ways? An Institutional Theory of Corporate Social Responsibility." *Academy of Management Review*, 32 (3): 946–67.

Deutsch, Claudia H. (2007) "Companies Giving Green an Office," *New York Times*, July 3. Available at: <http://www.nytimes.com/2007/07/03/business/03sustain.html?pagewanted=all> (accessed July 2014).

Dyllick, Thomas and Muff, Katrin. (2013) "Clarifying the Meaning of Sustainable Business," University of St Gallen and Business School Lausanne Working Paper.

Eccles, Robert and Serafeim, George. (2013) "The Performance Frontier: Innovating for a Sustainable Strategy," *Harvard Business Review* 91 (5): 50–60.

Eccles, Robert, Miller, Kathy, and Serafeim, George. (2012) "How to Become a Sustainable Company," *MIT Sloan Management Review* 53 (4): 43–50.

Edelman, Lauren and Suchman, Mark. (1997) "The Legal Environments of Organizations," *Annual Review of Sociology* 23: 479–515.

Ernst & Young. (2012) "The DNA of the CIO." Available at: <http://www.ey.com/GL/en/Services/Advisory/The-DNA-of-the-CIO> (accessed July 2014).

Esty, D. C. and Winston, A. S. (2006) *Green to Gold: How Smart Companies Use Environmental Strategy to Innovate, Create Value, and Build Competitive Advantage.* New Haven: Yale University Press, 2006.

Footprint Talent and WAP Sustainability Consulting. (2011) "The State of the CSO." Available at: <http://www.wapsustainability.com/WAP/Media_&_Links_files/The%20%State%20of%20the%20CSO%20Finnal.pdf>.

Greenbiz. (2013) "State of the Profession." Available at: <http://ugs.utah.edu/sustainability-certificate/State%20of%20the%20Profession%202013.pdf> (accessed July 2014).

Hoffman, Andrew and Bansal, Pratima. (2012) *Business and the Natural Environment.* Oxford: Oxford University Press.

IBM. (2011) "The Emergence of the CIO." Available at: <http://www-03.ibm.com/ibm/history/ibm100/us/en/icons/emergenceofcio/> (accessed July 2014).

Ioannou, Ioannis and Serafeim, George. (2012) "What Drives Corporate Social Performance? The Role of Nation-level Institutions," *Journal of International Business Studies* 43 (9): 834–64.

Kellogg, Katherine C. (2011) "Hot Lights and Cold Steel: Cultural and Political Toolkits for Practice Change in Surgery," *Organization Science* 22 (2): 482–502.

Lounsbury, Michael. (2001) "Institutional Sources of Practice Variation: Staffing College and University Recycling Programs," *Administrative Science Quarterly* 46 (1): 29–56.

McGraw-Hill. (2010) *Green Market Report*. Available at: <http://www.construction. com/AboutUs/2010/1112pr.asp> (accessed July 2014).

McWilliams, Abagail and Siegel, Donald. (2001) "Corporate Social Responsibility: A Theory of the Firm Perspective," *Academy of Management Review* 26 (1): 117–27.

Meyer, Alan. (1982) "Adapting to Environmental Jolts," *Administrative Science Quarterly* 27 (4): 515–37.

Miller Perkins, Kathy. (2013) "Sustainability and Culture: A Case Study of Dow Chemical and Nedbank," Working paper.

Mirvis, Philip and Googins, Bradley. (2009) "Moving to Next Generation Corporate Citizenship," *CCCD Century fur Corporate Citizenship Deutschland. Kollwitzstr* 73: 10435. Available at: <http://www.gn-cc.org/sites/gern.werk21system.de/files/ CCCDebatte%2001%20Moving%20to%20Next%20Generation%20CC%202009% 20engl.0.pdf>.

Myerson, D. and Martin, J. (1987) "Cultural Change: An Integration of Three Different View," *Journal of Management Studies* 24 (6): 623–47.

Nadler, David and Tushman, Michael. (1995) "Types of Organizational Change: From Incremental Improvement to Discontinuous Transformation," in D. A. Nadler, B. R. B. Shaw, A. E. Walton et al. (eds), *Discontinuous Change: Leading Organizational Transformation*. San Francisco: Jossey-Bass Pfeiffer, 15–34.

National Association of Corporate Directors. (2013) "C-Suite Expectations." Available at: <http://www.nacdonline.org/files/FileDownloads/PDF/C-Suite%20Expectations_ 1364247261983_2.pdf> (accessed July 2014).

Nidumolu, Ram, Prahalad, C. K., and Rangaswami, M. R. (2009) "Why Sustainability is Now the Key Driver of Innovation," *Harvard Business Review* 87 (9): 56–64.

PwC. (2012) "The Sustainability Executive: Profile and Progress." Available at: <http:// www.pwc.com/us/en/corporate-sustainability-climate-change/publications/sustain ability-executive-profile-and-progress.jhtml> (accessed July 2014).

PwC. (2013) "Evolution of the CFO." Available at: <http://pwc.com.au/consulting/ assets/publications/Evolution-CFO-Jul13.pdf> (accessed July 2014).

Skanska. "Green Building." Available at: <http://www.usa.skanska.com/Markets/ Green-building/> (accessed July 2014).

Spitze, James M. (2012) "How to Unlock the Power of the CIO," *Wall Street Journal*, August 1. Available at: <http://blogs.wsj.com/cio/2012/08/01/how-to-unlock-the- power-of-the-cio/> (accessed July 2014).

Thornton, Patricia and Ocasio, William. (2008) "Institutional Logics," in R. Greenwood, C. Oliver, and R. Suddaby (eds), *Handbook of Organizational Institutionalism*. London and Thousand Oaks, CA: Sage Publications, 99–129.

Tolbert, Pamela and Zucker, Lynn. (1996) "The Institutionalization of Institutional Theory," in S. Clegg, C. Hardy, and W. Nord (eds), *Handbook of Organization Studies*. London: Sage Publications, 175–90.

Warglein, Massimo. (2002) "Intra-organizational Evolution," in J. Baum (ed.), *A Companion to Organization Theory*. Oxford: Blackwell.

Weinreb Group. (2011) *CSO Back Story: How Chief Sustainability Officers Reached the C-Suite*. Available at: <http://www.weinrebgroup.com/wp-content/uploads/2011/ 09/CSO-Back-Story-by-Weinreb-Group.pdf>.

Willard, Bob. (2012) *The Sustainability Advantage*, 10th Anniversary Edn. Gabriola Island, BC: New Society Publishers.

Part IV
Exploring the Processes of Change

9 Two Roads to Green

A Tale of Bureaucratic versus Distributed Leadership Models of Change

Deborah Ancona, Elaine Backman, and Kate Isaacs

Over the past decade there has been a trend in the corporate world for companies to transition their environmental policies and practices from a matter of compliance and risk management to a "source of opportunity, innovation and competitive advantage" (Hoffman and Glancy, 2006; Porter and Kramer, 2006: 80). Leading companies are redesigning products and manufacturing processes to use resources more wisely, eliminate toxic inputs, and reduce waste by-products. In so doing, they are learning to anticipate regulations and position themselves competitively.

In this study, we examine how two well-known corporate entities, "Alpha" and "Beta," initiated and advanced company-wide green initiatives. Alpha is a large multinational company in the business equipment and services industry. Beta is a medium-sized, multinational company that produces a wide range of high-end consumer and industrial products. Both are known for being well managed; both have frequently been recognized as "Great Places to Work"; and both have received numerous awards for innovation.

Yet Alpha and Beta occupy different positions on the continuum of leadership logics that ranges from "command and control" to "cultivate and coordinate" (Malone, 2004). (The two ends of the continuum are summarized in Table 9.1 as ideal type models.) Alpha is trying to pull away from its traditional bureaucratic roots, with varying degrees of success, while Beta is constantly working to improve on its legacy of distributed leadership. These different leadership logics, each driven by a coherent bundle of core assumptions about leadership authority, role autonomy, and innovation processes, impact the way each company travels the "road to green."

At both companies, the Environmental Health and Safety (EH&S) department succeeded in influencing senior leaders to embrace green business opportunities as a strategic priority; at both, the resulting projects had access to manpower, funding, and political backing; and at both there was a sense of excitement about what could be achieved.

But despite these similarities, differences in the dominant leadership logics in the two companies led to their green initiatives unfolding in very different ways. Although Alpha had been moving towards more of a "cultivate-and-

Table 9.1 Comparison of organizational models

Organizational model	Traditional bureaucracy	Distributed leadership
Leadership logic	*Top-down "command and control"*: role-based "heroic" leadership: individual, leaders are responsible for major leadership functions and engage in top-down decision making	*"Cultivate and coordinate"*: leadership functions are performed by many people throughout the organization; decision making is top down *and* bottom up
Type of leader authority	*Positional authority*: formal leaders issue commands and expect compliance from subordinates; authoritative power is used, along with other forms of power	*Collaborative influence*: leaders influence others and cultivate their involvement without using authoritative power (note this does not imply that power is always used in benign ways)
Role autonomy	*Negotiated autonomy*: individuals have varying degrees of autonomy; must negotiate task and role decisions with superiors; superiors may or may not take individual interests, skills, and preferences into account	*Strategic autonomy*: all individuals have significant autonomy to select tasks and roles based on their skills and interests; they are expected and encouraged to choose in ways that serve both themselves and the organization
Innovation model	*Blueprint-control*: issue direction after some organizational input; top leaders determine vision, set specific innovation goals, assign tasks, and control timing and process	*Emerge-synthesize*: build internal support for shared vision; members propose goals, tasks, and project timing that are gradually formalized; leaders guide, support, and connect emergent efforts

coordinate" logic, bureaucratic rules, and a top-down mindset kept hi-jacking attempts at collaborative influence. What began as a bottom-up green initiative moved quickly to an implementation effort cascading down from the top to successively lower levels within each of its divisions through the company's annual planning and evaluation processes.

At Beta, the challenge was how to cultivate organization-wide excitement in a coordinated fashion without imposing change. Implementation there involved creating space and support for bottom-up green initiatives by individuals and small teams working within the company's business divisions.

At Alpha, the shift from a bottom-up to a top-down initiative led relatively quickly to a concentrated effort on a few high-priority projects approved by top managers, each designed to lead to radical improvements in the company's environmental performance. By contrast, Beta's collaborative leadership led to a slower start-up process focused on creating support throughout the organization and a new game board for playing the environmental innovation game—one designed to encourage, channel, and connect small, bottom-up innovations.

The differing positions of Alpha and Beta on the distributed leadership continuum created critical differences in how each company decided to adopt green as a strategic priority, the selection of initiative leaders, and the execution of key leadership functions. In this chapter, we describe how the two roads to green played out, highlighting how entrenched organizational models and leadership logics shape change trajectories. The results suggest that even when traditional bureaucracies try to move away from a top-down approach, rigid routines and command and control mindsets hamper movement into a looser, more innovative space. As for distributed leadership organizations, the results indicate that sometimes they need to create simple structures and rules so that innovation does not run wild. Finally, in terms of the specific challenge of going green, we highlight some of the danger points in such an effort, and suggest steps to counteract deeply entrenched patterns that can work against success.

Research design and relevant literature

This case study is part of a larger comparative field study of product innovation at Alpha and Beta. It employs an inductive design that allows case differences and similarities to emerge from the data, and draws upon two literature streams: one documenting the broader shift from bureaucratic to new organizational forms, and one identifying key leadership functions.

Bureaucratic versus distributed leadership

Recent work on organizational design has documented four trends that make it clear that the old bureaucratic form of organizing—with its clear rules, fixed division of labor, and hierarchy of offices—is giving way to a significantly modified organizational form:

- There has been a decline in formalization of job descriptions and task assignments, leading to an attenuation of the distinction between managerial versus non-managerial roles (Kelley, 1990; Powell, 2001; Snell and Dean, 1992; Youndt and Snell, 2004).
- Hierarchies have become flatter as organizations move from "jobs to projects," often self-managed by team members, rather than by supervisors (Powell, 2001; Pettigrew and Massini, 2003; Rajan and Wulf, 2006), and from relying on a small number of large, vertically integrated business units towards smaller, semi-autonomous "modular" business units each adapting to distinctive markets (Brown and Eisenhardt, 1997; Schilling and Steensma, 2001).
- There has been a huge expansion in the use of teams. This shift originated in Japanese-inspired quality improvement techniques, and became widespread after the 1990s with the use of cross-functional teams and taskforces (Donnellon and Scully, 1994; Osterman, 1994; Hackman, 2002; Strang and Kim, 2005).
- Internal and external boundaries have become more porous as teams and task forces with overlapping, cross-functional memberships and enterprise-wide collaborative technologies break down the traditional dividing lines of bureaucracy (Gulati et al., 2012).

The organizational context evolving from these four trends is very different from a traditional bureaucracy characterized by centralized strategy formulation, rigid organizational structures, and a "command and control" leadership logic. With more flexible job descriptions, flattened hierarchies, team-based work, and porous boundaries, newer organizational initiatives rely more on individual agency operating within overarching corporate goals with a "cultivate and coordinate" leadership logic (Brown and Eisenhardt, 1997; Eisenhardt et al., 2000).

This new organizational form and way of operating has various names, including "post-bureaucratic" (Heckscher, 1994), the "collaborative community" (Heckscher and Adler, 2006), the "networked organization" (Powell, 2003), "adaptive systems" (Heifetz et al., 2009), the "adhocracy culture" (Cameron and Quinn, 2011), and "collaborative enterprise," (Heckscher, 2007). We employ the term "distributed leadership organizations," a term derived from one of their central characteristics—multiple autonomous agents exerting leadership at many different levels to both instantiate and alter core organizational structures and processes.

Although there is intense interest in distributed leadership organizations, there are few fine-grained empirical field studies aimed at understanding how these forms actually operate. Furthermore, organizations do not simply flip a switch and shift from one form of leadership logic to another. The road from "command and control" to: cultivate and coordinate" is fraught with traps, as bureaucratic behavior lodged deep within standard operating procedures and mental models often blocks the way. This chapter aims to expand our understanding of two distributed leadership organizations, one in a period of transition and one firmly established in this space. By tracing how the green initiatives played out at Alpha and Beta, we come to understand how change and innovation efforts differ as organizations move away from the traditional bureaucratic structures that dominated organizational life in the twentieth century.

Leadership functions

Our analysis focuses on three aspects of green initiatives at the two companies: the decision to launch the initiative; the choice of initiative leaders; and the execution of key leadership functions. With regard to the last of these, the data is presented using the Four Capabilities Model, a framework that focuses on four leadership functions: relating, sensemaking, visioning, and inventing (Ancona et al., 2007). We chose this organizing framework because it highlights how a more experienced "cultivate and coordinate" organization operates to engage multiple individuals in the change process and how old "command and control" processes can reassert themselves through leadership practices, as well as because this model has been shown to help leaders develop new skills in a dynamic world (Ancona, 2011).

Relating refers to the form and nature of relationships among leaders and those they lead. Relating includes perspective taking—being able to see the world through the lens of others—as well as advocating your own point of view, and creating effective networks within and outside of your group (see Reagans and McEvily, 2003; Williams et al., 2007). The research presented here suggests that as organizations move from "command and control" to "cultivate and coordinate," relating needs to shift from telling people what to do to enrolling them as active change agents, and those agents need to develop broad relating within and outside of the organization.

Sensemaking refers to a leader's efforts to understand the context in which she is operating. This involves collecting data and mapping external conditions, including stakeholder needs and expectations, technological advancements, competitive threats, economic conditions, and political shifts (Weick et al., 2005; Ancona, 2011). This study suggests that in a "cultivate-and-coordinate" leadership organization sensemaking is distributed across multiple individuals on an on-going basis, as opposed to being the work of a specialized group at a particular moment in time.

Visioning is the ability to paint a picture of the future and frame the overall mission of the organization (House and Howell, 1992). Visionary leaders have been shown to help in the process of transformational change (Bass and Avolio, 1994), and to inspire employees with greater motivation and commitment to the job (Avolio et al., 2004). On the other hand, this study illustrates that when top management in a "command and control" model sees its role as dictating the vision and objectives for change, the result can be to supplant more bottom-up efforts.

Inventing includes the actions taken to make the vision a reality, creating new structures and processes to shift the focus of activity in a new direction (Cameron and Quinn, 2011). Our work suggests that when pushed by a top-down leadership mode, inventing can be quite constrained by set procedures and targets, unlike in a "cultivate and coordinate" mode, where the focus is specifically on creating a context in which others can invent.

The enactment of these leadership practices is highly differentiated across the Alpha and Beta sites, illustrating how such practices are both influenced by, and in turn influence, each organization's models and leadership logics.

Findings

MAKING THE DECISION TO GO GREEN

Alpha

Alpha is proud of its history of leadership on environmental issues. In the 1990s, the company made major changes in its internal processes to reduce waste, and worked with the Environmental Protection Agency to develop the Energy Star standards. Since the program's inception, Alpha's products have consistently received the highest Energy Star rating. Nevertheless, by 2005 the leaders of the EH&S group believed that Alpha's efforts should expand beyond a focus on Star certification to a broader effort to encourage all divisions to embrace the business case for green.

In 2006, EH&S began a major information collection effort—attending scientific meetings and collecting data from academics, NGOs, investors, regulators, competitors, and customers to identify important environmental issues and possible directions for promising business opportunities. They identified climate change, energy conservation, and waste reduction as major focus areas, prompting Lisa Scanlon[1], the leader of EH&S, to convince Alpha's corporate leaders to adopt a "green" initiative in 2007 as a major strategic priority.

When a corporate strategic priority is declared at Alpha, unit managers are expected to create relevant project goals, timelines, head counts, and individual assignments. When the green priority was presented during Alpha's annual planning cycle, the head of the research and development (R&D) division, Abby Shore, an avid environmentalist, embraced the new green thrust, and created a cross-level taskforce comprised of scientists and managers from each of the four R&D centers to kick off the division's green initiative.

Beta

Like Alpha, Beta felt it had a good sustainability record and could point to historical collaborations with government regulators to develop environmental standards in several of its target industries. By 2005, however, two long-time employees—Bill Anderson, who led the EH&S group, and John Gomes, an engineer with a long history in new product development—had come to believe that Beta was not fully capitalizing on green business opportunities. Consequently, the two men began working together to lay the groundwork for a new green initiative at the company.

All initiatives at Beta are driven by what the company calls "passionate champions." The company's employees have wide latitude to choose the projects they want to work on and to shape the scope of their work commitments by choosing to build or join small, multi-functional teams. The resulting teams select their own leaders through an emergent, negotiated process. Thus innovation relies not on appointed leaders, but on individuals who have a vision to create something new, and who can successfully influence others to join them in making that vision a reality.

Because people at Beta have a great deal of freedom to try new things, passionate environmental champions like Anderson and Gomes had been at work for years to advance green initiatives. But the company had no overarching environmental vision, so these local champions were not getting as much traction as they would have liked. As Anderson explained:

---

[1] All names used in this chapter have been changed for presentation purposes.

We've behaved environmentally responsibly for a long time. But it's been disjointed...if you've got a number of different objectives, and people doing it in their spare time, and if there's not clear and substantial leadership support then it's hard to make much progress.

At the time that Anderson and Gomes were beginning their collaboration, some of the company's most senior leaders were themselves sensing increased interest in environmental issues. Customers, end consumers, younger employees, and even casual visitors were asking Beta about its environmental practices. The senior leadership team realized that the company had no consistent answers for these stakeholders and was not able to "speak with one voice" about its environmental record, as the CEO put it.

Based upon discussions with customers and other CEOs, Beta's CEO joined Anderson and Gomes and their growing group of followers in a far-reaching, internal influencing campaign to make the case for Beta's adoption of an environmental responsibility statement. In 2008, this effort succeeded, and the company adopted the statement as a key strategic priority.

Key differences

While both Alpha and Beta arrived at the same decision to prioritize going green, they did so in very different ways. Alpha's top management group was influenced by the EH&S department, but once the company decided to move, the initiative became a top-down push that was supported and enforced with a focused change process and measures for success. In contrast, Beta started with two internal champions who created a campaign that gradually pulled the CEO and others into setting a new priority for the firm. Beta's process was more inclusive, organic, and slowly emergent. Alpha's sensing of environmental opportunity came from a small, specialized group, while Beta's was based on a swelling chorus of multiple employees and stakeholders all suggesting new directions and seeking to influence key leaders.

These initial differences set the stage for Alpha's road to green evolving as a top-down initiative run by formal leaders with a narrow focus, while Beta involved more people from varying roles collaborating formally and informally to chart the way forward.

CHOOSING A LEADER AND RELATIONAL NETWORK DIFFERENCES

Alpha

At Alpha, once the company's environmental strategic "plank" was adopted, responsibility for green innovation shifted away from EH&S. Although the EH&S leader, Scanlon, had a passion for environmental matters, deep expertise around green business opportunities, and significant relational networks that she had developed while developing Alpha's strategic proposal, she played only an advisory role in the implementation phase of the new green strategy.

This decision simply reflected how Alpha's bureaucratic rules came to dominate the structure and decision making around the decision to go green. EH&S—and its leader—were seen as fulfilling a "staff function" that fit into a clearly defined box, with specialized environmental responsibilities. As such, it was considered "too isolated" to lead a company-wide initiative. Once top management adopted the green strategic plank, they relieved EH&S of its early leadership, and gave leadership responsibility to line managers within the company's major divisions. In this chapter, we tracked how this process played out in one of these divisions—the research and development division (R&D)—comprised of four centers and some 800 scientists and engineers, led by the company's Chief Technology Officer (CTO), Abby Shore.

In 2007, Shore created a taskforce of scientists and managers from each research center and asked her special assistant, a "high-potential" leader named Janice Goodhue, to spend part of her time leading the new green effort in the R&D division. Shore felt this would be a "stretch assignment" for Goodhue that would help her develop new management skills and relational networks as she advanced to more senior leadership positions.

Goodhue had a personal interest in sustainability but lacked expertise in green technologies. Also, while Goodhue got assistance from EH&S and used her personal network to identify and quickly form a green team, she had much weaker internal and external networks of individuals interested and knowledgeable about sustainability than either Scanlon or Shore. With the choice of Goodhue as the leader of its green initiative, Alpha selected a high-potential leader, but lost much of the technical knowledge and pre-existing relational networks associated with sustainability.

Beta

Meanwhile at Beta, the leadership selection process was handled in a consultative, negotiated manner. Bill Anderson, the head of EH&S, had extended discussions with the company's CEO about leadership of the green initiative. After considering several options, including bringing in an outside person, Anderson, Beta's CEO, and others agreed that Anderson would be the best person for the job. Anderson explained the process as follows:

The CEO and I talked about how bringing in an experienced new hire to try to influence an enterprise-wide initiative does not have a good success rate. The environmental work just so happened to coincide with something else I'm doing in developing the next generation of leadership in EH&S. I could hand off some of my leadership obligations, which would allow me to take on more of a role in environmental responsibility and sustainability. We talked about it, and it made sense, so I made the commitment to champion this initiative and worked to identify people who would be valuable on a core team.

At Beta, as at Alpha, the EH&S group was focused primarily on regulatory compliance. But Anderson had broader environmental interests and had been pushing for an organization-wide green initiative for some time. In short, he brought passion, expertise, a deep network of relationships, internal credibility, and ready-to-go projects to the initiative:

Twelve years ago I led a team that started developing and implementing environmental management systems because of a business need. I've been sensitive to opportunities to move the environmental program forward. 'Stealthing' is recognizing the smaller opportunities that have value. Stealthing sometimes has negative connotations. It's really not negative because you get buy-in for these smaller initiatives. You start building programs that can connect in the long term. Part of our strategy was also to integrate into existing programs, such as the quality management system. Customers were saying that they weren't going to buy from us unless these processes were in place… this presented an opportunity to connect previous developed programs and continue to build upon them.

All of these individual pieces were based on local needs and opportunities. When these bigger needs developed you could quickly stitch them together into a more comprehensive model.

Key differences

There were striking differences in the individuals chosen to play crucial leadership roles in the green initiatives at Alpha and Beta. Both Goodhue and Anderson were skilled leaders, but they had vastly different resources in three areas: 1) the amount of interest and expertise in environmental issues (Anderson had a great deal; Goodhue had a steep learning curve); 2) a network of relationships that could help advance a green initiative (Anderson had a rich, existing network; Goodhue had to build hers up quickly); and 3) the time they had to devote themselves to the effort (Anderson worked the majority of his time on Beta's green initiative once he off-loaded his other responsibilities; Goodhue was assigned to her initiative only part-time).

The respective selections of Goodhue and Anderson illustrate the two different leadership logics at work. Alpha moved the initiative out of the EH&S "staff" function and into the company's business units. At the R&D division, CTO Shore assigned it to Goodhue, a high-potential manager. The rules around "who can lead" were dominated by considerations of where one sits in the hierarchy, role specialization, and readiness for managerial promotion. In contrast, Beta demonstrated more flexibility to match people and tasks, rather than being constrained by rigid job titles and organizational rules. In practice, this meant that Beta focused on choosing the person who could make the best leader, with little or no consideration to the staff/line distinction or role specialization.

SENSEMAKING

Any kind of change process involves external environmental scanning—"what's going on out there?"—and an assessment of internal capabilities—"what can we do in here?" Sensemaking melds data collection from multiple sources, with an ability to "map" the data and discern patterns, and the capacity to test and update the map of the external environment (Weick et al., 2005; Ancona, 2011).

In both organizations, people in the EH&S departments had done a great deal of sensemaking before the green initiatives became official, building an understanding within the broader organization about the need for "green" and the possible role that such an initiative could play strategically. While Beta opted to have EH&S lead its green initiative, each of Alpha's divisions, including R&D, appointed an internal candidate to lead its effort. These choices carried important consequences for sensemaking.

Alpha

Janice Goodhue, who was appointed by Shore to lead the R&D green initiative, had not been part of the first round of sensemaking led by Alpha's EH&S department. She was therefore coming to the initiative without much sense of the organizational history or existing knowledge base around green. To get up to speed, Goodhue recognized the need to move quickly and initiate broad sensemaking.

I started interviewing senior level R&D managers, because I wanted to understand where they feel green fits in and what they think is important. I talked to VPs or chief technology types because I knew they would have direct contact with customers and I wanted to keep that linkage. I also met with EH&S and the VP there. I wanted to be in line with the Alpha plank for green. They did a lot of research and a lot of background work, so I missed all of that. I came in around the time they were coming up with their conclusions so it was perfect. So I said, ok, tell me what you found out.

Goodhue then created an exploratory team, anchored by four senior managers representing the four R&D centers. These individuals were assigned by Shore and had varying levels of environmental interest. All were familiar with their center projects and had direct contact with customers. Goodhue then added a handful of team members who were passionate about environmental issues. These included several scientists working on small, existing green projects, and two volunteers from EH&S. Except for Goodhue, whose formal work assignment included part of her time for the green effort, all of the other team members were appointed or voluntary. Their participation was authorized, but "below the line"—not part of formal headcount for the project.

During 2007, this team pursued an extensive outreach effort to solicit green project ideas. Internally, they held open, face-to-face meetings in each of the four research centers; started a green blog; hosted a session at the division's annual research conference; and held a weeklong ideation jam open to several divisions. Goodhue enlisted Shore to help secure funds for a consultant who conducted external market research.

In the end, the team's findings paralleled the earlier findings of EH&S: opportunities lay in either reduction of waste or energy usage. They also discovered that while Alpha's customers were interested in greener technologies and products, they would not pay substantially more for them. In sum, Goodhue initiated an intense sensemaking effort that started from ground zero and included second-hand information that others had previously collected.

Beta

At the beginning of its green initiative, Beta already had in place an extensive green sensemaking capacity. This included not only Anderson's EH&S group, but a wide network of people across the company who were actively learning about customers, external expectations, competitive activities, internal capabilities, and technical advances in the environmental area. Anderson had become a key contact point for all these individuals. "People were calling up and going, hey we're not moving fast enough on this," he said.

Over time, Anderson had drawn several conclusions from these sensemaking efforts. He had come to believe that " . . . sustainability is a good fit with the culture of being a 'good' organization and with external expectations from consumers. And . . . customers want us to go beyond [what] the law [requires]." And then, "there's the financial side, because most of the issues related to sustainability deal with waste; if you can reduce your waste you can save money as well as have a positive environmental impact. Another consideration is the younger generation, who have expectations of being able to do something in this domain."

Once Anderson assumed leadership of Beta's environmental initiative, he expanded his informal sensemaking. He pulled together the many perspectives he had been collecting for years from inside and outside of Beta to come up with a more formal map and set of arguments about why "green" was important. Anderson saw Beta's embrace of the environment as a strategic imperative as "a perfect storm," describing the initiative as a "Venn diagram of passion, skills, and business need."

Key differences

Both Alpha and Beta made "going green" a strategic priority by undertaking extensive internal and external sensemaking. In this sense, both leaders practiced "cultivate and coordinate" by having people from multiple parts of the organization provide information and suggest possible innovations. At Alpha, however, Goodhue faced a much steeper learning curve than her counterpart at Beta. Ultimately, her team's sensemaking effort relearned much of what had already been discovered by Alpha's EH&S group. At Beta, Bill Anderson came to his leadership role with a broad and deep understanding of environmental issues—knowledge that had accumulated gradually with Anderson over a long period of time.

At Alpha, the sensemaking process was more targeted and more formal than at Beta. Goodhue and her team needed information quickly, and launched a variety of efforts to capture that information. However, not everyone thought the process was effective. One person complained, "It was too big a group and they were doing market studies. Anytime you do market studies you are shooting behind the duck because customers only know what they have. It was a big waste of time."

At Beta, information about and interest in environmental issues was embedded in pockets of learning and innovation across the company. Anderson and his team built on their existing informal knowledge base to create a more formal map with which to advance a green agenda. Anderson's role as a key person in the sustainability domain meant that his broad network of relationships helped with the mapping effort.

VISIONING

Research suggests that visioning is more effective to the extent that it is related to key organizational values, and presents an overarching goal and an image of the future that is a major shift from the status quo (Avolio et al., 2004). Both Alpha and Beta's visioning processes fit these criteria, but took very different forms.

Alpha

At Alpha, the green vision was bounded and specific from the beginning, with top leadership defining success in terms of developing radical new products that would constitute "big wins" in the marketplace. This vision then cascaded down to the divisions via the annual planning process, where the vision was interpreted as a need to move quickly to identify and develop target projects. Goodhue described her mission in these terms: "OK, my responsibility is to come up with these technologies that we're going to invest in, in 2008." Ultimately, the team Goodhue assembled decided to identify a small number of high-impact projects that would reduce energy usage or lead to significant waste reduction.

Beta

Beta's visioning process proceeded slowly, as do most initiatives at the organization. Leaders seek to influence their colleagues to move in a new direction or make a change at the organization. Anderson's first step in the change process was to gain organizational buy-in for a common vision for environmental responsibility. Over a period of years, he worked to build widespread support for the vision, which Beta eventually rolled out on a global basis. In Anderson's words, the vision was, "not to be used for marketing but as an internal compass to guide decision making and set expectations. We will expect ourselves to live up to these expectations."

Beta tries to cultivate a strategic mindset in all its people—an ability to hold in one's mind the organization's strategic vision and think about how one's efforts can contribute to that vision, leverage the organization's core capabilities, win in the marketplace, and make money, while simultaneously adhering to core values. Anderson leveraged this strategic mindset in the visioning process by "collecting examples of things that we've done well and communicating, educating, and getting buy-in." As he proceeded, Anderson sought to understand how the green initiative could simultaneously solve a number of strategic organizational needs, problems, and opportunities.

Anderson also sought to cultivate a strategic mindset in others who were already moving towards a green vision by connecting their efforts, legitimizing their activities, supporting them with new tools and organizational resources, and linking their activities to an emerging meta narrative. His efforts sought to enable both individual freedom and organizational focus, about which he said:

You have to figure out where the boundaries are to guide people and keep them moving in a direction that is consistent with the enterprise objectives while still allowing them the excitement and the freedom to work within those boundaries on the things that they're interested and passionate about.

Ultimately, Anderson's team identified four broad areas for green innovation: products, processes, new facilities, and facility operation and maintenance. The team's vision was to embed sustainability in how people across the organization sought to create change. Anderson notes:

We want a place where looking at the environmental footprint of products, processes, facilities, and operations is just a normal part of thinking. I'd like to have it be part of the normal thought process in building plants, in developing equipment, and in developing products. It's just the most cost-effective time to do it. It just needs to be part of the way we think.

Key differences

While the R&D division at Alpha was trying to move in the direction of "cultivate and coordinate," this shift in leadership logic was stymied as top leaders moved relatively quickly to define the core vision for the green initiative—a vision centered on ambitious product goals. With goals defined and temporal targets set, it becomes difficult to create a context in which people further down can collaborate to create their image of a sustainable future. This contrasted with Beta's broad vision, which was grounded in organizational values, and aimed to satisfy multiple stakeholder interests.

Anderson worked to build bottom-up momentum around the concept of going green, and invited all interested members of the organization to help define a strategic vision. Anderson built the vision based on his own thinking and by synthesizing ideas from a broad network. Employees were free to decide whether and how to innovate around the four focus areas of this vision, and were also influenced, supported, and rewarded to move in that direction.

The visioning process at Alpha and Beta illustrates the difficulties of breaking out of a traditional "command and control" mindset versus operating in a culture where "cultivate and coordinate" is practiced. In the former, heroic leaders are called upon to quickly figure out how to make the vision come to life through clear product commitments and deliverables, while in the latter, organizational members are encouraged to come up with ideas that fit a new strategic direction, with coaching from more experienced managers. In the former, the vision quickly becomes narrowly focused and is sent down to lower-level units for implementation, while in the latter the vision is broadly construed and aligned with organizational values, in order to invite widespread experimentation, as discussed next.

INVENTING

At Alpha, leaders quickly established specific focus areas after a short period of sensemaking and visioning. Leaders set timelines and goals that would require Alpha to produce revolutionary innovation in a short period of time. By contrast, Beta developed a broad vision and intention, supported existing green initiatives, and celebrated small wins. Timelines and targets were left to develop gradually, as project ideas became clear. In these organizations inventing a way towards the vision involved following their very different routines for implementing change.

Alpha

Goodhue's process for implementing Alpha's vision began with putting together a team of people to staff the project, consisting of leaders high in the organizational hierarchy, and others who were passionate and/or experienced with green projects. Unlike Anderson at Beta, who was already connected with Beta's passionate environmental champions, Goodhue's process for selecting her passionate champions was more serendipitous, "A guy emailed Abby Moore about his interest around green, and she forwarded it to me and said can you follow up with him. And I said, hey, let's channel this passion into actual research work. So I got him."

Although Goodhue collaborated with EH&S on a company-wide effort to build a bottom-up community focused on sustainability issues, Goodhue and her team focused primarily on gathering new technology and product ideas that reflected the ambitious vision of Alpha's senior leaders. In short, her task was less about changing mindsets and more about choosing specific areas of focus with prescribed target goals. In discussing the green blog she initiated, for instance, Goodhue said:

I asked researchers to input ideas of what they wanted to see as far as green innovation. We had over a hundred ideas coming out of this, when you combine all four centers. It was quite a lot...if you could think about being totally green what would you do? What I did from our previous team was give them some guidelines—50% less energy. What would you come up with? And how could you make it totally recyclable?

While this method certainly garnered input from all over the organization, it is not clear that the people who were submitting ideas were knowledgeable enough about customers and green technologies to make informed suggestions. Nonetheless, three project ideas emerged: a reusable version of a previously disposable-only product, a radical new green hardware product, and a software product that would track the cradle-to-grave environmental impact of office technologies/products. These projects were submitted to and approved by the R&D's senior management team, and then funded as strategic priorities.

The three projects were clustered under a single "green program" to be housed in one research center. The head of that center in turn appointed one of his most promising project leaders, Donna Hale, as the green program manager. Although Hale had only "a modicum of interest in sustainability," she was tapped for two reasons: promotion to a program manager role represented a developmental opportunity, and Hale's manager knew that she was extremely effective at recruiting volunteers for her projects. Indeed, Hale achieved the head-count target set by senior management for the green projects with significantly fewer people from the research center than originally anticipated.

As Hale assumed leadership of the green initiative, it was agreed that Goodhue's continued leadership role would be threefold: to support Hale by helping to secure additional resources should they be needed; to continue to serve as the main liaison to the senior management team: and to continue representing the division on EH&S's corporate green advisory board. Goodhue also became more involved in project implementation by providing guidelines for one of the teams that was working on the second of the three projects. As Goodhue described:

Our team gave them these guidelines, and one thing that they came up with was a technology which will give us the energy reduction we are looking for. It will also give us a way to take something that Alpha previously worked on in a technology, re-invent it in a new way and it will give us a big savings in power, which is what the customers are looking for.

Goodhue's guidelines were more about objectives to achieve, which would most likely require significant technology innovations, rather than a new way to think and act, which was more the focus of implementation at Beta. Alpha's approach to implementation was driven by the fact that Goodhue was trying to meet the needs and goals of the new, visible, corporate objective she had been tasked with achieving. According to one team member:

... [the question was] how can we go out there and do something that was completely disruptive? We're out for a 10x improvement...Abby [Alpha's CTO] said Alpha is going to prioritize and focus on green just like we focus on quality and cost and other performance attributes. This is important. We say, OK, where do we think the big hitters are? We go after the big hitters.

As it turned out in this case, however, giving the team a goal requiring them to create a disruptive technology did not achieve the desired results. Under pressure to create radical innovation, the team grabbed for answers, and ended up trying to resurrect a technology that had failed in the 1970s. In one person's words:

We were supposed to do something radical. And actually the word radical was giving us trouble because what that meant was people expected something very different. And anything we could think of was not going to fulfill that category. So one of the things that I did was say let's rethink this technology. In the nineteen seventies and eighties it was a big thing in our industry, and there's lot of Alpha patent. Alpha invented a lot of stuff. There were a bunch of problems [with] it. It was never quite as good [as another technology]. But one part of the technology had changed and the customer standard had changed. So 1—new technology, and 2—lower quality expectations. Like a hybrid car. For some customers if it didn't last so long it's ok if you have better energy usage. So I put together a research presentation.

Some Alpha team members thought at times that the composition of the team skewed the project selection process. As one team member noted:

It was kind of an insular team. These guys were incredibly senior guys. They are all Fellows or Principal scientists who've been here for 30 years...all mechanical people. So what spun off? A mechanical solution. There may have been more value in making a service that you could roll out to a larger community. That's what Alpha does. But (the mechanical solution) turned into something because it was a quick hit.

The three target projects moved fully into development mode, with mixed results:

1) The reusable product team encountered significant technical barriers to translating the technology into an affordable product. Additional market research revealed that the product would require a type of hardware that Alpha does not make. There was considerable stress within the team as these barriers became clear. Eventually the project manager met with the CTO and CEO to deliver the negative prognosis. Subsequently, there was a push to capture all the intellectual property developed, and Alpha began a low-profile search for a partnering company that made more compatible hardware.

2) The team focused on retooling some of its old technology to deliver a radical green hardware product made considerable technological progress, but over time it became clear that incorporating these technologies would require major and expensive changes in the design of Alpha's other products in order to maintain compatibility. Team members were skeptical that they could pull this off under the time constraints established by Alpha's leadership. "The business case hasn't been made yet to warrant the type of investment and development that would be needed. I feel a little bit like I'm spinning my wheels and I don't like that feeling. I don't feel like I'm being productive. I guess there's a little anxiety over working on something that probably isn't going to work." At the end of 2009, the project was discontinued after capturing any new intellectual property with the hope that it might lead to future licensing opportunities.

3) Although the environmental assessment software project required the least resources, it had the most positive outcome. The project team finished a first iteration of the product, and created a web tool that it believed could become part of an energy management service that Alpha could offer to other businesses. Further development, however, would require additional software engineers to develop and a buy-in from a business group to get off the ground. Eventually they were able to hand off the tool to a services group that was interested in incorporating the instrument in an on-going project.

One Alpha engineer suggested that the "big bets" approach may not be the right one when dealing with uncertainty, but perhaps Alpha could at least do a better job of learning from failure:

Alpha likes to develop thrusts that have these real long term benefits. Theoretically we shouldn't even be working on it unless we have a big wow. That doesn't always happen but it's our goal. It's very risky to sign up for something because we can't predict squat. We can't predict our market, we can't predict our customers, we can't predict our business, or technology. So we like to pick things that have these big audacious goals. So ok, well, we didn't make it all there but this has some incremental value that the business group can go take. We could compile a platform based just on things we know now while aiming higher.

In the end, while some incremental innovation did take place, the push from above to make breakthrough innovations put pressure on the implementation teams that resulted in some bad decisions. In the process of reaching for quick innovations, newer ideas were lost, and the team was afraid to speak up about the pitfalls they saw around their chosen innovation path. On the positive side, Alpha did experiment with a number of different solutions to "green," created some new intellectual property, and the company now knows more about what does not work. The hope is that future experiments will have a better yield.

Beta

When Anderson began leading Beta's green initiative, he created a core team of people from across the company who were already engaged and passionate about sustainability. Having worked in this domain for some time, he used his network to staff the team. People also started calling him. "When word leaked out that I was working on this I started getting phone calls—all kinds of people were interested in being involved," Anderson reported.

Anderson saw the purpose of his team as "changing the mindset of the company," and he looked for ways to support teams that were already working on environmental initiatives—serving as a team liaison; highlighting success stories; helping people develop expertise and a strong business case for their ideas; and ensuring that people got compensation rewards for working on such projects.

Beta's emergent style of implementation paralleled its approach to product innovation in general—rapid prototyping and testing to make ideas concrete, followed by collective vetting and pruning to focus on the most promising ideas. As ideas took shape, Beta would then formalize the product development cycle, and develop timelines for deliverables using a modified stage-gate process.

Beta's organizational culture encouraged openness and acceptance of negative information. Cumulative learning from failure tended to be rapid as people engaged in repeated small cycles of experiment-test-fail/succeed-experiment-again. Anderson summarized this ethos:

Where people fail is that their "quick win" is too big. It has to start small or you are not going to get a quick win. You need to start building your credibility and also learning because we don't know how to do this right out of the gate. And that's the beauty of it; we're not setting a five-year objective. We've got our vision; let's figure out what the next step is. When we make mistakes we can learn from them and then move forward. You gain credibility, you learn, you expand your network. You take on a project that's bigger, more impactful. If you make a mistake, you have the credibility and people say, I've worked with this guy before, it's not a big deal. With more wins, you get to a point where it becomes part of people's thinking. This is also a way of mitigating risk since you're not going to do something that's going to be high risk.

Beta was thus characterized by a perpetual state of frothy innovation, with ideas bubbling up continually from all corners of the organization. The company's challenge was finding ways to weed out less promising projects in order to focus on those that had the most potential. For product innovation, Beta had developed sophisticated organizational routines involving continual formal and informal vetting by leaders and peers to select projects that best fulfilled Beta's product development criteria. Projects were "selected" by identifying them as strategic areas of focus and devoting funding and other organizational resources to them. This happened only after a long process of advocacy by the project champion and collective refinement of the project idea. Anderson explained how Beta thinks about pruning out less-promising product ideas:

What we want to do is really focus people on things that they're passionate about and are the most meaningful things to do... Someone had a [recycling idea] ... but if you look at it from a life-cycle analysis it would require a lot of solvents and energy. You end up creating a significant amount of waste solvent. Even though there are people who are passionate about the product recycling program, when you looked at it from a business standpoint and from an environmental standpoint it really didn't make sense.

The environmental initiative was too early for a pruning process; there were simply not enough projects yet to compare them against one another. In this phase, Beta encouraged all project ideas for process and facility improvements that had a payback of two years or less. For products, Anderson's team was at the early stage of trying to influence Beta's R&D leaders to integrate environmental criteria into the product development process.

Key differences

At Alpha and Beta, both organizations swung into action to implement their visions for going green. Both experienced some successes and some failures, and both are continuing on. Alpha made things happen quickly up front, setting big goals and engaging a broad range of people to advance those goals. However, this process created resistance and confusion, and people felt they were slogging along unproductively on the politically hot project of the moment. Nonetheless, this approach did elevate "green" to a higher priority in people's minds, it did create a round of sensemaking that educated a new set of people on sustainability issues from a customer and business standpoint, and it did create new discussions, intellectual property, and learning around how the R&D division might move ahead.

Beta, in contrast, initiated an evolutionary process—stimulating a variety of ideas, developing and connecting them, seeking to retain only good ideas, and then institutionalizing the development process. The process is naturally slow and builds gradually over time. To date no breakthrough innovations have resulted. Nonetheless, there is now an organization-wide commitment to being more "green," numerous projects have emerged in line with this new commitment, and a set of tools, examples, coaches, and resources are now available to help people succeed in green projects.

Figures 9.1 and 9.2 present some of the major differences in how the four key leadership functions of relating, sensemaking, visioning, and inventing were executed at Alpha and Beta.

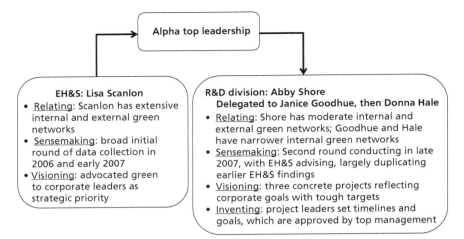

Figure 9.1. Alpha's green initiative

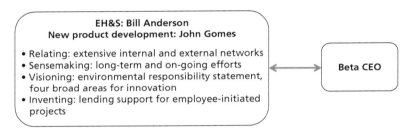

Figure 9.2. Beta's green initiative

SUMMARY

After a brief period of sensemaking, the R&D division at Alpha created a macro, top-down focus on three "stretch" projects, inviting people to flesh out the micro details. Beta instead developed a broad vision over a number of years and then looked to the many micro efforts and ideas that could eventually be synthesized into a macro strategy and focus. Compared to Alpha, Beta's process was more on-going as part of daily work, more experimental and tentative, and tended to produce smaller-scale innovations that could be rapidly killed or fixed.

The role of leadership at Alpha was to create a specific blueprint for change and control the process by setting tough deadlines, while at Beta leaders established guidelines for an emergent process and then supported and fused what grew as a result.

These different trajectories towards green evolved in ways that reflected the historic organizational models from which they emerged. Alpha made strides in the direction of a "cultivate and coordinate" leadership logic, but consistently got pulled back into the bureaucratic, "command and control" mode, while Beta enacted more of a distributed leadership model. Each leadership logic was instantiated in the way that people decided to go green, why and how they selected certain leaders, and in the way that relating, sensemaking, visioning, and inventing took place.

The "command and control" logic has power and authority to move initiatives from top to bottom, with individuals assigned to tasks in keeping with their role in the organization. People often take on stretch roles to make an impression on top management and to move up the management ladder. As project goals come down from above, the people who must meet those goals sometimes see them as separated from the technologies, customer needs, and interdependencies that one needs to understand project success. Nonetheless, employees carry on with their assigned tasks, resurrecting what they can from failing or modestly successful projects in order to succeed in a performance culture.

The "cultivate and coordinate" logic is slow to start, as those with new ideas try to negotiate their own roles and garner interest on the part of others. The relating function of leadership is critical in this organizational model, as many people must be consulted for key sensemaking, visioning, and inventing efforts. Because people have high role autonomy and cannot be assigned to tasks or ordered to perform, they must be influenced to adopt new ideas and ways of working. In turn, their ideas become part of the strategy. The ideas that emerge must be supported or dropped, tested and, if successful, woven together with other emergent ideas to create a coherent set of strategic offerings.

In sum, the road to green is different based on where you are on the continuum from "command and control" to "cultivate and coordinate." The dominant logic shows up in the on-going processes and structures of organizations, as well as in the very mindsets of people that influence day-to-day decisions. Even organizations trying to shed their "command and control" mentality may be pulled back into a bureaucratic mode as formal leaders configure human resources within a constrained set of roles and responsibilities. Innovation then takes place within a tightly constrained vision that propels innovation forward but, in this case, appears to have limited the creativity brought to bear on the task. When organizations are closer to the "cultivate and coordinate" logic, formal and informal leaders collaborate to create an environment that enables small experiments, celebrates small wins, and winnows out bad ideas. However, this process is slow, and it can be frustrating to try to influence so many people and guide them in one direction.

From an academic perspective, several key points emerge. First, future analyses need to combine a leadership and organizational lens to enable a broad understanding of how to implement change in a dynamic, complex environment. Second, making change in only one part of this interdependent system will not be enough to create lasting change; the system as a whole and its interdependent effects must be considered. For example, simply choosing a different leader will not shift the innovation pattern unless organizational norms are also changed. Third, organizations that are historically coming from a "command and control" logic can be hampered by a reliance on career managers rather than idea champions, innovation on demand under tight time constraints, a reliance on big wins, and a performance rather than a learning culture. Fourth, several micro-processes end up being critical to organizational change in a distributed system: emergent leadership; a widely shared strategic mindset; iterative learning; and the compilation of distributed sensemaking. We hope that future research can further explore these ideas.

Managerial implications

As firms move strategically to embrace sustainability, their leaders embark on a difficult path of change. Many are trying to shed their "command-and-control" mode of operating and innovate through "cultivate and coordinate." While this is an aspiration for many, the pathway to change in this new mode is not always clear. Here, we have tried to capture the micro-processes of leadership across different stages of the change process, comparing firms at different points on this continuum. Furthermore, firms coming from a bureaucratic lineage may be hi-jacked by deeply embedded modes of change that frustrate the desire to operate in a more distributed mode. Based on our findings, we offer ten key elements to creating change using a "cultivate-and-coordinate" leadership logic. We hope that managers moving towards this mode of operating can use this as a kind of checklist for change.

Creating change with a "cultivate and coordinate" logic

1. When people at lower levels of the firm have ideas on new strategic objectives that have been vetted and tested, let those people have a role in the change process. Change does not always have to be completely top down. This new mode of operating requires senior management that is open to ideas from below, a capacity for employees to be entrepreneurial, and the ability of managers to synthesize bottom-up efforts into a higher-level focus.

2. When assigning people to roles, consider who has the passion, knowledge, networks, and time availability to succeed—independent of that person's position in the hierarchy and organizational role. If this is not politically possible, then think about creating dyads or teams that include the necessary expertise to lead the initiative.

3. If sensemaking has been done and deep knowledge exists within, or outside, the organization, suggest that people engage in "vicarious learning" (Bresman, 2010) from others so they can build on, instead of duplicate, existing knowledge. Also, since the move to sustainability is

complex, sensemaking should be distributed with information coming from multiple functions, divisions, and levels continuously over time.

4. If you are implementing electronic brainstorming or voting or other processes to pull on the collective intelligence of multiple employees, make sure that those participating actually have the expertise required, and that the input gathered fits the task at hand. People need to understand the problem they are trying to solve, the key goals to be met, and the technological and financial constraints in order to weigh in effectively on product ideas and invent new ways to move forward.

5. Before assigning stretch goals and objectives, have an honest conversation with team members about their capacity to implement. Create a safe atmosphere so that progress reports and other communications are open and honest. Make sure that people understand the overarching vision that is driving the project, rather than just communicating targets and goals. Have people weigh in with their own ideas for goals and objectives.

6. Provide coaching and learning opportunities so that people can practice the decision making, entrepreneurial activity, and negotiating needed to work in this mode of operating.

7. Provide opportunities for employees to meet one another and network across the firm. The shift from a "command and control" to a "cultivate and coordinate" logic requires high levels of trust and connectivity to enable effective collaboration for distributed sensemaking, inventing, and visioning.

8. Remember that moving away from a "command and control" mode of operating does not mean that senior leaders cease to play a role in the change process, nor that chaos rules. Leaders create the environment and guidelines that enable others to step up and innovate.

9. Don't assume that employees in a "cultivate and coordinate" system will revolt at the idea of a top-down decision, if for example, there is a need to move quickly due to a clear and short window of opportunity or to weed out unproductive projects. Even though contrary to "cultivate and coordinate" norms, if leaders make their decisions transparent, get input, and share their sensemaking and reasoning, then top-down decision making can be successful on occasion. In fact, employees may be frustrated by the slowness of the decision-making process and welcome some quick action if the rationale is clear.

10. Achieving change in the area of sustainability will require some combination of "command and control" and "cultivate and coordinate." It will, by necessity, involve many organizational players that exist across the bureaucratic—distributed leadership continuum, including government agencies, universities, NGOs, companies, and dedicated teams. It will demand leaders who can both engage in top-down decision making to make shifts in environmental and energy policies and practices, as well as

in creating the structures, opportunities, and guidelines to compel and enable others to innovate and act within this space.

■ REFERENCES

Ancona, D. (2011) "Sensemaking: Framing and Acting in the Unknown," in N. Nohria, S. Snook, and R. Khurana (eds), *The Handbook for Teaching Leadership: Knowing, Doing, and Being*. Thousand Oaks, CA: Sage Publications, 3–21.

Ancona, D., Malone, T. W., Orlikowski, W. J., and Senge, P. M. (2007) "In Praise of the Incomplete Leader," *Harvard Business Review* 85 (2): 92–100, 156.

Avolio, B. J., Zhu, W., Koh, W., and Bhatia, P. (2004) "Transformational Leadership and Organizational Commitment: Mediating Role of Psychological Empowerment and Moderating Role of Structural Distance," *Journal of Organizational Behavior* 25 (8): 951–68.

Bass, B. M. and Avolio, B. J. (1994) *Improving Organizational Effectiveness through Transformational Leadership*. Thousand Oaks, CA: Sage Publications.

Bresman, H., (2010) "External Learning Activities and Team Performance: A Multi-Method Field Study," *Organization Science* 21 (1): 81–96.

Brown, S. L. and Eisenhardt, K. M. (1997) "The Art of Continuous Change: Linking Complexity Theory and Time-Paced Evolution in Relentlessly Shifting Organizations," *Administrative Science Quarterly*, 1–34.

Cameron, K. S. and Quinn, R. E. (2011) *Diagnosing and Changing Organizational Culture: Based on the Competing Values Framework*. New York: John Wiley & Sons.

Donnellon, A. and Scully, M. (1994) "Teams, Performance and Rewards: Will the Post-Bureaucratic Organization be a Post-Meritocratic Organization?," in *The Post-Bureaucratic Organization*. Thousand Oaks, CA: Sage Publications, 63–90.

Eisenhardt, K. M., Brown, S. L., and Neck, H. M. (2000) "Competing on the Entrepreneurial Edge," *Entrepreneurship as Strategy* 49–62.

Gulati, R., Puranam, P., and Tushman, M. (2012) "Meta-Organization Design: Rethinking Design in Interorganizational and Community Contexts," *Strategic Management Journal* 33 (6): 571–86.

Hackman, J. R. (2002) *Leading Teams: Setting the Stage for Great Performances*. Boston, MA: Harvard Business School Press.

Heckscher, C. C. (1994) "Defining the Post-Bureaucratic Type," in A. Donnellon and C. C. Heckscher (eds), *The Post Bureaucratic Organization: New Perspectives on Organizational Change*. Thousand Oaks, CA: Sage Publications, 14–62.

Heckscher, C. C. (2007) *The Collaborative Enterprise: Managing Speed and Complexity in Knowledge-Based Businesses*. New Haven, CT: Yale University Press.

Heckscher, C. C. and Adler, P. S. (2006) *The Firm as a Collaborative Community: Reconstructing Trust in the Knowledge Economy*. New York: Oxford University Press.

Heifetz, R. A., Grashow, A., and Linsky, M. (2009) *The Practice of Adaptive Leadership: Tools and Tactics for Changing your Organization and the World*. Boston, MA: Harvard Business School Press.

Hoffman, A. J. and Glancy, D. (2006) *Getting Ahead of the Curve: Corporate Strategies that Address Climate Change*. Arlington, VA: Pew Center on Global Climate Change.

House, R. J. and Howell, J. M. (1992) "Personality and Charismatic Leadership," *The Leadership Quarterly* 3 (2): 81–108.

Kelley, M. R. (1990) "New Process Technology, Job Design, and Work Organization: A Contingency Model," *American Sociological Review* 48 (2) (April) 191–208.

Malone, T. W. (2004) *The Future of Work*. Boston, MA: Harvard Business School Press.

Osterman, P. (1994) "Supervision, Discretion, and Work Organization," *The American Economic Review* 84 (2): 380–4.

Pettigrew, A. M. and Massini, S. (2003) "Innovative Forms of Organizing: Trends in Europe, Japan and the USA in the 1990's," in A. M. Pettigrew, R. Whittington, L. Melin, C. Sanchez-Runde, F. A. Van den Bosch, W. Ruigrok, and T. Numagami (eds), *Innovative Forms of Organizing: International Perspectives*. Thousand Oaks, CA: Sage Publications, 1–32.

Porter, M. E. and Kramer, M. R. (2006) "Strategy and Society," *Harvard Business Review* 84 (12): 78–92.

Powell, W. W. (2001) "The Capitalist Firm in the Twenty-First Century: Emerging Patterns in Western Enterprise," in Paul DiMaggio (ed.), *The Twenty-First Century Firm: Changing Economic Organization in International Perspective*, Princeton, NJ: Princeton University Press, 33–68.

Powell, W. W. (2003) "Neither Market Nor Hierarchy," in Michael J. Handel (ed.), *The Sociology of Organizations: Classic, Contemporary, and Critical Readings*, Vol. 315. Thousand Oaks, CA: Sage Publications, 104–17.

Rajan, R. G. and Wulf, J. (2006) "The Flattening Firm: Evidence from Panel Data on the Changing Nature of Corporate Hierarchies," *The Review of Economics and Statistics* 88 (4): 759–73.

Reagans, R. and McEvily, B. (2003) "Network Structure and Knowledge Transfer: The Effects of Cohesion and Range," *Administrative Science Quarterly* 48 (2): 240–67.

Schilling, M. A. and Steensma, H. K. (2001) "The Use of Modular Organizational Forms: An Industry-Level Analysis," *Academy of Management Journal* 44 (6): 1149–68.

Snell, S. A. and Dean, J. W. (1992) "Integrated Manufacturing and Human Resource Management: A Human Capital Perspective," *Academy of Management Journal* 35 (3): 467–504.

Strang, D. and Kim, Y.-M. (2005) "The Diffusion and Domestication of Managerial Innovations: The Spread of Scientific Management, Quality Circles, and TQM Between the US and Japan," in *The Oxford Handbook of Work and Organization*, Oxford: Oxford University Press, 177–99.

Weick, K. E. (1995) *Sensemaking in Organizations*, Vol. 3. Thousand Oaks, CA: Sage Publications.

Weick, K. E., Sutcliffe, K. M., and Obstfeld, D. (2005) "Organizing and the Process of Sensemaking," *Organization Science* 16 (4): 409–21.

Williams, H. M., Parker, S. K., and Turner, N. (2007) "Perceived Dissimilarity and Perspective Taking Within Work Teams," *Group & Organization Management* 32 (5): 569–97.

Youndt, M. A. and Snell, S. A. (2004) "Human Resource Configurations, Intellectual Capital, and Organizational Performance," *Journal of Managerial Issues* 16 (3): 337–60.

10 Leading Proactive Punctuated Change

Michael Tushman, Charles A. O'Reilly, and Bruce Harreld

This chapter focuses on leading proactive punctuated change. Based on the institutional and organizational change literatures and our extended involvement with IBM between 1999 and 2008, we suggest that proactive punctuated change can be effectively managed through an engineered social process designed and led by the senior leadership team. Where reactive punctuated change is driven by crisis conditions, the motivation and energy required to lead proactive punctuated change is rooted in an overarching aspiration coupled with a contradictory strategic challenge. The challenge to simultaneously explore and exploit provides the logic, tension, and requirement for experimentation that helps an extended management community collectively learn how to execute strategic organizational renewal. This change process involves disciplined conversations, actions, and associated learning by the senior team, diffusing these learning capabilities to the extended senior leadership team, and over time to the larger leadership community. We connect principles for leading proactive punctuated change to organizational change dilemmas associated with sustainability.

Leading punctuated change is one of the most important and least understood challenges to the modern firm and its leaders (Greenwood and Hinings, 1996; Agarwal and Helfat, 2009).[1] As environments shift, punctuated change is an inherent aspect of organizational evolution. Yet after decades of research, the mechanisms and dynamics of systemic punctuated change are still not well understood (Pettigrew, 1985; Tushman and Romanelli, 1985; Romanelli and Tushman, 1994; Eggers and Kaplan, 2009; Tripsas, 2009; Adner, 2012). Thus while building sustainable firms may be associated with considerable organizational benefits (for example, Cheng et al., 2014; Eccles et al., forthcoming), the process by which such system-wide change might be implemented are opaque.

Leading punctuated change is particularly problematic as those capabilities associated with exploiting a particular strategy are also associated with organizational inertia. Any strategic change must deal with the power and politics,

---

[1] By punctuated change, we mean integrated shifts in a firm's architecture; its structure, critical tasks and interdependencies, competencies, and culture (see O'Reilly and Tushman, 2008). Where punctuated changes may or may not involve strategic shifts, proactive punctuated changes are rooted in strategic change.

organizational processes, capabilities, and embedded agency dilemmas associated with inertia both within the firm and its institutional context (for example, Pfeffer, 1992; Miller, 1994; Nadler and Tushman, 1997; Greenwood and Suddaby, 2006; Benner, 2007; Collins and Hansen, 2011). These inertial dynamics are likely to be accentuated for change efforts, like sustainability, that link doing well with doing good (see Margolis and Walsh, 2001; Beer, 2009; Beer et al., 2011; Smith and Lewis, 2011; Eccles et al., 2012).

While we know much about the content of strategic change (for example, Barnett and Carrol, 1995; Hambrick et al., 1998; Weick and Quinn, 1999), we know much less about the process by which punctuated change is executed (Spillane et al., 2004; Greenwood and Hinings, 2006). Although management scholars have labeled types of change (for example, strategic, rhythmic, punctuated, transformational, divergent, or discontinuous) and offered checklists for leading change (for example, form a guiding coalition, shared commitments, create a burning platform, maintain control during the change process) (Kotter, 1995; Brown and Eisenhardt, 1997; Nadler and Tushman, 1997; Tushman and O'Reilly, 1997; Beer, 2009; Collins and Hansen, 2011; Eccles, et al., 2012), we know very little about the actual process and mechanisms by which incumbents execute either reactive or proactive punctuated change (see Joseph and Ocasio, 2012; Battilana and Casciaro, 2013, and Ramarajan et al., 2012 for exceptions).

Empirically, most punctuated changes are reactive; they are initiated under crisis conditions. Based on our work at IBM between 1999 and 2008, we suggest that proactive punctuated change (what we label as "strategic renewal") can be effectively managed through an engineered social process designed, owned, and led by the leader and his/her senior team. This change process involves disciplined conversations and associated learning by the senior team, building and shaping an extended senior team, and then diffusing the ownership and energy of change to a larger community of leaders. The motivation and energy required to lead proactive punctuated change is grounded in a compelling overarching aspiration coupled with a paradoxical strategic challenge (at IBM, to both explore into new domains as well as exploit existing capabilities). The challenge to simultaneously explore and exploit provide the logic and tension for experimentation that helped an engaged managerial community collectively learn how to execute proactive punctuated change.

We use IBM between 1999 and 2008 (the latter portion of Lou Gerstner's tenure and the early phase of Sam Palmisano's tenure) as a case in point of proactive punctuated change driven by the mandate of growth through innovation and executed through a top-down/bottom-up engineered social movement.[2] While incremental change can be managed from the bottom up, the

---

[2] This chapter is based on the on-going relationship between IBM (and Bruce Harreld who was the senior vice president of strategy) and HBS Executive Education (Michael Tushman collaborated with Charles O'Reilly on this extended engagement). While this client relationship is obviously associated

learning associated with punctuated change must be designed, owned, and energized by the senior team. While the impetus for system-wide change is initiated by the senior team's aspiration and paradoxical strategic challenge, the change is executed through an extended social movement.

At IBM, this social movement was instantiated through a series of workshops where senior leadership teams and their shared executives, informed by a common problem-solving methodology, collectively initiated, discussed, and learned about innovation and change in their local domains. We suggest that the methods by which IBM's extended senior leadership team learned how to execute proactive punctuated change is a more general change process that can be applied to the challenges of leading proactive sustainability transformations (see also Barley and Tolbert, 1997; Spillane et al., 2004; Scott and Davis, 2007; Sull and Spinosa, 2007; Eggers and Kaplan, 2009; Battilana and Casciaro, 2012; Ramarajan et al., 2013).

We suggest that strategic renewal is not an event, a set of steps, or a program, but an engineered social process anchored by an overarching aspiration and a paradoxical strategic intent that unfolds over time. This process is rooted in a series of concrete strategic challenges to the status quo (either performance gaps or strategic opportunities) at the unit and/or corporate level. These challenges uncover idiosyncratic root causes at the unit level as well as more systemic root causes at the firm level. Guided by the CEO's paradoxical strategic challenges, a common language and problem-solving tools, and disciplined follow-up, the extended management team collectively learns how to lead proactive change. This learning is grounded in collective cross-level and cross-firm experiences and conversations in solving real strategic challenges (see also Beer, 2009; Collins and Hansen, 2011; Kellogg 2011a, 2011b; Joseph and Ocasio, 2012; Gawer and Phillips, 2013).

Strategic renewal at IBM (1999–2008)

THE EVOLUTION OF STRATEGY FORMULATION AT IBM

In 1993, Lou Gerstner took over as the CEO of IBM. He was externally recruited to re-invent IBM. What once was the most admired firm in the world was reeling from both financial and competitive failure. An integrated series of strategic, leadership, organizational, and cultural actions initiated by Gerstner helped turn IBM around. By 1998, the firm had returned to financial stability and was growing its services and software businesses. Much has been written about this transformation (see Gerstner, 2002). We focus here on the

---

with issues of Tushman's and O'Reilly's objectivity, these concerns must be balanced with the substantial benefits of sustained access on issues related to innovation and change (see also Van de Ven, 2007; and Anteby, 2013).

subsequent strategic renewal of IBM initiated in 1999, late in Gerstner's tenure, and continued through 2008, the first half of Sam Palmisano's tenure.

The renewal initiated in 1999 was motivated by Gerstner's observation that IBM's growth had stalled. While IBM had been turned around financially in the initial phase of Gerstner's tenure, he felt it now had a growth crisis based on the firm's inability to take advantage of a series of breakthroughs developed in its laboratories. IBM's strategy group documented 29 distinct business opportunities based on technologies developed within the firm that it failed to commercialize. For example, IBM had been the first mover in routers, web infrastructure, voice recognition, RFID, and pervasive computing, only to lose to competitors like Cisco, Akamai, Nuance, and others. By 1999, the consequences of such missed opportunities were that IBM's growth had leveled off (see Harreld et al., 2007). The fact that IBM had led the world in patents had not been translated into sustainable growth.

Gerstner challenged Bruce Harreld, his senior vice president of strategy, to get at the roots of this growth issue. Harreld and four of his colleagues did an analysis of this corporate-wide innovation gap. Six root causes emerged: existing management systems focused energy on the short term; the firm was preoccupied with current customers and existing offerings; the IBM business model emphasized profit and sustained EPS (earnings per share) improvement, rather than higher price/earnings; the firm's market insight analytics were inadequate for embryonic markets; and the firm lacked processes for hosting new businesses, and even after new businesses were funded, most failed in execution. IBM's intense efforts to re-invent itself between 1993 and 1999 had a dark side. It had become a "disciplined machine" for short-term performance (i.e., exploitation), but had reduced its ability to innovate and grow through exploratory activities.

With these data, Gerstner asked Harreld to rethink IBM's strategic formulation process such that it was fact based, strategically informed, growth oriented, and had a disciplined approach to execution. As importantly, Gerstner insisted that the strategy process be owned by general managers (as opposed to their staff) (see Harreld et al., 2007). Harreld and his team, collaborating with Tushman and O'Reilly, developed the IBM Business Leadership Model (see Figure 10.1). The Business Leadership Model required general mangers to focus on either strategic performance gaps (for example, underperformance against plan or customer expectations) or strategic opportunities (for example, proactive shifts in business models).

Rather than the typical formalistic yearly review, the new strategic planning process engaged general managers in disciplined conversations with their strategy colleagues on the nature of their performance and/or opportunity gaps. These conversations focused on strategic insight, based on fact-based analyses of market conditions, innovation streams, and associated alternative business models, along with a careful analysis of execution options (the implications of various business models on the units' critical tasks, structure, culture, processes, competencies, and leadership behaviors). Under this

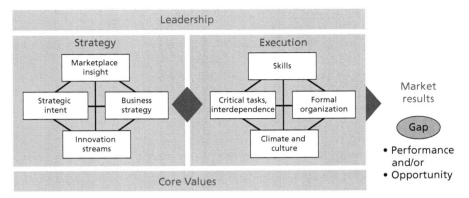

Figure 10.1. IBM Business Leadership Model

Source: Adapted from Harreld et al. (2007) (figure 1): 28.

revised strategic planning process, the role of Harreld's strategy team shifted from yearly evaluation to on-going conversations, based on jointly developed data, about innovation streams, new business models, and associated leadership capabilities and organizational architectures (this process of corporate/business unit interaction is similar to that described by Joseph and Ocasio (2012) at GE).

STRATEGIC LEADERSHIP FORUMS AND EMERGING BUSINESS OPPORTUNITIES

To execute this new strategic planning process with its emphasis on maintaining the firm's ability to exploit existing strategies and to simultaneously explore opportunities to leverage IBM's technological capabilities, Harreld initiated two related but distinct interventions: Strategic Leadership Forums (SLFs) and Emerging Business Opportunities (EBOs). SLFs were intensive workshops to engage both strategic and operational issues within and across IBM's business units. In these workshops, intact teams learned to employ the business leadership model and to explore the relations between streams of innovation (exploration and exploitation), senior team behaviors, ambidextrous designs, and change management. These SLFs were followed up with 30-day, 60-day, and 90-day reviews initiated through Harreld's office. EBOs were a series of efforts to strategically explore new business opportunities at the corporate level. EBOs were initially built to explicitly take advantage of cross-line-of-business opportunities, for example creating the life science and pervasive computing businesses (O'Reilly et al., 2009).

SLFs and EBOs involved every area of IBM (i.e., functions, geographies, and business units) and its most senior leaders in a series of experiments designed to both enhance the on-going cadence of IBM's "disciplined machine" and to "trick the disciplined organization" into exploring new strategic spaces (see Harreld et al., 2007). The SLFs and the EBOs were corporate interventions employed between 2000 and 2008. As these experiments began to have an impact on innovation outcomes, the SLFs and EBOs developed a reputation for impact and senior team involvement and, in turn, generated their own momentum.

Initial SLFs and EBOs (2000–2002)

The nature of the SLFs and EBOs shifted over time as IBM learned how to employ these interventions. Between 2000 and 2002, Harreld sponsored seven SLFs involving 34 intact teams. The initial SLFs were composed of sponsors and senior teams that Harreld knew would be a supportive community to help launch and co-create the SLFs. These sponsors also had performance or opportunity gaps so that if progress were made, the interventions would be visible and impactful to IBM. For example, Paul Horn, then head of IBM's research community, worked on technology-transfer issues for IBM Research, while Janet Perna and John Swainson brought their teams to work on major strategic issues in database management and in the Websphere business units, respectively. In this initial phase, one SLF was entirely dedicated to EBOs. Five early EBO initiatives (for example, life sciences and network processor) were brought together to work on their unique EBO challenges as well as to share learning across EBOs.

With the active involvement of Harreld's strategy team, the initial 34 business owners, and the two external faculty, early SLFs evolved into the following structure and process. Structurally, each SLF had corporate strategy and a group senior vice president as sponsors. Such dual senior sponsorship ensured that strategic performance or opportunity gaps were selected and that intact teams and appropriate other individuals joined the workshop. SLFs were funded both by Harreld's organization and by the sponsoring line executive's organization. Teams were selected by Harreld and a co-sponsoring senior vice president based on the firms strategic issues. Resistant leaders were actively encouraged to take advantage of these workshops. These initially resistant leaders either became more enthusiastic or were sanctioned by Harreld and his colleagues.

The SLF process evolved during these first two years (see Figure 10.2). By the end of 2002, Harreld and this early SLF community converged on a replicable methodology. Each SLF had between three and seven intact teams (roughly 90 individuals in total), each with a unique performance or opportunity gap. These teams were supplemented with other individuals who had relevant expertise for their gap. The teams met before the workshop to gather their own data on the unit's strategic situation and craft a clear gap statement. These pre-SLF meetings were facilitated by a strategy person as well as by an organizational effectiveness professional from the HR community. Teams

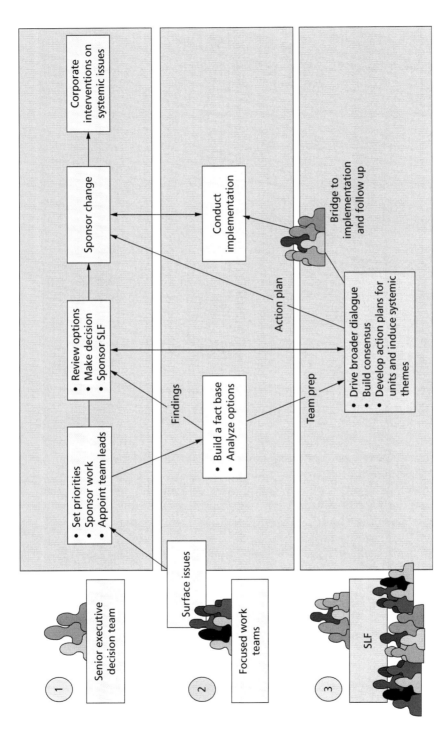

Figure 10.2. SLF and EBO process: top-down and bottom-up dialog and learning

Source: Adapted from IBM document.

came to SLFs primed on the nature of the issues to be discussed and armed with data on the strategic importance of their performance/opportunity gaps.

The SLFs were 3.5 days in duration and held in non-IBM settings. In these initial workshops, external faculty presented content on the challenges of dynamic capabilities, the IBM Business Model, strategic innovation and change, structural ambidexterity, culture, and leading change. The content sessions used non-IBM cases. The faculty modeled the process of disciplined problem solving through the cases and set up the challenges of building organizations that could simultaneously exploit existing capabilities and explore into new domains.

Over each 3.5-day workshop, each team spent 17 hours working their unique gap. In the non-academic sessions, each team did their own diagnostic work that led, in turn, to their own set of action plans and commitments. While each team did their own work, each day the teams reported back to the full community. These report backs, moderated by the executive sponsors, helped raise the level of work, as each group got immediate feedback from the corporate sponsors as well as from their peers in other teams. As participants heard multiple presentations, the SLF communities were able to uncover system-wide root causes as well as possible system-wide remedial actions. There was substantial social pressure to do quality strategic and diagnostic work. Each evening, the sponsors, faculty, and business owners met to debrief and make course corrections, so material and processes remained customized to each group. Finally, the process of articulating next steps and follow-up were built into the SLF methodology. Business owners were responsible for implementing their proposed actions. Their SLF facilitators assisted their implementation. Finally, business owners held structured follow-up sessions with Harreld's strategy colleagues, as well as their respective sponsors.

These SLF processes created a context for multiple types of learning. Learning at the unit level was initiated by top-down strategic challenges along with intensive cross-firm and cross-level dialog on the roots of these challenges. As each SLF had multiple teams, the report-back sessions encouraged communication across these extended communities. These community discussions surfaced a range of system-wide root causes of IBM's innovation performance gap. Thus, if several teams independently arrived at similar root causes, that convergence indicated a system-level root cause. Each SLF then generated insight for action at both the local and corporate levels of analysis. The SLF process triggered learning about innovation and change co-created and co-owned by multiple areas and levels in the firm.

SLF and EBO assessment (2002)

After this initial set of seven SLFs, O'Reilly and Tushman (assisted by a Graduate School of Education School student) did an SLF review. This review indicated that participants valued the business leadership framework and the common language employed to both develop provocative strategies and to build organizations capable of executing those strategies. Participants were struck by the complex interdependencies within and outside IBM. They were also struck with the leverage of bringing the right actors together, sponsored and pushed by corporate executives, to intensely grapple together with strategic issues. One of the most consistent observations was the importance of senior teams jointly owning their unit's strategy and having a hand in crafting their gaps, diagnoses, and action plans. They also noted the power of dedicated time and the ability to work together on strategic issues as intact teams with their relevant corporate executives (see Tushman et al., 2007; Kellogg, 2011a, 2011b).

This SLF review also generated a set of system-wide observations that were used to shape subsequent SLFs. Participants observed that while most of the firm's strategic opportunities involved cross-IBM interdependencies, the firm was organized and measured from a line-of-business, country, or functional point of view. Participants noted that the firm was optimized to exploit existing business but under-organized and managed for exploratory opportunities. Participants observed that "light-weight teams were given heavy-weight strategic opportunities." Participants also focused on the role of culture in stunting exploratory innovation at IBM. They observed that a culture of risk aversion and incremental change, the power of finance, a process mentality, low tolerance for mistakes, and little cross-line of business trust all colluded to diminish innovations that crossed firm boundaries. In contrast, the culture of collaboration, teamwork, and high expectations they experienced in the SLF was the kind of culture they felt could enhance innovation across the firm.

Finally, this interim review suggested a range of issues associated with the action-planning phase of the SLFs. Participants and faculty observed that across these initial SLFs, even though the root cause analysis often called for punctuated change, the proposed interventions were typically incremental in nature. Further, where actions on structure, roles, incentives, and processes were well specified, they were weak in dealing with cultural barriers, and weaker still in focusing on the role of the senior team as root cause of the performance gaps.

An interim review was also done for the EBOs. Harreld, his strategy colleagues, and the initial EBO leaders developed a set of best practices for EBOs going forward. This EBO design team learned that those EBOs with joint line and staff senior support and funding, that had seasoned EBO leaders, dedicated measures and milestones, disciplined reviews focusing more on strategy and emerging customer requirements than on financial measures, and had strict graduation criteria, were more impactful that those EBOs without these factors. These initial EBO experiments also required the CEO's support in signaling the importance of EBOs to prospective EBO leaders and to skeptical line/functional managers (see O'Reilly et al., 2009).

SLFs and EBOs, 2002–2008

These evaluation data suggested an emerging set of best practices in executing SLFs and EBOs. They also indicated that the SLFs and the EBOs were gaining traction in terms of organizational outcomes and credibility with influential senior executives across the firm. These data also indicated the power of SLFs to create the space and conditions for disciplined conversations about strategy and execution, the role of senior teams in driving change, and on the power of jointly developed and publically communicated diagnoses and action plans. These data also indicated there was a range of systemic factors hindering exploratory innovation and the associated execution of punctuated change within and across units.

These lessons on innovation and punctuated change overlapped with the promotion of Sam Palmisano to CEO in 2002. Palmisano articulated a growth agenda for IBM and his intention to have IBMers reinvigorate their heritage of "restless self-renewal." Palmisano also called on IBM to "re-invent itself again . . . even as it retained its distinct identity." Building on the firm's shared values of "client success, innovation that matters, and trust and personal responsibility," Palmisano suggested, "if there is one thing that IBMers agree on, it's that ours can be the greatest firm in the world."[3]

This energy by the new CEO for growth, innovation, cultural change, and renewal reinforced the importance of the SLF and EBO workshops. The SLFs and EBOs were tools to execute Palmisano's aspiration, based on the firm's rearticulated values. Armed with data from two years of experience with SLFs and EBOs and the CEO's call for growth and renewal, the next set of SLFs were more themed in nature. Between 2002 and 2005, 21 more SLFs were hosted, involving 150 teams and 2,500 executives. The themes included EBOs, technology, growth, industry standards, and cross-line-of-business integration. During this period, for example, three separate EBO-dedicated SLFs were hosted, involving 14 EBOs. These dedicated SLFs helped Harreld, his team, and an extended set of IBM leaders to learn how to execute EBOs across the corporation. By 2005, 80 percent of the top 50 IBM executives either attended or hosted an SLF (including Palmisano). During this period, more than 60 percent of the top 300 executives attended at least one SLF. As positions changed and challenges shifted during this period, many senior executives volunteered to attend multiple SLFs.

By 2005, the SLFs and EBOs were no longer experimental workshops. The language and methods of the business leadership model with its emphasis on gaps, disciplined problem solving, senior team responsibilities to re-invent their units through exploitation as well as exploration, and the power of conversations leading to disciplined action were diffused through the senior team. Influential leaders volunteered for both EBOs and SLFs. Those skeptical senior leaders either changed their point of view after having employed an SLF

---

[3] These values emerged from a "values jam" that involved 50,000 IBMers.

or were actively coached by Harreld and Palmisano on the career-limiting consequences of not engaging in these workshops. By 2005, SLFs were seen as an important tool to lead innovation and change. Further, EBOs were seen as a legitimate career step. Indeed, high-potential leaders had to demonstrate their ability to exploit through IBM's disciplined processes and cadences as well as effectively explore into new strategic spaces.

Given the momentum of the SLFs and EBOs, these workshops shifted from Harreld's direct sponsorship and were decentralized to the functions, geographies, and business units. Similarly, once the methodology was developed and tested at the corporate level, the logic of EBOs was decentralized into the functions, regions, and business units (O'Reilly et al., 2009). Over this period, more than 180 EBOs were in place across IBM's functions, regions, and business units. By 2005, EBOs alone had contributed more than $15 billion dollars in incremental IBM growth and were a more effective growth instrument than acquisitions (Harreld, et al., 2007; O'Reilly et al., 2009).

By 2008, 40 SLF sessions were run in this decentralized fashion, involving more than 5,000 IBM executives. The SLFs were institutionalized throughout the firm and led by middle-level managers who were able to leverage their more senior leaders to support and model leading punctuated change. This process of decentralizing SLFs and EBOs throughout the firm broadened the reach of senior leaders, developed leadership throughout the firm, and extended the language and orientation of the business leadership model more extensively (see Figure 10.3). For example, in IBM China, Henry Chow used the SLF methodology to engage his colleagues on accelerating growth in inland China. The EBOs and SLFs were associated with IBM's enhanced performance during this period (see Table 10.1).

LEADING PROACTIVE PUNCTUATED CHANGE AT IBM

Between 1999 and 2008, IBM renewed itself from a disciplined machine that excelled in incremental innovation to a firm that sustained its short-term targets even as it explored fundamentally different domains. This ability to lead proactive punctuated change was institutionalized throughout the firm; within functions (for example, R&D), geographies (for example, China or India), business units (for example, Tivoli or Lotus), and across-business units (for example, life sciences or pervasive computing). This strategic renewal was executed through a series of punctuated changes within each area of the firm.

During this nine-year period, the 180 EBO experiments and the 40 SLF workshops involving more than 150 intact teams created the material where more than 5,000 senior leaders learned about leading change in their own domains, helped others in their domains, and raised a set of system-wide issues that hindered IBM's ability to explore and exploit. Corporate executives used these data to take action at the system level to support more local (for example, functional, geographic, business-unit, and cross-business-unit) punctuated changes. During this period, IBM's executive leaders and its

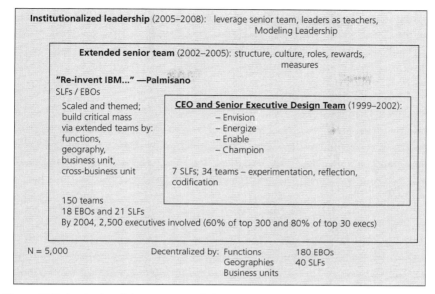

Figure 10.3. Institutionalizing punctuated change at IBM

Table 10.1 SLFs, EBOs, and IBM performance

	2002	2005	2010
Cum. no. of SLFs	7	23	40
No. of executive participants	350	1,800	5,000
No. of EBOs	7	23	180
EBO revenues (as % of IBM total)	6	19	24
IBM revenues ($billion)	81.2	91.1	99.9
Gross margin (%)	36.6	40.1	46.1
Earnings per share ($, diluted)	2.43	4.91	11.52

extended leadership team collectively learned and co-created a set of tools to more effectively lead punctuated change. This set of interrelated interventions led, over time, to the strategic renewal of IBM.

It may be that punctuated change at the corporate level can be executed through collective learning that is induced by senior leaders executing punctuated change within the firm's component units. Such learning about punctuated change is supported by a process, context, language, and set of tools where leaders and their teams both execute change and simultaneously learn from other teams about what helps and hinders punctuated change. Such experience-based conversations help an extended leadership community learn about leading punctuated change both at the unit level and at the corporate level. The impact of this senior team learning about leading punctuated change is institutionalized as these leaders, in turn, taught and coached their extended teams (see Figure 10.3).

This firm-wide strategic renewal was energized and legitimized by the new CEO, who articulated an emotionally engaging vision for the firm (one that was built on IBM's roots) and a new set of values, even as he articulated a growth opportunity gap. This proactive transformation was enacted through a set of experiments (i.e., SLFs and EBOs) that were constructed by Harreld and his colleagues, that led, in turn, to an ever-increasing set of senior leaders who learned to lead punctuated change by their own work in their teams and by sharing best (and worst) practices with their peers and corporate executives in highly engineered social settings. Similar to Kellogg's (2011a, 2011b) work on change in medical centers, the workshops associated with SLFs and EBOs were spaces where teams and their leaders collectively learned about leading punctuated change both in their units and across the firm.

This renewal was executed in a highly top-down fashion, even as the learning was actually done in a decentralized fashion. In effect, the IBM senior executive team proactively created a "burning platform" for change that captivated the hearts and minds of the extended organization. Further, as the SLFs and EBOs involved substantial time for conversation and collective learning, the extended team was able to give feedback on those systemic corporate issues that needed to be changed if the firm-wide renewal was to be executed. Thus, IBM's executive team and its extended senior team collectively co-created IBM's renewal through a combination of top-down as well as bottom-up leadership actions. The extended leadership team set the architecture, pace, and sequencing of these interventions over this extended period (see also Greenwood and Hinings, 1996; Nonaka, 2008; Joseph and Ocasio, 2012).

Institutionalizing innovation and punctuated change at IBM

The impetus for the post-2002 renewal at IBM was Palmisano's aspiration "that IBM can be a great company" and the new set of IBM values developed through the values jam. The new CEO observed that IBM had grown by "restless self-renewal" and could grow again based on innovation ("We create innovative technologies, and we help our customers apply them to transform what they do and how they do it"). Palmisano anchored this post-Gerstner renewal on the core identity of IBM as an innovator and IBMers as restless innovators (see Figure 10.3).

Palmisano empowered such innovation and renewal by further extending and supporting the strategy process Gerstner and Harreld had created. By 2002, Harreld and his strategy colleagues had already gathered data on those factors that helped versus hindered the SLFs and the EBOs. Over the last phase of Gerstner's tenure, the SLFs and EBOs had evolved into a learning and change process that had generated results and had helped create a culture among senior line and staff executives of collaboration, joint accountability, and teamwork, and a language around disciplined problem solving and leading innovation and change. These SLFs and EBOs were each experimental trials where participants and teams learned from their successes and failures, and importantly, Harreld and his corporate colleagues learned from these experiments. Anchored by Palmisano's aspiration for IBM, his growth-and-innovation mandate, and revised values for the firm, the SLFs and EBOs were accelerated and focused post 2002.

These workshops had an impact in every domain of the corporation and, as senior executives learned together about proactive punctuated change, this critical mass of senior executives then provided the energy to decentralize the EBOs and SLFs from the corporate level to countries, functions, business units. By 2005, most of the top 300 senior executives had been to one (or more) SLF or EBO. By 2008, these methods, language, and co-creation had involved more than 5,000 executives. These actions to decentralize the locus and ownership of change were driven even deeper into the firm through the use if idea jams (see Soske and Conger, 2010). This decentralized phase of learning to lead punctuated change was supported by senior leaders but driven by middle-level executives, who led change by teaching what they had learned from their executives. This cadre of middle manages enacting change in their local domains was crucial in institutionalizing change at IBM.

This proactive punctuated change at IBM was not a top-down, integrated change effort. Rather, it was top-down in energy and aspiration, in the articulation of an innovation-rooted performance gap, and an inspiring sense of what IBM and IBMers could be. Palmisano's aspirations were implemented through highly structured workshops where intact teams learned specific tools, languages, and skills for their specific strategic change effort. These workshops were not voluntary; they were driven from the top of the firm. Yet this change effort was also driven from the bottom up. The SLFs and EBOs, intact teams with two corporate sponsors (and associated facilitators), worked on their own root cause analysis and action planning. Moreover, since every SLF and EBO had multiple teams working simultaneously, these teams were able to experiment and learn from each other, hold each other accountable, and generate system-wide root causes that the sponsors took as action items (see Figure 10.4). In line with Kellogg's (2011a, 2011b) work on change in medical centers, the SLFs and EBOs provided the relational spaces as well as cultural and political tool kits, where a diverse leadership community came together to safely learn from each other as they worked on IBM's most pressing strategic issues.[4]

---

[4] After 2006, this process of leading system-wide change was reinforced by the Integration and Values Team. The top 300 executives from across the firm worked on a set of IBM-wide issues defined by the CEO (see Soske and Conger, 2010 for more detail).

Strategic Renewal at IBM (1999–2008)

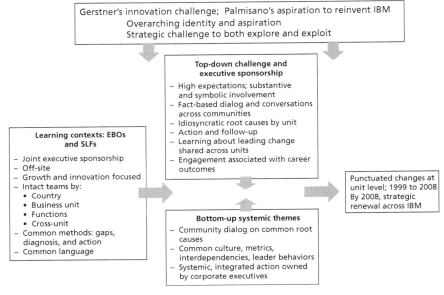

Figure 10.4. Strategic renewal at IBM (1999–2008)

Leading proactive punctuated change

Leading punctuated change through innovation, experimentation, and disciplined learning is not unique to IBM (see also Amis et al., 2004; Sull and Spinosa, 2007; Eggers and Kaplan, 2009; Gulati and Puranam, 2009; Beer et al., 2011; Battilana and Casciaro, 2012; Groysberg and Slind, 2012; Gawer and Phillips, 2013; Ramarajan et al., 2013). Extant literature and our experience at IBM suggest that there are multiple interrelated determinants of leading proactive punctuated change (see Smith et al., 2010; Tushman et al., 2010; O'Reilly and Tushman, 2011). These concepts can, in turn, be employed in leading change associated with sustainability.

SENIOR MANAGEMENT OWNERSHIP AND SUPPORT IS CRUCIAL

Without the most senior leaders on board, punctuated change gets bogged down by powerful forces associated with the status quo. Punctuated change requires the active, unequivocal, and sustained involvement of the firm's senior leadership team. At IBM, this change only gained traction after most senior levels of the firm focused their attention on institutionalizing change throughout the organization. Those senior leaders who did not support these changes (and the associated processes) either were let go or did not get promoted. Similarly, Ramarajan et al.'s (2013) research on gender and change in a professional service firm highlights the importance of sustained senior leadership support.

SENIOR MANAGEMENT ASPIRATION AND IDENTITY

Punctuated changes require an emotionally engaging vision or aspiration. This appeal to aspirations, emotion, and organizational identity is particularly important in executing paradoxical strategic challenges (see also Glynn, 2000, and Smith and Lewis, 2011). Palmisano's aspiration to make IBM "a great firm" again through both disciplined execution and experimentation helped unleash energy throughout the firm to lead innovation streams and, in turn, proactive punctuated change. Similarly, at Havas, David Jones has linked his firm's aspirations on youth empowerment (One Young World) to his clients' interests, as well as the role of the firm in society (Jones, 2012).

EXTENDING SENIOR TEAMS AND INSTITUTIONALIZING CHANGE

Senior leaders cannot lead change by themselves. Line management must eventually own and be engaged in the change effort. Punctuated change requires a social movement. Such a movement starts at the top, engages the top management team, and then involves an extended senior leadership team, and in turn, institutionalizes change throughout the firm. Senior leaders must be rewarded (or punished) and measured on their ability to manage punctuated change and to coach their subordinates in leading punctuated change (see also Amis et al., 2004; Battilana and Casciaro, 2012, 2013).

A CONTEXT FOR EXPERIMENTATION, LEARNING, AND CO-CREATION

Leading punctuated change is rooted in an extended team learning how to lead and co-create change. This community learning is facilitated by a context, structured process, set of tools, and a common problem-solving language. These workshops are most effective when held in a neutral location where participants are not interrupted and focus their full attention to the issues. Such workshops must have content on innovation, organizations, and change, as well as a disciplined process by which participants learn from each other, from external resources, from their work group colleagues who are also working on their own issues, and from their more senior sponsors. These workshops provide the space, legitimacy, cultural and political tools, and language for a heterogeneous group of leaders to experiment with ways to explore and exploit and to collectively learn how to execute punctuated change (see also Beer et al., 2011; Kellogg, 2011a, 2011b).

SENIOR TEAM SPONSORED WORKSHOPS AND FOLLOW-UP

These workshops must be owned and led by a senior leader. Without such senior governance in problem selection, team staffing, and finding co-sponsors, workshops are less effective. The senior sponsors must create a context where teams talk candidly about the real issues. Importantly, process must be built to follow up and monitor progress against commitments made at these workshops. Further, as so much systemic learning about change is generated at each workshop, the senior leader and his/her team have to integrate this learning and initiate appropriate change at the corporate level (see also Sull and Spinosa, 2007; Beer, 2009).

EXPLORATORY INNOVATION IS A CATALYST FOR STRATEGIC RENEWAL

Where proactive punctuated change can be managed with the same underlying processes as reactive change, its motivation is fundamentally different. In the absence of a crisis, the press of growth through exploratory as well as exploitative innovation is a powerful and concrete way to initiate strategic renewal. Since exploratory innovation is associated with a shift in strategy, it is also associated with system-wide organizational change. If ambidextrous organizational designs are able to host both exploitative as well as exploratory innovation, these designs are a powerful tool to create the context for proactive punctuated change. Further, the press of growth through exploration and exploitation push leaders to attend to contradictory strategies simultaneously; the need to explore and exploit as well as to manage incremental and also punctuated change. At IBM, the ability to be an ambidextrous leader, to manage incremental innovation as well as lead exploratory innovation and associated punctuated change, became a criteria for senior leadership promotions (see also similar ideas at GE, Prokesch, 2009).

Our experience at IBM is that leading innovation and punctuated change is less about steps and phases, and more about dialog, participation, contexts, conversations, and commitments that leaders and their teams make to each other in the service of executing their own local change efforts. These punctuated change efforts are energized by an emotionally engaging aspiration and a paradoxical strategic challenge—at IBM to both exploit as well as explore. This learning by doing, sharing this learning within the larger community, and senior team oversight helps create the social movement so central to punctuated change. While punctuated change is initiated from the top, it is executed through an extended social movement managed and designed by senior leaders and carried through the firm by an extended set of leaders who collectively initiate, reflect, and learn about leading change in their local domains.

This induced model or strategic renewal at IBM is consistent with the literature on strategic renewal of organizations in not-for-profit settings. This model of strategic renewal is consistent with Kellogg's (2011a, 2011b) work in medical centers, Battilana and Casciaro's (2012) work in medical centers, Glynn's (2000) work in the Atlanta Orchestra, Battilana and Dorado's (2010) work in community banking, and Eccles et al.'s (2012) work on sustainability. It may well be that this top-down, bottom-up change process, anchored in a paradoxical strategic challenge, and executed via orchestrated learning and a social movement across the firm is a general approach to leading proactive punctuated change.

As evidenced in several other chapters, sustainability needs to be embedded in all organizations' and institutions' agendas. Given the magnitude of potential negative impacts on our planet's livability and continued economic progress, waiting for a crisis to motivate change will only lead to disaster. It is likely that the principles of proactive punctuated change induced at IBM, and the larger body of literature on organizational and institutional change can be applied to the pressing challenges of creating sustainable organizations.

■ REFERENCES

Adner, R. (2012) *The Wide Lens: A New Strategy for Innovation*. New York: Portfolio/Penguin.

Agarwal, R. and Helfat, C. E. (2009) "Strategic Renewal of Organizations," *Organization Science* 20 (2): 281–93.

Amis, J., Slack, T., and Hinings, C. R. (2004) "The Pace, Sequence, and Linearity of Radical Change," *Academy of Management Journal* 47 (1): 15–39.

Anteby, M. (2013) "Relaxing the Taboo on Telling Our Own Stories: Upholding Professional Distance and Personal Involvement," *Organization Science* 24 (4): 1277–90.

Barley, S. R. and Tolbert, P. S. (1997) "Institutionalization and Structuration: Studying the Links Between Action and Institution," *Organization Studies* 18 (1): 93–117.

Barnett, W. P. and Carroll, G. R. (1995) "Modeling Internal Organizational Change," *Annual Review of Sociology* 21: 217–36.

Battilana, J. and Casciaro, T. (2012) "Change Agents, Networks, and Institutions: A Contingency Theory of Organizational Change," *Academy of Management Journal* 55 (2): 381–98.

Battilana, J. and Casciaro, T. (2013) "Overcoming Resistance to Organizational Change: Strong Ties and Affective Cooptation," *Management Science* 59 (4): 819–36.

Battilana, J. and Dorado, S. (2010) "Building Sustainable Hybrid Organizations: The Case of Commercial Microfinance Organizations," *Academy of Management Journal* 53 (6): 1419–40.

Beer, M. (2009) *High Commitment, High Performance: How to Build a Resilient Organization for Sustained Advantage*, 1st edn. San Francisco, CA: Jossey-Bass Pfeiffer.

Beer, M., Eisenstat, R. A., Foote, N., Fredberg, T., and Norgreen, F. (2011) *Higher Ambition: How Great Leaders Create Economic and Social Value*. Boston, MA: Harvard Business Review Press.

Benner, M. J. (2007) "The Incumbent Discount: Stock Market Categories and Response to Radical Technological Change," *Academy of Management Review* 32 (3): 703–20.

Brown, S. L. and Eisenhardt, K. M. (1997) "The Art of Continuous Change: Linking Complexity Theory and Time-Paced Evolution in Relentlessly Shifting Organizations," *Administrative Science Quarterly* 42 (1): 1–34.

Cheng, B., Ioannou, I., and Serafeim, G. (2014) "Corporate Social Responsibility and Access to Finance," *Strategic Management Journal* 35 (1): 1–23.

Collins, J. C. and Hansen, M. T. (2011) *Great by Choice: Uncertainty, Chaos, and Luck: Why Some Thrive Despite Them All*, 1st edn. New York: HarperCollins.

Eccles, R. G., Perkins, K. M., and Serafeim, G. (2012) "How to Become a Sustainable Company," *MIT Sloan Management Review* 53 (4): 43–50.

Eccles, R. G., Ioannou, I., and Serafeim, G. (2014) "The Impact of Corporate Sustainability on Organizational Processes and Performance," *Management Science* (forthcoming).

Eggers, J. P. and Kaplan, S. (2009) "Cognition and Renewal: Comparing CEO and Organizational Effects on Incumbent Adaptation to Technical Change," *Organization Science* 20 (2): 461–77.

Gawer, A. and Phillips, N. (2013) "Institutional Work as Logics Shift: The Case of Intel's Transformation to Platform Leader," *Organization Studies* 34 (8): 1035–71.

Gerstner, L. V. (2002) *Who Says Elephants Can't Dance? Inside IBM's Historic Turnaround*. New York: HarperBusiness.

Glynn, M. A. (2000) "When Cymbals Become Symbols: Conflict over Organizational Identity within a Symphony Orchestra," *Organization Science* 11 (3): 285–98.

Greenwood, R. and Hinings, C. R. (1996) "Understanding Radical Organizational Change: Bringing Together the Old and the New Institutionalism," *Academy of Management Review* 21 (4): 1022–54.

Greenwood, R. and Hinings, C. R. (2006) "Radical Organizational Change," in S. Clegg, C. Hardy, T. B. Lawrence, and W. R. Nord (eds), *The SAGE Handbook of Organization Studies*, 2nd edn. London/Thousand Oaks, CA: Sage Publications, 814–42.

Greenwood, R. and Suddaby, R. (2006) "Institutional Entrepreneurship in Mature Fields: The Big Five Accounting Firms," *Academy of Management Journal* 49 (1): 27–48.

Groysberg, B. and Slind, M. (2012) *Talk, Inc.: How Trusted Leaders Use Conversation to Power Their Organizations*. Boston, MA: Harvard Business School Press.

Gulati, R. and Puranam, P. (2009) "Renewal Through Reorganization: The Value of Inconsistencies Between Formal and Informal Organization," *Organization Science* 20 (2): 422–40.

Hambrick, D. C., Nadler, D. A., and Tushman, M. L. (1998) *Navigating Change: How CEOs, Top Teams, and Boards Steer Transformation*. Boston, MA: Harvard Business School Press.

Harreld, J. B., O'Reilly III, C. A., and Tushman, M. L. (2007) "Dynamic Capabilities at IBM: Driving Strategy into Action," *California Management Review* 49 (4): 21–43.

Jones, D. (2012) *Who Cares Wins: Why Good Business is Better Business*. New York: Pearson.

Joseph, J. and Ocasio, W. (2012) "Architecture, Attention, and Adaptation in the Multibusiness Firm: General Electric from 1951 to 2001," *Strategic Management Journal* 33 (6): 633–60.

Kellogg, K. C. (2011a) *Challenging Operations: Medical Reform and Resistance in Surgery*. Chicago, Ill.: University of Chicago Press.

Kellogg, K. C. (2011b) "Hot Lights and Cold Steel: Cultural and Political Toolkits for Practice Change in Surgery," *Organization Science* 22 (2): 482–502.

Kotter, J. P. (1995) "Leading Change: Why Transformation Efforts Fail," *Harvard Business Review* 73 (2): 59.

Margolis, J. D. and Walsh, J. P. (2001) *People and Profits? The Search for a Link between a Company's Social and Financial Performance*. Mahwah, N.J.: Lawrence Erlbaum Associates.

Miller, D. (1994) "What Happens After Success: The Perils of Excellence," *Journal of Management Studies* 31 (3): 325–58.

Nadler, D. A. and Tushman, M. L. (1997) *Competing by Design: The Power of Organizational Architecture*. New York: Oxford University Press.

Nonaka, I. (2008) *The Knowledge-Creating Company*. Boston, MA: Harvard Business School Press.

O'Reilly III, C. A., and Tushman, M. L. (2008) "Ambidexterity as a Dynamic Capability: Resolving the Innovator's Dilemma," *Research in Organizational Behavior* 28: 185–206.

O'Reilly III, C. A. and Tushman, M. L. (2011) "Organizational Ambidexterity in Action: How Managers Explore and Exploit," *California Management Review* 53 (4): 5–22.

O'Reilly III, C. A., Harreld, J. B., and Tushman, M. L. (2009) "Organizational Ambidexterity: IBM and Emerging Business Opportunities," *California Management Review* 51 (4): 75–99.

Pettigrew, A. M. (1985) *The Awakening Giant: Continuity and Change in Imperial Chemical Industries*. Oxford: Blackwell.

Pfeffer, J. (1992) "Understanding Power in Organizations," *California Management Review* 34 (2): 29–50.

Prokesch, S. (2009) "How GE Teaches Teams to Lead Change," *Harvard Business Review* 87 (1): 99–106.

Ramarajan, L., McGinn, K., and Kolb, D. (2013) "An Outside-In Internalization of Shifting Gender Logics in Professional Work," HBS Working Paper No. 13-051. Boston, MA: Harvard Business School.

Romanelli, E. and Tushman, M. L. (1994) "Organizational Transformation as Punctuated Equilibrium: An Empirical Test," *Academy of Management Journal* 37 (5): 1141–66.

Scott, W. R. and Davis, G. F. (2007) *Organizations and Organizing: Rational, Natural, and Open Systems Perspectives*, 1st edn. Upper Saddle River, N.J.: Pearson Prentice Hall.

Smith, W. K. and Lewis, M. W. (2011) "Toward a Theory of Paradox: A Dynamic Equilibrium Model of Organizing," *Academy of Management Review* 36 (2): 381–403.

Smith, W. K., Binns, A., and Tushman, M. L. (2010) "Complex Business Models: Managing Strategic Paradoxes Simultaneously," *Long Range Planning* 43 (2–3): 448–61.

Soske, T. L. and Conger, J. A. (2010) "The Shifting Paradigm of Executive Leadership Development," in K. Bunker, D. T. Hall, and K. E. Kram (eds), *Extraordinary Leadership: Addressing the Gaps in Senior Executive Development*. San Francisco, CA: John Wiley & Sons, 239–69.

Spillane, J. P., Halverson, R., and Diamond, J. B. (2004) "Towards a Theory of Leadership Practice: A Distributed Perspective," *Journal of Curriculum Studies* 36 (1): 3–34.

Sull, D. N. and Spinosa, C. (2007) "Promise-Based Management," *Harvard Business Review* 85 (4): 78–86.

Tripsas, M. (2009) "Technology, Identity, and Inertia Through the Lens of 'The Digital Photography Company'," *Organization Science* 20 (2): 441–60.

Tushman, M. L. and O'Reilly III, C. A. (1997) *Winning Through Innovation: A Practical Guide to Leading Organizational Change and Renewal.* Boston, MA: Harvard Business School Press.

Tushman, M. L. and Romanelli, E. (1985) "Organizational Evolution: A Metamorphosis Model of Convergence and Reorientation," *Research in Organizational Behavior* 7: 171–222.

Tushman, M. L., Fenollosa, A., McGrath, D. N., O'Reilly III, C. A., and Kleinbaum, A. M. (2007) "Relevance and Rigor: Executive Education as a Lever in Shaping Practice and Research," *Academy of Management Learning & Education* 6 (3): 345–62.

Tushman, M. L., Smith, W. K., Wood, R. C., Westerman, G., and O'Reilly III, C. A. (2010) "Organizational Designs and Innovation Streams," *Industrial and Corporate Change* 19 (5): 1331–66.

Van de Ven, A. (2007) *Engaged Scholarship: A Guide for Organizational and Social Research.* New York: Oxford University Press.

Weick, K. E. and Quinn, R. E. (1999) "Organizational Change and Development," *Annual Review of Psychology* 50: 361–86.

Part V
Leading Change in the Broader System

11 The Role of Multiplier Firms and Megaprojects in Leading Change for Sustainability

Amy C. Edmondson, Martine Haas, John Macomber, and Tiona Zuzul

Introduction

The environmental, social, and economic problems created by the world's rising levels of greenhouse gas emissions and natural resource depletion require new thinking about how to drive change for sustainability.[1] Awareness of the need for significant change to develop more sustainable organizations and communities has expanded dramatically in recent years. In response, many nations and organizations have pursued strategies to improve or preserve the natural environment. As a consequence, rivers are cleaner, air quality is better, and energy efficiency in cars, furnaces, and appliances is greater. Yet critical gaps remain. Companies and countries alike still largely pursue short-term goals at the expense of addressing long-term consequences of their decisions and actions, even when they are aware of the perils of those consequences. Despite gains in pollution control and in public awareness of environmental challenges, progress towards sustainability remains slower than desirable in many sectors of the economy. Moreover, concerns about social and economic sustainability are also growing, as the damaging consequences of inequality, poverty, and instability become increasingly evident.

We conceptualize sustainability as environmental, social, and economic conditions that can be maintained over an extended time horizon. We define *change for sustainability* as substantial efforts by single firms, pairs of firms, or groups of firms to develop and implement initiatives intended to improve environmental and social conditions in an economically viable way in the medium-to-long term. While there is abundant research on leading change inside organizations, our current understanding of how organizations drive larger-scale change aimed at increasing sustainability is limited. Our aim is to take a small step towards advancing such understanding. We do this by exploring initiatives in the *built environment* (that is, in the development of buildings and urban infrastructure) that have the potential to stimulate and

[1] See Friedman (2007).

encourage transformational change for sustainability. In particular, these initiatives catalyze larger-scale change by having an influence that is amplified through the involvement of many organizations, rather than confined within the borders of one organization.

This chapter has three aims. First, we highlight the roles of *multiplier firms* and *megaprojects* in driving change for sustainability in the built environment around the world. We offer a framework comparing and contrasting these two types of inter-organizational change catalysts, as a complement to research on sustainability initiatives within a single organization.

Multiplier firms, in this context, are organizations that develop, disseminate, and facilitate sustainability initiatives for a range of client or partner organizations. We argue that, by working with many organizations, multiplier firms can accelerate the spread of sustainability knowledge and practices across industries and geographies, and thereby have an impact on other firms over an extended period.

Megaprojects are finite-duration initiatives involving multiple diverse entities in the design and delivery of a large-scale development, such as a brand-new smart city, often over a period of many years. We argue that megaprojects' influence on sustainability results from their visibility, which may catalyze future sustainability projects, and from their size. Through efficient use of scarce resources like electricity and water, megaprojects can have a substantial effect on the sustainability of a region. During construction, green space, and transit choices in megaprojects, sustainability decisions are literally cast in concrete and forged in steel.

By drawing attention to the high potential of these activities for catalyzing large-scale change for sustainability, our framework extends work on sustainability-related change within single organizations to show how individual multiplier firms and megaprojects both can drive sustainability-related change through many organizations.

Second, we propose that megaprojects and multiplier firms seeking to produce change for sustainability can benefit from following what we call learning logic, in contrast to blueprint logic, to guide their strategies and actions. We draw on prior and current research on organizational change as the foundation for contrasting these two types of logics for leading change.[2] We conceptualize *blueprint logic* as a top-down or centralized approach aimed at implementing known techniques or solutions, using clear plans, well-defined tasks, and deadlines. Blueprint logic is appropriate when traveling a well-worn path about which considerable prior knowledge exists (for example, implementing a Total Quality Management (TQM) program), in the context of a single organization where the relationships between participants in the implementation process are well established.[3] In contrast, leaders employ *learning logic* when soliciting and using the ideas and innovations of multiple,

---

[2] See Edmondson (2012).   [3] See Westphal et al. (1997).

diverse participants to make progress on complex goals. In short, the logic behind the learning approach is to discover what works along the way, because effective techniques for driving or implementing improvements are not yet known. The distinction between learning logic and blueprint logic is not limited to the context of multiplier firms and megaprojects, but we suggest it as a helpful framework for understanding how to lead sustainability-related change initiatives, given their novel, uncertain, and complex nature.

Third, we draw from four case studies of multiplier firms and megaprojects in the built environment to illustrate how learning logic can be employed to facilitate large-scale change for sustainability. Two of the case studies focus on multiplier firms—Arup & Partners, a global engineering consultancy firm, and EnerNOC, a demand-response facilitator in the US electricity industry. The other two focus on recent and on-going megaprojects—the retrofitting of the Empire State Building, and the creation of a new sustainable city at Lake Nona in Central Florida. These four case studies stand out for a focus on sustainability that is unusual in their industries, where many firms focus on delivering projects or services with low "first costs" (i.e., initial capital expenditures). The cases are thus offered as examples of sustainability-related change initiatives. Our aim is not to make claims about the superiority of the approaches in these four cases relative to other approaches; we leave such comparisons to future research. Rather, we sought rich, illustrative examples to add texture to our arguments about the role of multiplier firms and megaprojects in driving large-scale sustainability-related change, and to illuminate the essential elements of a learning logic for leading change when facing an uncertain path forward.

Multiplier firms and megaprojects in the built environment

As urgency about environmental, social, and economic problems created by the world's rising levels of greenhouse gas emissions and natural resource depletion grows, the built environment is becoming an increasingly important context for large-scale change focused on sustainability. Levels of urbanization are accelerating: by 2008, more than 50 percent of the world's 6.7 billion inhabitants lived in cities, a proportion expected to rise to nearly 70 percent by the middle of the twenty-first century. Cities consume 60–80 percent of the world's energy production.[4] It is important to note that built spaces vary

---

[4] See "UN: World Population Increasingly Urban," available at: <http://www.cbsnews.com/news/un-world-population-increasingly-urban/> (accessed July 2014) and "USS GDP World Bank" website, <http://data.worldbank.org/indicator/NY.GDP.MKTP.DC> (accessed July 2014); also "United Nations Environment Programme" (2013), available at: <http://www.unep.org/greeneconomy/Portans/88/documents/ger/GER_12_Cities.pdf> (accessed July 2014).

widely in consumption of energy and emission of carbon, suggesting oppor-tunities for improvement for consistent achievement of the highest standards.[5] In sum, sustainability-focused change is both a necessity and an opportunity in the built environment.

Furthermore, the built environment is big business. The global value of new construction in the formal economy is approximately $4 trillion per year, or about a quarter the size of the $16 trillion US GDP. Annual revenue in the construction and engineering industry represents about 25 percent of the entire annual global investment in fixed capital.[6] At least this much economic value is added to the built environment each year. Two major areas of improvement exist: first, performing the work with better processes lowers first costs; second, performing the work with smarter designs that optimize energy, water, and traffic flows later provides recurring efficiencies in resource use—a key aspect of sustainability.

Despite its potential impact on sustainability for societies around the world, the construction industry remains a difficult context in which to promote dramatic change. The industry has long been characterized by mistrust, inefficiency, and lack of cooperation, in addition to an emphasis on first cost, rather than operating cost.[7] In contrast to these counterproductive industry dynamics, and at the leading edge of practice, recent years have yielded a number of visionary efforts to catalyze large-scale sustainability-related change in sectors related to the built environment. Multiplier firms and megaprojects are both emerging as potential catalysts of far-reaching sustain-ability change. Moreover, by affecting the built environment, often in well-publicized projects, their actions can also serve to educate the public about sustainability options.

MULTIPLIER FIRMS

Multiplier firms have the potential to accelerate the pace of change for sustainability by developing, disseminating, and facilitating sustainability ini-tiatives for (and with) a range of client or partner firms. Multiplier firms catalyze change for sustainability by building networks of inter-organizational relationships and spreading sustainability-related knowledge, practices, prod-ucts, and services through those networks via direct, intense interaction.

Two kinds of multiplier firms are especially prevalent in the built environ-ment. The first kind focuses on short-term client relationships of limited duration. Such firms typically develop specialized knowledge through working with some client organizations and then transfer it to others. Arup & Partners,

---

[5] See Glaeser and Kahn (2003).

[6] For examples, see Skolkovo, Moscow School of Management (2013). Available at: <http://iems.skolkovo.ru/en/research-platforms/publications/317-the-upcoming-four-trillion-dollar-infrastruc ture-gold-rush> (accessed July 2014) and "US GDP World Bank" website, available at <http://data.worldbank.org/indicator/NY.GDP.MKTP.CD> (accessed July 2014).

[7] See Rashid and Edmondson (2012): 129–50.

the global engineering consultancy firm described below, provides an example. The second kind of multiplier firm focuses on on-going partnership-based engagements of extended durations. Such firms enable partner organizations to achieve efficiencies in the utilization of resources that individual organizations could not or would not achieve alone. EnerNOC, the electricity demand-response facilitator firm, is an example of this kind of multiplier firm.

As both kinds of multiplier firms operate by building connections with and between client or partner organizations, research on inter-organizational networks is relevant for understanding their potential influence. As this research has shown, the dissemination and acceptance of innovative practices across industries often depends on the efforts of well-connected, central actors who can spread new processes and convey complex ideas throughout their networks.[8] By forging ties with multiple clients or partners, multiplier firms help build networks between organizations[9] and create communities of practice[10] that can drive larger-scale change and innovation. Multiplier firms export lessons about sustainability throughout their networks, shaping what their clients or partners do and how they do it; these organizations, in turn, influence other organizations. Multiplier firms thus have an impact on an exponentially growing number of projects and locations. If successful, multiplier firms may catalyze change for sustainability throughout multiple organizations within, and even across, industries.

MEGAPROJECTS

In the context of the built environment, megaprojects involve collaboration among a large and diverse group of organizations to conceive, design, finance, build, and operate large-scale projects. Such megaprojects include collaborative efforts to, for instance, create transportation infrastructure or planned cities; recent examples include the Big Dig in Boston, the Los Angeles Subway System, the Denver International Airport, Terminal 5 of the London Heathrow Airport, and New Songdo City.[11] The organizations involved in these collaborative efforts often include city and state governments, real estate developers, architects, engineers, construction companies, and technology specialists.[12] A group of organizations is assembled from scratch for each megaproject and dissolved upon project completion; the relationships are usually temporary, lasting from several months to several years. Thus, megaprojects involve establishing fluid ecosystems of organizations interconnected for the purposes and duration of a given project.[13]

---

[8] See Uzzi and Spiro (2005).   [9] See Uzzi (1997) and also Fleming et al. (2007).
[10] See Wenger (1998).
[11] See Lehrer and Laidley (2008) and also Brady and Davies (2010).
[12] See Lehrer and Laidley (2008) and also Van Marrewijk et al. (2008).
[13] See Van Marrewijk et al. (2008) and also Davies et al. (2009).

Megaprojects in the built environment invest many billions of dollars in shaping land and structures. Such projects typically require both high up-front costs and a long-term perspective on capital.[14] Historically, however, many megaprojects, along with most smaller-scale projects in the built environment, have placed little emphasis on maximizing resource efficiency in the operating phase, as opposed to the construction phase.[15] Moreover, many such projects are notorious for cost overruns and delays during construction.[16]

The diverse set of organizations that come together in megaprojects thus have significant, but largely underdeveloped, potential to catalyze broad and deep change for sustainability. The size of a megaproject can often justify spending more effort in early-stage planning, optimization, analysis, and team building, requiring collaboration and alignment of interests to achieve a better long-term result. Megaprojects also tend to be one-offs with little precedent—so their development requires innovation on many fronts at once. This creates an opportunity for multiple teams (representing multiple organizations) to realize new levels of sustainability performance. By working together across professional and industry boundaries, these teams and organizations have the potential to arrive at innovative solutions for environmental, social, and economic sustainability above and beyond what individual firms might generate.[17] Megaprojects can also catalyze broader change by allowing participating organizations to test and gain exposure to new sustainability solutions that they can refine and deploy in future projects. Additionally, their unusual scope and visibility means that they function as demonstration projects that can spread lessons learned.

In summary, megaprojects and multiplier firms both have great potential for catalyzing sustainability-related change as a result of direct and indirect involvement of numerous organizations in their initiatives. Some very large single firms (for example, Walmart) might be able to exert considerable influence through their own internally focused sustainability initiatives. The extent of the influence of most individual firm sustainability initiatives is limited, however, relative to the potential influence of multiplier firms and megaprojects, because of their less extensive and diverse external reach. Essential elements of single firms, multipliers, and megaprojects as catalysts for driving sustainability-related change are summarized in Table 11.1.

Next, we draw on four illustrative cases to describe how multiplier firms and megaprojects are beginning to drive change for sustainability in the built environment. We start by providing brief descriptions of two multiplier firms—Arup & Partners and EnerNOC—and two megaprojects—the Empire State Building and Lake Nona Medical City. We then turn to the literature on organizational change to gain insight into how multiplier firms and megaprojects can drive sustainability-related change successfully, and distinguish

---

[14] See Flyybjerg, Bent, Bruzelius, Nils, and Rothengatter, Werner (2003).
[15] See Herron et al. (2013).   [16] See Flyybjerg et al. (2003).
[17] See Lehrer and Laidley (2008); Van Marrewijk et al. (2008), and also Davies et al. (2009).

Table 11.1 Single firms, multiplier firms, and megaprojects as leaders of change for sustainability

	Leading change for sustainability *within one organization*	Leading change for sustainability via *multiplier firms*	Leading change for sustainability via *megaprojects*
Situation	Single organization deploys sustainability initiatives within the firm and its operations	Multiplier firm develops, disseminates, and facilitates sustainability initiatives for its clients or partners	Megaproject engages groups of organizations to work together to conceive, design, finance, build, and operate large projects with substantial sustainability focus
Nature and length of relationship between participants	Forever: Formal and hierarchical permanent operating company	Variable: Persists while useful to all parties; advising can go on for months; optimizing can go on for years	Temporary: Assembled from scratch each time with new relationships; dissolved on completion of project
Range of influence of the changes for sustainability	Usually limited: Within the firm and sometimes into parts of the supply chain	Wide: Intentionally well beyond the firm to many other clients and partners	Deep and wide: Primarily in the focal project and secondarily in the ability of firms to deploy learning to future projects
Magnitude and type of potential sustainability impact	Medium: Internal processes like electricity for lighting and cooling, supply chain improvements, for example in packaging	High: Best practice-driven improvements in processes, particularly around energy use and CO_2 savings	Very high: Long-term improvements in effective use of key scarce resources like electricity, water, land, and CO_2
Authority for implementing changes for sustainability	Executive: Chief Executive Officer, Chief Sustainability Officer, or other member of hierarchy leads change	Content experts: Experts and allies develop knowledge and disseminate best practices based on evidence	Participants: Project leaders influence communication but analysis, commitment, and implementation flows up from below

between two possible logics for leading such change: blueprint logic and learning logic. Subsequently, we revisit our four cases and discuss how these catalysts of large-scale, inter-organizational change have relied on the use of learning logic rather than blueprint logic to achieve results.

SPREADING EXPERTISE: ARUP & PARTNERS

Arup, founded in 1946 by Ove Arup with a focus on structural engineering, is a global consultancy with approximately 10,000 employees working in more than 90 countries. The firm specializes in the innovative design and specification of buildings, bridges, and urban plans that include the most compelling and up-to-date advances in sustainable practice. When new advances in sustainability are not yet widely known or well established, it is difficult for small design firms, or small building owners, to identify which advances to adopt. By developing, applying, and disseminating cutting-edge advances to its clients and partners, Arup spreads expertise and drives change in sustainability performance across multiple organizations.

Arup exemplifies a multiplier firm in the realm of sustainability-related change because it directly influences the sustainability practices of many other companies through its interactions with a growing network of clients. The company continually builds leading-edge knowledge as a result of the reputation it has earned as a "go-to" firm for challenging and innovative designs, like the Water Cube at the Beijing Olympics[18] or the deeply cantilevered structure at the Institute of Contemporary Art in Boston.[19] The firm also builds knowledge through its renowned forensics practice, which explores system failures in many projects by other design and engineering firms. Arup is involved in a large number of different projects at any one time; its leaders and employees thus continually learn from these projects.

By aggressively cataloging its experiences and spreading learning gleaned from some clients to other clients, Arup disseminates this knowledge through its network of inter-organizational relationships. Many consulting firms spread knowledge about techniques such as structural analysis or adoption of new building materials. However, Arup is unusual in its commitment to exploring and disseminating learning about efficient use of resources like water and power in operations, setting the firm apart as a leader in multiplying the impact of changes that foster sustainability.

FACILITATING MULTIPARTY EFFICIENCIES: ENERNOC

EnerNOC, a demand-response facilitator in the US electricity industry is a multiplier firm that connects many disparate entities in a network that optimizes energy usage and reduces the need for new power plant construction.[20] In the US, electric utilities are expected to build enough generating capacity and have enough fuel on hand to satisfy "peak demand," or the peak electricity called for by consumers and corporations—an event that usually occurs sometime each July when air conditioning demand is at its highest. Utilities therefore must build a large quantity of "peaking-power" generators to accommodate spikes in consumer demand. Although they are expensive to build and own, these peaking-power generators only get used a few times per year. They typically use the dirtiest fuel sources, since these are the easiest to turn on and off quickly (it is easier, for instance, to start and stop a diesel generator than a nuclear power plant or hydroelectric dam).

Demand-response services like EnerNOC enlist corporate customers in optimization arrangements that distribute the load across firms and days, or require firms to reduce electricity usage during a peak time. EnerNOC pays

---

[18] See Eccles et al. (2010).
[19] For examples, see <http://www.Arup.com> (accessed July 2014).
[20] For more details, see Toffel et al. (2012), in addition to EnerNOC (2013) and Macomber (2013).

corporate electricity users a year-round fee to entice them to be in the program. When a peaking event occurs, EnerNOC either coordinates with corporate users to shift their big draw to another day, or requires them to reduce usage (by turning off selected lights, running air conditioning set points at warmer temperatures for a few hours, or shutting down some machinery). EnerNOC thus manages to cross new efficiency frontiers through its advanced use of information technology (as it analyzes large amounts of data to get a detailed idea of the collected power demand of all of the businesses in its system, and then optimizes power delivery) and its advanced financial layering (as it finances its operations through very diverse sources, including standby fees and utility payments collected from participating organizations).[21]

By pulling together, organizing, and providing incentives for multiple organizations across a network, EnerNOC is a multiplier firm that enables sustainability gains greater than the sum of gains that each individual organization could accomplish alone. At present, EnerNOC manages about 65 GW of electricity (about 30 times the capacity of the Indian Point Energy Center nuclear power plant in New York state) and, according to the company website, has saved over 16 million tons of CO_2 through demand-response and other services.[22] Demand-response is difficult to coordinate across many entities, and seldom deployed in the US. The willingness and ability of EnerNOC to build a business that connects multiple parties, all of whom pay to participate, is unusual and, if successful, will lead to extensive savings in both concrete and steel (construction of plants) and carbon (burning of dirty fuels for peak power). This is an advance in change for sustainability enabled by a multiplier firm that connects otherwise-disparate parties to optimize behavior in a way that the parties cannot accomplish on their own.

RETROFITTING AN ICON: THE EMPIRE STATE BUILDING

The Empire State Building in New York City is one of the most recognized buildings in the world, yet by 2008 it had become outdated in terms of energy efficiency, water usage, air filtration, and physical attractiveness of the office floors for corporate tenants. The building was spending in excess of $11 million per year just for energy.[23] In a $500 million megaproject, Empire State Building LLC (ESB) (now Empire State Realty Trust) renovated and updated the Empire State Building to become a Class A office building and a showcase from the inside, not just from the outside. This megaproject involved dozens of parties—engineering firms, architects, corporate tenants, real estate brokers, interior designers, furniture and equipment vendors, and utility

---

[21] For more details, see Toffel et al. (2012), in addition to EnerNOC (2013) and Macomber (2013).
[22] For examples, see <http://www.enernoc.com/> (accessed July 2014).
[23] See the Official Site of the Empire State Building. (2014) "Empire State Building Sustainability Program." Available at: <http://www.esbnyc.com/sites/default/files/ESBPlacematFINAL.2.pdf> (accessed July 2014).

companies—who came together to retrofit the iconic building for greater sustainability. The renovated building was expected to effectively reduce energy use by 38 percent—and to save 150,000 tons of CO_2 emissions over the life of the improvements.

According to industry groups like the Real Estate Roundtable, this emphasis on energy efficiency is unusual in an environment where landlords pay for capital costs and tenants pay for energy costs. Usually neither party has an incentive to invest in energy efficiency, and this problem has famously stalled energy retrofit work in buildings all over the world. The Empire State Building leadership was unusual in its zeal to address the problem, in its deployment of specialists from the National Resources Defense Council and the Clinton Global Initiative to work with both landlords and tenants, and in its insistence on open analysis and reporting on the public website, sharing of information between the parties involved, and full disclosure of learning from the project, rather than patenting or hiding discoveries.

With this unusual attention to energy efficiency, the megaproject participants discovered and shared sustainability measures that extended well beyond the prior state of the art. For example, the team initially expected to use the Leadership in Energy and Environmental Design point system of the US Green Buildings Council (LEED) scoring system to assess interventions on a simple point-score basis. LEED is an effective assessment system for high-level evaluations in situations with less complexity, but it proved insufficient for this megaproject. As a result, the team members instead used cost–benefit analysis of multiple systems and multiple new technologies. Most of the engineering, product, and consulting firms involved (and even corporate tenants with offices in many other cities) were subsequently able to spread both this cost–benefit approach and the specific lessons learned about materials and methods, thereby accelerating the spread of knowledge of what worked, the analytical toolkit, and the culture of this megaproject to subsequent renovation and tenant improvement projects. Lessons from the Empire State Building thus had far greater reach than might first appear likely. The megaproject was also publicized extensively, amplifying its impact on future sustainability efforts in the built environment.

CREATING A SUSTAINABLE CITY: LAKE NONA

The goal for the Lake Nona Medical City megaproject was to develop a new, sustainable research and residential cluster in Central Florida that integrated the entire value chain in the health-care industry. This megaproject was spearheaded by Tavistock Group (Tavistock), an international private investment organization. Tavistock leaders aspired to attract a viable ecosystem of leading health-care institutions involved in research, education, and delivery to comprise one of the world's most important bench-to-bedside research clusters on a 7,000-acre plot of largely undeveloped land. They hoped to create 30,000 jobs in the region, and to build 10,000 environmentally sustainable homes for the community's projected 25,000 residents, many of whom would move into the region because of jobs available in the cluster.

An important guiding principle for the megaproject was the collaborative involvement of diverse public and private organizations. Tavistock began by forming Lake Nona Property Holdings and the Lake Nona Institute to work together to develop the community and manage its partnerships. These organizations worked closely with the major tenant organizations in Lake Nona to recruit employees and find opportunities for joint research. State and local governments assisted with zoning and regulatory requirements and provided funding based on the community's potential to generate jobs. The local school system administrators collaborated on the building of new public schools for the cluster, including a high school equipped with technologies provided by community partners. Large technology companies, including General Electric (GE) and Cisco tested and deployed smart and sustainable technological solutions, and several local developers and construction companies worked on the construction of the community.

As of 2013, nine years after the project's launch, Lake Nona is well on its way to meeting its ambitious goals. The community was planned and almost fully developed, using design and construction that followed principles of sustainability. The health-care cluster attracted a number of private- and public-sector residents, including Nemours Children's Hospital, the first new United States Veterans Affairs (VA), the Sanford-Burnham Medical Research Institute, the University of Central Florida's brand new medical school, and the University of Florida Research and Academic Center. The residential community was close to completion, with homes suitable for a range of income levels along with mixed-use urban spaces to bring communities together.

Lake Nona's emphasis on sustainability as well as collaboration separates it from most traditional real-estate developments. Environmentally, the community has demonstrated an alternative to typical large-scale developments. In addition to 44 linear miles of bike and walking trails, every road in Lake Nona has a bike lane, all major buildings in the community must be certified as LEED Silver or higher, and all new homes are energy efficient. The living spaces, the residential neighborhoods, and the schools use energy-efficient technologies and were designed to reduce energy consumption and encourage residents to lead healthier lives. Among other solutions, GE developed custom LED streetlights for Lake Nona, and the community features the largest single deployment of LED lights in the United States. Cisco designated Lake Nona as one of nine "Smart + Connected Communities," and anticipated deploying a sensor network to enable the collection and intelligent use of data. In a speech on February 29, 2012, City of Orlando Mayor Buddy Dyer emphasized that Lake Nona was on track to create over 30,000 jobs and to have a major ten-year economic impact on the region. The projected economic impact of the community has risen from the 2005 estimate of $5 billion per year to $7.6 billion.

Leading change for sustainability in the built environment

Reflecting on these four cases of multiplier firms and megaprojects undertaking unique journeys towards greater sustainability, we consider what lessons they offer for those interested in leading large-scale change for sustainability. To do this, we briefly review prior research on organizational change, including recent work on sustainability-related organizational change. This review highlights two basic approaches to leading change, one that we characterize as driven by blueprint logic, and one driven by learning logic. We propose that learning logic is more conducive to driving large-scale change for sustainability than blueprint logic, and illustrate how this plays out in our case studies. The key features of these two types of logics for leading change are summarized in Table 11.2.

BLUEPRINT LOGIC VERSUS LEARNING LOGIC

Research on leading organizational change presents numerous models that fall into two broad categories based on the degree, clarity, and formality of their prescriptions. One category encompasses well-planned change, while the other relates to emergent change.[24] Planned change, a more traditional managerial approach, builds on the early work of psychologist Kurt Lewin, who conceptualized change as a three-step process—"unfreezing" current behaviors and processes, shifting to new ones, and then "refreezing" with the desired changes in place.[25] Models of planned change tend to assume an initial stable state, followed by a change process of specified steps to reach a particular end state.[26] Firms can enact internal organizational change for well-understood improvement goals through top-down implementation of targets and deadlines, and by promoting employee effort.[27] Advice for leaders undertaking planned changed includes consolidating change leadership responsibilities among senior executives, clear communication of a vision and the content of the planned change, modeling new behaviors, and selecting or removing employees based on their adherence or resistance to change practices.[28] This approach involves what we term "blueprint logic," in which the goals of change are well understood, as are best practices for achieving those goals. Under these conditions, leaders can develop clear plans and targets, and push them to fruition by gaining buy-in from and exerting authority over the members of their organization.

---

[24] See Baron and Hannan (2002).   [25] For examples, see Lewin (1958: 197–211).
[26] See Baron and Hannan (2002).
[27] See Baron and Hannan (2002) for a discussion of blueprints for employee motivation and reward in a situation characterized by direct monitoring, peer or cultural control, and formal processes and procedures.
[28] See Baron and Hannan (2002), Van der Voet et al. (2013), and also Kotter (1990).

Table 11.2 Contrasting approaches to leading change for sustainability

	Blueprint logic	Learning logic
Novelty of change goals	Low	High
Number of organizations involved	One	One or more
Best practices	Known	Unknown
Clarity of plans and targets	High	Low
Leadership authority	Centralized	Distributed
Leadership goals	Seek buy-in	Seek experimentation

Blueprint logic can be effective for leading organizational change when knowledge about the context and about successful processes is well developed. To illustrate, consider a suburban water utility seeking to improve its efficiency. Water utilities deliver a predictable and narrowly defined set of services with well-understood processes and technologies. In one illustrative case, managers recognized that their organization's cost performance was 30 percent worse than that of leading competitors in the industry.[29] Sensibly, they set out to benchmark a best-in-class water utility and thereby found transferable process solutions. This enabled them to apply organizational work processes used elsewhere to their own operations, the very essence of blueprint logic. The change goal was to systematically implement clearly prescribed solutions, and good leadership and disciplined implementation allowed them to succeed in that goal.

Not surprisingly, in an increasingly dynamic and complex world, models of planned change have been criticized recently for their reliance on a top-down regimented approach. Planned change, with its blueprint logic, is seen as inflexible in the face of unexpected conditions. Blueprint logic does not easily accommodate the diverse contributions that reflect experiences and expertise available from members of the organization during the process of change. Some have suggested that planned change does not allow for a continuously changing environment, as it seeks to follow the strict timing and objectives of senior-level leaders.[30] This type of change management can be more appropriate for incremental changes in familiar contexts than for extensive change in contexts where proven models don't yet exist. Further, critics acknowledge that planned change presumes that all participants agree with the change and are able and ready to act to implement it.[31]

This criticism has spawned a new literature on emergent change, which advocates an approach to organizational change that is fluid and flexible, rather than deterministic and planned. This literature suggests that by encouraging and incorporating bottom-up learning and action, change will better reflect and respond to the complexities and dynamism in an organization's

---

[29] Edmondson and Hajim (2003).   [30] See Baron and Hannan (2002).
[31] See Baron and Hannan (2002).

operations and environment.[32] In emergent change, leaders inspire and support the change process, rather than prescribing and mapping it out. Action is local, variable, and somewhat uncoordinated, but focused on creating changes that are aligned with a common vision. Individuals experiment with new approaches in whatever part of the organization they manage or support. These experiments are a source of organizational learning. The leadership of emergent change processes is also distributed, involving individuals throughout an organization, who work to facilitate others' participation by communicating the need for change, fostering discussion, acting as role models, ensuring that people feel safe expressing their ideas, solving problems, learning from each other, and finding solutions.[33]

We refer to the underlying logic driving emergent change as "learning logic." As previously noted, learning logic is needed when knowledge about how to achieve organizational goals is incomplete. This is often the case in novel contexts, where setting targets can be challenging because of a lack of shared templates or accepted definitions of success. In such novel and complex contexts, effective change calls for exploration rather than exploitation.[34] Additionally, when multiple units or even organizations are working together to achieve shared goals, leadership is distributed more widely than concentrated, and leaders must drive change by seeking and supporting experimentation by the parties involved.

To illustrate, consider the case of a hospital leadership team seeking to lead change targeted at 100 percent patient safety.[35] There is no blueprint for how to alter hospital work processes to successfully accomplish this goal. Optimal care delivery processes vary greatly from patient to patient, and multiple professionals with specialized knowledge interact to provide care. The simultaneous uncertainty and complexity of the patient-care delivery process has given rise to visible failures in health care, and finding ways to ensure patient safety in hospitals has proved challenging.[36] Hospitals that succeed in dramatic safety improvement do so by embarking on an emergent change process that follows learning logic to solve this challenging problem.

While the research discussed so far has examined organizational change in general, a small but growing body of research focuses specifically on sustainability-related change. This work considers change efforts that balance environmental, social, and economic perspectives. Three features distinguish sustainability-related change from change management more generally.[37] First, in sustainability initiatives, a known risk is "greenwashing"—or a focus on external image enhancement rather than on material improvement. Second, the vision or goal for sustainability is often unclear and hard to define for

[32] See Edmondson (2012).
[33] See Edmondson (2012), Baron and Hannan (2002), and also Van der Voet et al. (2013).
[34] See March (1991).   [35] See Bohmer (2003) and Edmondson and Roberto (2003).
[36] See Edmondson (1996): 5–28 and also Tucker and Edmondson (2003): 55–72.
[37] See Lueneburger and Goleman (2010).

participants in such initiatives. Third, sustainability initiatives typically involve multiple participants and stakeholders, inside and often outside a focal organization, rather than being limited to specific groups or functional roles with an organization. These features imply that learning logic may be more appropriate for leading sustainability-related change than blueprint logic, given the emphasis of the learning logic on managing novel goals and multiple parties.

Sustainability-related change research places great emphasis on leadership and the values and competencies required for leading such change.[38] Adaptive leadership is seen as a helpful approach when there is no defined answer or plan to implement.[39] In our terms, adaptive leadership follows learning logic that emphasizes inclusion and experimentation over implementation or execution. Major themes in sustainability change leadership include creating a vision or sense of urgency, changing the mindset of the employees, connecting employees to the vision, building an alliance among employees with enthusiasm for the vision, developing a plan, enabling action and learning, maintaining commitment through modeling, and removing barriers for empowerment.[40]

The themes that can be seen in the small but growing body of research on leading sustainability-related change thus seem to point to the potential value of learning logic, in particular, for driving such change. At the same time, most research on leading change for sustainability has focused on efforts to improve environmental, social, or economic performance *within* firms. For change involving multiple firms, blueprint logic is even more inadequate. Multiple firms undergoing a change journey together, even one that is focused on a shared initiative, create enormous complexity and uncertainty. We thus build on prior work to emphasize the value of learning logic for leading sustainability-related change in multiplier firms and megaprojects. Specifically, we propose that multiplier firms and megaprojects can best drive large-scale change for sustainability in ways that reach well beyond their own activities, by following learning logic.

LEADING CHANGE FOR SUSTAINABILITY IN MULTIPLIER FIRMS AND MEGAPROJECTS

We suggest that a top-down blueprint approach to leading change in multiplier firms and megaprojects is unlikely to be effective for several reasons. First, leaders of multiplier firms and megaprojects have few successful precedents or models to emulate. At the outset, answers are elusive; changing technologies limit knowledge of the best change metrics. Ideas and solutions must emerge as the work unfolds. Well-defined plans, with specific tasks and deadlines, are impractical when little is known.[41] Second, multiplier firms and

---

[38] See Lueneburger and Goleman (2010).   [39] See Heifetz (1994).
[40] See Heifetz (1994) and also Senge et al. (2008).
[41] See Sitkin et al. (1994): 537–64, for a discussion of how traditional quality-control techniques are not well suited to highly uncertain situations, which instead call for learning-oriented practices that promote innovation.

megaprojects operate in complex environments and involve multiple, diverse participants, giving rise to unpredictable interactions and events. The only certainty is that the unexpected will occur. The multiplier firms and megaprojects we studied—Arup, EnerNOC, ESB, and Lake Nona—operated in dynamic networks and ecosystems where any participating organization could opt out. Engaging participants was critical to success. An approach developed and driven forward by a single organization would risk failing to incorporate unique ideas and experiences offered by each partner. Managing relationships through centralized control might thereby alienate partners and extinguish creativity.

By consciously using learning logic rather than blueprint logic, energetic and thoughtful leaders of multiplier firms and megaprojects may be better able to work with (rather than resist) the challenges they face in novel and complex initiatives, transforming them into learning opportunities. Clients and partners can self-select into a situation where they intentionally engage a multiplier firm or sign up for involvement in a megaproject. Leaders can promote innovation by encouraging everyone to offer ideas and solutions. Fluid relationships mean that parties are not locked into hierarchies, processes, or roles, and can improvise as needed.

Turning to the four cases we studied, the leaders of these multiplier firms and megaprojects clearly faced challenging tasks. The novelty and complexity of their change goals—spreading sustainability knowledge across multiple client organizations, coordinating multiple parties to achieve efficiency gains, retrofitting an iconic building, and developing a new sustainable community—were high. Outcomes were dependent on successful interactions with a large and shifting set of collaborators. They lacked proven examples of best practices, and faced unclear targets and plans. Moreover, their leaders had to encourage collaboration and change via distributed authority: the leaders of Arup, EnerNOC, ESB, and Lake Nona had little formal authority over the activities of their clients and partners. Lacking blueprint for change, and with complex networks of participation, the leaders of these multiplier firms and megaprojects engaged in learning process through which they, as well as the broader communities of organizations with which they worked, developed new knowledge about how to produce change.

Leading change following a learning logic requires taking an observant and tentative stance. Given that few answers are known in advance, the essential leadership task is to motivate people to work hard to discover new answers together. Consider what organization and project leaders can do to encourage this to happen. We organize these leadership activities into three categories—*articulating a vision, inviting participation,* and *encouraging experimentation.*[42] Using this organizing framework, we examine how the multiplier firms and megaprojects we studied employed a learning logic to discover and implement new processes and practices to drive change for sustainability.

---

[42] See Edmondson (2012) esp Chapter 8.

Launching Change: Articulating a Vision

To engage stakeholders to enact change, leaders of the multiplier firms and megaprojects in the four cases we examined had in common the articulation of a compelling vision to motivate participants to want to help bring it about. Each vision was both audacious (setting challenging and unprecedented aspirations) and inclusive (emphasizing the benefits to all involved parties). In no case, however, did a leader's vision specify *how* it should be achieved. Consistent with learning logic, leaders left room for process experimentation, iteration, and emergence.

EnerNOC's business model, for instance, is predicated on multiple participants buying into a single vision—the premise that a third party can create enough savings in energy use and capital costs that everyone—the utility company, the electricity consumer, and EnerNOC—does better than they would working alone. EnerNOC emphasizes and promotes this vision: "EnerNOC helps commercial, institutional, and industrial organizations use energy more intelligently, pay less for it, and generate cash flow that benefits the bottom line through our complete suite of energy intelligence software and solutions," as the company's promotional materials explain. This vision opens many possibilities: the application of sensors, sharing of consumption data, sharing of demand projections, sharing of capital cost information, and alteration of consumption behavior to smooth out spikes in demand, driving system-level change for sustainability. This is embodied in EnerNOC's tagline: "We're changing the way the world uses energy." It is a bold vision, and one that promises change for multiple stakeholders.

The Empire State Building's comprehensive approach to sustainability was led by the CEO of Empire State Realty Trust, Tony Malkin, who began the project with a bold and inclusive vision. Malkin described the vision behind the Empire State Building megaproject:

> To define intelligent choices, which will either save money, spend the same money more efficiently, or spend additional sums for which there is reasonable payback through savings. Addressing these investments correctly will create a competitive advantage for ownership through lower costs and better work environment for tenants. Succeeding in these efforts will make a replicable model for others to follow.[43]

Although Malkin created this vision, he did not set precise metrics or methods for achieving it, such as engineering and payback analyses, nor did he dictate the exact equipment to be purchased, or design features to be incorporated, or design-and-construction processes to be followed for each tenant project. Instead, those decisions were left to those closest to the data. In a correspondence with one of the authors, Malkin later recalled, "We shared and we share

---

[43] See the Official Site of the Empire State Building, "Empire State Building Sustainability Program" (2014). Available at: <http://www.esbnyc.com/sites/default/files/ESBPlacematFINAL.2.pdf> (accessed July 2014).

everything on our website, patented nothing, and demanded open sharing." Malkin's role, in short, was to set the vision, provide resources and convene the relevant parties to learn from shared novel experiences.

Similarly, to achieve their ambitious goals, Lake Nona's leaders articulated a vision that emphasized the creation of a collaborative culture for managing this megaproject. Tavistock did not develop blueprints for the community and ask partners to plug in their solutions. Instead, executives sought to develop a vision for the community, and attract partners who could expand and modify that vision. In an interview with the authors, a Lake Nona executive explained:

In the typical merchant builder scenario, there is the developer, who, before they spend their money, will try to minimize their risks. They'll try to get the land preleased, presold, then build the roads and infrastructure and then make their profit at the end and move on. There is a saying in the development business, that "the pioneers get the arrows, the settlers get the land." But for us—we're not in this to mint money. We're in this to make a difference in the world . . . . We view ourselves as having a tremendous amount of responsibility to doing something special with this land.

Partners involved in the project emphasized that Tavistock leadership did not micro-manage the development of the community. Instead, they described the leadership as "accelerators," "conductors," and "builders of collaboration." Tavistock executives commonly reflected, "We want to be a conductor and let other people play their instruments."[44]

Enrolling Others in Change: Inviting Participation

Enacting a learning logic, the leaders of the multiplier firms and megaprojects we studied invited involvement and ideas from employees, partners, and beyond. Because they functioned in novel territory, inviting such participation was essential to allowing discovery of new and better solutions and processes needed to implement change for sustainability.

Arup & Partners, for instance, has a clear culture of encouraging ideas and innovation from anyone. The contributor might be an employee, a client, an outside consultant, or a building product manufacturer like Otis Elevator or Owens-Corning insulation. This is very different than having a "company method" or template for fee-based service delivery, as some large professional service organizations do in order to be able to swap staff in and out and deliver consistent, if sometimes overly standardized, client solutions. Arup organizes itself from its core to invite ideas not only through an open attitude, but also through an intentional structure. Rather than a vertical hierarchy, the firm has a rotating set of board members and trustees who guide the direction of the company but are closely attuned to its operations and encourage the voices of

---

[44] Interview conducted by Amy C. Edmondson and Tiona Zuzul, September 2011.

workaday engineers. "Everybody in Arup feels totally empowered to have a view on everything," says one employee.[45]

The Empire State Building team was set up with multiple players, multiple tasks, multiple technologies, and multiple iterations specifically to encourage new ideas, and rigorous evaluation of their usefulness. Although the project's leadership set its vision, unusual partners were enlisted to generate, analyze, and find new ideas. The Clinton Climate Initiative and the Rocky Mountain Institute were engaged both to focus attention on the project and to help generate new ideas about sustainability and innovation that typical developers do not consider. The landlord also collaborated with the National Resources Defense Council and its team of techno-economic analysts, who helped assess possible interventions. A vendor team including Johnson Controls, Jones Lang Lasalle, and Serious Materials worked closely to assess ideas about the building, providing both existing data and new learning to product companies and tenants alike. By inviting ideas and contributions from these unusual partners, the megaproject's leadership team was able to make progress on their vision for retrofitting an icon.

Similarly, Lake Nona leaders worked with organizations that ranged from construction specialists to technology companies and medical institutions. The Lake Nona Institute did not approach each partner with a specific plan for how they could contribute to the community. Instead, the team engaged each partner in a conversation about the possibilities. Once they did this, members of the two organizations sat together to think about how their capabilities could be combined to be innovative and add value to the community and to both of them. This led to the development of solutions not envisioned in early plans. An executive at Lake Nona Institute, for instance, explained how the idea for one of Lake Nona's major health-related initiatives—a large-scale, longitudinal study on the health and wellness of community residents—emerged through conversations with a major corporate partner:

We initially came together at a strategic level. But as we talked and worked together, we began to think of initiatives that weren't discussed at the beginning. It's an interesting process—beyond just defining and working on a specific project, we allow time to have conversations on what else we could do. Now there are maybe four different initiatives that have evolved that weren't even part of our original discussion—including the wellness study.[46]

Producing Change: Encouraging Experimentation

Finally, leaders of the multiplier firms and megaprojects we studied encouraged experimentation and sought to lower the natural fear that inhibits

---

[45] Quote by Arup Americas Chairman, Mahadev Ramen in Voner (2013), "The Sky's the Limit." Available at: <http://www.metropolismag.com/September-2013/The-Skys-the-Limit/index.php?cparticle=2&siarticle=1> (accessed July 2014).

[46] Interview conducted by Amy C. Edmondson and Tiona Zuzul, February 2012.

willingness to try out new things that might fail. By doing so, they ensured their emergent ideas were evaluated and tested through each multiplier project and megaproject.

At Arup & Partners, change and experimentation are deeply intertwined with the company culture. As one senior member of the firm explained, "We love to explore new things, test theories, experiment with design. A certain number of those things fail, but we have a greater tolerance for that risk and failure."[47]

EnerNOC's approach invites both internal and external innovation. The firm supports and funds the development of technologies for managing energy more effectively. For example, they offer a software and communication platform for other parties to use in building applications, and they make user data (aggregated and anonymized) available to spur new optimization technologies. The communication platform includes EnerNOC Open, where outside engineers can collaborate to advance energy management innovation. EnerNOC Open hosts open source code, provides a forum to share details on the latest smart grid standards such as OpenADR 2.0, Zigbee, and XMPP, and enables collaboration among individuals and organizations to accelerate the development of energy management applications. The data collaboration, as well, is tuned to encourage innovation and experimentation. According to Hugh Scandrett, Vice President of Engineering at EnerNOC:

We want to create an ecosystem where smart, passionate [outside] developers can change the way the world uses energy. Just like developers flock to build new apps for iOS or Android, we're hoping that by driving standards adoption and sharing source code, we can ignite a new wave of innovation industry-wide.[48]

In this way, EnerNOC explicitly works to strengthen its multiplier role by trying to draw in many other firms to help build knowledge about energy management, participate in the core business, and disseminate knowledge through the industry.

In the Empire State Building megaproject, Malkin hoped to collaborate to make changes to every aspect of the building on a "whole system" basis. Rather than assigning individual parties specific tasks, he pushed for multiple meetings, quick decisions, and engagement of many parties—but did not advocate solutions. He stimulated the learning process but did not specify outcome details. Early days were marked by tension and disagreement. But through continued iterations by equipment firms, and detailed and objective analysis, tenants and representatives alike came to identify the best interventions. The team was surprised by some of the innovative cost-effective findings that emerged: for example, installing reflective barriers behind radiator units

---

[47] See the Official Site of the Empire State Building, "Empire State Building Sustainability Program" (2014). Available at: <http://www.esbnyc.com/documents/sustainability/ESBOverviewDeck.pdf> (accessed July 2014).
[48] See EnerNOC (2013).

effectively sent heat back into the interior instead of out through the exterior walls, while individual-user plug load monitors helped to reduce personal power consumption.

Leaders of the Lake Nona megaproject similarly gave participants considerable freedom to experiment with different solutions. In an interview with the authors, an executive explained:

There's a remarkable mix of people on our team. We focus on throwing out crazy ideas, figuring out what's achievable and what makes sense. That's been part of our secret sauce. One of the things that's different about here than other places I've worked—there's sort of this culture of not being afraid to dream big ideas. Nobody here is afraid to come up with big ideas.[49]

Lake Nona encouraged partners to develop new ideas and technologies. The initial plans for Lake Nona, for instance, did not include LED streetlights, but the idea emerged in conversations, and Tavistock and GE leaders both recognized its value. GE developed new LED lighting systems for Lake Nona, compressing its product development period from 18 to 6 months to fit the tight construction schedule. Such experimentation sometimes led to failures: after GE had already shipped and installed several fixtures, for instance, testing indicated a possibility of technical issues. But failures were seen as opportunities for improvement, consistent with learning logic. In this case, GE recalled and reworked the fixtures. Lake Nona emerged with 100 percent functional LED lighting designed to their requirements, and GE had a new product it could sell in other markets. A GE executive explained the unusual nature of this approach:

One of the great things about Lake Nona is they're willing to try things. "Let's just try it." And that's how you get to innovations. Let's pilot, let's try, let's see what works, what doesn't work and then we can make the changes to get a product or a solution out. There's always this level of brainstorm is going on. "Hey, would this work? Hey, what do you think about this? Let's discuss it. Let's talk about it."[50]

Ultimately GE leaders saw Lake Nona as an opportunity to deploy and test some of their existing and new Ecomagination™ and Healthymagination™ technologies at a significant scale in a "living laboratory." While they earned revenue from the technologies deployed in Lake Nona, they also appreciated the opportunity to innovate and test solutions for future urban projects. Lake Nona's impact on sustainability thus extended beyond the community: by engaging in experimentation during this megaproject, participating organizations gained experience with sustainable solutions and technologies they could deploy in the future. Moreover, other organizations could learn from their experiences.

---

[49] Interview conducted by Amy C. Edmondson and Tiona Zuzul, September 2011.
[50] Interview conducted by Amy C. Edmondson and Tiona Zuzul, September 2011.

Conclusion

As pressures on local and global resources intensify, researchers and practitioners alike need to develop insight into more effective methods to drive change for sustainability. The management literature on leading organizational change generally, and on leading sustainability-related change in particular, has largely concentrated on how change can be driven within a single organization. In contrast, in this chapter we have examined multiplier firms and megaprojects as catalysts with the potential to accelerate the pace of sustainability-related change across organizations, industries, and nations.

IMPLICATIONS FOR PRACTICE

We have argued that when multiplier firms are involved in sustainability-related change, the spread of new knowledge and new practices is accelerated. Multiplier firms like Arup and EnerNOC work to uncover new ways to advance change for sustainability and then they disseminate and facilitate use of this knowledge. Similarly, megaprojects that engage in sustainability-related change accelerate the scope and extent of such change by bringing many diverse organizations together to develop new solutions for enhancing sustainability that each can adjust and apply to future projects, and by serving as demonstration projects. Megaprojects like the Empire State Building and Lake Nona illustrate the power of assembling new teams from scratch, without preconceived hierarchies and relationships, and making smart choices in concrete, steel, glass, and dirt that reduce energy, water, electricity, and CO_2 on a long-term basis. Given the potential importance of multiplier firms and megaprojects for driving sustainability-related change at a scale that outstrips the efforts of single firms, our goal is to attract further interest in studying and improving leadership of these activities as potential sources of large-scale change for sustainability.

Furthermore, building on past and current research on organizational change, we use our case study research to propose that leading sustainability-related change successfully requires learning logic to engage people in discovering and implementing new solutions. The nature of the work and the fluid inter-organizational relationships that characterize multiplier firms and megaprojects makes the deployment of a top-down blueprint logic very difficult, since each new initiative involves starting afresh every time with a new situation and new players, with all parties participating voluntarily, rather than under direction from above. At the same time, these features make the use of learning logic in leading change more necessary and more promising.

We also identified three leadership activities that fostered shared learning—*articulating a vision, inviting participation and ideas,* and *encouraging experimentation*—and illustrated them with our four case studies. As the examples from Arup, EnerNOC, the Empire State Building, and Lake Nona suggest, none of these activities is easy; each of these four organizations invested substantial financial, organizational, and reputational resources—along with relentless follow-up and tracking—to turn their worthy aspirations into real accomplishments. Each confronted failures along the way to innovation and successful change.

IMPLICATIONS FOR RESEARCH

The multiplier firms and megaprojects we studied each drove initiatives with the potential to generate truly substantial and long-lasting change for sustainability in energy, electricity, water usage and CO_2 reduction. Each has also led to organizational learning and greater organizational effectiveness in the form of increases in sophistication and competitiveness for many of the parties involved. However, they are case studies, and each is unique in important ways. Future research is needed to identify and clarify the opportunities that multiplier firms and megaprojects may present for influencing large-scale changes in sustainability performance in societies around the world. We hope that future research will involve larger samples to assess the impact of multiplier firms and megaprojects on sustainability, and to measure the extent of their impact. First, however, research is needed to provide additional insight into the full variety of different organizational forms that multiplier firms and megaprojects might take, and to understand what managerial practices increase their effectiveness in driving change. Practitioners can help develop new knowledge too through thoughtful interventions and innovative experiments. Leaders of multiplier firms and megaprojects, employing learning logic, can effectively lead change that promotes sustainability.

■ REFERENCES

Baron, James N. and Hannan, Michael T. (2002) "Organizational Blueprints for Success in High-Tech Start-Ups," *California Management Review* 44 (3): 8–36.
Bohmer, Richard M. J. (2003) "The Dana-Farber Cancer Institute Teaching Note," HBS Case No. 603-092. Boston, MA: Harvard Business School Press.
Brady, Tim and Davies, Andrew. (2010) "From Hero to Hubris—Reconsidering the Project Management of Heathrow's Terminal 5," *International Journal of Project Management* 28 (2): 151–7.
Davies, Andrew C., Gann, David, and Douglas, Tony. (2012) "Innovation in Megaprojects: Systems Integration at London Heathrow Terminal 5," *California Management Review* 51 (2): 101–25.
Eccles, Robert G., Edmondson, Amy C., and Karadzhova, Dilyana. (2010) "Arup: Building the Water Cube," Harvard Business School Case 410-054. Boston, MA: Harvard Business School Press.
Edmondson, Amy C. (2012) *Teaming: How Organizations Learn, Innovate, and Compete in the Knowledge Economy.* San Francisco: Jossey-Bass Pfeiffer.

Edmondson, Amy C. (1996) "Learning from Mistakes is Easier Said Than Done: Group and Organizational Influences on the Detection and Correction of Human Error," *Journal of Applied Behavioral Science*: 5–28.

Edmondson, Amy C. (2012) "Leadership Makes it Happen," *Teaming: How Organizations Learn, Innovate, and Compete in the Knowledge Economy*. San Francisco: Jossey-Bass Pfeiffer, 257–85.

Edmondson, Amy C. and Hajim, Corey. (2003) "Large-Scale Change at the WSSC," HBS Case No. 603-056. Boston, MA: Harvard Business School Press.

Edmondson, Amy C. and Roberto, Michael A. (2003) "Children's Hospital and Clinics Teaching Note," HBS Case No. 303-071. Boston, MA: Harvard Business School Press.

Empire State Building. (2014) "Empire State Building Sustainable Program" Available at: <http://www.esbnyc.com/sites/default/files/ESBPlacematFINAL2.pdf> (accessed July 2014).

EnerNOC. (2013) "EnerNOC Launches Microsite to Drive Collaboration and Innovation in Energy Management," press release, January 17.

Fleming, Lee, King, Charles, and Juda, Adam I. (2007) "Small Worlds and Regional Innovation," *Organization Science* 18 (6): 938–54.

Flyybjerg, Bent, Bruzelius, Nils, and Rothengatter, Werner. (2003) *Megaprojects and Risk: An Anatomy of Ambition*. Cambridge: Cambridge University Press.

Friedman, Thomas L. (2007) *The World is Flat: A Brief History of the Twenty-First Century*. New York: Picador/Farrar, Straus and Giroux.

Glaeser, Edward E. and Kahn, Matthew E. (2003) "Sprawl and Urban Growth," Harvard Institute of Economic Research Working Papers, No. 2004. Cambridge, MA: Harvard University Press.

Heifetz, Ronald A. (1994) *Leadership without Easy Answers*, Vol. 465. Boston, MA: Harvard University Press.

Herron, Jock, Edmondson, Amy C., and Eccles, Robert G. (2013) "Beyond Platinum: Making the Case for Titanium Buildings," in Andrew Hoffman, eds, *Constructing Green: The Social Structures of Sustainability*. Cambridge, MA: MIT Press, 77.

Kotter, John P. (1990) *A Force for Change: How Leadership Differs from Management*. New York: Free Press.

Lehrer, Ute and Laidley, Jennefer. (2008) "Old Mega-Projects Newly Packaged? Waterfront Redevelopment in Toronto," *International Journal of Urban & Regional Research* 32: 786–803.

Lewin, Kurt. (1958) "Group Decision and Social Change," in E. E. Maccoby, T. M. Newcomb, and E. L. Hartley (eds), *Readings in Social Psychology*. New York: Holt, Rinehart, and Winston, 197–211.

Lueneburger, Christoph and Goleman, Daniel. (2010) "The Change Leadership Sustainability Demands," *MIT Sloan Management Review* (Summer): 49–55.

Macomber, John D. (2013) "Building Sustainable Cities," *Harvard Business Review* 91 (7/8) (July/August): 40–50.

March, James G. (1991) "Exploration and Exploitation in Organizational Learning," *Organization Science* 2(1): 71–87.

Rashid, Faaiza and Edmondson, Amy C. (2012) "Risky Trust: How Multi-Entity Teams Develop Trust in a High-risk Endeavor," in R. Kramer and T. Pittinsky (eds), *Restoring Trust*. New York: Oxford University Press, 129–50.

Senge, Peter M., Smith, Bryan, Kruschwitz, Nina, Laur, Joe, and Schley, Sara. (2008) *The Necessary Revolution: How Individuals and Organizations are Working Together to Create a Sustainable World.* New York: Random House Digital, Inc.

Sitkin, Sim B., Sutcliffe, Kathleen M., and Schroeder, Roger G. (1994) "Distinguishing Control from Learning in Total Quality Management: A Contingency Perspective," *The Academy of Management Review* 19: 537–64.

Skolkovo Moscow School of Management. (2013) "The Upcoming Four-Trillion-Dollar Infrastructure Gold Rush." Available at: <http://iems.skolkovo.ru/en/research-platforms/publications/317-the-upcoming-four-trillion-dollar-infrastructure-gold-rush> (accessed July 2014).

The Associated Press. (2008) "U.N.: World Population Increasingly Urban." Available at: <http://www.cbsnews.com/news/un-world-population-increasingly-urban/> (accessed July 2014).

Timmer, Dagmar, Buckler, Carolee, and Creech, Heather. (2007) *Becoming a Sustainability Leader.* Winnipeg: International Institute for Sustainable Development. Available at: <http://www.iisd.org/publications/pub.aspx?pno=863> (accessed July 2014).

Toffel, Michael W., Fabrizio, Kira, and van Sice, Stephanie. (2012) "EnerNOC: DemandSMART," Harvard Business School Case 613-036. Boston, MA: Harvard Business Press.

Tucker, Anita L. and Edmondson, Amy C. (2003) "Why Hospitals Don't Learn from Failures," *California Management Review* 45: 55–72.

United Nations Environment Programme. (2013) "Cities." Available at: <http://www.unep.org/greeneconomy/Portals/88/documents/ger/GER_12_Cities.pdf> (accessed July 2014).

Uzzi, Brian. (1997) "Social Structure and Competition in Interfirm Networks: The Paradox of Embeddedness," *Administrative Science Quarterly* 42 (1): 35–67.

Uzzi, Brian and Spiro, Jarrett. (2005) "Collaboration and Creativity: The Small World Problem," *American Journal of Sociology* 111 (2).

Van der Voet, Joris, Groeneveld, Sandra, and Kuipers, Ben S. (2013) "Talking the Talk or Walking the Walk? The Leadership of Planned and Emergent Change in a Public Organization," *Journal of Change Management* 14: 1–21.

Van Marrewijk, Alfons, Clegg, Stewart R., Pitsis, Tyrone S., and Veenswijk, Marcel. (2008) "Managing Public–Private Megaprojects: Paradoxes, Complexity, and Project Design," *International Journal of Project Management* 26 (6): 591–600.

Voner, Ian. (2013) "The Sky's the Limit," *Metropolis Magazine.* Available at: <http://www.metropolismag.com/September-2013/The-Skys-the-Limit/index.php?cparticle=2&siarticle=1> (accessed July 2014).

Wenger, Etienne. (1998) *Communities of Practice: Learning, Meaning, and Identity.* Cambridge: Cambridge University Press.

Westphal, James, D., Gulati, Ranjay, and Shortell, Stephen M. (1997) "Customization or Conformity? An Institutional and Network Perspective on the Content and Consequences of TQM Adoption," *Administrative Science Quarterly* 42: 366–94.

World Bank. (2014) "US GDP World Bank." Available at: <http://data.worldbank.org/indicator/NY.GDP.MKTP.CD> (accessed July 2014).

12 Managing Shifting Goal Consensus and Task Ambiguity in Making the Transition to Sustainability

Alfred A. Marcus and Andrew H. Van de Ven

"The *only* truth which I have ever found out for myself is, I think, this one: of the unavoidability of conflicting ends..." Isaiah Berlin, as quoted in A. Kelly, "Getting Isaiah Berlin Wrong," the *NY Review of Books* (2013).[1]

Introduction

For most corporations, the transition towards greater social, economic, and environmental sustainability does not occur in one fell swoop with a single change initiative; instead, it entails undertaking many change projects that vary over time in levels of ambiguity and consensus to relevant stakeholders within and outside of the organization. We use the classic Thompson and Tuden (1959) typology which has been supported by many additional studies (see Courtney, 2001; Schoemaker, 2002; Marcus, 2006; and Raynor, 2007) to determine what types of decision and change strategies are appropriate for managing projects that vary in task ambiguity and goal consensus. Relying on this typology and using case study examples, we illustrate how sustainability projects shift in task ambiguity, goal consensus, and control over time.

The major practical implications are that managers should expand their repertoire from hierarchical leadership and planned change to include pluralistic leadership and dialectical change in order to manage the shifting periods of project conflict, ambiguity, and shared power. During implementation, sustainability projects often go through periods when there is low goal consensus among key stakeholders and high project ambiguity. These periods call for a strategy of partisan mutual adjustment, which favors leaders who simultaneously compete and cooperate with the leaders of other organizations.

---

[1] Available at: <http://www.nybooks.com/articles/archives/2013/jun/20/getting-isaiah-berlin-wrong/?pagination=false> (accessed July 2014).

We call this "running in packs." It is analogous to bicycle racers who cue their pace to one another and take turns breaking wind resistance until the ending sprint. Overall, our chapter emphasizes that understanding sustainability requires going beyond models and theories of planned change under conditions of consensus about shared purpose, that centralized leadership is not adequate to the task, and that organizational leaders need to rely on models and processes of constructive conflict resolution and pluralistic leadership. We start with a discussion of the transition to sustainability, move on to the need to manage multiple parallel projects, provide the case examples, and conclude with five suggestions about how to manage this transition.

The transition to sustainability

The transition to sustainability signifies an on-going business commitment to demonstrate respect for the environment, while contributing to economic development and showing regard for people and communities (Roome, 1998; Barbier, 2010; Daily and Walker, 2000; Hall et al., 2010; Marcus et al., 2011). The concept of sustainability is an evolving one driven by many factors, including NGO pressure and the need that corporations have to preserve their legitimacy and enhance their reputations. Paul Polman, the CEO of Unilever, claims that his company has reaped many economic benefits from the transition to sustainability programs (Gunther, 2013) that have helped his company introduce new products, lowered its costs, and motivated his employees. As demonstrated by many writers (Hoffman, 1997, 2000; Laszlo, 2005; Marcus, 2005; Orsato, 2009;), sustainability makes good economic sense in some instances. There is research which shows that companies that maintain a high commitment to sustainability perform significantly better than companies that do not (Eccles et al., 2011). Nonetheless, the premise that companies can serve the planet and people while providing good returns to shareholders does not pass every test.

The primary challenge arises in implementation. Implementing a sustainability strategy is a huge test that has been under-studied by management scholars. It is not enough for the leaders of an organization to declare their commitment to sustainability. The implementation journey they face will be difficult. Typically, it involves multiple parallel projects prone to setbacks and conflict. We focus on implementing different projects of varying degrees of goal consensus and task clarity that change over time. Across projects, and over time, both goal consensus and task clarity shift—often as a consequence of external and unavoidable reasons. The cases in this chapter—Google, BP, and the German Feed-In tariff, although different in many respects, illustrate how these shifts may occur.

Each combination of high/low goal consensus and high/low task clarity, requires different leadership styles and decision-making processes. Leaders of organizations must have the different leadership styles and decision-making processes that are required and be adaptable. In particular, the combination of low agreement and high uncertainty—a combination that often characterizes sustainability programs at some point—calls for a strategy of partisan mutual adjustment, which favors leaders who can work over time with other leaders to bridge the gap between divergent goals.

Multiple parallel projects involving different levels of ambiguity and consensus

We contend that the journey to sustainability typically consists of multiple parallel projects that involve different levels of ambiguity and consensus. These projects often involve discord. The discord often results in the exercise of power which all too often ends in stalemate. In this sense, the transition to sustainability is not that different from the innovation journey that Polley et al. (1999) have portrayed. Sustainability, then, is as a type of innovation journey involving multiple parallel projects that experience different levels of ambiguity and consensus.

MULTIPLE PARALLEL PROJECTS

The multiple parallel projects unfold in different organizational units over time and they also involve other organizations (Willums and Goluke, 1992; Prakash, 2000). As the journey takes place (Van de Ven, et al., 2008), not all projects in an organization's portfolio will develop similarly; they will change over time. A single managerial approach does not fit them all.

Like other organizational transformation initiatives, a sustainable enterprise may start with a long-term overarching strategy that is meant to move the organization towards sustainability (Eccles et al., 2011). It may also move from the bottom up with employee-initiated projects that are not strategically driven, but rather decentralized and experimental in nature (Burgelman and Sayles, 1986). Even when an overall corporate mission and strategy towards a sustainable enterprise is set, the details of such a strategy often are unspecified and typically are assigned to sub-unit managers, who develop their own operational plans and projects and generate their own ideas for achieving this strategy.

No central strategic unit—no matter how synoptic—can possibly anticipate and coordinate all the operational activities that are entailed in any large-scale organizational transformation like sustainability (Lindblom, 1965). Strategies for sustainability therefore are likely to be both deliberate and emergent

(Mintzberg, 2007). Operational activities will adapt and redirect the implementation of the transformation effort over time.

LEVELS OF AMBIGUITY AND CONSENSUS

The multiple parallel projects that organizations undertake in their sustainability journey will vary in their levels of ambiguity and consensus at different points in time. Thompson and Tuden's (1959) well-known typology of strategies for decision making and change (see Figure 12.1) is useful for distinguishing projects in an organization's sustainability portfolio according to these criteria. This typology has been supported and used in a large number of management studies (see Courtney, 2001; Schoemaker, 2002; Marcus, 2006; and Raynor, 2007).

Decision-making strategies associated with different types of projects are found in the cells in the Figure 12.1. Judgmental strategies of consensus decision making and planned change are on the left side in the figure. Unfortunately, we find that management scholars and practitioners have not paid sufficient attention to situations in the right of the figure. These are situations where stakeholders disagree on project goals and engage in negotiation and partisan mutual adjustment to address their differences.

		Agreement on ends or goals	
		High agreement	Low agreement
Uncertainty of means to achieve ends	Low uncertainty	Computational or programmed decision making (e.g. energy efficiency and conservation projects)	Bargaining or negotiated decision making (e.g. efforts to make environmental regulation more cost-effective and protective of the environment as in the Clinton administration's Project XL)
	High uncertainty	Judgmental or non-programmed decision making (e.g. building construction and reconstruction, capital acquisitions, and/or distribution channel contracting)	Partisan mutual adjustment (e.g. what took place after the explosion at BP's Texas City refinery, leaks in its Alaska pipelines, and the Deepwater Horizon oil rig spill)
		Prevailing norms: rationality and efficiency	Prevailing norms: social power and influence

Figure 12.1. Typology of decision-making strategies with sustainability examples

Source: adapted from Thompson and Tuden (1959)

A computational strategy

When the means to achieve given project ends are generally known and there is agreement about project goals, then decisions and activities can be specified in advance of their execution using a computational strategy that is most efficiently performed in a technical way through organizational routines. For example, most people agree about the importance of energy conservation (Marcus, 1992) and these programs can be implemented in a fairly routine way (Henn, 2010). Maintenance personnel or technological sensors turn off the lights, water, and heaters when they are not needed. Organizational systems, rules, and regulations typically implement programmed decisions that may be optimized by means of computational algorithms.

Collegial decision making

When the means to a desired project end are ambiguous, however, programmed decisions are inadequate. Under these conditions, project decisions cannot be reduced to a series of programmed decisions, as in Simon's (1973) idea of ill-structured problems. Decisions are typically made via processes that emphasize discretionary collegial decision making among experts and/or professionals (Thompson and Tuden, 1959; Courtney, 2001; Schoemaker, 2002; Marcus, 2006; and Raynor, 2007). For example, many projects that affect firm sustainability, such as building construction and reconstruction, capital acquisitions, and supply chain contracting require careful study and professional judgment, often from teams of experts who deal with the uncertainties. This judgmental process typically follows a teleological model of planned change where people search, screen, select and then implement a solution that they view as best achieving an agreed-upon objective based on their experience and judgment (Van de Ven and Poole, 1995; Maxwell et al., 1997).

Bargaining

However, at one stage or another many projects in a typical sustainability portfolio experience conflict among key stakeholders (Sexton et al., 2001; Marcus et al., 2002; Boutilier, 2009; Yaziji and Doh, 2009). When the preferred outcomes of conflicting parties are reasonably well known, a bargaining strategy may be employed. For example, in the 1990s, the US government's Environmental Protection Agency (EPA) and many companies made substantial progress towards making environmental regulation both more cost effective and more protective of the environment (Marcus et al., 2002). However, they got locked into unproductive power struggles that prevented them from achieving progress.

Partisan Mutual Adjustment

When the goals of conflicting parties are highly ambiguous or rapidly changing, then decisions are made through what Lindblom (1965) has called "partisan mutual adjustment." British Petroleum (BP), as we discuss in the section "Case examples," faced a number of related incidents in which partisan mutual adjustment played a dominant role—the explosion at its Texas City refinery, the leaks that occurred in its Alaska pipelines, and the massive Deepwater Horizon oilrig spill in the Gulf of Mexico. Central to understanding what happens when there are disagreements of this type between companies and citizens is the process of dialectical change (Van de Ven and Poole, 1995), where the resolution of conflict or contradiction between the opposing parties, each attempting to achieve its own ends, may yield outcomes that are not to the satisfaction of any of the parties. If there is resolution, it may be highly unstable and take long periods of time to accomplish.

When parties have legitimate power and conflicting interests, they tend to engage in political strategies and tactics of partisan mutual adjustment. Lindblom (1965) discussed a variety of partisan mutual adjustment strategies, including adaptive adjustment (where parties seek no response from others and instead accommodate and try to avoid fights), and manipulated adjustments (where parties try, but do not generally succeed, in directly engaging in negotiation, compensation, reciprocity, and various forms of direct and indirect manipulation).

Davis et al. (2005) and Hargrave and Van de Ven (2006) discuss how such political strategies vary by stages. Distributive strategies are common during power mobilization stages, as pluralistic actors seek to gain sufficient power in order to engage in conflict. When conflicting parties have gained sufficient power to confront one another, then integrative negotiation strategies may be used, but they will not always be successful. These political strategies have no underlying capacity to produce "rational" or "win–win" solutions (Marcus and Fremeth, 2011) good for the economy, environment, and society. Unfortunately, conflict involving direct confrontation and struggle among opposing parties within institutional constraints does not necessarily yield good results (Marcus et al., 2002).

Power is the means by which these disagreements often get played out. Their legacy may be continued resentment, lingering grievances, and on-going efforts to overturn temporary compromises that have been reached. As Hargrave and Van de Ven (2006) discuss, in the short term, conflict may remain latent or be squelched by dominant actors, until challengers are again able to mobilize sufficient power. They must mobilize power by engaging in political strategies and collective action tactics to generate additional support for their demands (Yaziji and Doh, 2009).

A necessary condition for conflict to re-emerge is that opposing parties have sufficient power to confront dominant parties and engage in additional struggle. But political relations then become hard-wired and institutionalized. They are reproduced through taken-for-granted arrangements and routine behaviors, unless opposing parties again generate enough power to re-engage in struggle. Thus, relationships among conflict, power, and political behaviors are recursive; institutions shape the forms that conflict takes and power is central to the process of institutional change, if change takes place to any degree and in any substantive way (Hargrave and Van de Ven, 2006).

All-too-frequent stalemate

When the disagreements among the parties about the domain or goals of a project are substantial, coalitions regularly shift as the parties engage in power contests to implement their preferences (Pfeffer, 1978). Long struggles over such decisions are time consuming. Many of the people involved feel very uncomfortable with the conflict. To squelch the conflict, precedent becomes very important (Pfeffer, 1978: 14). The upshot is that stalemate and inertia often set in.

Sustainability projects may be blocked temporarily or permanently. If reasonable compromises are reached, they establish precedents for future decisions that are hard to undo. Compromises avoid reopening negotiations that may be painful for the parties, who may view reopening old conflicts as unproductive. So long as the existing balance of power is reasonably stable, precedents prevail. When the balance shifts dramatically, there will be attempts to re-open negotiations, to remove precedent, and to establish a new basis for future actions. However, if the burden on time and organizational energy is great, this shift does not take place. Many organizations therefore start on sustainability journeys that they do not complete. They become hemmed in by premature closure that is buttressed by precedent and are blocked from making progress.

Case examples

The case examples that follow are representative of those found in the collections of Post et al. (1992); Reinhardt and Vietor (1996); Rowledge et al. (1999); Russo (2008); Hamschmidt and Pirson (2011), and Hoffman (2013). Here we choose to analyze two cases found in the Hoffman collection and then introduce a third case presented at the Green Economy conference held at the University of Minnesota in April 2010.[2] These cases illustrate that the sustainability projects in which these companies were involved developed unevenly over time, with conflict over goals and ambiguous means arousing

---

[2] Available at: <http://www.leadership.umn.edu/news/annual_conferenece_agenda.html> (accessed July 2014). This case was developed by Rolf Wuestenhagen.

stakeholder voice and opposition (Boutilier, 2009; Sarkis et al., 2010; Marcus and Fremeth, 2011). The life span of these sustainability projects varied in their degree of consensus and ambiguity. The decision makers adapted by adopting different decision strategies and change processes over time.

In the first two cases—Google and BP—the companies took the first initiative. They tried to establish a new consensus around sustainability, only to be thwarted by errors and opposition to their plans. In the third case—the German Feed-In Tariff Law—society made the first move. The consensus for sustainability originated in a social movement outside the corporate sphere, only to be upended by companies who organized to oppose it. The resolution in the first case aided the company and society, in the second case, neither was better off, and in the third the prevailing equilibrium was destabilized and restored.

The first case (Google) shows the alternation between consensus and conflict. The consensus was among Google's top management team and employees to have sustainable campuses in terms of carbon emissions. This project starts in the top left quadrant of Figure 12.1. However, Google was forced into a conflict mode when challenged by a magazine article about its energy consumption and emissions. The issue evolved into conflict where there was low agreement about ends, though continued high agreement about means. The project evolved. It involved bargaining and negotiated decision making (see Figure 12.2). Subsequently, the issue entered a new consensus mode as Google entered into partnerships with environmental organizations and invested in a series of clean energy start-ups and projects. Its sustainability journey again shifted.

The BP case too, started in a consensus mode (Augustine, 2008) driven by the firm's top leader, CEO John Browne, as a result of contacts he had with

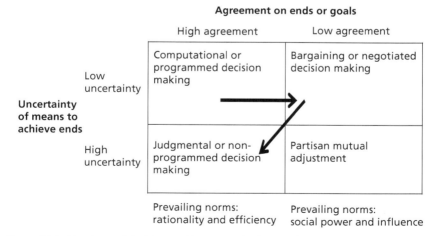

Figure 12.2. Typology of decision-making strategies in Google example

Source: adapted from Thompson and Tuden (1959)

environmental organizations and the scientific community. This sustainability project started in the bottom left quadrant (see Figure 12.3). The company hired new managers who were knowledgeable and committed to the environment. It broke ranks with organizations that opposed actions to reduce greenhouse gas emissions and joined an organization that supported the Kyoto Accord. BP was the first petroleum company to voluntarily certify its greenhouse emissions with the California Climate Action Registry, and like Google, it invested in renewable energy—not as much as environmentalists would like—but nonetheless it made a significant commitment to these investments.

However, BP then stumbled into a series of conflicts. The first of these conflicts concerned its decision to expand capacity to process oil derived from Canadian tar sands at its Whiting, Indiana plant. Many actors became involved: the Indiana governor, Indiana's Department of Environmental Management, the US EPA, the media, protestors, representatives from the US House of Representatives, Argonne National Laboratory, and Purdue University. The project was now in the right top quadrant of low agreement about ends, low uncertainty about means, and bargaining (see Figure 12.4). BP had to make concessions to diverse stakeholders, despite reservations about the technical feasibility of the concessions it made.

Unlike Google, which reached understanding with its critics, BP experienced additional troubles. These were an explosion at its Texas City facility, leaks in its Alaska pipelines, and the massive Deepwater Horizon oilrig spill in the Gulf of Mexico (Huyn et al., 2012). Outside investigators did thorough examinations of company practices and operations, both John Browne and his successor CEO were forced to resign, and BP and its partners in the Deepwater Horizon project, Transocean and Halliburton, ended up blaming each other for this final disaster. The sustainability initiatives of BP had migrated.

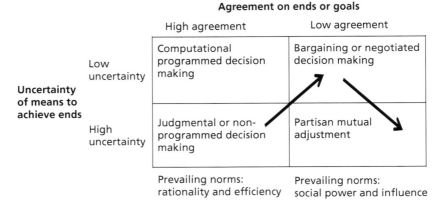

Figure 12.3. Typology of decision-making strategies in BP example

Source: adapted from Thompson and Tuden (1959)

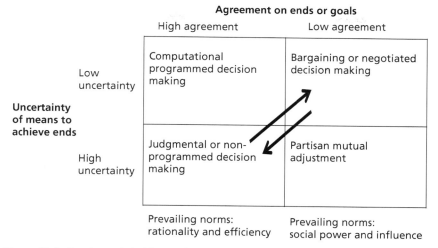

Figure 12.4. Typology of decision-making strategies in German Feed-In Tariff example

Source: adapted from Thompson and Tuden (1959)

Though they took very different forms, the dialectics that played out in the Google and BP cases were similar. These companies took the initiative to become more sustainable. They appeared to be starting down this road with good intentions, but in each instance they suffered setbacks. Google managed them fairly well. Of course, its setbacks were less serious than those of BP. It achieved a rapid recovery and restoration of the prior equilibrium. There was a positive synthesis with the views of stakeholder groups. In BP's case, on the other hand, one setback was followed by another, even more serious than the previous one.

The pattern in the German Feed-In Tariff project (Wustenhagen and Bilharz, 2006) was different from that of Google or BP in that it started outside the company. Consensus among environmental organizations, business trade associations, political parties, and the German public drove German utilities down a path towards greater sustainability. There was high agreement about ends, high uncertainty about means, and judgmental decision making (see Figure 12.4). As in the Google and BP cases, however, this consensus broke down. The Feed-In Tariff project moved to the top right quadrant of the table. German utilities, government agencies, industry groups, and citizens concerned that wind and solar power developments would hurt their property values, called for the Feed-In Law to be amended, watered down, or eliminated. This attack generated an equally strong reaction from the law's supporters. They included environmental groups, the German solar and wind power industries, local governments, activists, and the steel industry, a major supplier to the wind power developers. Ultimately, the supporters of the tariff defeated attempts made to change the law. They helped get the Bundestag to pass a new and stronger Renewable Energy Sources Act, which entailed an even greater commitment to the tariff.

To illustrate these transitions within sustainability projects we now discuss them in more detail. We show the common patterns based on shifting positions in the typology.

Computational decision making: Google

Google's founding principles included sustainability—from the very start it had employee-initiated projects organized under the title of "Google Green" (Bunker et al., 2012). Many of the projects affect the operations of its campuses. They encompassed commuting (high-tech, low-impact employee shuttles, electric corporate car sharing, and bicycles), eating (sourcing food locally, supporting sustainable seafood, and reducing waste), and buildings (eliminating toxic materials, smart design, and performance measurement, including LEED certifying its buildings). Employees also tried to accelerate the adoption of plug-in hybrid vehicles by means of a project called RechargeIT. The company goal has been to be "carbon neutral." It measured how much of its energy comes from renewable sources. The aim was to achieve a 35 percent reduction by 2012. Google bought carbon offsets and the Mountain View campus in California had a 1.6-megawatt photovoltaic solar array that produces 3 million kWh of energy annually.

Judgmental decision making: BP and the Feed-In Tariff

Unlike Google, BP's initiatives were driven from the top down and not from the bottom up (Augustine, 2008; Huyn et al., 2012). Interested in the environmental movement, then-CEO John Browne spent time learning about climate change, and his company was the first in the oil business to acknowledge the risks of global warming. In 1996, BP left the Global Climate Coalition, an organization that opposed actions to reduce greenhouse gas emissions, and joined the Business Environmental Leadership Council, which supported the Kyoto Accord. Under Browne, BP tried to foster a new culture. It attempted to hire management with strong environmental beliefs and endeavored to be a cleaner and more progressive oil company, one with extensive pollution prevention efforts. In 1998, the company purchased Amoco, and in 2000 created a new slogan: "Better people, better products, beyond petroleum." It invested in wind, solar, biofuels, gas-fired power generation, and hydrogen. It aimed to expand its solar subsidiary fourfold by 2007 and spent billions to develop renewable energy. Its advertisements acknowledged oil's harmful environmental effects. In 2006, it became the first energy company to voluntarily certify its greenhouse gasses inventory with the California Climate Action Registry. By investing so heavily in the environment, it hoped to be in a better position to influence and take advantage of the new laws covering climate change that it considered to be inevitable. When BP took this action, the American Petroleum Institute treated it as a traitor and said that the company had "left the church." Despite these efforts, by 2008 only about 7 percent of its capital spending was in renewables and the company's interest in opening Arctic National Wildlife Refuge to drilling aroused the suspicion of some environmental groups, who considered BP guilty of "green washing." Fearful of a campaign that would question its use of the phrase, "Beyond Petroleum," BP, in an attempt to appease its critics, backed away and said what it was doing was just "a start."

Rather than the push for sustainability coming from the business side, the push in the German Feed-In Tariff case originated from a shift in public attitude in Germany just prior to and after reunification (Wustenhagen and Bilharz, 2006). In the 1980s, increasing awareness of climate change and the Chernobyl accident altered public perceptions of nuclear and coal electricity generation. German environmental organizations like Friends of the Earth helped to organize citizens concerned about these issues and began to advocate for alternatives. The German Association for the Promotion of Solar Power (Forderverein Solarenergie) developed the concept of "cost covering payment" for electricity generated by renewable energy technology. This concept ultimately was applied in Feed-In Laws at federal and local levels. The 3,500 owners of small hydro power plants, many of whose members were politically conservative, organized small and medium-sized German firms in support of the Feed-In Law, and the German Green Party obtained backing from other major parties in the Bundestag, including the Christian Democrats. It promoted the Feed-In Law statute as one that would level the playing field for all sources of electricity by setting the Feed-In rates at levels based on the external costs of conventional power generation. Politicians were increasingly concerned with public opinion that wanted to do something about climate change, and the utilities did not exercise power in opposition. The Feed-In Tariff Law that was passed in 1990 received unanimous support in the Bundestag, with the Christian Democrats joining the Social Democrats and Greens in voting for the measure. It required utilities to connect generators of electricity from renewable energy technology to the grid—a significant step, as they were under no obligation to do so previously. It also required utilities to buy the electricity at specific rates favorable to the renewable electricity generators.

Bargaining: Google, BP, and the Feed-In Tariff

Environmental groups such as Greenpeace started to criticize Google. Their claim was that the company was keeping the actual details of its energy consumption and greenhouse gas emissions a secret. Google's response was that this information is a trade secret that can be used by its competitors and therefore it should not be forced to release it. In 2009, however, *Harper's Magazine* ran an article which asserted that the real reason for Google's secrecy was the extent of its emissions. The company was not really committed to the goals it espoused. Each search on its engine released 7 grams of carbon dioxide into the atmosphere (Bunker et al., 2012). Google's retort was that it was not responsible for all of the releases; the computer user had to share in the responsibility. Google was only responsible for 0.2 grams of carbon dioxide per search. However, with the growth in use of its data centers, the company could not stem the tide of increased environmental group criticism and media scrutiny.

Six years after its rebranding effort began, BP decided to expand capacity to process Canadian tar sands at its Whiting, Indiana plant (Augustine, 2008). BP's plan was to invest $3.8 billion to expand the facility, including $1.4 billion for environmental improvements. At first, Indiana Governor Mitch Daniels welcomed the initiative because of the positive economic impact on the state. Indiana's Department of Environmental Management (IDEM) and the EPA were on board to approve a water permit for the facility after BP notified county and city officials, received comments, and subjected its permit to multiple peer and other reviews. But the *Chicago Tribune* published an article called "BP Gets Break on Dumping in Lake," which led to protests, organized boycotts, more investigative news articles, and a petition campaign opposing the permit. The advocacy group Alliance for the Great Lakes, the *New York Times*, and The US House of Representatives, led by Illinois' Rahm Emmanuel and Vernon Ehlers, joined the effort to stop the permit.

BP countered with meetings with other members of the House of Representatives and with officials of the Indiana environmental agency. It agreed to a proposal involving cooperation among Argonne National Laboratory and Purdue University to explore emerging technologies for water pollution prevention. However, the EPA was not satisfied and it organized a summit in Chicago with government and environmental leaders. The boycotts and public uproar were having an impact. They were tarnishing the green image the company was trying to foster, so BP eventually agreed to limit its discharges. It warned that if it had to cancel the project, jobs might be lost. The concession it made on its water discharges, however, did not deter environmentalists from asking for additional air-quality permit changes. No matter what BP did, it did not seem to be enough.

At the same time that the controversy was taking place in Indiana, BP was receiving bad press from a 2005 explosion at its Texas City facility, which claimed the lives of 15 workers and injured more than 170 people (Huyn et al., 2012). This was the worst industrial accident in the US in a decade. The explosion raised the scrutiny of investigators because of the many possible legal violations that were suspected. Investigators did find that the firm's refineries in Texas, which it had inherited from Amoco, were seriously mismanaged. Employees were not openly reporting accidents or safety concerns because of a company culture that relied on fear and intimidation to keep sensitive matters quiet.

Though utilities were not happy about the Feed-In Law, they viewed it as primarily aimed at a small number of generators and therefore did not at first see it as a major disruptive issue. The utilities and their allies had always been hostile to alternatives that might threaten to disrupt the system. They dominated the traditional German electricity supply system, which had been set up to generate electricity from coal and nuclear sources. Government had supported generation from coal and nuclear sources through a series of incentives for coal and nuclear electricity generation after the 1970s energy shocks. The traditional electricity system did not present promising political opportunities for renewable energy advocates. It was surprising how easily the Feed-in Tariff Law passed. The law passed soon after German reunification, when most utilities were preoccupied with the transition. Consequently, although the opponents of the Feed-In Tariff Law were quite powerful, they failed to protest. After the Feed-In Tariff Law was passed, the utilities and government officials, especially those in the Ministry of Economic Affairs (MEA), started to voice their opposition to the law. The MEA proposed to reduce Feed-In Tariff rates for renewables in 1997 and the association of German utilities lodged a complaint with the European Commission claiming that under the laws of competition, the Feed-In Tariff Law was unfair. The Federation of German Industry (BDI) claimed that it would hurt German competitiveness and create unnecessary burdens, and citizens begin to raise NIMBY issues with regard to wind turbines cluttering rural landscapes.

Judgmental decision making: Google and the Feed-In Tariff

Google relented and made public how much carbon it emitted and how much electricity it consumed. It argued that compared to other sectors in society it was not a major carbon emitter (Bunker et al., 2012). It reported that its servers were among the most efficient in the world and that they used half the energy of a typical center. Even so, it could not refute arguments that its emissions were high, in fact as large as that of the entire country of Laos (Bunker et al., 2012), and that while each search was low in emission, use of Gmail and watching videos on YouTube had very high footprints. For its transparency,

Google received praise from environmentalists, including Greenpeace, which urged others to follow Google's lead. Partnering with organizations like the Climate Savers Foundation and the Green Grid, Google aimed to establish a set of best practices and make improvements in its data centers by such means as controlling airflow, adjusting thermostats, and relying on free cooling such as that provided by the Columbia River in Oregon. While its conflict with these environmentalists was raging, the charitable arm of Google had supported projects aimed at generating renewable energy at prices lower than coal. It provided more than $100 million to non-profits and companies that were touting their breakthrough utility-scale solar and wind power projects (Bunker et al., 2012). The motivation was not simply charitable. The company took advantage of federal tax credits and subsidies. It experimented with projects to reduce its own energy use and its for-profit arm invested in renewable energy projects of its own.

Google proper (not its charitable foundation) invested in alternative energy in order to realize a financial return (Bunker et al., 2012). Among its most prominent investments was the one it made in 2008 in Brightsource, a developer of solar thermal power towers ($10 million) and in Brightsource's inaugural utility-scale solar project ($168 million). Other investments were made in Makani Power (high-altitude wind) and Potter Drilling (geothermal drilling). In 2010, Google acquired a 35-percent stake in the transmission infrastructure company Atlantic Wind Connection, and it invested $38.8 million into North Dakota utility-scale wind-scale projects of Next Era's, from whom it agreed to buy wind energy to offset its carbon emissions. In 2011, Google invested in a Clean Power Finance fund that would assist homeowners in placing solar panels on their roofs and in a SolarCity fund that would provide lease financing for residential solar projects. It also invested in Southern California wind projects.

In response to the attack on the tariff, the German renewable industry increased its lobbying efforts. The association of solar producers threatened to go abroad in the absence of domestic market expansion. Jobs would be lost just when Germany, in the post-unification period, needed them the most. Other renewable firms allied themselves with environmental groups in defending the Feed-in Law. The equipment and machinery producers and the German wind energy association were powerful lobbying groups. They worked with regional associations and helped to organize protests in response to government threats to reduce renewable energy subsidies in 1997. Activists held protests and encouraged local governments to force the utilities to enter into long-term contracts with renewable suppliers, even when those contracts guaranteed highly favorable rates to the renewable producers. The activists emphasized that support for renewables helped to create jobs and economic growth. The German Wind Energy Association claimed that 50,000 jobs had been created and that the government underestimated the negative impact of fossil fuels. Wind was the biggest customer of the German steel industry after automobiles.

This pressure bore fruit. The Renewable Energy Sources Act passed in 1997 gave justification for further support of renewables by explicitly referring to the fact that conventional electricity generation entailed significant external social and environmental costs paid for by the public. The new 1997 law established long-term 20-year guaranteed tariff rates to investors in renewables. However, to address concerns of excessive costs and illegal (based on EU competition law) support for renewables, the tariff rates was set to decline over time. Though some compromises had been struck with the opponents of renewables, this law resulted in substantially increased diffusion of wind and solar technologies throughout Germany and it fueled the growth of sustainable power investment and production throughout the world.

Partisan mutual adjustment: BP

In 2006, BP's image continued on a downward spiral. The public became aware of a large oil leak in its Alaska pipeline. Up to 267,000 gallons of oil had been allowed to escape into Alaska's North Slope tundra (Huyn et al., 2012). Clearly, there was a mismatch between the image BP was trying to convey and its actual operational record. The steelworkers' union stated that for years it had been warning the company about such an accident, but its voice had been systematically ignored. In 2007, BP announced plea bargains over the tragedy in Texas City and the Alaska pipeline leak and admitted to legal violations. CEO John Browne was forced to resign. Tony Hayward, head of exploration and production, replaced him, but not long thereafter, another disaster struck.

The Macondo 252 well site in the middle of the Gulf of Mexico ruptured. BP contracted with Transocean to drill this well below 5,000 feet of seawater and down into 13,000 feet of seabed. BP licensed the Deepwater Horizon rig from Halliburton. This partnership did not work to the benefit of these companies. The rig went up in flames, killing 11 crew members and seriously injuring 17, and the companies blamed each other for what took place. The causes soon became well known—technical and procedural failures and poor management oversight. BP, Transocean, and Halliburton were all held responsible. Many technical barriers had been breached, including the cement at the bottom of the well, the mud in the well and in the riser, and the blowout preventer (Huyn et al., 2012). With this blow, BP's image as an oil company at the forefront of the transition to sustainability had fallen apart.

Case lessons

From these cases, we can see that the transition to sustainability consists of a series of incidents that alternate between consensus, conflict among partisan stakeholders over time, and turnaround or additional challenges. They alternate among different levels of agreement about ends, uncertainty about means, and the decision-making strategies that major protagonists use.

We also can see that the projects companies carry out are not carried out in isolation, nor can they be. They bring into play resources, knowledge, technologies, institutional actors, and arrangements that transcend the boundaries and capabilities of a single organization. We draw two lessons from the cases. The first is that sustainability is a collective and not an individual accomplishment. The second is that a simple application of stakeholder theory is not an adequate way to manage the conflicts that arise.

A COLLECTIVE, NOT INDIVIDUAL, ACCOMPLISHMENT

The cases show that achieving sustainability goals is a collective, not an individual, accomplishment (Hoffman, 2000). The participants are many. They are in the media and government; they are in environmental organizations (Yaziji and Doh, 2009); they are protestors. They are also a company's ostensible partners—companies like Transocean and Halliburton that let BP down in the Gulf of Mexico oil spill disaster. As the cases demonstrate, the collective actors who engage in sustainability projects are not necessarily a set of like-minded people who share common purposes or goals. Instead, diverse and partisan actors in the public and private sectors are involved. They have different interests, perform divergent roles, and are embedded in path-dependent and often opposing social, technical, and political processes that do not necessarily coalesce to all of the parties' benefit. This collective process can evolve into conflict and partisan mutual adjustment, much of it not pleasant either for organizations or their leaders (Hargrave and Van de Ven, 2006).

To cope, we maintain that organizations should "run in packs." That is, the success of their sustainability projects is highly dependent on the development of a well-functioning sustainability infrastructure of supportive actors (Hoffman, 2000). We develop this point further later in the chapter.

The cases indeed suggest that the time, cost, and risk incurred by organizations in developing their sustainability projects are directly related to progress in establishing institutional arrangements for sustainability at the infrastructure level (Van de Ven et al., 2008). In the first two cases, organizational employees (Google) and top leaders (BP) tried to develop this type of infrastructure in a conscious and intentional way before the fact, only to have counter movements come to life and challenge their primacy. In the third case, the infrastructure was built outside the coalition of interests that historically had supported the utility industry in Germany. The counter-movement to the established infrastructure came first and the utility industry had to respond in a reactive way. The counter-movement rejuvenated the supporters of alternative power. In the BP case, the counter-movement's supporters kept expanding during the planned Whiting expansion. From a relatively small group in

Indiana, they encompassed new actors in Illinois and nationally. As the new actors became engaged, BP kept losing credibility. It had to retreat and had few resources to draw upon when the Deepwater Horizon tragedy occurred. In the BP Whiting case, the company's degrees of freedom quickly contracted. After the Texas City accident, the pipeline leak, and the Gulf of Mexico oil spill, BP had virtually no room left for maneuver. Its operational lapses depleted it of the credibility it had meticulously tried to build up with other organizations, with its own employees, and with the public.

After the property damage and the loss of life and injuries in these incidents, BP could no longer plausibly claim that it was making the transition to a sustainable future. Google, in contrast, by virtue of its many investments in alternative energy, was able to recapture its image as a sustainability leader after being challenged. The effort by the German utility industry to push back on the Feed-In Law, which came after a new and counter-organizational ecosystem had built momentum, largely faltered. Instead, this effort resuscitated and gave new life to its opponents.

BEYOND STAKEHOLDER THEORY

In managing the transition to sustainability, stakeholder theory gets it wrong in that it puts the focal organization at the center. The stakeholder model may work if the projects an organization undertakes are clear and conflict is minimal, but when there is ambiguity and discord, its assumptions do not hold. Its assumptions are that organizational memories are long lived and managers have capacity to mold durable ties based on values and principles and agreements of give and take. With sufficient creativity, all of the stakeholder groups to which a corporation relates can be satisfied.

Stakeholder theory misses the problems of collective action theory, tradeoffs, the limits of control that a focal organization has, and the importance of broader networks, over which the focal organization has little influence. It assumes that many different types of organizations with vastly different purposes can be brought together into a unified coalition. Collective action problems (Olson, 1965; Ostrom, 2000) are overcome not by spontaneous self-organization (Axelrod, 1997) or government authority, but instead by the wisdom of focal organizations. But the transition to sustainability cannot necessarily be orchestrated so readily. Managing sustainability projects where the potential for consensus about goals is low and the likelihood of ambiguity about means is high requires sharing leadership among conflicting actors and creating an atmosphere of information sharing, trust, and joint problem solving (McEvily and Marcus, 2005). If managing sustainability projects is to be constructive, it requires engaging social movements, as opposed to squelching the opposition by means of hierarchy or force.

The dialectical processes of change require an openness to learn from an organization's ostensible adversaries (Davis et al., 2005). Examples of social movements playing a central role in current issues that involve the transition to sustainability include the proponents for preserving the environment who oppose the advocates for the Keystone pipeline. They include supporters of water supply protection who clash with champions of technologies like fracking for ensuring energy security. Due process means that these divergent voices are heard. In these settings, the extent to which any leader or single organization has complete power is limited. The constructive management of such dialectical processes depends on the ability of the actors to adjust to each other's perspectives.

Five suggestions on managing the transition to sustainability

As Hargrave and Van de Ven (2006) maintain, conflict, power, and politics are central to a dialectical theory of change. Conflict can generate change, but not necessarily as it might just easily result in stalemate. Organizational leaders should decide the kind of project—in the Thompson and Tuden sense—with which they are dealing. They will have to adjust the project to the setting and rely on computational decision making in the case of high agreement and low uncertainty projects, non-programmed judgment in the case of high agreement and high uncertainty projects, bargaining in the case of low agreement and low uncertainty projects, and partisan mutual adjustment in the case of low agreement and high uncertainty projects. Once they understand the type of project they confront, we have five suggestions for how to approach the sustainability journey.

1) *Periods of conflict and ambiguity are common during the implementation of sustainability projects.* Sustainability may sound like a rallying cry that unites people, but it is actually one of the most divisive issues facing the world today. A prime example of this type of frustrating conflict was the inability of the US government to pass cap-and-trade climate legislation in 2009. Many organizations tried to get this legislation passed, including BP. Many other organizations opposed it. In the end, it was not passed. This failure upended many business plans that had been created in the expectation that this legislation would be a reality. Organizational leaders can increase their odds of successful outcomes by gaining skills in creative conflict resolution among pluralistic actors with legitimate but divergent interests and power bases.

2) *As the sustainability journey unfolds, many setbacks, obstructions, and blockages are encountered over time.* Simple commands and computational decisions are only possible when sustainability projects are clearly understood and agreed up. Management scholars too often emphasize unity of command and cooperation (Barnard, 1938), and tend to not pay sufficient attention to systematic treatments of conflict in strategic organizational change. As the

cases show, the best strategic plans go awry. No matter how powerful firms may seem, there will be countervailing power, checks on what they do, and balances on what they can accomplish. The transition to sustainability does not consist of a predictable linear sequence of events or stages. Instead, based on Van de Ven's studies of innovation (Van de Ven et al., 2008) it is more likely that the process consists of a non-linear cycle of divergent and convergent activities that may be repeated over time and at different organizational levels. While leaders cannot control this process, they can learn to better maneuver the setbacks, obstructions, and conflicts by practicing and developing skills for these hurdles when they arise.

3) *The sustainability journey entails making strategic decisions about which activities to be engaged in and which to avoid.* While decisions of whether to engage or lead involve balancing costs and the benefits on a project-by-project basis, their impact on organizational performance are likely to be uncertain. Moreover, few organizations have the resources, competencies, and legitimacy to be engaged in a lead role in all sustainability infrastructure initiatives. Thus, though having a seat at the table may be useful, most organizational leaders will decide to occupy it only selectively or sporadically, focusing on some projects but not others, and choosing to be leaders on some projects and neutral or passive on others. On some issues, leaders may want to maintain flexibility and be reactive, rather than taking a leadership position.

While influenced by calculations of costs and benefits, these choices are inherently ambiguous and cannot be fully anticipated. Some of the benefits from being proactive can be measured, but others are intangible. Intangible benefits include obtaining early warning about problems, gaining intelligence about emerging issues, and learning. The knowledge gained might translate into influence, legal protection, and/or legitimacy, but then again it might not. It might lead to innovation, to an understanding of markets and business opportunities that otherwise would be ignored, but it does not necessarily have to lead in this direction.

4) *A mental map of the sustainability landscape is useful for understanding and managing the process.* This landscape includes the organizational infrastructure for sustainability that exists in a particular domain in terms of the roles that various private- and public-sector actors play in the development and implementation sustainability projects in which they are involved (Boutilier, 2009). This infrastructure, or ecosystem, varies by project and stage of development over time. The goals, interests, and motives of many different types of actors must be understood. Private actors have profit-making goals, while public-sector actors have responsibilities to create public goods and collective resources. Private actors engage in proprietary research and perform development, manufacturing, marketing, and distribution functions. Universities and research institutions provide scientific facts and opinions, training, and human resources. Financial institutions play key roles in generating liquidity and creating insurance that are needed in order to develop and implement risky sustainability initiatives (Hoffman, 2000). Studies of

industry emergence show that both public and private actors perform key roles in building various components of the infrastructure: intellectual, financial, and technological endowments, institutional norms, laws, and standards and education of consumers and the public at large (Garud et al., 2013).

Because these infrastructure components do not emerge evenly, they often become "bottlenecks" to the emergence of the overall infrastructure. Moreover, the actors involved are often not moving in the same direction with regard to sustainability goals (Prakash, 2000). The creation of this infrastructure for sustainability is well beyond the reach of single organizations. It thereby requires that organizations "run in packs" and participate with many private, public, and non-profit organizations whose interests may complement, oppose, or are indifferent towards each other. Organizational leaders who "run in packs" are likely to be more successful than those who go it alone. As we have so far indicated, "running in packs" presents organization leaders with many challenges about how, with whom, and when to cooperate. Understanding the pack, the organization's role in it, and the extent to which the pack gives the organization power are critical to the success of the sustainability projects that organizational leaders undertake.

5) *Divergent periods of sustainability implementation require pluralistic leadership.* Managing a portfolio of sustainability projects with ambiguous goals and conflicting stakeholder groups challenges the leaders of organizations to gain skills and experiences in pluralistic leadership and dialectical processes of change (Van de Ven and Poole, 1995; Hargrave and Van de Ven, 2006). The strategic logic of pluralistic leadership is the logic of complexity (Lengenick-Hall and Wolf, 1999). In other words, the logic that leaders apply in projects where people agree is not relevant in other settings of conflict among multiple stakeholders. Though achieving sustainability is a collective, not individual, achievement, this collective endeavor does not consist of a set of like-minded people who share common purposes or goals. Instead, it consists of many diverse and partisan actors in public and private sectors that have different interests, perform divergent roles, and are embedded together in the development of ecosystems and infrastructures for sustainability, where the relative influence of the actors depends on how much bargaining power and freedom they have.

Conclusion to Managing Shifting Goal Consensus and Task Ambiguity in Making the Transition to Sustainability

The challenges discussed in this chapter are exacerbated by the complexities leaders of organizations face when they are managing not one, but a portfolio of sustainability projects. These projects vary in degrees of consensus and ambiguity among stakeholders, and hence require different decision strategies. The Thompson and Tuden (1959) typology outlines different strategies of decision making and change that organizational leaders have used. This typology is useful in selecting and applying different strategies for projects that vary in consensus and ambiguity. It is also useful in switching strategies over the life span of sustainability projects as degrees of consensus and ambiguity change and unfold over time. When there are different levels of agreement or disagreement about goals and different levels of uncertainty about the means to achieve these goals, decision makers should rely on different methods of choice. As their organizations transition to sustainability, they must anticipate the obstacles, prepare for them, choose when and when not to be proactive, have mental maps of the organizational ecosystem, work with other relevant organizations, and acquire pluralistic leadership skills.

These observations lead us to propose that managing sustainability projects requires an expanded repertoire of leadership skills from hierarchical leadership and planned change to pluralistic leadership and dialectical change (Van de Ven and Poole, 1995). It also requires learning how to shift between these strategies as support for sustainability projects rises and falls over time. John Browne himself now seems to better recognize these insights (Browne and Nuthall, 2013). A company cannot just proclaim its adherence to sustainable values and goals. It must do much more.

To support this, academic scholars need to develop and test models of pluralistic leadership and constructive methods of dialectical change and conflict resolution. For the most part, scholars have focused on models and theories of planned change under conditions of consensus on shared purpose and centralized leadership. As we have seen, these conditions apply for relatively short periods of the sustainability journey. Scholars need to go beyond these situations to developing models and processes for constructive conflict resolution and pluralistic leadership.

ACKNOWLEDGMENTS

An earlier version of this chapter was presented at the conference on "Change and Sustainability" at Harvard Business School, May 9–10, 2013. We thank Rebecca Henderson, Michael Tushman and Judy Marcus for useful comments on this chapter.

REFERENCES

Augustine, G. (2008) "Whiting Refinery: Beyond Petroleum (A) BP and the Whiting Refinery: Beyond Petroleum (B)," case 1-428-727 and mini-case 1-428-736. Erb Institute, University of Michigan.

Axelrod, R. (1997) *The Complexity of Cooperation*. Princeton, NJ: Princeton University Press.

Barbier, E. (2010) *A Global Green New Deal*. Cambridge: Cambridge University Press.

Barnard, C. (1938) *The Functions of the Executive*. Cambridge, MA: Harvard University Press.

Boutilier, R. (2009) *Stakeholder Politics*. Sheffield, UK: Greenleaf Publishing.

Browne, J. and Nuthall, R. (2013) "Beyond Corporate Social Responsibility: Integrated External Engagement," *McKinsey Quarterly* (March). Available at: <http://www.mckinsey.com/insights/strategy/beyond_corporate_social_responsibility_integrated_external_engagement> (accessed July 2014).

Bunker, B., Foster, J., Levine, J., Sanchez, R., Sethi, G., and Tan, G. (2012) "Google's Shift into Renewables," case 1-429-226. Erb Institute, University of Michigan.

Burgelman, R. A. and Sayles, I. A. (1986) *Inside Corporate Innovation: Strategy, Structure, and Managerial Skills*. New York: Free Press.

Courtney, H. (2001) *202/20 Foresight*. Cambridge, MA: Harvard University Press.

Daily, G. and Walker, B. (2000) "Seeking the Great Transition," *Nature* 403: 243–5.

Davis, G. F., McAdam, D., Scott, W. R., and Zald, M. N. (2005) *Social Movements and Organization Theory*. Cambridge: Cambridge University Press.

Eccles, R. G., Ioannou, I., and Serafeim, G. (2011) "The Impact of a Corporate Culture of Sustainability on Corporate Behavior and Performance," Working paper no. 12-035. Boston, MA: Harvard Business School Press.

Garud, R., Tuertscher, P., and Van de Ven, A. H. (2013) "Perspectives on Innovation Processes," *Academy of Management Annals* 7. Available at: <http://www.tandfonline.com/doi/abs/10.1080/19416520.2013.791066> (accessed July 2014).

Greenwood, R., Oliver, C., Sahlin, K., and Suddaby, R. (eds). (2008) *The Sage Handbook of Organizational Institutionalism*. Los Angeles, CA: Sage Publications.

Gunther, M. (2013) "Unilever has a Green Thumb," *Fortune* 167: 124–32.

Hall, J., Daneke, G., and Lenox, M. (2010) "Sustainable Development and Entrepreneurship: Past Contributions and Future Directions," *Journal of Business Venturing* 25: 439–48.

Hamschmidt, J. and Pirson, M. (2011) *Case Studies in Social Entrepreneurship and Sustainability: The Oikos Collection*, Vol. 2. Sheffield, UK: Greenleaf Publishing.

Hargrave, T. J. and Van de Ven, A. H. (2006) "A Collective Action Model of Institutional Innovation," *Academy of Management Review* 31 (4): 964–88.

Henn, R. (2010) "Living Homes," case 1-428-714. Erb Institute, University of Michigan.

Hoffman, A. (1997) *From Heresy to Dogma; An Institutional History of Corporate Environmentalism*. San Francisco: The New Lexington Press.

Hoffman, A. (2000) *Competitive Environmental Strategy*. Washington, D.C.: Island Press.

Hoffman, A. (2013) *Strategies for Sustainable Development Course*. Erb Institute, University of Michigan.

Huyn, J., Kaplan, J., Katpally, S., Pierce, B., and Pierson, B. (2012) *BP: Beyond Petroleum?* Erb Institute, University of Michigan.

Kelly, A. (2013) "Getting Isaiah Berlin Wrong," *NY Review of Books*. Available at: <http://www.nybooks.com/articles/archives/2013/jun/20/getting-isaiah-berlin-wrong/?pagination=false> (accessed July 2014).

Laszlo, C. (2005) *The Sustainable Company*. Washington, D.C.: Island Press.

Lengenick-Hall, C. and Wolf, J. (1999) "Similarities and Contradictions in the Core Logic of Three Strategy Research Streams," *Strategic Management Journal* 20: 1109–32.

Lindblom, C. E. (1965) *The Intelligence of Democracy: Decision Making Through Mutual Adjustment.* New York: Free Press.

Marcus, A. (1992) *Controversial Issues in Energy Policy,* Beverly Hills, CA.: Sage Publications.

Marcus, A. (2005) "Research in Strategic Environmental Management," in Sanjay Sharma and J. A. Aragon-Correa (eds), *Corporate Environmental Strategy and Competitive Advantage.* Northhampton, Mass: Edward Elgar Publishing.

Marcus, A. (2006) *Big Winners and Big Losers,* Upper Saddle Rive, N.J.: Wharton School Press.

Marcus, A. and Fremeth, A. (2011) "Institutional Void and Stakeholder Leadership," in J. Burger (ed.), *Science and Stakeholders: Solutions to Energy and Environment Issues.* Heidelberg: Springer.

Marcus, A., Geffen, D., and Sexton, K. (2000) "A New Competence in Environmental Management: Lessons from Project XL in Minnesota," in Eric Orts (ed.), *Environmental Contracts: Comparative Approaches to Regulatory Innovation in Europe and the United States.* Amsterdam: Kluwer.

Marcus, A., Geffen, D., and Sexton, K. (2002) *Reinventing Environmental Regulation: Lessons from Project XL,* Resources for the Future. Washington, D.C.: Johns Hopkins University Press.

Marcus, A., Shrivastava, P., Sharma, S., and Pogutz, S. (eds) (2011) *Cross-Sector Leadership for the Green Economy: Integrating Research and Practice on Sustainable Enterprise.* New York: Palgrave MacMillan.

Maxwell, J., Rothenberg, S., Briscoe, F., and Marcus, A. (1997) "Green Schemes: Corporate Environmental Strategies and their Implementation," *California Management Review* 39: 118–34.

McEvily, B. and Marcus, A. (2005) "Embedded Ties and the Acquisition of Competitive Capabilities," *Strategic Management Journal* 26: 1033–55.

Mintzberg, H. (2007) *Tracking Strategies:...Toward a General Theory.* Oxford: Oxford University Press.

Olson, M. (1965) *The Logic of Collective Action.* Cambridge, MA: Harvard University Press.

Orsato, R. (2009) *Sustainability Strategies: When Does It Pay to be Green?* New York: Palgrave MacMillan.

Ostrom, E. (2000) "Collective Action and the Evolution of Social Norms," *J. Econ. Perspectives* 14: 137–58.

Pfeffer, J. (1978) *Organizational Design.* Arlington Heights, IL: AHM Publishing.

Polley, Douglas E., Raghu, Garud, and Venkataraman, Sankaran. (1999) *The Innovation Journey.* New York: Oxford University Press.

Post, J., Buchholz, R., and Marcus, A. (1992) *Managing Environmental Issues,* Englewood Cliffs, N.J.: Prentice-Hall.

Prakash, A. (2000) *Greening the Firm.* Cambridge: Cambridge University Press.

Raynor, M. (2007) *The Strategy Paradox.* New York: Doubleday.

Reinhardt, F. and Vietor, R. (1996) *Business Management and the Natural Environment.* Cincinnati, OH: Southwestern.

Roome, N. (ed.). (1998) *Sustainability Strategies for Industry.* Washington, D.C.: Island Press.

Rowledge, L., Barton, R., and Brady, K. (1999) *Mapping the Journey.* Sheffield, UK: Greenleaf Publishing.

Russo, M. (ed.). (2008) *Environmental Management: Readings and Cases*. Los Angeles, CA.: Sage Publishing.

Sarkis, J., Brust, D., and Cordeiro, J. (2010) *Facilitating Sustainable Innovation Through Collaboration*. Heidelberg: Springer.

Schoemaker, P. (2002) *Profiting from Uncertainty*, New York: The Free Press.

Sexton, K., Marcus, A., Easter, K., and Burkhardt, T. (eds). (1999) *Better Environmental Decisions: Strategies for Governments, Businesses, and Communities*. Washington, D. C.: Island Press.

Sexton, K., Murdock, B., and Marcus, A. (2001) "Cooperative Environmental Solutions: Acquiring Competence for Multi-Stakeholder Partnerships," in *Environmental Agreements: Process, Practice, and Future Trends*. Sheffield, UK: Greenleaf Publishing, 54–72.

Simon, H. A. (1973) "The Structure of Ill-Structured Problems," *Artificial Intelligence* 4: 191–201.

Thompson, J. D. and Tuden, A. (1959) "Strategies, Structures, and Processes of Organization Decision," in J. D. Thompson et al. (eds), *Comparative Studies in Administration*. Pittsburgh, PA: University of Pittsburgh Press.

Van de Ven, A. H. and Poole, M. S. (1995) "Explaining Development and Change in Organizations," *Academy of Management Review* 20: 510–40.

Van de Ven, A. H., Polley, D. E., Garud, R., and Venkataraman, S. (2008) *The Innovation Journey*. New York: Oxford University Press.

Willums, J. and Goluke, U. (1992) *From Ideas to Action: Business and Sustainable Development*. Geneva: ICC Publication No. 504.

Wustenhagen, R. and Bilharz, M. (2006) "Green Energy Market Development in Germany: Effective Public Policy and Emerging Customer Demand," *Energy Policy* 34: 1681–96.

Yaziji, Michael and Doh, Jonathan. (2009) *NGOS and Corporations: Conflict and Collaboration*. Cambridge: Cambridge University Press.

13 Sustainability and Organizational Change

An Institutional Perspective

Royston Greenwood, P. Devereaux Jennings,
and Bob Hinings

Introduction

Sustainability, as we mean it, refers to "development that meets the needs of the present without compromising the ability of future generations to meet their own needs" (Bruntland, 1987: 43). If one assumes that moving towards sustainability represents a significant form of organizational change, then there are two overarching approaches that can be taken about how that change might be accomplished. The two approaches are distinguished by whether they focus upon the organizational or the institutional level of analysis. The former—the organizational level—approach asks how any such important organizational change can be achieved, wittingly? That is, it asks what senior managers can and should (usually) "do" if they wish to fundamentally change an organization—i.e., to move it from one state (such as one that is unresponsive to issues of sustainability) to another (where sustainability figures prominently)? This approach considers aspects of the organization—such as its structural complexity, its existing resource commitments, the reproductive impulse of on-going routines, and the play of political resistance—as problematical obstacles, and explores the role of managers in framing change strategies so as to overcome them. Leaders of organizations are portrayed as important players in orchestrating change.

The second—institutional level—approach is very different. This approach emphasizes the contextual (rather than intra-organizational) circumstances that enable, push, or inhibit organizations from moving from one state to another. The actions of managers within organizations, whether deliberate or otherwise, are seen as secondary in this change process. Broader, socio-cultural factors are at work in defining and legitimating acceptable organizational ideas and behaviors, particularly deeply engrained ones. As such, managers play only one of two roles in this institutional process. A hard institutional stance portrays them as "puppets" or "dupes" acting out, unthinkingly, taken-for-granted prescriptions. A softer, more agentic stance sees managers as interpreting and shaping those prescriptions, even if managers are not normally the driving force behind them (Barley, 2008; Maguire and Hardy, 2008). As a result of our own research on institutional theory (for example, Greenwood et al., 2011) and sustainability (for example, Hardy and Maguire, 2008), we lean more towards the latter, more nuanced position.

Institutional accounts seem well matched with the macro level of analysis involved in sustainability and with the degree of difficulty in achieving it. This chapter puts forward an institutional account of organizational change focused upon the challenge of introducing and embedding ideas of sustainability. In doing so, we emphasize sustainability from an environmental point of view, while acknowledging that environmental sustainability entails social sustainability (for example, see McWilliams and Siegel, 2011). We begin in the section "Institutional change" by outlining the institutional perspective and in particular what it says about the challenge of introducing change. We trace the shift from the perspective's early emphasis upon stability and institutional maintenance to more recent analyses that highlight the circumstances and mechanisms that enable, indeed trigger and promote, institutional and organizational change. We ask how this perspective indicates the means by which the ideas and practices of sustainability could become taken for granted and widely practiced. We then turn to an institutional account of organizational change and conclude by suggesting six implications of importance for senior managers seeking to improve their organization's sustainability.

Institutional change

BEGINNINGS

While not the earliest model of institutional change (for example, see Weber, 1922 [1919] or Selznick, 1949) the work of Meyer and Rowan (1977), Meyer and Scott (1983), and DiMaggio and Powell (2000) launched a line of work that received sufficient consensus to be identified as the most widespread early model of institutional change (for a review, see Greenwood et al., 2008). Meyer and Rowan observed that, within any given sector or industry, organizations use similar organizational forms. They explained this observation by pointing to the influence of the social context within which organizations are embedded. That context contains "powerful institutional rules" that define appropriate and acceptable forms of organizing.

In effect, Meyer and Rowan alerted theorists to the fact that organizations are not simply production systems, functioning in an environment comprised of suppliers, consumers, and competitors, but social and cultural systems embedded within an "institutional" context, comprising social expectations and prescriptions of what constitutes appropriate ("legitimate") behavior, supported by an institutional infrastructure of actors including the state, professions, interest groups, the media, public opinion and so forth, that monitored and cajoled organizations to adopt those behaviors. The behavior of organizations, in consequence, cannot be understood without taking into account the influence of this institutional context. Moreover, this influence is resonant and resilient. Organizations are not free-floating islands of rationality or units of political expediency; instead, they are seriously constrained by social expectations and the properties of legitimacy. In examining how or why individual organizations adopt new ideas or practices, it is thus necessary to understand the role and consequences of these field-level isomorphic and policing mechanisms.

From its early days, institutional analyses have focused upon *field-level* processes. Fields are "...a community of organizations that partakes of a common meaning system and whose participants interact more frequently and fatefully with one another than with actors outside the field" (Scott, 1995: 56). The idea of fields having "common meaning" systems has since become associated with the idea of "institutional logics" (Friedland and Alford, 1991; Thornton et al., 2012), defined as sets of reasonably coherent socially constructed rules, norms, and beliefs that define field membership, specify institutional or "collective" identities (Glynn, 2008) and that lay down patterns of appropriate conduct. Logics, in this sense, shape how actors interpret reality and provide the criteria for socially "legitimate" behavior. They prescribe and proscribe acceptable collective purposes and the appropriate organizational arrangements by which those purposes should be pursued. Or, as Battilana et al. (2009: 65) simply put it, a logic "is a field's shared understanding of the goals to be pursued and how they are to be pursued."

While market, religion, family, and community were all domains of social life that could be assessed at the field level and that had logics governing them (see Thornton et al., 2012 for a review), in the early model of institutions the natural environment was only implicitly, not explicitly, acknowledged as being part of these domains. Weber (1913, 1922)—and much later Scott and Meyer (1983)—underscored the naturalistic components of institutional orders and that various domains, such as religion, with its naturalistic underpinnings, might influence market domains. Similarly, Selznick (1949) documented that values followed by community leaders were an extension of the domains in which leaders operated—in the case of the TVA, highly agrarian ones. Yet it was not until the mid-1990s that a few institutional theorists explicitly proposed that the natural environment could be assessed as a field (or parts of fields) and that logics governed the operation of the natural environment in those fields (for example, Jennings and Zandbergen, 1995; Frank, 1997; Hoffman, 1999).

THE EARLY MODEL OF INSTITUTIONAL CHANGE: PRESCRIPTIONS AND CONVERGENCE

Contained within these early expressions of institutional theory is a process model of *convergent* change built around prescriptions and convergence, as was first explicated by Tolbert and Zucker (1983): for a later articulation, see Tolbert et al. (1996); for a review of subsequent work, see Boxenbaum and Jonsson (2008). Tolbert and Zucker examined the diffusion of personnel reforms across municipalities in the US and suggested that institutionalization follows three identifiable stages: *pre-institutionalization* (habitualization); *semi-institutionalization* (objectification); and *institutionalization* (sedimentation). Pre-institutionalization is the emergence of behaviors specific to a problem. Although some imitation between organizations may occur, there is no sense of obligation to do so; on the contrary, behaviors are appraised for their pragmatic functionality (i.e., whether they work). Knowledge of a new organizational arrangement, moreover, is restricted to small numbers of neighboring or interlocked organizations.

Eventually, in this model of change, a social consensus emerges over the value of particular social arrangements, followed by increasing rates of their adoption. In this semi-institutionalization stage, diffusion occurs because organizations mimic those perceived to be successful, but eventually the motivation to adopt shifts to a "more normative base" (Tolbert et al., 1996: 183). That is, the more that a new arrangement is adopted, the more it becomes regarded as an appropriate response and acquires cognitive legitimacy. There is too, the emergence of a supporting infrastructure of institutional intermediaries and referent audiences (associations, critics, consultants, etc.) that detail and enforce social prescriptions. Full institutionalization occurs when diffusion is almost universal and the new arrangement has become taken for granted. At this point, organizations within a field are not only constrained by institutional intermediaries, but, in their behaviors, act out and thus reproduce those structures, albeit sometimes imperfectly (Barley and Tolbert, 1997).

For sustainability advocates, this earlier model of institutional change is discouraging because it implies that long-standing arrangements that deny sustainability ideas and practices, sustainability as a logic, and institutional mechanisms for sustainability will be difficult to change (Hoffman and Ventresca, 2002). A more optimistic stance, however, is to see this earlier model as highlighting the factors that could be targeted if change were to be secured (Jennings and Zandbergen, 1995; Frank et al., 2000). It spotlights the importance of social legitimacy and the importance of field-level infrastructures that can inhibit or encourage organizational change. It implies that, if legitimation of "sustainability" as a central or complementary logic in a field could be garnered, then the adoption, diffusion, and longevity of sustainability ideas and practices would be more likely to be assured.

THE MORE RECENT MODEL OF INSTITUTIONAL CHANGE: COMPLEXITY AND DIVERGENCE

In fact, institutional change does occur. Prodded by DiMaggio (1991), institutional theorists have sought to understand the circumstances by which such change unfolds. Making sense of this extensive and sprawling literature is difficult (for a review, see Greenwood et al., 2008; Battilana et al., 2009), but two questions have attracted attention and are of relevance to our purpose here. First, where and how do initiatives that challenge existing logics initially arise? Put another way, how does "reflexivity" occur, thus opening up possibilities and places for institutional change? Second, how are new ideas successfully "theorized" and accorded legitimacy? If a central prerequisite of institutional change is to incorporate or reprioritize a new logic, how is that accomplished? Once these questions have been asked, attention can then turn to understanding why some organizations are receptive to new ideas whereas other organizations are more resistant to them. The following discussion of these issues is summarized in the institutional model of organizational change depicted in Figure 13.1.

Question 1—reflexivity

Given the emphasis of early institutional accounts upon taken-for-granted logics and their associated practices, the starting point for any theory of institutional change has to be an account of how and why some actors are able to exercise "reflexivity"—that is, *how they get "outside" prevailing ideas and consider alternatives.* This is the "paradox of embedded agency" (Battilana et al., 2009). Three approaches to this paradox have been developed.

The first and earliest approach sees reflexivity occurring as a response to exogenous "jolts" (Meyer, 1982; Meyer et al., 1990). The exogenous jolts that have been examined include world wars (Baron et al., 1986; Dobbin, 1992), social upheavals (Skogpol, 1994; Voss and Sherman, 2000) and the entry of

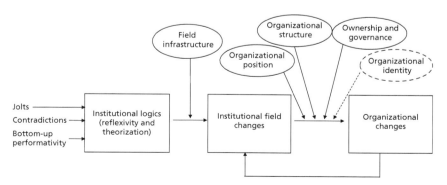

Figure 13.1. The newer model of institutional change

new players into an organizational field (Starr, 1982; DiMaggio, 1988; Thornton and Ocasio, 2008). In the case of sustainability, technical failures—such as nuclear accidents (Perrow, 1999) or chemical spills (Weir, 1987)—lead to reflexivity. The basic thesis is that such jolts disturb preconceived and taken-for-granted ideas and prompt reflection about possible alternative ways of doing things—much as profoundly erratic weather shifts have precipitated wider consideration of climate change.

A second explanation for the occurrence of reflexivity builds upon the idea that fields contain multiple logics, and proposes that reflexivity and deinstitutionalization arise not from exogenous shocks but from endogenous tensions and contradictions within a field (Jennings and Zandbergen, 1995; Seo and Creed, 2002; also see Giddens, 1984). According to Friedland and Alford (1991), society is composed of several "institutional orders"—such as the market, family, religion—each associated with distinctive institutional logics. Importantly, any organizational field may be subject to the influence of more than one institutional order and thus of multiple logics. Moreover, sometimes these logics are—or are assumed to be—contradictory in their implications. Organizations thus face the challenge of coping with incompatible institutional demands. Those located at the interstices of competing logics are especially likely to perceive opportunities for change, especially if their identity is not conditional upon one logic rather than another. Hoffman (1997: 1999), for example, documented how various logics of environmental management (for example, industrial, regulatory, CSR, and strategic) arose in the chemical industry after periods of contestation, each logic only partly embodying elements of the prior logic.

The third and more recent approach to reflexivity focuses upon initiatives and improvisations—often unplanned and often loosely coordinated—that arise in the "performativity" of day-to-day "practices" (for example, Lounsbury and Crumley, 2007; Smets et al., 2012). Such "bottom-up" improvisations are driven by the need to get things done—as illustrated by Zietsma and Lawrence in their study of forest practice code elaboration, which preceded the forestry field's transformation (Zietsma and Lawrence, 2010). According to these studies, modifications to practices can arise and slowly coalesce and crystallize at the "coalface" (Barley, 2008) into new ways of doing things. Under certain circumstances, these coalface improvisations become adopted more formally by the host organization and subsequently move to the level of the field. The common conclusion of the practice improvisation approach is that change is both highly dispersed in its origins and heterogeneous in the forms that it takes. Hence, there is continual improvisation, learning, and thus reflexivity.

As accounts of reflexivity—whether arising from exogenous shocks, endogenous contradictions, or bottom-up performativity—and its role in institutional change have developed, an important shift in imagery has occurred (and one that has implications for our later discussion of *organizational* change). The early imagery implied that field-level institutional change was the replacement of one dominant logic by another—even though it has long been recognized that organizations typically face multiple logics (for example, see D'Aunno et al., 1991; Hoffman, 1999). The more recent imagery accepts the *on-going* (albeit, possibly contested) presence of *multiple* logics. Instead of fields being portrayed as fundamentally stable, they are depicted as persistently in flux—"legitimacy is not a state but a constant struggle" (Rozbicki, 1998: 25)— although the likelihood and pace of change has been observed to vary from field to field (Delbridge and Edwards, 2008; Marquis and Lounsbury, 2007; Thornton and Ocasio, 2008; Purdy and Gray, 2009; Reay and Hinings, 2009; Dunn and Jones, 2010). Nevertheless, "institutional complexity" (Greenwood et al., 2011), rather than enduring institutional homogeneity is now seen as increasingly common and as the mechanism of institutional change.

The emergence of sustainability fits well with this research thrust in that it is often portrayed as an attempt to somehow reconcile/blend/balance two or more logics—usually those of business efficiency (a market logic) and some form of environmental and/or community logic (Bansal, 2005; Hoffman and Jennings, 2011; Jennings et al., 2012). Sustainability, in this sense, is usually not seen as being very compatible with existing economic logics in most industrial sectors (Gladwin et al., 1995; Hulme, 2009). Instead, it is viewed as a logic and set of prescriptions in competition with extant economic practice.

Question 2—"theorization"

By itself, reflexivity is not a sufficient condition for institutional change. Theorization is also needed and is, we propose, distinctive of the institutional perspective. Tolbert et al. (1996) propose that theorization involves two major tasks: specification of a general organizational failing, in order to challenge the adequacy of existing arrangements; and justification of new organizational arrangements as a widely appropriate solution. Theorization is thus the rendering of ideas into compelling formats and is critical for the ascription of legitimacy to them (Strang and Meyer, 1993). It is the process whereby new ideas and practices gain legitimacy and the means by which "renegotiations of meaning take place" (Aldrich and Fiol, 1994: 649). Successful theorization "increases the zones of acceptance by creating perceptions of similarity among adopters and by providing rationales for the practices to be adopted" (Rao et al., 2003). For example, the creation of new categories related to sustainability backed by key constituents further enables the acceptance process. Such is the case with "grass-fed" beef, as supported by local ranchers and consumers over "normally raised" beef, which was often for less local consumption (Weber et al., 2008). Theorization, thus, is the stage where competing versions like grass-fed versus normally raised struggle for superiority. The contribution of institutional theory is the attention it gives to socio-cultural processes and, increasingly, the rhetoric of language connected to higher-order institutional logics as means by which novelty is rendered acceptable and preferable

(Suddaby and Greenwood, 2005). These linguistic-discursive processes attach social approval to novelty.

Birkinshaw et al. (2008) remind us that theorization is necessary both within an organization and externally. Because of their especial interest in field-level processes, however, most institutional analyses attend to the latter in the attempt to understand how institutional (rather than organizational) change is theorized, and have centered their attention upon two more specific questions regarding theorization: "*Who* can successfully theorize?" and "*How* do they do so?"

Who can theorize? Several theorizing agents have been identified: management consultants (Abrahamson, 1991; Sahlin-Anderson and Engwall, 2002), the media (Davis, et al., 1994; Rao et al., 2003) professional associations (Greenwood et al., 2002; Jones, Maoret, Massa and Svejenova, 2012; Goodrick and Reay, 2010), corporations (Munir and Phillips, 2005), critics and journalists (Rao, Morin and Durand, 2003), and historians (Khaire and Wadhwani, 2010)—to which might be added academics. Especial emphasis has been placed upon the role of social movements as agents of theorization (for a review, see Schneiberg and Lounsbury, 2008). For example, in their study of DDT, Maguire and Hardy (2009) note how opponents of DDT discursively problematized its use. This external theorization, of which Rachael Carlson's *Silent Spring* is but one example, put pressure on the industry to defend its practices (Maguire and Hardy, 2009; Hoffman and Jennings, 2011).

The list of theorizing agents is long, but not all actors/organizations are equally successful in commanding attention, for which various explanations have been offered—including references to an organization's status, its size and visibility, and its ability to deploy resources (cultural, political, financial, and formal regulatory authority). Common to successful theorization efforts, however, is that proponents have "discursive legitimacy" (Hardy and Phillips, 1998). That is, that they are acknowledged by members of the field as having the right to exercise "voice."

The importance of having discursive legitimacy is highlighted in Lefsrud and Meyer's (2012) examination of the climate change debate, which shows the role and frames of professional engineers and geophysicists in creating variance in the meaning of climate change and its associated risks. This study reveals that certain segments of scientists have become useful tools for skeptics of climate change because they have legitimacy as scientists (also see Hoffman and Jennings, 2011). The general point is that for successful theorization to occur the identity (and thus the legitimacy) of those theorizing the need for change matters, and that the legitimacy of sustainability as a new logic depends upon the nature of their association and identification with the logics in play.

How do they theorize? Much recent work has examined *how* theorization is accomplished. For the most part, these studies focus upon the use of cultural symbols and language—"discourse" (Phillips et al., 2004)—as proponents and opponents contest the appropriateness of existing and nascent templates of behavior (Greenwood et al., 2002; Maguire et al., 2004; Suddaby and Greenwood, 2005). The role of language in the theorization process is regarded as "fundamental" because "discourses make certain ways of thinking and acting possible, and others impossible or costly" (Phillips et al., 2004: 638; see also Clark and Jennings, 1997). Language, in other words, is a means "to persuade constituencies of the desirability and appropriateness of institutional deviance" (Suddaby and Greenwood, 2005: 37). Successful institutional entrepreneurs, therefore, are those "skilled enough to craft a compelling message advocating for change" (Etzion and Ferraro, 2010: 1092; Lefsrud and Jennings, forthcoming).

But how is a compelling message constructed? One line of study draws upon social movement theory and its emphasis upon "framing." Lounsbury (2001), for example, shows how a viable infrastructure for recycling did not develop until activists reframed (re-theorized) recycling as a *for*-profit service; that is, the framing had to connect with the interests and market logic of critical players in order to garner legitimacy. Similarly, Weber et al. (2009) report how the anti-genetic movement in Germany "described biotechnology as a threat not only to the environment but to the moral good of pure untouched nature, and they tapped into a deep-seated suspicion of eugenics..." It was the use of these "culturally resonant frames" that helped to mobilize support and provided access to critical resource holders and influential decision makers.

Etzion and Ferraro (2010), in their longitudinal study of the Global Reporting Initiative for sustainability reporting practices, highlight two particularly successful "discursive strategies" deployed in the sustainability debate. One strategy used the analogy of financial reporting in order to associate a sustainability "audit" with an already highly legitimated practice (even drawing verbatim from the International Standard Committee Board's reporting principles). The second strategy framed "social ills and environmental degradation... as issues that have an impact on businesses' economic performance," in order to distance ("decouple") the GRI guidelines "from the more politically sensitive agenda of sustainability" (Etzion and Ferraro, 2010: 1,100).

A second line of inquiry into how theorization can be accomplished draws upon rhetorical theory (for example, Green, 2004; Suddaby and Greenwood, 2005; Erkama and Vaara, 2010; Goodrick and Reay, 2010). Green (2004) distinguishes between three forms of "discursive justification"—*pathos* (an appeal to emotion), *logos* (an appeal to logic and pragmatic legitimacy), and *ethos* (an appeal to ethical legitimacy)—and discusses their implications for persuasion. For example, pathos is high on attention capture but is transient in its effects, whereas appeals to ethos are more durable, but low on attention capture (although, see Bansal, 2005). Hence, Green suggests that the sequence in the use of these justifications will affect the success or otherwise of theorization efforts. An example of the aligning of language to the setting is contained in studies documenting the relationship between regulatory processes and the field-level diffusion of affirmative action and due process (Dobbin, 1992, 1993; Edelman, 1990, 1992; Edelman et al., 1992; Dobbin et al., 1993; Edelman and Suchman, 1997). Given the ambiguity of regulatory policies, including environmental ones, personnel practitioners interpreted those practices and persuaded managers that they should be perceived not as "red tape" but as ways of improving efficiency (for example, by better linking employee skills to jobs and responsibilities). Recently, in their large-scale study of several thousand French firms, Delmas and Pekovic (2013) documented the importance of human resource managers' commitment and creation of training programs in order to realize productivity gains following the adoption of ISO 14001 policies.

Before leaving this discussion of theorization, a final point that deserves mention is that successful theorization is not simply the skilful linguistic appeal to higher-order values and ideals. It also has a political dimension, as pointed out by Maguire et al. (2004: 671; see also Zilber, 2008; Jennings et al., 2013):

> ...in addition to persuasively theorizing the new practices they are promoting as logical solutions to identified problems, institutional entrepreneurs in emerging fields need also to theorize political chains of cause and effect. They must make clear to stakeholders the political consequences of supporting or not supporting the new practices.

By drawing attention to political theorization, Maguire et al. (2004) are doing two things. First, they are reminding us that institutional change is not achieved solely through the use of persuasive language. Institutions are not simply the cognitive outcomes of discursive struggles but are "settlements of political struggles...fuelled by the mobilization of challenges around competitive projects and logics" (Schneiberg and Lounsbury, 2008). Actions, in other words, are also involved. Sometimes these actions are highly contentious, as shown by Hoffman's study of "institutional war" in the US chemical industry (1999). Developments in Alberta's Oil Sands (Coleman et al., 2012), such as the proposed XL pipeline from Alberta to Texas, is another example of a highly contentious struggle involving actions and discourse. Actors within the field's boundary employ highly creative, yet oppositional tactics to buffer the field from outside interests, such as e-non-governmental organizations or high-profile others, such as James Cameron, who has been publically critical of the Oil Sands. Second, Maguire and Hardy are accentuating that theorization of a particular case—such as the importance of sustainability and the threat posed by expanding Oil Sands development—involves not simply rhetorical skill, but the spelling out of the political implications for those ultimately responsible for policies and regulatory decisions.

FIELD INFRASTRUCTURE AS A TYPE OF "MODERATING" EFFECT

Thus far, the argument has been that institutional change is the consequence of disturbance to the underpinning logics within an organizational field. That disturbance, which may arise from exogenous shocks, endogenous contradic- tions, or bottom-up performativity, precipitates reflexivity. If accompanied by successful theorization, institutional change may occur. For the sustainability debate, it means that reflexivity—the problematizing of existing arrangements— has to be accomplished through persuasive theorization by discursively legitim- ated advocates. Importantly, this link between reflexivity and theorization on the one hand, and institutional change on the other, is influenced by the infrastructure of the organizational field, which can enable or hinder change and may shape its pace and linearity. Some fields are more receptive to change than others. For example, Purdy and Gray (2009) argue that a field with relatively little structure—i.e. the absence of associations, conferences, etc.—means that organizational norms and practices will be poorly specified, allowing for com- peting logics to exist and to engage in continual contestation and struggle. In contrast, Jennings et al. (2005) show that the development of a legal infrastruc- ture around water laws goes hand in hand with the elaboration of water law regulations and their application, with regulation stimulating further bur- eaucratization of water administration via the need for rule refinement and interpretation.

Despite the importance of field infrastructures, it is beyond the scope of this chapter to review in detail what we know (which is rather modest) about field- level differences (for a summary, see Scott, 2001; Greenwood et al., 2011). But it is worth noting the recent interest in "field-configuring events" (FCEs), such as trade shows, conferences, award ceremonies, and tournaments; and in government support institutions (GSIs) such as public research institutes and training centers (see McDermott et al., 2009). Lampel and Meyer (2008) highlight the significance of FCEs in developing and diffusing novel ideas. These temporary social organizations are significant because they are vehicles for discursive struggles. They are particularly important in developing social networks that allow for the expression and dissemination of new ideas and the social reconstruction of norms and standards. As such, they are mechanisms that bring together actors to reshape fields (Anand and Jones, 2008). Maguire and Hardy (2009) note that FCEs provide those rare and important time- compressed opportunities for the interaction of actors holding different visions of the future. Participants in FCEs produce accounts and "narratives" that describe the way that fields should be theorized and organized, and provide opportunities for proponents of novel ideas to access and persuade those with power to give legitimacy to new practices (McInerney, 2008; Thornton et al., 2012). Schüßler et al. (2013), for example, have shown the role of FCEs as catalysts of change for climate policy. But in doing so they highlight the importance of the specific conditions in which debate occurs. Climate change conferences organized by the UN, for example, may paradox- ically prevent as well as allow the embedding of field-level change, depending upon the structure of the conferences. For change to occur, "interactional openness" (which generates learning and trust) has to be combined with "temporal boundedness" (which generates creativity and momentum).

Organizational change

At the level of the organization, institutionalists have explored two themes. The earliest theme examines the heterogeneity of organizational responses to similar institutional contexts and asks why organizations differ in their *receptivity* to new ideas/logics. Why, for example, do some organizations more willingly adopt practices that promote environmental sustainability, whereas others remain highly resistant? Put another way, why are only some organizations embracing the sustainability logic? The central insight for institutional theory to this line of questions is that receptivity to any logic is affected by various organizational attributes that work as filters upon how institutional demands are interpreted and understood. A more recent theme explores how profound change can be *implemented*.

ORGANIZATIONAL RECEPTIVITY

It is known that organizations do not respond uniformly to institutional demands. The early portrayal within institutional theory of organizations converging upon a common archetypal set of practices is now seen as an oversimplification. Instead, organizations vary in their responses, albeit within circumscribed limits. In consequence, the need to understand the heterogeneity of organizational responses to seemingly similar institutional demands has moved to the forefront of recent institutional discussion (Lounsbury, 2001; Marquis and Lounsbury, 2007; Delbridge and Edwards, 2008; Thornton and Ocasio, 2008; Purdy and Gray, 2009; Reay and Hinings, 2009; Dunn and Jones, 2010; Pache and Santos, 2010; Thornton et al., 2012). Much of this research examines how and why organizations make sense of multiple prescriptions and proscriptions that are pushed upon them by field-level processes.

For us, the question of how and why organizations respond to the sustainability logic is an inquiry into the *relationship* between an organization and the field (or fields) in which it operates. What happens inside the organization, in other words, is, for the most part, the consequence of those relationships. The ties that link an organization to its institutional context affect how an organization will understand and respond to ideas about appropriate behavior. And, those relationships/ties are structured, in part, by various attributes of the organization which "filter" institutional signals. Four attributes in particular have been highlighted: the organization's *position* within a field; its organizational *structure;* its form of *ownership and governance;* and its *identity* (Greenwood et al., 2011: 339; also see Scott, 2001).[1]

---

[1] *Identity* is considered quite important by us, but left to other contributors to this volume (e.g., Glynn et al. Chapter 6 Staying the Same While Changing: Organizational Identity in the Face of Environmental Challenges) to discuss in detail.

Field position

One of the earliest interpretations of why some organizations are more open to new ideas and practices centers upon the implication of an organization's "structural position" within a field. This interpretation has two variants, but they share the common theme that some organizations are both more embedded—and thus caught—within existing institutional arrangements. Embedded firms are, in institutional terms, "central," whereas others are more "peripheral" (Leblebici et al., 1991; Rao et al., 2000; Maguire et al., 2004). The thesis is that organizations on the periphery will be less informed by and/or knowledgeable of prevailing logics and thus more likely to exercise reflexivity and be willing to accommodate pressures for change. Centrally located firms, in contrast, are more aware of institutional expectations, are more fully and continually exposed to the social reproduction of those expectations, benefit more from them, and thus are more fully embedded. Moreover, centrally located firms are often highly visible and subject to detailed critical scrutiny from field-level audiences such as the media, which can work to keep them within the bounds of dominant logics (for an interesting example of this process, see Ahmadjian and Robinson, 2001, who show how large, elite Japanese firms were the most reluctant to abandon the traditional commitment to permanent employment). Several studies confirm this general thesis of peripheral players as the more likely source of "institutional entrepreneurship" (for a review, see Hardy and Maguire, 2008). An interesting sustainability example is Sine and Lee's (2009) study of wind power adoption, which shows the critical, joint role played by independent power producers and environmental social movements in building this new industry "off grid," then gradually linking it to the main sources of power production.

A counter to this view of peripheral organizations as being more receptive than central organizations to new logics is provided by Greenwood and Suddaby (2006; also see Greenwood et al., 2002), who detail how elite (central) firms within the accounting industry responded to, and co-developed new patterns of service and an organizational form that rebalanced the traditional professional logic with a more commercial logic. An interesting insight from this study is that central firms are often more able to exercise reflexivity because their networks of contacts "bridge" institutional fields and thus bring them into contact with new ideas and practices; *and* they are often sufficiently large that they are beyond the reach and scope of a field's regulatory agencies. Hoffman (2001), for example, has argued that the creation and adoption of new environmental practices by core players in the chemical industry, along with their linkage to government sanctions (laws, regulations, and enforcement) have been fundamental for the rise of new environmental management logics in that industry.

Organizational structure

Ideas do not simply "flow into" an organization. Institutional prescriptions and demands are "carried" by actors. Early institutional studies, for example, looked at the role of interlocking directorates as carriers of ideas (Davis, 1991; Palmer et al., 1993). Recent work has broadened this thesis that ideas—new and old—need "representation" within an organization if they are to have influence (Pache and Santos, 2010). That is, the receptivity of an organization to new ideas—such as sustainability—is, in part, dependent upon whether proponents of those ideas reside within the organization. New logics, it is argued, need championing within the organization by "representatives" if they are to have influence beyond ceremonial acknowledgment (Pache and Santos, 2010). Pursuing this idea, institutionalists have explored the role of different actors within organizations. For example, in their study of large Canadian firm environmental practice, Sharma and Henriques (2005) documented the association between different types of firms with different types of stakeholders (for example, reactive with media and proactive with community). Bansal and Roth (2000) showed that, in addition to regulatory pressure and economic good sense, corporate leadership's commitment to sustainability was an important reason for companies going green. Similarly, Lounsbury (2001) found that universities that have made the greater commitment to waste recycling are the ones that employ staff with the relevant expertise and thus who have the commitment to develop and advocate for the introduction of new, more sustainable practices. A key point of these studies is that organizational receptivity to the prescriptions of different logics depends upon their formal and explicit representation within the firm.

However, representation alone is only part of the story. An assumption of the representation thesis is that "representatives" retain their commitment to particular ideas and that they continue to enhance their understanding of them. Yet, it has been shown that this assumption is questionable. Gabbioneta et al. (2013), for example, observed that professionals in large organizations, especially those with high status, may be more susceptible to gentle pressure to compromise their professional norms because such organizations provide a form of "structural assurance" that its actions are acceptable. Similarly, Flood (2012: 192; see also Lewis, 1990; Smets et al., 2012) reports that large law firms "incubate their lawyers to act in particular ways." Hence, as Greenwood et al., (2011: 342) point out:

...the receptivity of organizational members to a given logic is affected by the thickness of ties—such as conference attendance, club memberships, training programs, etc.—linking them to the field-level institutional infrastructure...what matters, in other words, is not simply whether a logic is represented within an organization, but the thickness of the ties between organization members and field-level referent audiences; the thicker the tie, the more likely the logic will insinuate itself into the organization.

Hoffman's work on environmental NGOs (Hoffman, 2011; Hoffman and Bertels, 2007) neatly develops and illustrates these points. In the US, *eNGOs are tightly networked in particular cliques that include particular Fortune 500 firms*. As a result, the F500 firms' policies regarding the environment come to reflect the policies of these cliques (Hoffman and Bertels, 2007). In fact, the way in which the science of climate change is portrayed and by whom is also affected by such eNGO networks (Hoffman and Bertels, 2007; Lefsrud and Meyer, 2012).

The importance of ties between an organization and the field-level institutional infrastructure is not solely concerned with the latter providing normative and material support. As pointed out earlier, field-level actors—such as professional associations—not only provide support, they monitor and *police* implementation (Jennings et al., 2002). Connections between firms and field-level agencies can thus assist in the evolution and on-going retention of contested logics. The effectiveness of collective self-regulation, however, is by no means assured. King and Lenox (2000: 702) summarized the institutional argument underpinning self-regulation:

The essence of this argument is that the institutional structure that accompanies self-regulation can control behavior through more informal coercive, normative, and mimetic means... First, coercion can be achieved through more informal mechanisms, such as showing or public exposure... Second, self-regulation can support the emergence of new norms and values that change members' preferences for collectively valued actions... Finally, when collectively valued actions are also privately beneficial, industry self-regulation can facilitate the transfer of best practices...

Evidence from King and Lenox's study of the US chemical industry, however, is, at best, equivocal. Bansal and Roth (2000) suggest that whether firms comply with field regulations depends in part upon "field coherence," an idea also found in Pache and Santos (2013a), who stress that it is "centralized" fields—that is, those where there is a clearly dominant institutional logic—that are able to monitor and police the behavior of field members. In fields characterized by multiple incompatible logics where there is a lack of an accepted status hierarchy between logics, the ability of field agencies to monitor and enforce institutional demands is problematic. As Crilly et al. (2012) point out: "Competing stakeholder expectations... weaken the pressures on firm to comply with policy and thus increase their discretion over how to respond." Crilly et al. (2012) go further and emphasize that there is often an asymmetry of information favoring organizations (over field-level actors), which enables them to conceal their responses from regulatory agencies. Similarly, in fields where there is a transition among plural logics, there is often a lack of clarity about legal rules (laws and regulation), which increases the likelihood that actors might engage in non-compliance and lowers the enforcement intensity by government agencies (Jennings et al., 2002, 2011).

Ownership

A different approach to understanding why some organizations are more receptive to ideas and practices associated with the sustainability logic focuses upon the *type of ownership*. Several studies have shown the significance of *who* owns the firm. Studies have shown how family-owned businesses incorporate into their decisions the norms of "community," rather than exclusively those of the market logic (for example, Gomez-Mejia et al., 2007; Greenwood et al., 2010). As a result, family firms tend to be better environmental stewards (Berrone et al., 2009). Similarly, religious organizations prioritize particular values, as indicated by Walsh et al. (2003: 874) who found that "religious values that orient Catholic universities might prompt their faculty to focus on a more expansive set of business–society relationships than their peers at universities celebrated by the business community in the *Business Week* rankings." The form of ownership, in other words, serves to filter and/or give relative salience to incompatible and novel ideas.

A complementary approach to understanding the role of ownership and governance emphasizes not who owns an organization, but the *form* of that ownership (Fligstein, 2001). For example, the partnership form of governance, deployed by law firms and accounting firms, and by not-for-profits, "are distinguished by participation in decision processes that is wider and more inclusive than would be expected in the more hierarchically ordered publicly traded corporation" (Greenwood et al., 2011: 345—hence the higher likelihood of multiple ideas and views being brought into decision processes). For this reason, the partnership format might enable receptivity to new ideas. Alternatively, it has been argued that within professional service firms there can be considerable resistance to the introduction of "corporate" logics because of the norms of collegiality associated with the "partnership" form of ownership and governance (Pinnington and Morris, 2002). In other words, such structures not only allow for participation, they symbolize commitment to collegial forms of behavior (much as do universities) which might act *against* consideration of emerging alternative logics that appear to prioritize more self-interested norms. This assumption guided Lefsrud and Meyer's (2012) interpretation of the resistant position to climate change data taken by many geophysicists and geologists: if the profession does not accept the data as being sufficiently "scientific," then the likelihood of the profession embracing open-minded approaches to natural environment issues, actors, and technologies will be low.

There has also been a long-term interest within the social and environmental sustainability literature in whether forms of corporations—particularly, MNCs—are likely to pursue different types of policies and operate differently across non-home countries. Early work seemed to indicate that MNCs would transport pollution and social inequities (for example, low-wage labor) to non-home locations (Cardoso and Faletto, 1979; Piore and Sabel, 1984); but in more recent years, there is evidence of more complex effects (Porter and Van der Linde, 1995). King and Shaver (2001) showed that while foreign MNCs operating in the US may generate more waste, they also process more waste. In an analysis of GE's portfolio of more versus less environmentally oriented operations, Gehman (2012) found that, over time, GE has spun off the less environmentally sound operations—often internationally—as part of "category cleaning," though GE still retained arms-length ties with these operations.

IMPLEMENTING ORGANIZATIONAL CHANGE

A central assumption of institutional accounts is that disturbances at the field level create opportunities for actors within organizations to introduce new ideas, or to re-order their relative salience. Ideas of sustainability, in other words, are easier to introduce (they are recognized more readily and accorded more legitimacy) to the extent that field-level debates are occurring. Surprisingly, until relatively recently there have been few studies of *how* such changes are accomplished.

The list of such studies, however, is growing (for example, Lounsbury, 2001; Glynn, 2008; Battilana and Dorado, 2010; Erkama and Vaara, 2010; Spicer and Sewell, 2010; Kellogg, 2011; Smets et al., 2012; Jay, 2013; Wright and Zammuto, 2013) and all of these studies highlight the relationship between organizations and the organizational field—which, as we have pointed out, is distinctive of the institutional theory approach. But they also dig into the organization in an attempt to provide guidance on how change can be successfully introduced. Two approaches illustrate a clearly "institutional" approach to the implementation of organizational change. The first approach, for which we use Kellogg's (2009, 2011) work as an example, in many ways reflects the themes of field-level change. The second approach, for which we use as examples the works of Battilana and Dorado (2010) and Pache and Santos (2013b), focuses upon "hybrid" organizations—i.e., organizations that explicitly seek to combine practices and ideas from multiple logics—and attempts to understand how and when such organizations can be successfully deployed.

Implementing organizational change

An apposite illustration of an institutional approach to how organizational change my be accomplished is provided by Kellogg's (2011) analysis of how less powerful members within an organization—in her study, hospital interns—were able to change deeply institutionalized, industry-wide work practices by drawing on field-level discourses. She argues that such change requires the availability *and* the skillful use of cultural *and* political tools:

Cultural toolkits are composed of symbolic elements such as frames, identities and tactics that can be brought into organizations from other settings by any organization member. In contrast, political toolkits...are composed of material elements such as accountability systems, staffing systems, and evaluation systems that depend on the formal authority of more powerful organization members for their introduction into particular organizations. Changes over time in an organization's broader institutional context shape changes in cultural and political toolkits inside organizations. (Kellogg, 2011: 483.)

This study highlighted that organizational change is an expression of the relationship between an organization and its institutional context. For organizational change to occur, reflexivity—an awareness of possibilities—has to be aligned with the skillful use of discursive and political strategies (theorization) so as to persuade audiences of the legitimacy of proposed changes. That is, the legitimacy of ideas depends upon their attachment to the emerging generally accepted social norms *outside* the organization (also see Lounsbury, 2001 on the promotion of recycling in universities).

In an earlier study, Kellogg (2009) highlighted a second requirement of successful organizational change—and, again, it is one that echoes our discussion of field-level change. Kellogg points to the importance of "relational spaces" within hospitals, where junior physicians were able to meet and develop their ideas and their sense of community. These "spaces" could be seen as performing the same role as field-configuring events at the field level. They are the places where otherwise disconnected supporters of new ideas can meet, informally or otherwise, and then build an emerging community of support. The importance of relational spaces is illustrated in Weber et al.'s (2008) analysis of grass-fed beef production. The category system for grass-fed beef classifies producer and consumer relations—i.e., puts a cognitive and normative structure on those relations—which then allows individual organizations to implement these new methods of raising and selling cattle by connecting grass-fed beef products to these categories.

Taken together, the two Kellogg studies illustrate how implementing change at the organizational level *mirrors* the mechanisms and processes observed at the level of the field.

Creating hybrid organizations

A different institutional dig into the implementation of organizational change explores the circumstances that enable the successful use of "hybrid" arrangements. Most organizations are hybrids to some degree, in the sense that they incorporate multiple logics; hospitals and universities are obvious examples. Recent institutional attention to hybrids, however, largely stems from an interest in how organizations cope with the arrival of a new logic, especially one previously considered as incompatible with the dominant organizational purpose and way of operating. The emergence of the sustainability logic is a clear example of a new logic running against an embedded one, in this case the commercial logic.

Hybrids are often seen as "by nature arenas of contestation" (Pache and Santos, 2013b: 2), bringing together "key elements of different logics that may have little in common and may even be in conflict" (Tracey et al., 2011). In many respects, attempts by firms to embrace sustainability practices can be seen in the same light—they are translating themselves into hybrids—i.e., organizations that incorporate both commercial and sustainability logics within their structures and decision processes. For example, Jay (2013) looks at a public–private hybrid that combines the logics of government bureaucracies, non-profit organizations, and business firms as they deal with climate change.

Given the recency of this interest, it is not surprising that understanding of hybrids is modest (for a review, see Battilana and Lee, 2014). Nevertheless, several interesting findings have emerged. Battilana and Dorado (2010) examined two microfinance organizations that sought to combine the logics of business and of poverty alleviation by providing loans for business ventures to low-income entrepreneurs. They found that combining the two logics was highly problematical in one of the two organizations, in which the business logic gradually asserted priority. The successful organization avoided this outcome by hiring personnel whose minds were not captured by either of the two logics, and then used consistent socialization processes to develop a strong organizational identity that gave prominence to both logics. For new organizations, adoption of this prescription for success might be possible, but for established organizations its relevance would be more limited. This study (see also Tracey et al., 2011) indicates the difficulty of retaining a balance between logics, especially when the market logic is involved. That logic—at least in contemporary Western society—tends to exert significant pressure against other logics.

Hence, the challenge of maintaining balance is fundamental to the introduction of sustainability practices. The institutional argument would be that in order to nurture balance and prevent commitment to sustainability becoming ceremonial rather than substantive, two arrangements are essential: first, the appointment of explicit and dedicated proponents (representatives) of the sustainability logic (Lounsbury, 2001); and second, the building of strong ties to field-level proponents of that logic (Greenwood et al., 2011).

Different insights are offered by Pache and Santos (2013a). This study is also concerned with the choice of practices and structures from several logics, but Pache and Santos are interested in how an organization can secure legitimacy from the field-level advocates of incompatible logics; that is, the focus is outward looking, rather than internal to the organization. Pache and Santos compared four French work-integration social enterprises that combined practices of the social welfare logic with practices implicated by the commercial logic. These logics, in the French context, are associated with differences in legal status, ownership structures, profit destination (shareholders versus the enterprise), governance, use of professionals versus volunteers, and so on. Pache and Santos offer two key insights about the management of hybrids. First, successful hybrids "selectively couple" practices from both logics and blend them together because doing so signals their compliance to the field-level audiences prescribing and monitoring each logic. Hence, they gain legitimacy from both audiences. Second, the particular combination of practices coupled together depends upon the history of the organization. Those organizations that emanated from the commercial sector would, relative to those from the social welfare sector, emphasize the adoption of social welfare practices; whereas those from the social welfare sector would do the opposite and emphasize commercial practices. In other words, recently created hybrids pay special attention to those field-level audiences that are more likely to be skeptical of their intentions.

Most "green organizations" appear to be some form of hybrid: that is, they incorporate sustainability and corporate logics, to varying degrees (Hoffman and Georg, 2011). Research has moved in the direction of examining how this combination has been created and its effects in different types of organizations. This includes giving attention to NGO–business partnerships (Georg and Irwin, 2002; Kong et al., 2002) and public–private partnerships for the environment (Koppenjan and Enserink, 2009). But this research, with the exception perhaps of Henn and Hoffman (2013), has yet to be linked as explicitly to hybridity.

Guidelines for linking institutional change to sustainability

We are now in a position to return more explicitly to some of theoretical implications of our institutional change model for moving a field and a firm towards sustainability—and not simply to use sustainability research as examples for illustrating points about the institutional model. We offer six implications of importance for senior managers seeking to improve their organization's sustainability.

1. **Organizational change is significantly dependent upon first generating field-level institutional change**. This is the most fundamental point of our approach. It implies that a senior manager must view issues like climate change and social inequality as truly field-level problems, ones involving environmental and community logics, and then accept that the manager's logic is embedded in that field. Senior management policy and action must be positioned around the field's broader consensus about such issues and how they should be handled. One cannot, for instance, simply ignore data on climate change (for example, CO_2 levels, mean temperature change, sea-level increases, and the disappearance of Arctic ice): one must engage with these data and explain a firm's degree of acceptance (and non-acceptance) in order to generative distinctive sustainability policies and practices. Rick George of

SUNCOR for years debated the data on climate change, yet acknowledged local impacts and pledged SUNCOR to remediation of them. This distinctive position, in the end, won SUNCOR more friends than enemies among climate change groups.

Given that the popularity of and consensus around such issues as climate change tend to wax and wane, a senior manager must track the issues with opinion polls, consultations, and social media (even Twitter), and s/he must form a dynamic, longitudinal picture of the issues in order to best time his or her organization's action. Generally speaking, a field's constituents are likely to care about the system when the system is increasingly stressed. These stresses are often cyclical (for example, seasonal). Depending on the ecosystems in which the firm is involved, a senior manager should be able to anticipate some of these cycles of attention and pre-empt their negative effects on her/his firm.

2. **Field-level change can arise from exogenous (jolts) or endogenous (contradictions and bottom-up performativity) sources.** Most environmental sustainability issues start from outside the field via an exogenous shock, but periodic jolts then remain in the field due to reflexivity, theorization, and other knock-on effects concerning the jolts (Misutka et al., 2013). Such is the case of the climate-change associated greenhouse gas GHG problem. It appeared in the field in the mid-1990s with the discussion around the Kyoto Protocol and now is being re-worked in the field in a variety of ways, including through eNGO issues with the degradation of specific ecosystems, like the Arctic, and green party issues about renewable sources of issues. Social sustainability issues, in contrast, tend to start with contradictions in logics. A standard contradiction that leads to social sustainability issues is equality as a value underpinning community logics versus inequality that is part of market logics, for market logics normally require competition and unequal outcomes.

Outside jolts often require more immediate adaptation—even acquiescence— on the part of a senior manager and her/his firm than do inside jolts. Outside jolts often elicit a narrower range of responses, because there is far less time to reflect upon and theorize about them. In contrast, endogenously generated issues usually involve more lead time for and a wider range of responses. A senior manager therefore needs to craft different sets of responses to each type of field-level change. Today, few senior managers of major operations can be found without some version of a crisis management protocol for dealing with climate-related or ecosystems disasters, such as toxic spills. Most executives of major firms also have elaborate views on key, on-going field-level issues like climate change, and draw upon these views frequently.

3. **Field-level institutional change requires (a) "reflexivity"; (b) successful "theorization"; and (c) a supportive institutional infrastructure.** These related institutional factors imply that in order to gain competitive advantage, a senior manager must increase his/her active awareness of environmental and social issues, use the language appropriate to them, and craft new concepts and practices around them. Traditionally, senior managers have been less able to recognize and translate exogenous and endogenous into vibrant within-field

discourse and novel practice, compared to doing so in an institutional field such as, say, banking. The climate change information that was discussed in the Rio Accord and led to the Kyoto Protocol came to be heavily debated ten years later, stalling true progress in the US on cleaner air. Some already theorized programs are a useful place for a senior executive to overcome such inertia. The Natural Step (Robert, 1989) offers a coherent set of terms, theory, and associated practices for sustainability that has gained currency in the institutional field. More recently, former Sierra Club President, Adam Werbach (2009) has developed a training program about the basics of sustainability and how to negotiate on its behalf within a firm, which he has used with thousands of executives. A senior manager would benefit from learning about either and translating their sets of practices into those applicable for her or his firm.

In addition, given the underdeveloped nature of the institutional infrastructure for environmental and social issues, compared to that for more standard legal and business issues, a senior manager has the opportunity to create, and then engage with, field-level organizations devoted to sustainability. Today, transnational organizations are essential for generating and diffusing discourse and practice concerning environmental and social issues. By generating a transnational organization in a new issue area—such as one concerned with the rapidly declining critical oceanic nutrients (plankton and brine shrimp), or perhaps with the lack of financial and legal rights for poor entrepreneurs receiving microfinance—senior managers can make a big difference in an institutional field for sustainability.

4. **There is typically a heterogeneity of responses to institutional demands... and also a variety of opportunity spaces for institutional and astute institutional entrepreneurs/organizations.** A senior manager today must recognize that where sustainability is concerned there is much greater breadth and latitude for strategic response in institutional fields than previously existed. Two decades ago, there was more emphasis on regulation, compliance, and isomorphic response, with governments making up for market failure by inserting themselves in various industrial sectors. Currently, governments are more likely to allow a range of responses. In energy sectors, there are emissions permits with volume and time varying ceilings, cap-and-trade systems, carbon offsets, and carbon taxes. A senior manager must, therefore, strategize more fully to explore and exploit institutional possibilities. S/he needs to conceptualize a whole portfolio of approaches to sustainability based on the institutional development of the various subfields and how entrepreneurial a management wishes to be with regard to these different domains.

This new situation is not without its own perils. On the one hand, the heterogeneity in the sector allows a senior manager and his/her firm to craft unique positions within specific fields for sustainability (for example, greenhouse gases, water quality, genetically modified foods) and also a more unique, overall identity for the firm. These days firms that claim to be "different" in the way they handle these issues is large, compared to thirty years ago, when there were only a few firms like Patagonia and the Body Shop with sustainability-oriented approaches. On the other hand, without much commonality in idea, practice, and identity among firms within an institutional field, not only will a firm's particular approach become difficult for stakeholders to discern, but the field will not have enough collective focus to pursue a coherent set of sustainability practices. The trick for a senior manager, then, is to find—or construct—these central tendencies via reflexivity and theorization and to position his or her firm more uniquely around them. For years, BP Oil earned "green dividends" by trumpeting its lead in emissions reduction technologies and clean energy via their green marketing campaigns compared to other "oil majors," even if eventually the lack of investment in maintenance and safety undermined that effort.

5. **Organizational-level change is a consequence of four, more proximate factors: (1) organizational positions; (2) organizational structures (that determine whether logics are "represented"); (3) ownership and governance arrangements; and (4) the identity of the specific organization.** In the case of fields involving sustainability logics and their manifestations, a senior manager needs to use his/her firm's position in the field's infrastructure and its network linkages with field members to pursue various sustainability opportunities. As mentioned, peripheral positions may yield higher rates of experimentation, as they have with forestry practices; whereas more central positions may lead to competitive dynamism and attempts at disruption in the core, as they did with GE's creation and widespread use of Six Sigma. At the same time, a senior manager needs to be sure to selectively represent the institutional field in that structural position: not all voices from the field can or should be heard inside the firm. Instead, institutional theory suggests that those voices aligned with key areas of discourse and theorization at the field level, along with the firm's specific sustainability initiative, need to be brought inside the organization and given a role in shaping its operation. In the case of forestry, this was true in British Columbia when environmentalists were brought into the pulp and paper company, MacMillan Bloedel, via the Joint Solutions Project, and it was true for the Japanese manufacturing organizations that brought in Malcolm Baldridge to train them in Six Sigma.

A senior manager of an organization in a field involved with sustainability may also need to modify the firm's ownership and governance to align with the field. Sustainability-related fields are well known for having many strong stakeholders who have theorized and promoted extensive methods of consultation and representation. As a result, a senior manager of a firm in such a field should expect to have more advisory committees, formal consultation techniques, and a more diverse board than s/he would in a firm in, say, high technology. There is also evidence that family firms and firms with other strong links to the community are likely to embrace sustainability and, in turn, for fields that are involved with sustainability to allow such forms of ownership to flourish. As a result, a senior manager should anticipate that the field's members and the firm's employees will likely expect more participation and a more benevolent style of management in the firm. The Body Shop was well known for giving employees one day off per week to pursue social and environmental initiatives. Green firms as a whole appear to have more progressive HR policies, including more training and flexible schedules, than non-green ones.

6. **The implementation of change inside the organization involves (a) similar processes and mechanisms . . . to those operating at the field level; and (b) the skillful hybridizing of practices . . . to enhance the organization's legitimacy.** Reflexivity and theorization are essential for institutional change at the organizational level. Thus, as noted earlier, using language and mobilizing actors around new ideas and practices are essential skills for senior managers hoping to generate institutional change. Various external and internal sustainability experts can help. These experts have spent time thinking about sustainability and offer a ready-made language and set of mobilization techniques for a senior manager. For example, at Mountain Equipment Co-op (MEC), senior managers encourage co-op members in various communities interested in sustainability to pitch new initiatives, such as using organic fibers and heritage building sites. Similar policies are used at Patagonia and REI. In this way, many field-level processes can be translated into firm-level ones.

Once there is representation of field-level voices in the firms—especially of expertise via use of professionals—a senior manager may feel compelled to hybridize his/her firm. Such is the case with Khosla Ventures, a VC originally more dedicated to investing in high technology, which then moved heavily into biofuels. Today, even with the downturn in clean technology, Khosla Ventures has kept part of its portfolio in the clean-energy sector. The VC's CEO, Vinod Khosla, former co-founder and CEO of Sun Microsystems, continues to be an important voice both in the clean-energy and high-tech industry. Senior managers like Khosla must identify new "balance points" for hybrid firms around competing logics and to empower members to reach such points.

Conclusion to sustainability and organizational change

With these various field- and firm-level actions, the senior manager should be able to move her/his firm further in the direction of sustainability, where sustainability is development that meets the needs of the present without compromising the ability of future generations to meet their own needs. As we have seen, sustainability changes over time as a field evolves, depending on the degree of the heterogeneity of that field and firm-level practice. Currently, the field is becoming ever more global, with linkages among its economic, environmental, and social systems. Such linkages normally imply the need for increased coordination and cooperation. Yet we are also seeing increasing calls for more regulation and control. How then can we avoid returning to the unproductive oscillation between cooperative versus command and control approaches that characterized the 1970s and 1980s?

To match with this evolving, new set of sustainability pressures, ideas, and practices, some experts suggest it is important to find key configurations among firms in fields that allow for "generative" clusters, ones where the hybrids are tripartite, being composed of economic, social, and environmental practices, as they hold the most promise. Such is the case of particular co-gen energy regions of Germany, where social and economic experiments in manufacturing have led to energy efficiencies. Another case is in Costa Rica, where farmers, tourism firms, and biological reserves have formed durable cooperatives (for example, around Monteverde). Identifying the balance point among these systems and sets of generative practice across them will allow such complex organization to flourish. Indeed, the institutional approach is well suited to assessing the new pluralism among logics of sustainability. It has always wrestled with the paradox of the closing iron cage due to inexorable institutional forces versus the highly disruptive nature of large-scale institutional change. Our chapter's goal has been to illuminate this dynamic in the context of sustainability. We hope the reader departs with a greater understanding of it and somewhat different methods for handling sustainability issues.

▨ ACKNOWLEDGMENTS

We would like to thank Kate Kellogg for insightful comments on an early draft of this chapter, Manely Sharifian for her efforts with the references, the editors for their commitments to and thoughts about the chapter, and our colleagues at the University of Alberta, who, like us, have endeavored to develop institutional theory and combine it with sustainability.

▨ REFERENCES

Ahmadjian, Christina L. and Robinson, Patricia. (2001) "Safety in Numbers: Downsizing and the Deinstitutionalization of Permanent Employment in Japan," *Administrative Science Quarterly* 46 (4): 622–54.

Aldrich, Howard E. and Fiol, Marlene C. (1994) "Fools Rush In? The Institutional Context of Industry Creation," *Academy of Management Review* 19 (4): 645–70.

Anand, Narasimhan and Jones, Brittany C. (2008) "Tournament Rituals, Category Dynamics, and Field Configuration: The Case of The Booker Prize," *Journal of Management Studies* 45 (6): 1036–60.

Bansal, Pratima. (2005) "Evolving Sustainably: A Longitudinal Study of Corporate Sustainable Development," *Strategic Management Journal* 26 (3): 197–218.

Bansal, Pratima and Clelland, Iain. (2004) "Talking Trash: Legitimacy, Impression Management, and Unsystematic Risk in the Context of The Natural Environment," *Academy of Management Journal* 47 (1): 93–103.

Bansal, Pratima and Roth, Kendall. (2000) "Why Companies Go Green: A Model of Ecological Responsiveness," *Academy of Management Journal* 43 (4): 717–36.

Barley, Stephen R. (2008) "Coalface Institutionalism," in Royston Greenwood et al. (eds), *Handbook of Organizational Institutionalism*. London: Sage Publications, 491–518.

Barley, Stephen R. and Tolbert, Pamela S. (1997) "Institutionalization and Structuration: Studying the Links between Action and Institution," *Organization Studies* 18 (1): 93–117.

Baron, James N., Dobbin, Frank R., and Jennings, P. Devereaux. (1986) "War and Peace: The Evolution of Modern Personnel Administration in US Industry," *American Journal of Sociology* 92 (2): 350–83.

Battilana, Julie and Dorado, Silvia. (2010) "Building Sustainable Hybrid Organizations: The Case of Commercial Microfinance Organizations," *Academy of Management Journal* 53 (6): 1419–40.

Battilana, Julie, Leca, Bernard, and Boxenbaum, Eva. (2009) "How Actors Change Institutions: Towards a Theory of Institutional Entrepreneurship," *The Academy of Management Annals* 3 (1): 65–107.

Battilana, Julie and Lee, Matthew. (2014) "Advancing Research on Hybrid Organizing," *Academy of Management Annals* 8: 397–441.

Berrone, Pascual, Cruz, Cristina, Gomez-Mejia, Luis R., and Larraza-Kintana, Martin. (2010) "Socioemotional Wealth and Corporate Responses to Institutional Pressures: Do Family-controlled Firms Pollute Less?," *Administrative Science Quarterly* 55 (1): 82–113.

Birkinshaw, Julian, Hamel, Gary, and Mol, Michael J. (2008) "Management Innovation," *Academy of Management Review* 33 (4): 825–45.

Boxenbaum, Eva and Jonsson, Stefan. (2008) "Isomorphism, Diffusion and Decoupling," in Royston Greenwood et al. (eds), *Handbook of Organizational Institutionalism*. London: Sage Publications, 78–98.

Brundtland, G. (1987) *Our Common Future: Report of the 1987 World Commission on Environment and Development*. New York: United Nations.

Clark, Vivien and Jennings, P. Devereaux. (1997) "Talking About the Natural Environment," *American Behavioral Scientist* 40 (4): 454–64.

Crilly, Donal, Zollo, Maurizio, and Hansen, Morten T. (2012) "Faking It or Muddling Through? Understanding Decoupling in Response to Stakeholder Pressures," *Academy of Management Journal* 55 (6): 1429–48.

D'Aunno, Thomas, Sutton, Robert I, and Price, Richard H. (1991) "Isomorphism and External Support in Conflicting Institutional Environments: A Study of Drug Abuse Treatment Units," *Academy of Management Journal* 34 (3): 636–61.

Davis, Gerald F. (1991) "Agents Without Principles? The Spread of the Poison Pill Through the Intercorporate Network," *Administrative Science Quarterly* 36 (4): 583–613.

Delbridge, Rick and Edwards, Tim. (2008) "Challenging Conventions: Roles and Processes During Non-Isomorphic Institutional Change," *Human Relations* 61 (3): 299–325.

Delmas, Magali A. and Pekovic, Sanja. (2013) "Environmental Standards and Labor Productivity: Understanding the Mechanisms that Sustain Sustainability," *Journal of Organizational Behavior* 34 (2): 230–52.

DiMaggio, Paul J. (1988) "Interest and Agency in Institutional Theory," in Lynne G. Zucker (ed.), *Institutional Patterns and Organizations: Culture and Environment.* Cambridge, Mass.: Ballinger Publishing, 3–22.

DiMaggio, Paul J. (1991) "Constructing an Organizational Field as a Professional Project: US Art Museums, 1920–1940," in Walter W. Powell and Paul J. DiMaggio (eds), *The New Institutionalism in Organizational Analysis.* Chicago, IL: University of Chicago Press, 267–92.

DiMaggio, Paul J. and Powell, Walter W. (2000) "The Iron Cage Revisited Institutional Isomorphism and Collective Rationality in Organizational Fields," *Advances in Strategic Management* 17: 143–66.

Dobbin, Frank R. (1992) "The Origins of Private Social Insurance: Public Policy and Fringe Benefits in America, 1920–1950," *American Journal of Sociology* 97 (5): 1416–50.

Dobbin, Frank, Sutton, John R., Meyer, John W., and Scott, Richard. (1993) "Equal Opportunity Law and the Construction of Internal Labor Markets," *American Journal of Sociology* 92 (2): 396–427.

Dunn, Mary B. and Jones, Candace. (2010) "Institutional Logics and Institutional Pluralism: The Contestation of Care and Science Logics in Medical Education, 1967–2005," *Administrative Science Quarterly* 55 (1): 114–49.

Edelman, Lauren B. (1990) "Legal Environments and Organizational Governance: The Expansion of Due Process in the American Workplace," *American Journal of Sociology* 95 (6): 1401–40.

Edelman, Lauren B. (1992) "Legal Ambiguity and Symbolic Structures: Organizational Mediation of Civil Rights Law," *American Journal of Sociology* 97 (6): 1531–76.

Edelman, Lauren B. and Suchman, Mark C. (1997) "The Legal Environments of Organizations," *Annual Review of Sociology* 23: 479–515.

Edelman, Lauren B., Abraham, Steven E., and Erlanger, Howard S. (1992) "Professional Construction of Law: The Inflated Threat of Wrongful Discharge," *Law and Society Review* 26 (1): 47–83.

Erkama, Niina and Vaara, Eero. (2010) "Struggles over Legitimacy in Global Organizational Restructuring: A Rhetorical Perspective on Legitimation Strategies and Dynamics in a Shutdown Case," *Organization Studies* 31 (7): 813–39.

Etzion, Dror and Ferraro, Fabrizio. (2010) "The Role of Analogy in the Institutionalization of Sustainability Reporting," *Organization Science* 21 (5): 1092–107.

Fligstein, Neil. (2001) "Social Skill and the Theory of Fields," *Sociological Theory* 19 (2): 105–25.

Flood, J. (2012) "Transnational Lawyering: Clients, Ethics, and Regulation," in Leslie C. Levin and Lynn Mather (eds), *Lawyers in Practice: Ethical Decision Making in Context.* Chicago, IL: University of Chicago Press, 176–96.

Frank, David John, Hironaka, Ann, and Schofer, Evan. (2000) "The Nation-State and the Natural Environment over the Twentieth Century," *American Sociological Review* 65 (1): 96–116.

Friedland, Roger and Alford, Robert R. (1991) "Bringing Society Back in: Symbols, Practices and Institutional Contradictions," in Walter W. Powell and Paul J. DiMaggio (eds), *The New Institutionalism in Organizational Analysis.* Chicago, IL: University of Chicago Press, 232–63.

Gabbioneta, Claudia, Greenwood, Royston, Mazzola, Pietro, and Minoja, Mario. (2013) "The Influence of the Institutional Context on Corporate Illegality," *Accounting, Organizations and Society* 38: 484–504.

Gehman, Joel. (2012) "Categorical Cleaning: An Exploratory Study of Sustainability Induced Divestitures, 1992–2010," paper presented at the annual meeting of Academy of Management, Boston, Massachusetts, August 3–7.

Georg, Susse and Irwin, Alan. (2002) "Re-Interpreting Local-Global Partnerships," In T. de Bruijn and A. Tukker (eds), *Partnership and Leadership—Building Alliances for a Sustainable Future.* 61–76, Dordrecht, Netherlands: Kluwer Academic Publishers, 61–76.

Giddens, Anthony. (1984) *The Constitution of Society: Introduction of the Theory of Structuration.* Chicago, IL: University of California Press.

Gladwin, Thomas N., Kennelly, James J., and Krause, Tara-Shelomith. (1995) "Shifting Paradigms for Sustainable Development: Implications for Management Theory and Research," *Academy of Management Review* 20 (4): 874–907.

Glynn, Mary Ann. (2008) "Beyond Constraint: How Institutions Enable Identities," In Royston Greenwood et al. (eds), *Handbook of Organizational Institutionalism.* 413–30. London: Sage Publications, 413–30.

Gómez-Mejía, Luis R., Takács Haynes, Katalin, Núñez-Nickel, Manuel, Jacobson, Kathryn J. L., and Moyano-Fuentes, José. (2007) "Socioemotional Wealth and Business Risks in Family-Controlled Firms: Evidence from Spanish Olive Oil Mills," *Administrative Science Quarterly* 52 (1): 106–37.

Goodrick, Elizabeth and Reay, Trish. (2010) "Florence Nightingale Endures: Legitimizing a New Professional Role Identity," *Journal of Management Studies* 47 (1): 55–84.

Green, Sandy Edward. (2004) "A Rhetorical Theory of Diffusion," *Academy of Management Review* 29 (4): 653–69.

Greenwood, Royston and Suddaby, Roy. (2006) "Institutional Entrepreneurship in Mature Fields: The Big Five Accounting Firms," *Academy of Management Journal* 49 (1): 27–48.

Greenwood, Royston, Suddaby, Roy, and Hinings, Christopher R. (2002) "Theorizing Change: The Role of Professional Associations in the Transformation of Institutionalized Fields," *Academy of Management Journal* 45 (1): 58–80.

Greenwood, Royston, Oliver, Christine, Suddaby, Roy, and Sahlin-Andersson, Kerstin. (2008) *The SAGE Handbook of Organizational Institutionalism.* London: Sage Publications.

Greenwood, Royston, Magán Díaz, Amalia, Xiao Li, Stan, and Céspedes Lorente, José. (2010) "The Multiplicity of Institutional Logics and the Heterogeneity of Organizational Responses," *Organization Science* 21 (2): 521–39.

Greenwood, Royston, Raynard, Mia, Kodeih, Farah, Micelotta, Evelyn R., and Lounsbury, Michael. (2011) "Institutional Complexity and Organizational Responses," *The Academy of Management Annals* 5 (1): 317–71.

Hardy, Cynthia and Maguire, Steve. (2010) "Discourse, Field-Configuring Events, and Change in Organizations and Institutional Fields: Narratives of DDT and the Stockholm Convention," *Academy of Management Journal* 53 (6): 1365–92.

Henn, Rebecca L. and Hoffman, Andrew J. (2013) *Constructing Green: The Social Structures of Sustainability.* Cambridge, MA: MIT Press.

Hoffman, Andrew J. (1999) "Institutional Evolution and Change: Environmentalism and the US Chemical Industry," *Academy of Management Journal* 42 (4): 351–71.

Hoffman, Andrew J. (2001) *From Heresy to Dogma: An Institutional History of Corporate Environmentalism.* Stanford: Stanford University Press.

Hoffman, Andrew J. (2011) "Talking Past Each Other? Cultural Framing of Skeptical and Convinced Logics in the Climate Change Debate," *Organization and Environment* 24 (1): 3–33.

Hoffman, Andrew and Bertels, Stephanie. (2007) "Who is Part of the Environmental Movement?," in Thomas P. Lyon (ed.), *Good Cop Bad Cop: Environmental NGOs and their Strategies Towards Business*. 48–69. Washington, DC: RFF Press, 48–69.

Hoffman, Andrew J. and Georg, Susse. (2012) "A History of Research on Business and the Natural Environment: Conversation from the Field," In *Business and the Natural Environment: Critical Perspectives in Business and Management*. London: Routledge, Available at: <http://ssrn.com/abstract=2038429> (accessed July 2014).

Hoffman, Andrew J. and Jennings, P. Devereaux. (2011) "The BP Oil Spill as a Cultural Anomaly? Institutional Context, Conflict, and Change," *Journal of Management Inquiry* 20 (2): 100–12.

Hoffman, Andrew and Jennings, P. Devereaux. (2012) "The Social and Psychological Foundations of Climate Change," *Solutions* 4 (3): 58–65.

Hoffman, Andrew J. and Ventresca, Marc J. (2002) *Organizations, Policy and the Natural Environment: Institutional and Strategic Perspectives*. Stanford: Stanford University Press.

Hulme, Mike. (2009) *Why We Disagree about Climate Change: Understanding Controversy, Inaction and Opportunity*. Cambridge: Cambridge University Press.

Jay, Jason. (2013) "Navigating Paradox as a Mechanism of Change and Innovation in Hybrid Organizations," *Academy of Management Journal* 56 (1): 137–59.

Jennings, P. Deveraux and Zandbergen, Paul A. (1995) "Ecologically Sustainable Organizations: An Institutional Approach," *Academy of Management Review* 20 (4): 1015–52.

Jennings, P. Devereaux, Zandbergen, Paul A., and Martens, Martin L. (2002) "Complications in Compliance: Variation in Environmental Enforcement in British Columbia's Lower Fraser Basin, 1985–1996," in Andrew J. Hoffman and Marc J. Ventresca (eds), *Organizations, Policy, and the Natural Environment: Institutional and Strategic Perspectives*, 57–89. Stanford: Stanford University Press, 57–89.

Jennings, P. Devereaux, Schulz, Martin, Patient, David, Gravel, Caroline, and Yuan, Ke. (2005) "Weber and Legal Rule Evolution: The Closing of the Iron Cage?," *Organizational Studies* 26 (4): 621–53.

Jennings, P. Devereaux., Zandbergen, Paul A., and Martens, Martin L. (2011) "An Institutional View of Process Strategy in the Public Sector," in Pietro Mazzola and Franz Kellermann (eds), *Handbook of Strategy Process Research*, North Hampton, MA: Edward Elgar, 492–517.

Jennings, P. Devereaux, Coleman, Charlotte K., Misutka, Patricia J., and Hoffman, Andrew J. (2012) "Institutional Maintenance of Logics in Alberta's Oil Sands," paper presented at the annual meeting of Academy of Management, Boston, Massachusetts, August 3–7.

Jennings, P. D., Greenwood, R., Lounsbury, M., and Suddaby, R. (2013) "Institutions, Entrepreneurs, and Communities: A Special Issue on Entrepreneurship," *Journal of Business Venturing* 28 (1): 1–9.

Kellogg, Katherine C. (2009) "Operating Room: Relational Spaces and Microinstitutional Change in Surgery," *American Journal of Sociology* 115 (3): 657–711.

Kellogg, Katherine C. (2011) "Hot Lights and Cold Steel: Cultural and Political Toolkits for Practice Change in Surgery," *Organization Science* 22 (2): 482–502.

Kellogg, Katherine C. (2012) "Making the Cut: Using Status-Based Counter-tactics to Block Social Movement Implementation and Microinstitutional Change in Surgery," *Organization Science* 23 (6): 1546–70.

King, Andrew A. and Lenox, Michael J. (2000) "Industry Self-Regulation Without Sanctions: The Chemical Industry's Responsible Care Program," *Academy of Management Journal* 43 (4): 698–716.

King, Andrew A. and Shaver, J. Myles. (2001) "Are Aliens Green? Assessing Foreign Establishments' Environmental Conduct in the United States," *Strategic Management Journal* 22 (11): 1069–85.

Kong, N., Salzmann, O., Steger, U., and Ionescu-Sommers, A. (2002) "Moving Business/Industry towards Sustainable Consumption: The Role of NGOs," *European Management Journal* 20 (2): 109–27.

Koppenjan, Joop F. M. and Enerink, Bert. (2009) "Public–Private Partnerships in Urban Infrastructures: Reconciling Private Sector Participation and Sustainability," *Public Administration Review* 69 (2): 284–96.

Lampel, Joseph, and Meyer, Alan D. (2008) "Guest Editors' Introduction," *Journal of Management Studies* 45 (6): 1025–35.

Leblebici, Husayin, Gerald, R. Salancik, Copay Anne, and King, Tom. (1991) "Institutional Change and the Transformation of Interorganizational Fields: An Organizational History of the US Radio Broadcasting Industry," *Administrative Science Quarterly* 36 (3): 333–63.

Lefsrud, Lianne and Jennings, P. Devereaux. (forthcoming) "Being Entrepreneurial in Your Storytelling: An Institutional Tale," in Scott Newbert (ed.), *Small Businesses in a Global Economy: Creating and Managing Successful Organizations.* Westport, CT: Praeger.

Lefsrud, Lianne M. and Meyer, Renate E. (2012) "Science or Science Fiction? Professionals' Discursive Construction of Climate Change," *Organization Studies* 33 (11): 1477–506.

Lewis, M. (1990) *Liar's Poker: Rising through the Wreckage on Wall Street.* New York: Penguin Books.

Lounsbury, Michael. (2001) "Institutional Sources of Practice Variation: Staffing College and University Recycling Programs," *Administrative Science Quarterly* 46 (1): 29–56.

Lounsbury, Michael and Crumley, Ellen T. (2007) "New Practice Creation: An Institutional Perspective on Innovation," *Organization Studies* 28 (7): 993–1012.

Maguire, Steve and Hardy, Cynthia. (2009) "Discourse and Deinstitutionalization: The Decline of DDT," *Academy of Management Journal* 52 (1): 148–78.

Maguire, Steve, Hardy, Cynthia, and Lawrence, Thomas B. (2004) "Institutional Entrepreneurship in Emerging Fields: HIV/AIDS Treatment Advocacy in Canada," *Academy of Management Journal* 47 (5): 657–79.

Marquis, Christopher and Lounsbury, Michael. (2007) "Vive la Résistance: Competing Logics and the Consolidation of US Community Banking," *Academy of Management Journal* 50 (4): 799–820.

McDermott, Gerald Andrew, Corredoira, Raphael A., and Kruse, Greg. (2009) "Public–Private Institutions as Catalysts of Upgrading in Emerging Markets," *Academy of Management Journal* 52 (6): 1270–96.

McWilliams, Abagail, and Siegel, Donald S. (2011) "Creating and Capturing Value Strategic Corporate Social Responsibility, Resource-Based Theory, and Sustainable Competitive Advantage," *Journal of Management* 37 (5): 1480–95.

Meyer, Alan D. (1982) "Adapting to Environmental Jolts," *Administrative Science Quarterly* 27 (4): 515–37.

Meyer, Alan D., Brooks, Geoffrey R., and Goes, James B. (1990) "Environmental Jolts and Industry Revolutions: Organizational Responses to Discontinuous Change," *Strategic Management Journal* 11 (5): 93–110.

Meyer, John W. and Rowan, Brian. (1977) "Institutionalized Organizations: Formal Structure as Myth and Ceremony," *American Journal of Sociology* 83 (2): 340–63.

Meyer, John W. and Scott, W. Richard (eds.). (1983) *Organizational Environments: Ritual and Rationality*. Beverley Hills, CA: Sage.

Misutka, Patricia J., Coleman, Charlotte K, Jennings, P. Devereaux, and Hoffman, Andrew J. (2013) "Processes for Retrenching Logics: The Alberta Oil Sands Case, 2008–2011," *Research in the Sociology of Organizations* 39: 131–63.

Nattrass, B. and Altomare, M. (1999) *The Natural Step for Business: Wealth, Ecology and the Evolutionary Corporation*. Gabriola Island, BC: New Society Publishers.

Pache, Anne-Claire and Santos, Filipe. (2010) "When Worlds Collide: The Internal Dynamics of Organizational Responses to Conflicting Institutional Demands," *Academy of Management Review* 35 (3): 455–76.

Pache, Anne-Claire and Santos, Filipe. (2013a) "Embedded in Hybrid Contexts: How Individuals in Organizations Respond to Competing Institutional Logics," *Research in the Sociology of Organizations* 39: 3–35.

Pache, Anne-Claire and Santos, Filipe. (2013b) "Inside the Hybrid Organization: Selective Coupling as a Response to Competing Institutional Logics," *Academy of Management Journal* 56: 972–1001.

Palmer, Donald A., Jennings, P. Devereaux and Zhou, Xueguang. (1993) "Late Adoption of the Multidivisional Form by Large US Corporations: Institutional, Political, and Economic Accounts," *Administrative Science Quarterly* 38 (1): 100–31.

Perrow, Charles. (1999) *Normal Accidents: Living with High Risk Technologies*. Princeton, NJ: Princeton University Press.

Phillips, Nelson, Lawrence, Thomas B., and Hardy, Cynthia. (2004) "Discourse and Institutions," *Academy of Management Review* 29 (4): 635–52.

Pinnington, Ashly and Morris, Timothy. (2002) "Transforming the Architect: Ownership Form and Archetype Change," *Organization Studies* 23 (2): 189–210.

Piore, M. and Sabel, C. (1984) *The Second Industrial Division*. New York: Basic Books.

Porter, Michael E. and Van der Linde, Claas. (1995) "Toward a New Conception of the Environment-Competitiveness Relationship," *The Journal of Economic Perspectives* 9 (4): 97–118.

Purdy, Jill M. and Gray, Barbara. (2009) "Conflicting Logics, Mechanisms of Diffusion, and Multilevel Dynamics in Emerging Institutional Fields," *Academy of Management Journal* 52 (2): 355–80.

Rao, Hayagreeva, Morrill, Calvin, and Zald, Mayer N. (2000) "Power Plays: How Social Movements and Collective Action Create New Organizational Forms," *Research in Organizational Behavior* 22: 237–81.

Rao, Hayagreeva, Monin, Philippe, and Durand, Rodolphe. (2003) "Institutional Change in Toque Ville: Nouvelle Cuisine as an Identity Movement in French Gastronomy," *American Journal of Sociology* 108 (4): 795–843.

Reay, Trish and Hinings, C. Robert. (2009) "Managing the Rivalry of Competing Institutional Logics," *Organization Studies* 30 (6): 629–52.

Rozbicki, Michał. (1998) *The Complete Colonial Gentleman: Cultural Legitimacy in Plantation America*. Charlottesville and London: University Press of Virginia.

Schneiberg, Marc and Lounsbury, Michael. (2008) "Social Movements and Institutional Analysis," in Royston Greenwood et al. (eds), *Handbook of Organizational Institutionalism*. London: Sage Publications, 650–72.

Schüßler, Elke, Rüling, Charles, and Wittneben, Bettina. (2013) "On Melting Summits: The Limitations of Field-Configuring Events as Catalysts of Change in Transnational Climate Policy," *Academy of Management Journal*. doi: 10.5465/amj.2011.0812.

Scott, W. Richard. (1995) *Institutions and Organizations: Ideas and Interests*. London: Sage Publications.

Scott, W. Richard. (2001) *Institutions and Organizations: Ideas and Interests*, 2nd edn. London: Sage Publications.

Selznick, Philip. (1949) *TVA and the Grass Roots: A Study of Politics and Organization*. Princetown, N.J.: University of California.

Seo, Myeong-Gu, and Douglas Creed, W. E. (2002) "Institutional Contradictions, Praxis, and Institutional Change: A Dialectical Perspective," *Academy of Management Review* 27 (2): 222–47.

Sharma, Sanjan and Henriques, Irene. (2005) "Stakeholder Influences on Sustainability Practices in the Canadian Forestry Industry," *Strategic Management Journal* 26: 159–80.

Sine, Wesley D. and Lee, Brandon H. (2009) "Tilting at Windmills? The Environmental Movement and the Emergence of the US Wind Energy Sector," *Administrative Science Quarterly* 54 (1): 123–55.

Skocpol, Theda. (1994) *Social Revolutions in the Modern World*. Cambridge: Cambridge University Press.

Smets, Michael, Morris, Tim, and Greenwood, Royston. (2012) "From Practice to Field: A Multilevel Model of Practice-Driven Institutional Change," *Academy of Management Journal* 55 (4): 877–904.

Spicer, André and Sewell, Graham. (2010) "From National Service to Global Player: Transforming the Organizational Logic of a Public Broadcaster," *Journal of Management Studies* 47 (6): 913–43.

Starr, Paul. (1982) *The Social Transformation of American Medicine*. New York: Basic Books.

Strang, David and Meyer, John W. (1993) "Institutional Conditions for Diffusion," *Theory and Society* 22 (4): 487–511.

Suddaby, Roy, and Greenwood, Royston. (2005) "Rhetorical Strategies of Legitimacy," *Administrative Science Quarterly* 50 (1): 35–67.

Thornton, Patricia H. (1999) "The Sociology of Entrepreneurship," *Annual Review of Sociology* 25: 19–46.

Thornton, Patricia H. and Ocasio, Wiliam. (2008) "Institutional Logics," in Royston Greenwood et al. (eds), *Handbook of Organizational Institutionalism*. London: Sage Publications, 99–129.

Thornton, Patricia H., Ocasio, William, and Lounsbury, Michael. (2012) *The Institutional Logics Perspective: A New Approach to Culture, Structure, and Process*. Oxford: Oxford University Press.

Tolbert, Pamela S. and Zucker, Lynne G. (1983) "Institutional Sources of Change in the Formal Structure of Organizations: The Diffusion of Civil Service Reform, 1880–1935," *Administrative Science Quarterly* 28 (1): 22–39.

Tolbert, Pamela, Zucker, Lynne G., Clegg, Stewart R., Hardy, Cynthia, and Nord, Walter R. (1996) *Handbook of Organization Studies*. London: Sage Publications.

Tracey, Paul, Phillips, Nelson, and Jarvis, Owen. (2011) "Bridging Institutional Entrepreneurship and the Creation of New Organizational Forms: A Multilevel Model," *Organization Science* 22 (1): 60–80.

Voss, Kim and Sherman, Rachel. (2000) "Breaking the Iron Law of Oligarchy: Union Revitalization in the American Labor Movement," *American Journal of Sociology* 106 (2): 303–49.

Walsh, James P., Weber, Klaus, and Margolis, Joshua D. (2003) "Social Issues and Management: Our Lost Cause Found," *Journal of Management* 29 (6): 859–81.

Weber, Klaus, Heinze, Kathryn L., and DeSoucey, Michaela. (2008) "Forage for Thought: Mobilizing Codes in the Movement for Grass-fed Meat and Dairy Products," *Administrative Science Quarterly* 53 (3): 529–67.

Weber, Klaus, Rao, Hayagreeva, and Thomas, L. G. (2009) "From Streets to Suites: How the Anti-biotech Movement Affected German Pharmaceutical Firms," *American Sociological Review* 74 (1): 106–27.

Weber, Max. (1913) *The Protestant Ethic and the Spirit of Capitalism*, trans. Talcott Parsons [1968]. New York: Scribner and Sons.

Weber, Max. (1922) *Economy and Society*, Vols 1 and 2, trans. Talcott Parsons [1968]. New York: Bedminster.

Weir, David. (1987) *The Bhopal Syndrome: Pesticides, Environment, and Health*. San Francisco: Sierra Book Club.

Werbach, Adam. (2009) *Strategy for Sustainability: A Business Manifesto*. Boston, MA: Harvard Business Press.

Wright, April L. and Zammuto, Raymond F. (2013) "Wielding the Willow: Processes of Institutional Change in English County Cricket," *Academy of Management Journal* 56 (1): 308–30.

Zietsma, Charlene and Lawrence, Thomas B. (2010) "Institutional Work in the Transformation of an Organizational Field: The Interplay of Boundary Work and Practice Work," *Administrative Science Quarterly* 55 (2): 189–221.

Zilber, Tammar B. (2008) "The Work of Meanings in Institutional Processes and Thinking," in Royston Greenwood et al. (eds), *Handbook of Organizational Institutionalism*. London: Sage Publications, 151–69.

■ INDEX

Bold entries refer to Figures or Tables

Printed and bound by CPI Group (UK) Ltd, Croydon, CR0 4YY